D0886841

Chinese Revolutionary

Memoirs of a
Chinese Revolutionary

◔ ◔ ◔

Wang Fan-hsi

◔ ◔ ◔

Translated and with an Introduction by
GREGOR BENTON

COLUMBIA UNIVERSITY PRESS
NEW YORK

Columbia University Press Morningside Edition
Columbia University Press
New York   Oxford

Library of Congress Cataloging-in-Publication Data

Wang, Fan-shi, 1907–
[Shuang-shan hui i lu. English]
Memoirs of a Chinese revolutionary / Wang Fan-hsi ;
translated and with an introduction by Gregor Benton.
p.   cm.
Transltion of: Shuang-shan hui i lu.
Previously published: Chinese revoluitionary : memoirs,
1919–1949. Oxford ; New York : Oxford University Press, 1980.
Includes index.
ISBN 0-231-07452-2.
ISBN 0-231-07453-0 (pbk.)
1. Wang, Fan-hsi, 1907–
2. Communists—China—Biography.
3. Communism—China—History.
4. China—Politics and government—1912–1949.
I. Title.
DS778.W3445A3   1991
335.43′3′092—dc20
90-25606
CIP

Morningside Edition 1991

Contents

● ● ●

Preface to the Morningside Edition

❦ ❦ ❦

I was overjoyed to learn that Columbia University Press is preparing to make available for American readers a new edition of the English translation of my memoirs, first published by Oxford University Press in 1980.

The news could hardly have come at a better time, now that we are witnessing the general collapse of Stalinism. Starting in the late spring and early summer of 1989, earthshaking changes have taken place and are continuing to take place in countries of the "socialist" camp: changes so sudden and dramatic that everyone – Stalinist and anti-Stalinist alike – has tried hard to find an explanation for them.

To understand Stalinism's present collapse, in my opinion we must first grasp how the Stalinist system came into being. The main content and central story of this book tells how a Chinese revolutionary and his comrades set out after 1927 to oppose both the theory and the practice of Stalinism, at first in the Soviet Union and then in China. Needless to say, it does not give a rounded and comprehensive picture of its subject, but even so it shows graphically how Stalinism and its Maoist variant were born, began to flourish, and eventually triumphed both in the Soviet Union and in China. What's more, it might in some degree help predict the future of the system of Stalinism.

I would like to use this preface to review a number of new issues, as well as some old issues that were once thought to have been settled but have now been raised afresh by the new developments in the "socialist" camp. Is Stalinism really the equivalent of socialism? Does its collapse prove the bankruptcy of socialism and communism? Can and will it be capitalism that replaces Stalinism? Is capitalism from now on inviolable and irreplaceable? Will socialism and communism go down in history as reactionary illusions? Let me start by saying that my answer to these questions is in all cases no. I have spent the greater part of my life and effort in the struggle for socialism and against Stalinism, but that is not the main reason why I answer as I do. Under the new circumstances, even old questions must be freshly pondered and answered in the light of new facts. I have spent much energy considering these questions, and considering the answers that others have given to them. And my conclusion has not changed: I still believe that the bankruptcy of Stalinism is in no way equivalent to the bankruptcy of socialism. Nor do I believe that capitalism is "immortal and unending." On the contrary, I see no reason to change my view that the future of humankind depends on the realization of true, i.e., non-Stalinist socialism.

Unfortunately I am too old and tired to deal with these ideas in any detail, and in any case a short preface is not the right place to deal with such weighty issues. So to compensate a little, I would like to quote a passage written fifty-two years ago by George Orwell while reviewing *The Communist International*, by Franz Borkenau:

"Dr Borkenau thinks that the root cause of the vagaries of the Comintern policy is the fact that revolution as Marx and Lenin predicted it and as it happened, more or less, in Russia, is not thinkable in the advanced western countries, at any rate at present. Here I believe he is right. Where I part company from him is when he says that for the western democracies the choice lies between Fascism and an orderly reconstruction through the co-operation of all classes. I do not believe in the second possibility, because I do not believe that a man with £50,000 a year and a man with fifteen shillings a week either can, or will, co-operate. The nature of their relationship is quite simply, that the one is robbing the other, and there is no reason to think that the robber will suddenly turn over a new leaf. It would seem, therefore, that if the problems of western capitalism are to be solved, it will have to be through a third alternative, a movement which is genuinely revolutionary, i.e. willing to make drastic changes and to use violence if necessary, but which does not lose touch, as Communism and Fascism have done, with the essential values of democracy. Such a thing is by no means unthinkable. The germs of such a movement exist in numerous countries, and they are capable of growing. At any rate, if they don't, there is no real exit from the pigsty we are in."[1]

I am not an Orwellite, but apart from where he agrees with Borkenau that the revolution predicted by Marx and Lenin cannot

[1] Sonia Orwell and Ian Angus, eds., *The Collected Essays, Journalism and Letters of George Orwell*, Vol. 1, *An Age Like This, 1920–1940*. Harmondsworth: Penguin Books, 1970, pp. 387–88.

break out in the western democratic countries, I agree with most of what he says here and moreover applaud it, though naturally where he says "communism" I would say Stalinism. It's a fact that society consists of different classes, and it is illusory to expect the robbers and the robbed to cooperate freely and even more so to expect the robbers to "turn over a new leaf" of their own free will. Orwell's third road between fascism and Stalinism – a radical and if necessary violent class revolution to overthrow the robbers and at the same time to preserve by all means possible the democratic rights won across centuries of struggle – is indeed a way from the "pigsty" and the only path to equality, freedom, and democracy, and to the realization of a socialist future.

But what relevance do Orwell's comments have for the proposals made over the years by the Trotskyists? It is commonly believed that the difference between Trotskyists and Stalinists is that the former are not only more radical than the latter but even more frightful, even more dictatorial and centralist, even less interested in democracy. This point of view is not only wrong but even a deliberate perversion of the truth. Though I would not presume to claim that what Orwell in his essay calls "the germs of a movement" is a reference to Trotskyism or to a trend of opinion including Trotskyists, I must point out that Trotskyism does represent such a force. In my story I describe something of the Trotskyists' thinking and activity between 1927 and 1949. Readers can decide for themselves—at least where China is concerned—whether we fit the ugly picture drawn of us. Here I wish to say only one thing more: It was none other than Trotsky and his comrades who first (starting in 1923) and (through the proposals advanced and the criticisms made in Trotsky's *New Course*) most consistently came out against the degeneration of the Soviet state; it was they who all along exposed as an illusion the idea of "building socialism in one country"; it was they who first and most implacably called for a struggle against bureaucratic dictatorship, who demanded a workers' and peasants' democracy, and who called for a multiparty system in the Soviet councils and the right to form factions in the Communist Party; and it was they who consistently fought against bureaucracy and for democracy, right through until they were dismissed from office, expelled from the Party, and jailed, deported, executed or assassinated.

In short, over the past seventy years the Trotskyists – and only the Trotskyists – have been the group that struggled without regard to the cost for Orwell's "third way."

Could it be that in the world today, no matter whether it be the existing and now disintegrating "socialist" countries, standing blindfolded on the brink of an uncertain future, or the superficially prosperous capitalist countries, which in reality are host to all sorts of irresolvable contradictions – that in the world today the only way forward is in the policies already mapped out for us in documents of the Trotskyists? Probably not, for human affairs are too complex and "Old Man History" is too cunning for any individual or group to be able in advance to formulate an exit from crises that have not yet happened; new policies must constantly be developed to suit reality's everchanging needs. I am deeply convinced, however, that as long as construction of our society continues to rest on an opposition of robbers and robbed, repressers and repressed, the basic programmatic strategies laid down by the Trotskyists and by Marx cannot go out of date.

In the main, this new edition follows the old one, save for a few minor corrections of typographical and other errors. Apart from that, the translator has rewritten some passages in his original introduction and added others to it. The main difference between this and the Oxford edition is the reinstatement of the final chapter, "Thinking in Solitude," dropped in 1980 to save space. And I have appended a translation of the preface to the French translation of this book.

Here I would like to say a special word of thanks to Alexander H. Buchman, but for whose tireless efforts over more than two years this edition of my book would never have seen the light of day. Alex Buchman is my old friend from more than fifty years ago in Shanghai, where we worked together in opposition to the Japanese imperialists who were then committing aggression against China.

I would also like to take the chance to express my long overdue thanks to Gregor Benton, whose faithful and creative translation of my memoirs not only made them available for the English-speaking world but allowed them to be rendered into German and French, so that they could make the acquaintance of an even wider circle of new friends. Gregor Benton is not only my literary collaborator but a support in my life without whose help I would have encountered even more difficulties during my fifteen years of exile in Western Europe.

Wang Fang-hsi
Leeds, April 1990

Preface to the French Edition

● ● ●

When I wrote these memoirs thirty years ago in Macau, without even the most elementary research facilities to help my memory, I never guessed that what first saw life as a rough mimeograph would not only be pirated in China but would be translated into Japanese, English, German, and now French. Of course I am delighted and there is much that I would like to say. I wrote no specific preface for any of the three previous translations, save for a short postscript to the English one. I did not plan to write a preface for the French translation either, until it occurred to me that I could use the opportunity to reply to some of my reviewers.

Their criticisms and comments have mainly been friendly and appreciative, but a few have been hostile, and it is these that I shall address.

One critic called my book a sort of dirge to Chinese Trotskyism. Another called it a mere footnote to the history of the Chinese Revolution. A third said that it described a tragedy in which a small number of fanatics battled desperately for a lost cause.

Whether or not a cause is lost cannot be judged by short-term considerations or by this or that victory or defeat. Political movements must be judged above all by their program. If the program of a political movement meets objective needs and withstands the test of time, its cause is not lost; on the contrary, if the program is wisely implemented, the cause will prosper.

The program from which the world Trotskyist movement emerged, and for which it has been fighting, derives from the theory of permanent revolution. This theory has been proved right by past revolutions and shown by current events to be as indispensable today as it ever was.

The two great revolutions of this century – the Russian and the Chinese – won power by implementing the strategy of permanent revolution. In Russia the Bolsheviks did so with their eyes open, in China the Maoists did so blindly, and against their own declared intentions. Both parties seized power in the course of "bourgeois-democratic revolutions" and established "dictatorships of the workers and peasants": workers' states, but in a specifically conditioned sense, for these states are ruled by tyrannical bureaucracies (in Russia as a result of the defeat of the revolution after the death of Lenin, in China from the very beginning of the new regime). However, the founding of these states laid the basis for a future development, through political revolution, toward socialism.

Trotskyists everywhere have tirelessly advocated that working-class revolutionary parties can and should seize power in economically backward countries in the course of bourgeois-democratic revolutions; that the states thus formed can only be consolidated and developed by democracy and internationalism; and that socialism cannot be built unless the new state furthers the cause of world revolution and its leaders see their struggle as part of a future system of world socialism, i.e., see that socialism cannot be built in just one country.

So the betrayal of the revolution in Russia and the monstrous perversion of socialism in China do not prove that it is wrong to take power in poor countries in line with the strategy of permanent revolution. On the contrary, they prove the theory of permanent revolution right, by showing that socialism cannot be built in a single country, especially if that country is economically backward. They also show that regimes in post-capitalist societies that lack democracy and internationalism cannot consolidate even a relatively progressive state, let alone a socialist state. On the contrary, such regimes will fall prey to Stalinist and Maoist "new feudalism" or, even worse, to "communism" of the Pol Pot sort, i.e., a society crushed by mass murder.

So the cause of Trotskyism is by no means lost, nor need it be. Only the program of the Trotskyists, with its commitment to socialist democracy and internationalism, can lead China, the Soviet Union, and other "socialist" countries from the blind alley they are now in (and from which they are vainly trying to extricate themselves by superficial reforms).

So I see no reason to regret my life. I am proud of my small role in what some would call a tragedy. I will not guess about the future. Are my memoirs a dirge? Or are they a short overture to the symphony of true socialism throughout the world? Only history will tell.

Wang Fan-hsi
August 1987

Translator's Introduction

❃ ❃ ❃

Wang Fan-hsi wrote these memoirs in 1957, thirty-one years after joining the Chinese Communist Party (CCP), seven years after the establishment of the People's Republic, and five years after the crushing by the new regime of the Trotskyist organization that he had helped to found. At the time he was living alone, in poverty and exile, in the tiny Portuguese colony of Macau in Southern China. A friend painstakingly scratched the original mimeographed edition of his book character by character onto flimsy wax stencils, yielding a mere twenty copies of the text. The quality of the paper was poor and the faded blue print barely legible to the dwindling band of Trotskyists across the Pearl River in Hong Kong who were his readers.

Now, thirty-three years on, with the author in his early eighties, the fate of his friends, his movement, and his book has changed for the better. In the lightless years of the Mao dictatorship, the darkest spot behind the blackout on the history of the Chinese Revolution was reserved for Trotskyism. In 1952 the Trotskyists in China were swept up by the security police and jailed (in some cases for the next twenty-seven years) as "counter-revolutionaries." This was not the first time that they had disappeared behind bars for their beliefs. Many had also spent in jail the best part of the 1930s, then as revolutionaries against the Nationalist dictatorship of Chiang Kai-shek. Both times the bulk of their archive had vanished with them into government vaults, beyond the reach of most historians. On the rare occasions that Trotskyists were paraded in government-sponsored history books after 1949, it was as grotesque caricatures epitomizing national and political treason. Those few Trotskyist leaders who had slipped abroad before the clampdown did their best to keep alive the Trotskyist critique of CCP policy. But they lacked information and resources, and in any case they had been consigned (not least among their fellow revolutionaries) to the remotest margins of political life by the Maoist victory.

Then, in 1979, Cheng Ch'ao-lin and eleven other Trotskyists, jailed as counter-revolutionaries in 1952 and presumed dead by many, stepped unexpectedly into freedom.[1] In the same year Chinese historians took the first timid steps toward rehabilitating Ch'en Tu-hsiu, founder of both the CCP (in 1921) and (in 1931) its Trotskyist offshoot, which Wang had helped lead. Why the milder view of Ch'en? Mainly it was part of a wider trend to recognize the strengths as well as the weaknesses of Chinese communist leaders who had ended their careers in political disgrace, and to write an objective history of the CCP before the last of its veterans went to "meet Marx." So, starting in 1979 (Ch'en's hundredth birthday), a fresh version of Ch'en's political biography was released episode by episode to the Chinese public. First, his role in the May Fourth Movement of 1919 (then celebrating its sixtieth anniversary) and in founding the CCP was officially acknowledged. Then the historian Hsiang Ch'ing and others wrote that Ch'en's "right opportunism" in the mid-1920s was mainly the result of Comintern meddling (for by 1979 the taboo on criticizing Stalin and the Comintern had been lifted). Some historians even defended Ch'en's controversial stand on the Chinese Eastern Railways Incident of 1929, when he criticized the Central Committee's slogan of "armed defense of the Soviet Union." Finally, a number of studies have shown up as a groundless slander the 1938 charge that Ch'en Tu-hsiu took money from the Japanese.

By the 1980s even Ch'en's Trotskyism was no longer entirely taboo, and some mainland historians gingerly began to lift the curtain on it, so revealing a complex, original movement, a failed experiment in urban revolution in the land of rural revolution, that throws light from many interesting new angles of familiar questions of the Chinese Revolution. In the course of academic debate, the official view on Trotskyism has noticeably softened. In Mao's days it was classified as "counter-revolutionary"; now it is simply "wrong." In the new, more liberal climate some Chinese writers

---

[1] Traditionally August Blanqui, the French revolutionary who spent thirty-three of his seventy-five years in prison (and so became known in France as l'enfermé), is regarded as the record holder for political imprisonment. Cheng Ch'ao-lin had beaten Blanqui's record by one year when he stepped from prison in June 1979 after twenty-seven years, to add to the seven he had already served under Chiang Kai-shek. But there are almost certainly worse cases in the world than Cheng's.

have dared to strip away the lies and prejudices from Trotskyism and the Chinese Trotskyists, and memoirs by Trotskyist leaders have appeared in the Chinese press, including a restricted *nei-pu* edition of this book and another, now in its second edition, of the memoirs of Cheng Ch'ao-lin.

Even so, Ch'en and the Trotskyists remain a vexed issue in China's party-history schools, admired by some but deeply feared and hated by many, especially senior party officials whose view of them was prejudiced by the campaign launched in 1938 by the Stalinist Wang Ming to discredit the Trotskyists as venal traitors to party and country. What's more, because of their democratic critique of Chinese society and Stalinist politics they have become metaphors incarnate for a host of unresolved problems in Chiense politics. It was no accident that the students on T'ien-an-men Square in May and June 1989 drew their inspiration from the May Fourth Movement of 1919, which Ch'en Tu-hsiu led, and that they even copied Ch'en's famous slogan calling for science and democracy. So though the movement that culminated in the massacre of June 4 shows that Ch'en's legacy still lives, it set back the prospect – seriously mooted before the crisis – of a full rehabilitation of Ch'en and his Trotskyist disciples, whose return to limbo symbolizes the present blockage of China's evolution toward greater freedom.

Of the founding generation of Chinese Trotskyists, Wang Fan-hsi (born 1907) and Cheng Ch'ao-lin (born 1901) are still alive, but they are too old to take an active part in political life or even to keep up a regular commentary on it; and though Cheng is still hale and lucid and has been assigned to membership of Shanghai's People's Political Consultative Conference, he is still partly muzzled. However, Wang's and Cheng's memoirs have become objects of great admiration among Chinese academics allowed to read them,[2] and there has been a steady flow of articles – some surprisingly objective and unbiased – on the history of the Chinese Trotskyists. At the same time, many foreign writings sympathetic to Trotskyism have appeared in Chinese translation.[3] Outside China, literature by or about Chinese Trotskyists is now growing. Wang's book has already appeared in Japanese, in German, and in French, and prep-

[2] Cf. Lee Feigon, book review, *Theory and Society*, 1983, no. 2: 259–65.

[3] Gregor Benton, "Two Purged Leaders of Early Chinese Communism," *The China Quarterly*, June 1985, no. 102, pp. 317–28, at p. 318, fn. 9.

arations are under way to publish Cheng's in several languages, starting with German and English. The new literature on Trotskyism commands an eager readership on mainland China, where layer after layer of the official leadership has been discredited in the public eye, where the crisis of faith in Stalinism and Maoism is deep and general, and where younger historians and political thinkers have been emboldened by the post-Mao talk of the need for greater democracy, liberated thought, and truthful scholarship. On Taiwan, in Hong Kong, and among the diaspora of Chinese communities overseas too interest – measured by publications – in Ch'en and the Trotskyists is now rising.

Memoirs are commonly defined as that form of writing in which the author effaces himself except to verify an event by his presence, as distinct from autobiography, which is the "faithful portrait of a soul in its adventures through life." Since Wang is not just the connecting thread but a main focus of the events he describes, his book occupies a position midway between the two genres. Like Trotsky he would say of it that "it is not a dispassionate photograph of my life, but a component part of it. In these pages, I continue the struggle to which my life is devoted." If self-effacement is a distinguishing feature of the memoir, then Wang's book has it almost to a fault, for it passes over in complete silence the several deep personal tragedies suffered by its author. To some this may convey the forbidding impression of a man of unbending will and singleminded devotion to a cause. Only a closer reading of the text – the generosity of its characterization, the scrupulous balance of its judgment, and the complete absence of bitterness, even in the depths of defeat – reveals a person of warmth and compassion, to whom "nothing human is alien."

Like most Chinese revolutionaries of his generation, Wang's basic attitudes were shaped and colored by the May Fourth Movement that took its name from the demonstrations of May 1919 against the Peking Government's surrender of Chinese interests to Japan. May Fourth revitalized Chinese political life, and helped pave the way for the foundation of the Chinese Communist Party in July 1921. It also transformed Chinese cultural life in the broadest sense, rejecting traditional Confucianism in favor of a modern humanistic, scientific, and democratic outlook. The new spirit found rich and passionate expression in the writing of the period. Ch'en Tu-hsiu, its main representative, called on Chinese youth to be "independent, not servile; progressive, not conservative; dynamic, not passive; cosmopolitan, not isolationist; utilitarian, not emptily formalistic; scientific, not merely imaginative." In 1919 Ch'en's paper, New Youth, summed up the aims of the movement in a stirring Declaration of Beliefs: "The new society we have in mind is characterized by honesty, progress, positiveness, liberty, equality, creativity, beauty, goodness, peace, love, mutual assistance, joyful labor, and devotion to the welfare of humanity. In it all those phenomena that can be described as hypocritical, conservative, passive, restrictive, privileged, conventional, ugly, detestable, combative, frictional, inert, gloomy, and oligarchic will gradually be reduced in importance and eventually disappear."

By the time Wang arrived at Peking University in 1925 the May Fourth Movement had long since polarized into two main tendencies, one arguing for the formal study of "issues" and liberation "drop by drop, bit by bit," and the other (led by Ch'en Tu-hsiu, by now General Secretary of the CCP) favoring "isms" and revolutionary political engagement. In Peking Wang opted once and for all for the latter, so that his personal fate became inextricably bound to that of communism in China, whether inside or outside the established party. From then on his life was a hectic succession of strikes, polemics, constant changes of name and alias, and jail.

Until several years after the death of Mao Tse-tung in 1976 Wang's book was the only full-length autobiography to be published by a veteran of the Chinese Revolution, leaving aside men like Chang Kuo-t'ao who had quit the cause. The main reason for this singularly poor crop of biographical writing is that the CCP, once in power, immediately press-ganged history into the service of the state, so none dared write as individuals about the past. The "autobiographical" materials published by party committees in multivolume collections were invariably either hagiographies or short articles on specific topics written to meet the orthodox political requirements of the day. So for a long time Wang's book was unique, and the only available personal record of certain key periods in the history of the CCP, such as the struggles in Moscow in the late 1920s. It is of course also a valuable source for the history of Chinese Trotskyism, which was by far the most important branch of the International Left Opposition outside Russia.

In compiling these memoirs Wang could not always consult the necessary documents. He had managed to take some of the records of his organization with him into exile, but he lacked access to many sources relating to both the Trotskyist movement and the official party. Wherever possible this English edition has been checked and revised against the original evidence, and in the process Wang's memory has proved to be generally reliable. As a historical record, his book is marred by none of the Orwellian evasions, omissions, and falsifications of Maoist historiography.

Wang's political life as a communist began with the Revolution of 1925–27, when the youthful CCP, on instructions of the Moscow-based Comintern, worked for national unification and independence in alliance with the Kuomintang (or Nationalist Party). The terms of this alliance were in practice disadvantageous to the CCP, for they required its strict political subordination to the Nationalist leaders and the virtual submersion of its membership and organization into the Kuomintang. In 1920, at the Second Comintern Congress, Lenin had called on communist parties in colonial countries to resist bourgeois attempts to control the mass movement, and to carry out vigorous propaganda for the idea of Soviets. To square their positions with Leninist orthodoxy and to counter Trotsky's criticisms of the Chinese alliance, the Comintern majority in Moscow argued that the Kuomintang was not a bourgeois party but a "bloc of four classes" (bourgeoisie, workers, peasants, and petty bourgeoisie) and the "only serious national revolutionary group in China."

International considerations were an important factor in the formulation of the Comintern's policy for the Chinese Revolution. In the words of one classic study of the period, "by the time Russia actively intervened in China, the Revolution in Russia itself was in full retreat and the new nationalist Russia had begun to emerge. The Soviet bureaucracy . . . did not come to the East in search of new proletarian conquests. It came looking for new allies, new bulwarks, new fronts on which to blunt the hostile pressures of the Western powers."[4]

In early 1926 growing social and political tensions began to lay

---

[4] Harold Isaacs, *The Tragedy of the Chinese Revolution.* New York: Atheneum, 1968 (2nd rev. ed.), p. 49.

bare the underlying divisions between a Kuomintang leadership committed to defending the economic interests of the rich and a communist party whose constituency was mainly among the urban and rural poor. In July Chiang Kai-shek launched the Northern Expedition, to overthrow warlord rule in the areas to the north of the Kuomintang's base in Kwangtung. The highly politicized Nationalist armies, reorganized with Soviet help, quickly defeated or neutralized their badly-organized and disunited warlord adversaries, most of whom owed their position to sheer force of arms and were prey to the manipulations of powerful foreign interests. But in March, before launching the expedition, Chiang had staged a limited preemptive coup against the communists in Canton, by which he strengthened the position of the right wing within the Kuomintang.

In the spring of 1927, in a second and far bloodier coup, Chiang delivered a crushing blow to the communist movement in Shanghai. At the time Trotsky argued that the CCP should immediately declare its political and organizational independence of the Kuomintang, and should set up Soviets to lead the agrarian revolution in those parts of China where it was still under way. He thought that bold measures of this sort might still swing the tide against Chiang. But Stalin, adamant that his original strategy for China was "the only correct line," continued to call for an alliance with the Kuomintang – no longer, of course, with Chiang Kai-shek, but with its "left wing," in Wuhan, which had split with Chiang in late 1926. In a matter of months, however, the military backers of the Wuhan Government carried out their own murderous coup against the communists. Shortly afterwards both wings of the Kuomintang were reunited in Nanking in a national government that was in effect controlled by Chiang.

Trotsky had challenged the positions of the Soviet majority leaders throughout the three years of the CCP-Kuomintang united front, though not always with the same degree of energy and directness. Before 1926 he had confined his criticisms to the ruling bodies of the Soviet party, hampered by Stalin's rule that there should be no record or public report of leadership discussions, and by divisions within the minority opposition group. By late 1926, however, he was openly predicting that an anti-communist coup was imminent in China.

Nearly half the Chinese students in Moscow during this period accepted Trotsky's criticisms of the Comintern.[5] Like him, they now

[5] There is disagreement about the number of Chinese Trotskyists in Moscow. According to Comintern sources, there were only twenty-nine at the Chinese University in Moscow (*Materials for the Seventh World Congress.* Moscow: Bureau of the Comintern Secretariat, 1935: 702). According to the one-time CCP leader Chang Kuo-t'ao, a student called Li handed over a list of more than one hundred Trotskyists to the Stalinist authorities on defecting from the opposition (*Mingpao Yüeh-k'an*, 1968, vol. 3, no. 7: 87). According to Yueh Sheng (*Sun Yat-sen University in Moscow and the Chinese Revolution.* New York: Center for East Asian Studies, The University of Kansas, 1971, pp. 164 ff.) a list of eighty to ninety students was submitted to the party authorities by a traitor, but apparently there were others apart from these. There were twenty party cells at Sun Yat-sen University; of the twenty-odd students in Yueh Sheng's own cell, all but two or three were oppositionists. Yueh Sheng says that only a few Chinese Trotskyists died in the camps, though the number who died in prison "was not known"; the majority, "after surviving terrible hardships, were sent back to China." Wang Fan-hsi himself puts the number of Chinese oppositionists in Moscow at between two and three hundred. In May 1981 Wang wrote a short note about Yueh Sheng's book: "Only recently did I come across this book by Yueh Sheng, i.e. Sheng Yüeh, alias Sheng Chung-liang, one of Wang Ming's 'Twenty Eight Bolsheviks', who left the CCP in 1935. In 1929, when the Chinese Trotskyist organization in the University and its members were mercilessly crushed by the Wang Ming group with the help of the GPU, Sheng was the member of the Party Committee specially responsible for dealing with the Trotskyists. In Chapter 13 of his book he discusses some of the same events as I do in this book, and there are discrepancies between his account and mine. According to him, the man who committed suicide was not the man who actually handed over the list of secret Trotskyists. The suicide was Chao Yen-ching (Sheng forgot his name and only remembered that he was a native of Honan and had been a teacher and a school principal), who killed himself after making a half-hearted confession to Sheng and Ignatov, the Secretary of the Party Bureau. And the man who – several days after Chao's death – handed over the list was called Li P'in. So the arrest by the GPU of the Chinese Trotskyists happened not before but after Chao's suicide. Sheng is probably right, for whereas I heard the story from two Chinese Trotskyists who escaped from Siberia back to China, he knew the facts first-hand and was deeply implicated in the episode 'from start to finish.' Sheng does not say whether the number of 'some eighty to ninety' was the total of Chinese Trotskyists in the University (or in Russia). So was it? I knew Li P'in well, and I know that he was not a member of the leading committee of the secret Trotskyist organization in the University. (The actual person responsible for organizational affairs was Fan Chin-piao, who appears in Sheng's

blamed Stalin and the majority leaders for ordering the CCP into
the Kuomintang; for refusing to allow the communists to organize
the peasants independently during the Northern Expedition, or to
form Soviets in early 1927; for wrongly characterizing Wuhan as a
"revolutionary center" after the split with Chiang; and for refusing
to admit, for factional reasons, that the Chinese Revolution had
been defeated.

This last point was rich in implications for the immediate future
of the revolution. If it was true that there had been no defeat, then
the struggle was free to rise to new levels, with insurrections in the
cities backed by peasant armies in the countryside. This was in effect the course on which the CCP leaders now embarked.

The Trotskyists, in contrast, argued that a massive defeat had been
suffered and that the Chinese Revolution was not remotely near a
"new high tide." For them, the immediate tasks were to rebuild
the shattered trade unions, reestablish the party in the towns, and
forge new links to the workers. Central to these tasks was the struggle
for an all-powerful national (or constituent) assembly elected by
universal secret ballot, since this alone could bring together the
disparate economic and political struggles. These were the strategic
aims that shaped the course of Chinese Trotskyism in the first nine
years of its life.

Why did the Trotskyists fail to become a major political force in
China after their expulsion from the CCP? They have been criticized for failing to grasp the importance of serious and sustained
practical work in the countryside in this period. But not even the

---

book as Fan Ken-piao.) So Li was in no position to provide a complete list, for
as Sheng himself says, 'the Trotskyites at Sun Yat-sen University were knitted
into an underground organization which had only vertical, but no lateral, organizational connections. That is to say, members of one cell did not know
what other cells there were or who belonged to them. . . . Thus, any cell member who wavered in his loyalty was in a position to betray only his own cell
members.' So Li P'in could not have known all the members and there were
almost certainly more than 'eighty to ninety' Chinese Trotskyists in Moscow. I
cannot say exactly how many there were in late 1929, but I know for sure that
in the summer of that year when I was a member of the leading committee
there were more than one hundred Chinese Communists in the various universities and institutes of the Soviet Union who had become Trotskyists, and I
was told that in the six months after my return to China the secret organization
grew."

leaders of the official party, Mao included, had yet abandoned the idea of recapturing the towns as a precondition for a nationwide revolutionary upsurge, even though by 1931 Kuomintang repression had forced them to withdraw the bulk of their forces to the countryside. It was only after several years, and in the teeth of much opposition in the CCP leadership, that the Maoists – having ended up by accident among the peasants – finally elaborated their famous strategy for "encircling the towns with the villages."

In any case, it was not that the Chinese Trotskyists failed to understand the role of the peasantry in Chinese history, but that – from their own point of view – they understood it all too well. The mission of the CCP in its infancy, shouldered in 1931 by the Trotskyists, was – so they believed – to break the pattern of the Chinese past, which appeared to them doomed to repeat an endless cycle of dynastic decay, peasant revolt, and renewal under a new despotic line. Ch'en Tu-hsiu's communists in 1921 thought that they had found in the new urban classes – the bourgeoisie, the proletariat, the critical intelligentsia – a way to break this vicious circle. Which is why Ch'en's Trotskyists insisted after 1927 – save for a brief interval in 1938, under the exceptional circumstances of the Japanese invasion – on sticking to the cities, and why they never once considered abandoning them in the long term for the villages. Far from being mired in intellectual sloth, they actively resisted a turn to the countryside and insisted on striving for a new way to redeem Chinese society and the Chinese nation, rather than follow the old and fruitless one. They failed, partly because the class of industrial workers on which they tried to fasten was too small, too little spread (in just two or three big cities), and too demoralized by defeat and terror to pay much attention to them. In a word, they were prophets before their time.

Wang still believes today that the failure of the Chinese Trotskyist movement in the early 1930s was due more to its lack of numbers and material support from outside (unlike the CCP, which received financial and other backing from the Soviet Union), and to state repression, which resulted in the imprisonment of nearly all its leading members, than to any basic flaw in its strategic thinking. It is hard to see how the Chinese Trotskyists, squeezed between the Kuomintang and the CCP, could have established a political space for themselves in those early years. To an extent they may have hastened their own downfall by concentrating their efforts exclusively on the towns. True, they understood the need for agitation in the villages, but first they wanted to sink sturdy roots in the metropolitan littoral, for they were Marxists in the classic mold and their members were too few to dissipate across the vast Chinese countryside. Even after the Japanese invasion they stuck to their belief that there could be no revolution outside urban culture. But by then China's industrial base along the coast had been destroyed. "In numbers, in material strength, and in spirit," Ch'en Tu-hsiu wrote to Trotsky some time in 1939, "[the workers] have gone back to where they were thirty to forty years ago."[6]

So the Trotskyists played no role in the continuing agrarian revolution and, unlike the official party, had no rural sanctuaries to retreat to when pressure from the Kuomintang became intolerable. Wang admitted in 1973 that the Trotskyists would have done better "to open up new battlegrounds in the countryside, where the masses were in higher spirits and the repression was less harsh, with the aim of preserving our cadre and recruiting new militants,"[7] while continuing to devote their main efforts to restoring and strengthening underground work in the cities through the struggle for a constituent assembly. But it is worth remembering that where individual Trotskyists did participate in armed communist detachments in the countryside in the early 1930s, they were hunted down and exterminated by the CCP political police.

Would the official party have benefited by adopting policies that the Trotskyists were pressing on it in the early 1930s? Many of the Trotskyist criticisms of the official line were well-founded. Mao himself wrote in November 1928 from the Chingkang Mountains that he and his comrades were suffering from "an acute sense of loneliness," and that to put an end to "this lonely life . . . it is necessary to launch a political and economic struggle for democracy involving the urban petty bourgeoisie."[8] But the CCP, having refused to make such a call for democracy, could neither unify the

[6] Shuang Shan, ed., T'uo-luo-tz'u-chi tang-an-chung chih Chung-kuo t'ung-chih ti hsin, 1929–1939 (Letters in the Trotsky Archives to Chinese Comrades, 1929–1939). Hong Kong, 1981, p. 77.

[7] This sentence is quoted from an unpublished manuscript titled "On the Causes of the Triumph of the CCP and the Failure of the Chinese Trotskyists in the Third Chinese Revolution" (1973).

[8] Mao Tse-tung, Selected Works. London (Lawrence and Wishart), 1954, vol. 1, p. 99.

various scattered struggles in town and countryside nor seriously undermine the stability of Kuomintang rule in its urban strongholds. So it became increasingly isolated and was eventually forced to abandon its rural bases to the advancing Kuomintang armies. Its catastrophic defeat in 1934 and the subsequent hunt for scapegoats in its ruling bodies are the best indication that its political strategy could not have led to success against the Kuomintang in China as it was before the Japanese occupation.

So in the early 1930s both parties of Chinese communism hurried down their different roads to disaster. For all its greater resources, the Red Army had been whittled down to just a few thousand men and women when it eventually landed up in its new northwestern sanctuary in 1935, at the end of the legendary Long March, and the communist party in the towns had been destroyed; while the brave but tiny band of Chinese Trotskyists, jailed and tortured as revolutionaries by the Kuomintang and shot as counterrevolutionaries by the CCP, had been wiped from the political map.

In July 1937 the Japanese transformed the entire situation in China by embarking on a final push to bring the whole of the country under their control, after six years of aggression against Chinese territories in the northeast. One result of this invasion was a partial resumption of the alliance between the Kuomintang and the CCP. But the Chinese communists had learned the lessons of their earlier bitter experiences, and took precautions to ensure that the second united front did not end up in the same way as the first. In the war years they boldly and skilfully swung the military and political balance more and more their way, so that by 1945 they were poised to seize huge areas of the country and to prepare the way for the final communist victory in 1949.

The war created conditions that the communists, with their previous military and political experience in the rural areas to the south, were uniquely equipped to exploit. The entire political life of China now assumed military form, and political issues were settled ever more by the gun. Earlier the CCP's rural strategy had failed mainly because of its inability to mount a simultaneous challenge to the Kuomintang political order in the towns. But now the Japanese invasion had cut the Kuomintang off from the industrial and commercial nerve centers of China, forcing it to retreat to the backward southwest of the country and so depriving Chiang of one of his chief advantages over the communists. By championing the cause of national resistance more actively than the Kuomintang, whose reactionary policies and corrupt government in the war years progressively alienated popular support, the CCP was able to attract ever wider sections of Chinese society.

But the Trotskyists viewed the CCP's activities in this period with contempt, denouncing the new alliance as a shameless sell-out of the revolution. From their own vantage point this was a reasonable conclusion, for on paper its terms allowed for the "reorganization" of the Red Army into the national forces, an end to "class struggle," and the merging of communist and Kuomintang territories. What the Trotskyists could not know was that the Maoists, even-though reluctant to disagree openly with the Comintern proposals (pushed by Stalin's emissary Wang Ming), had not the slightest intention of giving up their military or territorial independence. So the revival of this united front in 1937, as Wang Fan-hsi later concluded, was "by and large a matter of tactical manoeuvre rather than a strategic turn in orientation."[9]

One reason the Chinese Trotskyists so badly misread the situation was that their eyes were fixed on the big cities, where Wang Ming's faction dominated party work. Another was that they had already written off the CCP as a "petty bourgeois," "peasant" party as early as 1934, and therefore failed to pay sufficient attention to the continuing differentiation that was going on within it.

The Chinese Trotskyists themselves concentrated their wartime activities on Shanghai, organizing the workers under the very noses of the Japanese invaders. Although Wang's own efforts to involve himself in military work came to nothing, others who had been cut off from Shanghai by the war organized and led Trotskyist guerrilla detachments in various parts of China. But none survived the struggle, and little is known of them except that their forces were crushed between the millstones of the CCP and the Japanese. Despite this cheerless experience, Wang continued to argue in later writings that the Trotskyist leadership should have actively encouraged and coordinated the setting up of armed detachments. "It is impossible to say for certain," he wrote, "whether we could have built up a force strong enough to compete with that of the CCP, but at least we would have not ended up as we did. During the War our organization was practically obliterated. Some of our cadres

[9] Ssu-hsiang wen-t'i ("Some Ideological Questions"). Hong Kong, 1957.

even starved to death, and we made no active contribution to the resistance. After the War we were too weak to take advantage of the pre-revolutionary situation that had opened up, and adopted an entirely passive attitude towards the civil war between the CCP and the Kuomintang."[10]

Thus the Chinese Trotskyists wrote themselves out of the final pages of the Chinese Revolution, so that they were relegated to the role of mere bystanders during the titanic battles of the late 1940s. Was their contribution to modern Chinese history therefore "written in wind and running water," or are there elements of lasting value in it?

Since 1949 Wang has argued that the actual course of the Chinese Revolution broadly confirmed the Trotskyist theory of permanent revolution (according to which the bourgeois-democratic revolution would grow over with no intervening stages into socialist revolution), rather than the theory of New Democracy, which was in essence the Chinese version of Stalin's theory of revolution in stages.[11] The dynamic of the revolution, both in town and countryside, was indeed radically anticapitalist, and Mao's prediction that New Democracy (and hence elements of capitalism) would last for "several decades" was rapidly disproved by the tempo of social transformation in China, which was completed in just a few years. The irony is that this fundamental tenet of Trotskyist theory was put into practice not by the Trotskyists themselves but by the Maoists, who arrived at it more or less through trial and error. So despite the Trotskyists' practical failure, their criticisms of the political positions of the official leadership of the CCP are not without significance and value. Perhaps the most convincing proof of the force of this criticism is that during later inner-party disputes the Maoists unconsciously echoed many of the arguments that the Trotskyists had developed years before.

[10] Wang Fan-hsi, "On the Causes of the Triumph of the CCP. . . ."

[11] Wang argues his case in Shuang Shan (pseud.) *Mao Tse-tung ssu-hsiang lun-kao* (*Studies on Mao Tse-tung Thought.*) Hong Kong (Hsin-ta ch'u-pan-she), 1973, esp. ch. 7; Ts'ai-lien (pseud.), "Liang-chung pu-tuan ke-ming lun" ("Two Theories of Permanent Revolution"), appendix to Yi Yin (i.e. Cheng Ch'ao-lin) *Pu-tuan ke-ming lun ABC* (*ABC of Permanent Revolution*). Hong Kong (Hsin-ta ch'u-pan-she), 1958, pp. 61–71; and in his own Translator's Introduction to Leon Trotsky, *Hsin lu-hsiang* (*The New Course*). Hong Kong, 1958.

But on the strategic questions of war and the peasantry the Trotskyists were unable to meet the changing needs of the situation
after 1937. Their failure to develop their own armed forces robbed
them of the chance to participate in the war of resistance, and left
them defenseless against their enemies. Linked to this was their
failure to work among the peasants. Their mistake was not, I repeat, that they ignored the peasants. On the contrary, after 1927
one of the main Trotskyist charges against the Comintern leaders
was that they had actively opposed a deepening of the agrarian
revolution. But in the early 1930s the Trotskyists had argued, justi-
fiably in the light of their tiny numbers and the immense difficulties of establishing military bases in the villages, that before attempting to win influence and leadership over the peasants it was
necessary to establish a firm base among the urban proletariat. After
the Japanese invasion this strategy was no longer feasible, and in
fact became the main obstacle to political success. The Trotskyists
failed to see that the workers had been politically neutralized as a
cumulative effect of the 1927 defeat, the ensuing Kuomintang
repression, and, most decisively of all, the Japanese occupation of
China's main towns; and that for the revolution to succeed it was
not only possible but essential to begin organizing the peasants,
even before the movement in the towns revived.

At the root of this failure lay an excess of orthodoxy. Although
some Trotskyist leaders, Wang among them, were acutely aware
that the war had rendered many of the old formulas out-of-date,
and tried (however unsuccessfully) to respond to this new situation, others clung to what they saw as the traditional Marxist analysis, arguing that the peasantry was backward and conservative, and
that armed struggle would have to wait until the conditions were
right for an insurrection of the urban workers. So in 1937–38 the
newly-restored Provisional Central Committee of the Trotskyists
continued to concentrate exclusively on urban work and to oppose "military adventurism" of any kind – a position that Wang
has criticized as a "very grave and absolutely unforgivable political
mistake." Some Trotskyists, for example P'eng Shu-tse, still clung
to these "orthodox" positions even after 1949, insisting that the
strategy of their movement had been essentially correct and that
the CCP victory had nothing to do with its guerrilla war strategy,
but was instead a result of the "exceptional historical circum-

stances" created by the Japanese invasion and the World War.[12] Mao Tse-tung, in contrast, scorned "foreign dogmas" and in his formative years was by his own admission largely ignorant of Marxist theory. Eclectically combining elements of rebellious Chinese tradition with some postulates of Marxism and modern military thinking, he developed an original and highly successful theory of revolutionary war as waged from the countryside.

But through their advocacy of the theory of permanent revolution, socialist democracy, and internationalism, the Trotskyists in China kept alive a tradition that the Maoists had long since abandoned: the new democratic, humanist, and universalist values of May Fourth, now subsumed into the politics and morality of Marxism. The Maoist leaders, on the other hand, dismissed this tradition as "bourgeois," and fought to extinguish it, rather than to develop it further. For Ch'en Tu-hsiu and many revolutionaries of Wang's generation, it was ultimately the CCP's retreat from the intellectual conquests of the early period of the revolution that ruled out any prospect of a reconciliation with it.

Chinese communism began life as fervently internationalist, under the influence both of the Russian Revolution and of May Fourth, whose main leader Ch'en Tu-hsiu denounced "selfish nationalism and patriotism" as "inferior goods" from Japan, to be boycotted along with other Japanese products. The official leaders of the CCP first transformed this policy of internationalism into slavish obedience to Moscow and later promoted nationalist and even xenophobic sentiments within the party. But the Trotskyists maintained a consistently internationalist approach, adamantly refusing to compromise with the deeply ingrained chauvinism of Chinese politics.

The influence of the Chinese Trotskyists in the cultural and literary fields was far greater than their political influence. Even Lu Hsün, the giant of modern Chinese letters, was strongly influenced by Trotsky's ideas on literature and art. Writers close to Trotskyism engaged in fierce polemic with the CCP and its supporters, whom they accused of seeking to strap literature into a political straitjacket. Strong echoes of this debate were heard in the CCP's war-

---

[12] Wang subjected these views to withering criticism in "On the Causes of the Triumph of the CCP and the Failure of the Chinese Trotskyists in the Third Chinese Revolution," 1973.

time capital of Yenan, where writers influenced by Lu Hsün and Trotsky argued that literature should remain critical even within a revolutionary society. Such was the depth of their support that they became the main target of Mao's famous Talks on Art and Literature, in which he advanced the thesis that the task of literature was not to expose the "dark side" of revolutionary society, but to reflect its "bright side," and to extol the masses. One of these Yenan writers, Wang Shih-wei, who argued in favor of revolutionary humanism and egalitarianism in an essay called "Wild Lily," was eventually executed. But Shih-wei's arguments resurfaced irrepressibly during the student unrest of 1957, after his articles had been republished as "negative study materials" in an official literary journal, and again in the 1980s, when all the earlier slanders against him were openly retracted; and finally in 1990 he was reportedly rehabilitated.

Probably the Chinese Trotskyists' main point of interest for critical Chinese communists today is their consistent promotion of the idea of socialist democracy, in relation both to the revolutionary state and to the internal regime of the revolutionary party. As early as August 1929 Ch'en Tu-hsiu had reminded CCP leaders that "democracy is a necessary instrument for any class that seeks to win the majority of its side." But the official party soon abandoned the principle of democratic organization, as a result both of Russian influence and of the switch to a mainly military struggle waged from the most backward parts of the Chinese countryside.

Between 1936 and 1938 and again in late 1939 or early 1940 Wang had a vigorous exchange of views with Ch'en Tu-hsiu on the issue of democracy. Sometime in 1936 Ch'en Tu-hsiu, then in prison, smuggled out an article on democracy to the Trotskyists in Shanghai, where Wang published it in *Huo-hua* (*Spark*) together with some of his own critical comments. Then, three or four years later, Wang again discussed this same question with Ch'en, by then in Szechwan, in letters that he sent him from Shanghai. Ch'en's replies to Wang[13] and others who had written to him in similar vein were later published by Hu Shih in a collection of Ch'en's last articles and letters.[14]

[13] Ch'en addresses Wang as Lien-ken (one of Wang's many aliases) in his correspondence.

[14] Ch'en Tu-hsiu, *Shih-an Tzu-chuan* (*Shih-an's Autobiography*). Taipei: Chuan-chi Wen-hsüeh Ch'u-pan-she, 1967.

Trotskyism is often thought of as a left-wing variant of communism, but it was not only Trotsky's analysis of the failure of the Chinese Revolution but his advocacy of the democratic slogan for China after 1927 that attracted Ch'en Tu-hsiu, who had started his political career as a radical democrat, to the opposition. In the mid- to late 1930s two crucial events—the Moscow show trials and Stalin's alliance with Hitler—caused Ch'en to rethink many of the basic views on democracy advanced by Lenin and by Trotsky. Ch'en concluded that Lenin's complete denial of the value of democracy was at least in part responsible for Stalin's bureaucratic crimes and that dictatorship of any sort, revolutionary or counter-revolutionary, is incompatible with democracy. Whereas in orthodox Leninist terms the dictatorship of the proletariat is simultaneously—at least for the workers—the most extensive form of democratic government, Ch'en no longer bothered to distinguish the various democratic rights from democracy as the bourgeois governing form—an example, in Wang Fan-hsi's view, of Ch'en's tendency to push his ideas to an extremity. After his move to Szechwan in 1938, it seemed to his comrades in Shanghai that Ch'en Tu-hsiu had returned in his declining years to his "first love" in "pure democracy." For Wang and other Trotskyists, democracy was not abstract but bounded by class and time, whereas for Ch'en Tu-hsiu after 1938 it was a more or less transcendental concept expressed in universal institutions. Even so, Wang Fan-hsi did not dismiss out of hand Ch'en's formulations, and instead strove to develop along Marxist lines the elements in them that he found to be perceptive and valuable; just as Trotsky continued to admire Ch'en, and even mentioned him as a possible member of a special committee of the Fourth International that he wanted to form.[15] Between the two of them, Ch'en and Wang raised – decades in advance of the mainstream of communist dissent – issues that bear directly on the invariably vexed relationship between socialist government and democratic freedoms. Ch'en's last views have been preserved, but Wang's replies to Ch'en published in *Spark* and the letters he wrote

---

[15] See Jean van Heijenoort, *With Trotsky in Exile: From Prinkipo to Coyoacán.* Cambridge, Mass.: Harvard University Press, 1978, p. 143. This special committee, elsewhere called the General Council, was intended to be an honorary organization; it never came into being.

to him before Ch'en died, in which he tried to reconcile the necessity of radical revolution with democratic rights, have apparently been lost. Fortunately, in an article written in Macau in 1957,
Wang summarized, in seven points, positions derived from those
that he had advanced in the late 1930s in his exchange with Ch'en.
The article in which he elaborated these seven theses was originally intended as the second part of the final chapter of these
memoirs, but to save space Wang dropped them from the 1957
Chinese edition of his book; and in 1980 even the truncated chapter was dropped (also for reasons of space) from the Oxford En-
glish-language edition (though it has been reinstated here under
the title "Thinking in Solitude"). Wang's seven theses were as follows:

"1. Under present historical conditions if the proletariat through
its political party aims to overthrow the political and economic
rule of the bourgeoisie, it must carry out a violent revolution and
set up a dictatorship to expropriate the expropriators. So in nine
cases out of ten it is bound to destroy the bourgeoisie's traditional
means of rule – the parliamentary system. To complete such a
transformation 'peacefully,' through parliament, is practically if not
absolutely impossible.

"2. A proletarian dictatorship set up in such a way neither must
nor should destroy the various democratic rights – including ha-
beus corpus; freedom of speech, the press, assembly, and association; the right to strike; etc., etc. – already won by the people under the bourgeois democratic system.

"3. The organs of the dictatorship elected by the entire toiling
people should be under the thoroughgoing supervision of the
electors and recallable by them at all times; and the power of the
dictatorship should not be concentrated in one body but should
be spread across several structures so that there is a system of checks
and balances to prevent the emergence of an autocracy or mono-
cracy.

"4. Opposition parties should be allowed to exist under the dictatorship as long as they support the revolution. Whether or not
they meet this condition should be decided by the workers and
peasants in free ballot.

"5. Opposition factions must be tolerated within the party of the
proletariat. Under no circumstances must organizational sanctions,

secret service measures, or incriminatory sanctions be used to deal with dissidents; under no circumstances must thought be made a crime.

"6. Under no circumstances must proletarian dictatorship become the dictatorship of a single party. Workers' parties organized by part of the working class and the intelligentsia must under no circumstances replace the political power democratically elected by the toilers as a whole. There must be an end to the present system in the communist countries, where government is a façade behind which secretaries of the party branches assume direct command. The ruling party's strategic policies must first be discussed and approved by an empowered parliament (or soviet) that includes opposition parties and factions, and only then should they be implemented by government; and their implementation must continue to be supervised by parliament.

"7. Finally, ... since political democracy is actually a reflection of economic democracy and no political democracy is possible under a system of absolutely centralized economic control, ... to create the material base for socialist democracy a system of divided power and self-management within the overall planned economy is essential.

"All these points are not in themselves enough to save a revolutionary power from bureaucratic degeneration; but since they are not plucked from the void but rooted in bloody experience, they should – if formulated with sufficient clarity – (a) help workers and peasants in countries that have had revolutions to win their anti-bureaucratic struggle when the conditions for the democratization of the dictatorial state have further ripened; and (b) enable new revolutionary states from the very outset to avoid bureaucratic poisoning."[16]

After 1949 the old Trotskyist polemic about the nature of the Chinese Revolution (proletarian or bourgeois-democratic, permanent or staged?) and the strategy and tactics to pursue in it was relegated to the history books, but the other main issue that had exercised Ch'en and Wang in the 1930s – the relationship between socialism and democracy – became a central and burning issue for

---

[16] Shuang Shan "Ts'ung Ch'en Tu-hsiu ti 'tsui-hou i-chien' shuo-ch'i" ("On Ch'en Tu-hsiu's 'Last Views' "), in *Ssu-hsiang wen-t'i* (*Some Ideological Questions*). Hong Kong, 1957, pp. 5–6.

young people in China, especially in the universities. Opposition to the personality cult, to repression of dissent, and to the lack of civil and human rights has remained a central plank in the platform of the surviving handful of Chinese Trotskyists over the past four decades, and now that their views are beginning to become known again in China (mainly as a result of the publication of their memoirs) people are beginning to take their criticisms and proposals seriously.

Wang's memoirs draw to a close in 1952, which was an exceptionally somber and depressing year for the movement he had helped to create. Thrown into complete confusion by the unexpected Maoist victory, many Chinese Trotskyists at first argued that the new regime in Peking would never advance beyond its merely bourgeois character. But as if to mock their predictions the new state soon began to move in a radically anticapitalist direction, establishing itself in an apparently unassailable position. Only one thing maintained Wang in his unshakable opposition to the Maoists and in his shining optimism even in the depths of failure: his belief that a system in which decision-making powers were vested in a tiny elite and in which dissent was met with crude repression would inevitably sow the seeds of its own destruction. The situation had a certain irony. In turning its back on the urban culture that had produced it, the CCP had been able to discover rich new seams of revolutionary energy; but it returned in 1949 to confront the workers as an alien force, with new and ugly features acquired during two decades of armed struggle in the countryside. The Trotskyists, who had stayed on in the cities to share the trials and sorrows of the proleatriat, had failed utterly to establish themselves as a significant factor in the revolution; but they had kept alive the universalist spirit of May Fourth and classical Marxism.

Wang's expectations of new social tensions and political crises in China were soon fulfilled. Although Maoism subsequently showed itself to be more differentiated and resourceful than he had imagined, the Hundred Flowers campaign of 1957, the upheavals of the Cultural Revolution, the mass protests in T'ien-an-men Square in April 1976, the stormy emergence of an unofficial opposition in 1979, the growth of a strong democratic trend of opinion in the CCP in the 1980s, and the "Peking Commune" of 1989 that shook the CCP regime to its foundations revealed deep currents of unrest

in Chinese society, and raised issues of democracy, legality, representation, and control that point like daggers at the very heart of
the CCP's political system. For Wang these explosions of dissent
have been a retrospective vindication of his life's work, and are the
first bitter-sweet fruits of victory in defeat.

[Revised May 1990]

CHAPTER I

My First Contact with New Ideas

◔ ◔ ◔

The town in which I was born was a strange mixture of backwardness and enlightenment. Hsia-shih lay on the railway line between Shanghai and Hangchow, and it was one of the main rice-markets in Western Chekiang. Silk produced by the peasants from quite a wide area around it was bought by local merchants to be resold in Shanghai. Commercial capital had therefore long been dominant in the area, and all the most powerful figures in the community were merchants. For centuries local scholars had been looked down on unless they also owned a pawnshop, bank, or large amounts of land. The stench of money prevailed over the fragrance of the book, and there was no cultural life to speak of. In a town of 30,000 inhabitants there were only two higher primary schools. Mine was regarded as the highest educational institution in the town since its headmaster was both rich and learned − he had passed the second grade in the Imperial examinations and most of the teaching staff were respected members of the local gentry. But the headmaster's methods were very old-fashioned. In the school hall there was a tablet in honour of Confucius inscribed with the words 'Divine Sage of the Greatest Perfection', and we children had to bow down in front of it when we arrived in the morning and before we went home in the afternoon. Although the curriculum included natural science, music, and English for the older pupils, pride of place still belonged to Chinese literature, and in particular to the *Analects* of Confucius and Mencius. I only studied the *Analects*, which were taught by an old *hsiu-ts'ai* (a holder of the lowest degree in the Imperial examinations), who was versed in the Confucian classics and in traditional Chinese medicine. He was a very conscientious and fastidious teacher, and made us learn Chu Hsi's textual commentary by heart.

In 1919, when the May Fourth Movement[1] broke out, I was

[1] On 4 May 1919 Peking students went on strike, demonstrating against the decision reached on China at the Versailles Peace Conference and against the Chinese Government's acceptance of Japanese demands. May Fourth represented a turning-point in Chinese history, and signalled the awakening of many Chinese intellectuals to the need for change.

twelve years old. News from the Shanghai market could cause a commotion within a matter of hours in the local tea-shops, but 'trouble-making' by Peking students attracted little attention. Shut up as we were inside the four walls of the school, it is not surprising that the ideological ferment of the outside world took some time to seep through to us. But there was no way of holding up the inevitable, and a year or two later the new ideas took the school by storm.

It so happened that at the time the county's Education Inspector was eager to seize control of our primary school. With the support of a member of the local gentry he managed to oust the old headmaster from his post. But he was unable to gain the sympathy of the rest of the townspeople, and when he came to take over as headmaster the teachers resigned *en masse*, and local scholars declined his offers of appointments. As he was therefore forced to seek his teaching staff elsewhere, he recruited a batch of recent graduates of the Hangchow First Normal School to teach us.

Hangchow First Normal School, a training college for secondary school teachers, was the Peking University of Chekiang province. With Ch'angsha First Normal School, where Mao Tse-tung studied, it was one of the two most powerful provincial outposts of the new ideological movement which centred on Peking University. The Principal of Hangchow First Normal School, Ching Heng-yi, was rather similar in character to the President of Peking University, Ts'ai Yüan-p'ei. He harboured no prejudices, and was prepared to tolerate all outstanding individuals, whatever their views. His own thinking was enlightened and democratic. One of his best-known students, Shih Ts'un-t'ung, became famous for an anti-Confucian article he wrote, *Against Filial Piety*. This was published in the school magazine and gained the First Normal School quite a reputation among radical intellectuals of the period. But the military, civil, and police authorities in Chekiang Province, who had long considered the Hangchow First Normal School a thorn in their flesh, seized this chance to start up a campaign of harassment. To protect his teachers and students Ching Heng-yi threatened to resign, and eventually did so. The students, who wanted him to stay on, boycotted lectures and demonstrated. After they had assembled on the school playing-fields, they were surrounded by soldiers and police. This confrontation, which became famous throughout China, went on for several days.

One of the graduates from the Hangchow First Normal School that our new headmaster appointed was a leader of that struggle, and he became my teacher in the graduation class. The others were also followers of the new movement. On the first day of term we noticed that the tablet to Confucius had been removed, and that the Confucian classics had been taken off the curriculum. The four or five new teachers were only about ten years older than we were. Standing there in their long linen gowns, they did not seem at all forbidding. The solemn atmosphere of the school under the old headmaster was clearly a thing of the past, and those of us who were now under the 'new dynasty' could not help feeling rather upset by what we saw. Students whose families could afford private tuition stayed away from school out of loyalty to the old headmaster. Most of us who remained were poor, and at first we received these representatives of the May Fourth Movement with a mixture of disappointment and apprehension. This feeling did not last for long, however, and after a couple of months we began to hero-worship them.

We no longer feared our teachers, as we had in the old days. On the contrary, they were like friends to us. We found it easy to grasp the things they taught us, unlike the classical texts which we had studied previously. We greedily devoured Ch'en Tu-hsiu's and Hu Shih's articles on the literary revolution, Chou Tso-jen's essays, and the poems in modern Chinese by Liu Pan-nung and others. (I should add that the teachers never once told us about Lu Hsün's writings, and we did not even hear his name mentioned; I myself only heard of Lu Hsün and began to read him after 1925.) We were especially fond of hearing them talk about their lives as students and the struggle in Hangchow. It was not long before we began to experiment with new activities inside our own school: we set up a school council, ran our first library, subscribed to newspapers and magazines from Shanghai and Hangchow, wrote out our own school newspaper by hand and pasted it up on the school wall. We even opened a school shop (dubbed the 'business management training department' by our English teacher) where we sold exercise books, pencils, and sweets.

I left primary school at the age of fourteen, and like many others of my generation clashed with my father about my future career. He was something of a scholar, and had gained the degree of hsiu-ts'ai during the last Imperial examinations ever held. He had many friends among the educated local gentry, but because he was not from a wealthy background they never really accepted him as an equal, even when he was drinking and swapping poems with them, and he resented this. Hence the two sides to his character: he looked down upon his friends as merchants pretending to be scholars, but he was also determined to compete with them in amassing a fortune. When he got drunk he often used to remark cynically to us children: 'There's not much percentage in being a scholar, they'll only respect you if you've got money.' When I had finished my primary school studies (generally considered as the equivalent of a *hsiu-ts'ai* degree under the old Ch'ing dynasty), he insisted that I should study business and refused to let me go on to middle school. Another reason for his decision was the state of our family finances: my father simply did not have enough money to pay for me to study at Hangchow, the provincial capital. He therefore arranged for me to receive training in an import and export business in Shanghai.

In my outlook and my aspirations I was very unlike my father. I think I must have been born an idealist. As a child, I had loved novels of heroism, and adored a great-uncle who had been in the army and who had told me about his father's adventures fighting for the Taipings.[1] Now a year or so of education in the spirit of the May Fourth Movement had turned me into a high-flying idealist, 'infected with the sickness of the epoch'. Given my mental state, it was inevitable that I would refuse to accept the future which my father had mapped out for me. When he told me that he had found me an apprenticeship in Shanghai where I could study English and learn about the import-export trade I found the courage to blurt out: 'I don't want to go into business, I want to go to Hangchow to study!' Relations between us became tense and remained so for months. Finally we arrived at a compromise: he would let me go on to middle school as long as I agreed to study commerce. I therefore entered Hangchow Commercial Middle School.

This school was on the same site as Hangchow First Normal School. Both used the buildings which under the Ch'ing dynasty had housed the Imperial examination rooms, and were separated by a wall. Physically I was on the eastern side of the wall, but my heart was on the western side. The curriculum of the commercial school did not arouse the slightest spark of interest in me. I especially detested book-keeping, abacus work, and the course on how to recognize counterfeit coins. The atmosphere in the school was

[1] The great peasant rebellion (1850–64) against Manchu rule, led by Hung Hsiu-ch'üan.

utterly philistine. There were no student activities, and even less intellectual life than there had been in my primary school under the old regime. After over a year breathing the fresh air of the May Fourth Movement I felt suffocated in my new surroundings. I still had no definite idea about what I wanted to study, and I was not in the least concerned about what profession I should follow. What I really cared about was scholarship and knowledge in general, especially the 'new' variety. Therefore I read every modern book I could get my hands on, not caring whether it was literature, philosophy, or science. Since I could not afford to buy books, I would go and browse in the bookshops every Sunday, or borrow from the West Lake Library. Few of these books were easy to understand, and some of them were very difficult, often as a result of bad translation; but, whether I could digest them or not, I swallowed them all. In my two years at the commercial school I did not even learn how to use the book-keeper's ruler for drawing lines in the account books. But I already knew the names of a string of famous thinkers, from John Dewey and Bertrand Russell to Henri Bergson and Rabindranath Tagore, as well as classical thinkers like Socrates and Plato. I had even read some of their works in Chinese translation. My interests were moving further and further away from commerce, and to stay on in that school would have been pure torture for me.

Fortunately, that was not to happen. During the second term of my second year, we students went on strike against the Principal, and I was elected as one of our representatives. We achieved our demands, but at the end of term our representatives were all expelled. I was originally among those expelled but, because the Chinese literature teacher, who was a friend of my father, spoke up for me, I was in the end quietly advised to leave. To my surprise my father was not at all angry, and he willingly allowed me to transfer to a privately-run, ordinary middle school. After that I had nothing more to do with commerce.

A year later my father died, and the next year, 1925, just before I graduated from middle school, the May Thirtieth Movement erupted. On 30 May 1925, Shanghai students staged a mass demonstration in support of workers on strike at a Japanese cotton mill. While marching into the city centre they were fired on by British police. Several died and still more were wounded. As a result a furious anti-imperialist movement swept first Shanghai and then the rest of China. This was the prologue to the Second Chinese Revolution.

I was then eighteen years old. In the two years leading up to May Thirtieth I had continued to read indiscriminately whatever came to hand, but like many other young people of my generation I came under the influence of the newly-formed Creation Society[1] and gradually developed a particular interest in literature. I was very fond of Yü Ta-Fu's work and whether I was aware of it or not I was profoundly influenced by his romantic and decadent style. Because of my father's death and my family's worsening financial plight, I was all the more ready to identify with the unhappy hero of Yü Ta-fu's novel *Degradation*. Among my fellow students there were some who liked to write, and there were even one or two adherents of the new school. Six months before the events of May Thirtieth, three other students and I produced a paper called *Red News*. I cannot say for certain why we used the word 'red' – our thinking was still far from 'red', and so were the contents of the paper. I recall that one of the articles was a translation from the English I made of the introduction to a history of philosophy published in the Home University Library series. Those of us who collaborated on the paper had no fixed ideological positions, and our politics could best be described as nationalist. But the name of the paper created considerable alarm and, as it was banned by the school Principal, the first issue was also the last.

Red ideas were in fact already circulating in Hangchow at that time. The address of the Communist Party organ *Guide Weekly* was given openly as Hangchow Law School. An Ts'un-chen (later re-named An T'i-jen), one member of the teaching staff (later murdered by Chiang Kai-shek in Shanghai), was a well-known member of the Communist Party, and several people from my home town were carrying out Communist activities under the guise of doing Kuomintang work. The Socialist League of Youth was already in existence, and had a small group at Hangchow First Normal School, run by my childhood friend Hsü Chih-hsing. I was in constant touch with this group, but I never joined it, since I used to look down upon people who engaged in political activity. I believed strongly in 'study for study's sake', and I felt that the pursuit of politics and the search for knowledge were mutually exclusive. I had chosen the latter, and

[1] The Creation Society was a literary group, organized in the summer of 1921 by Kuo Mo-jo, Yü Ta-fu, and other students returned from Japan and France. At first it espoused 'art for art's sake' and romanticism, but later it moved to the left and finally advocated 'proletarian literature'.

intended to devote myself heart and soul to research. One or two of the students in my middle school had become politically active and joined the Kuomintang: they thought themselves a cut above everyone else, but they were very poor students, which only strengthened my prejudices.

These views of mine reflected the differentiation then taking place within the main current of the new ideological movement, although it was not until some years after May Fourth that I personally came into contact with the ideas which it represented. By the time that I caught up with and came to accept these ideas, the new ideology had itself changed and developed further. The *New Youth*[1] group had split, and its two leading figures, Ch'en Tu-hsiu and Hu Shih, had parted company and gone their separate ways. The former advanced towards Marxism, while the latter remained stuck at the bourgeois-democratic stage. The former made the leap from thought into action, and from the literary to the political revolution; the latter wanted to conserve the 'purity' of ideology, and was opposed to scholars sullying themselves with politics. Ch'en Tu-hsiu, Li Ta-chao, and others had set up the Chinese Communist Party (CCP) in 1921, and made an alliance with the revolutionary nationalist Sun Yat-sen and his Kuomintang in the south; Hu Shih and others had joined Liang Ch'i-ch'ao's 'Study Clique', which based its political hopes with the warlord government in the north.

I was completely unaware of this process of differentiation and regrouping in the Chinese intellectual world. Even though Hang-chow was a provincial capital where new publications from Peking could quite easily be obtained, it was still very backward. Insofar as the teachers and students of Hangchow were of the new school, most of them did not advance beyond accepting the general spirit of May Fourth. In Hangchow the dividing line between the new and the old was, and remained, between those who were for Science and Democracy, and those who were against them, between those who attacked Confucius and those who revered him. It was therefore only natural that the young people ideologically awakened by the May Fourth Movement in Hangchow tended to drift into Hu Shih's camp (i.e., Liang Ch'i-ch'ao's camp), rather than Ch'en Tu-hsiu's. Their attitude towards the handful of 'Kuomintang elements' was hostility and contempt. This was because the latter were not 'faithful to the cause

[1] *New Youth* was the name of a magazine edited by Ch'en Tu-hsiu.

of learning' and instead spent their time 'messing about' with politics.

Before the spring of 1925 I was also one such unwitting follower of the Hu Shih school. However, the experience of the May Thirtieth Movement brought a radical and decisive change in me. When the tragic events of May Thirtieth took place in Shanghai, we were busy taking our end of school examinations. At first we did not pay much attention to what was happening, but when we heard that the protests were gathering momentum, and that students, merchants, and workers were staging strikes and creating unprecedented turmoil, we felt we had to do something, if only not to be outdone by the Shanghai students. The atmosphere in my school became heated and the students excited. Contacts began to grow between one school and another, and everyone thirsted for action. Some three or four days after the Shanghai killings, a delegation from the Shanghai Students' Union arrived in Hangchow and told us in detail what had happened. Hangchow students responded immediately by electing two delegates from each school to form the Hangchow Students' Union (representing middle school and college students). Since I used to take part in public speaking competitions, and had once won the all-Hangchow schools public speaking prize, my fellow students considered that I had the necessary qualifications for being a delegate and duly elected me. The other delegate was one of the Kuomintang 'elements'. At first I was not too keen on being a delegate, because of the prejudice I mentioned earlier: I was afraid of appearing vain. And to my surprise, at the inaugural meeting of the Hangchow Students' Union I was put in charge of the propaganda department. This both alarmed and embarrassed me: how on earth would I be able to revise for the school-leaving examinations, let alone prepare for university entrance? But these feelings were short-lived. As soon as I started work, the struggle between the students and the local authorities in Hangchow intensified daily, and I threw myself wholeheartedly into my new role, putting the question of examinations and university to one side for the moment.

My work for the Hangchow Students' Union lasted for only two months, from the beginning of June until I left Hangchow at the end of August to sit the entrance examinations for Peking University. But my experiences in those two months profoundly influenced my life and my thinking. In short, I left the Hu Shih camp for that of Ch'en Tu-hsiu. During those two months my whole time was taken up with work, and yet the experience taught me more than ten years' reading. The struggles which take place during periods of great historical importance are like huge furnaces which instantly reduce to ashes all unhealthy or inappropriate thoughts or feelings and enhance one's better qualities. A student movement in a provincial capital, especially at that time, was not particularly significant, either in itself or in terms of its wider repercussions. But because this movement occurred within the context of other epoch-making struggles and was seen to be part of a nation-wide anti-imperialist and anti-warlord upsurge, it took on a very different meaning. For someone like myself, who had only just taken the first step into the realm of ideas, it was of decisive significance. I very soon realized that the theory of 'study for study's sake' was a false one; true learning should be integrated into and should serve action. I also realized that people who are politically oppressed cannot possibly engage in pure scholarship, as what they learn must have as its focal point the struggle to remove that oppression. I reached this awareness partly through my own experience in the course of the struggle and partly through my contacts with those people whom I had formerly looked down on as 'show-offs'. I found that most of them were not only more able than I, but were also more learned. The 'true' learning which had for several years now been my declared aim in life – a hotchpotch of Dewey, Russell, Bergson, and others – was now revealed as an ill-informed mess of confused ideas. It was during this period that I first came into contact with Marxism. Two friends from my home town who were working in the Kuomintang lent me some elementary social science pamphlets which struck me as examples of practical and useful learning, worlds apart from what I had been studying before.

My short period of student activity in Hangchow taught me something which has stood me in good stead all my life: that it is impossible to draw any distinguishing line between struggles waged against internal enemies and those waged against external ones. Victory over the first is an indispensable pre-condition for victory over the second. I remember that at the first meeting of the Hangchow Students' Union one important question under discussion was whether or not to express solidarity with the Shanghai students by boycotting lectures. The delegates were split two ways on this question. Some argued that, since the struggle was against an external adversary (British imperialism), we should not use the boycott weapon, which was more suited to dealing with internal matters such as government corruption or reactionary measures by the school administration. In their opinion, to go on a lecture strike to oppose the British in the international settlements in Shanghai was the equivalent of shooting an arrow without a target. 'The British won't care if you boycott classes,' they said. 'You will simply be spiting yourselves. If we really want to oppose imperialism, we must drop the idea of a lecture strike and study harder in order to arm ourselves.' Arguments of this sort were very attractive at first. But those delegates who in one way or another had connections with outside political organizations were firmly in favour of the boycott. Their argument was quite simple: if we did not go on strike, then all talk of resisting imperialism was hot air. I was among those in favour of going on strike, but in my heart of hearts I was more convinced by the other argument; I only favoured a boycott because I wanted to see some action.

The strike resolution was passed by a narrow majority, and the entire student body was organized into hundreds of small units, each of which agitated in theatres, tea-shops, parks, and on the streets. The mobilization was very thorough. It even affected the students of the ultra-conservative girls' middle schools in Hangchow. At first we even tried to get the shopkeepers to close down their shops, but without much success. Finally, the Hangchow students' movement held its biggest demonstration ever, numbering seven to eight thousand people, including primary school pupils in their early teens and a number of townspeople.

The Military Governor of Chekiang province was a very shrewd and cunning northern warlord called Sun Ch'uan-fang. Since the whole country was in a mood of extreme militancy, he did not dare to repress us openly and even came to us to express his 'sympathy'. During the demonstration he sent soldiers with loaded rifles slung over their shoulders to 'protect' us. He also summoned a delegation of students, and told them that he was as patriotic as the next man, but that we should leave foreign affairs to the responsible authorities and devote our energies to our studies. At first it was very difficult, especially for those of us who were teenagers, to see through his treachery; but we gradually became aware of what he was up to behind the scenes. The delegates of a physical training college, whose principal was in collusion with the provincial authorities, began to sabotage the Students' Union by behaving disruptively. Then a teacher at my school who was an ardent supporter of the students' movement was sacked, and I myself received a warning in a roundabout way. I was told that if I did not forgo my political activities I would be refused a graduation certificate.

By the time I handed over my responsibilities in the Hangchow Students' Union propaganda department to my successor and left for Peking, I had already purged myself of the last vestiges of Hu Shih's and Liang Ch'i-ch'ao's values, and had gone over completely to the left-wing positions of Ch'en Tu-hsiu, even though I had still not yet joined the Communist Party.

Two Years of University Life

●●●

Graduating from middle school was for me a very different experience from primary school graduation, since by then there was no one attempting to map out my future. My father had been dead for more than a year, and in that respect I was completely free to do as I chose, but family finances were much worse than before and this placed new constraints on me.

My brother, who was only six years older than I, had assumed the heavy burden of supporting the family. A young man in his early twenties, he was expected to deal with the many financial problems which arose after my father's death. In a little town like ours, where money was so important, it was humiliating for him to have to face our father's creditors, and he became very aware of the cruelty of human and social relations. He constantly grumbled about this to me and declared that it was his intention to restore the family fortunes. As a part of his plan, he approved of my wish to sit the university entrance examination, and promised to do everything he could to help me.

Five members of the graduation class, myself included, were going to sit the examinations in Peking. Just before I left, my brother and my mother managed to scrape together fifty silver dollars for me. Since a third-class ticket to Peking cost nearly twenty dollars, I had no idea how I would manage on only thirty dollars after I arrived in Peking. The other four students started out from Hangchow, and we met up together on the way. My brother came along to the station to see me off, and travelled with me for a short stretch before returning home. On the train neither of us spoke a word, except when he urged the other four to look after me. He got off at Chiahsing and waited for a while at the train window, not knowing what to say. As the train moved off, he stood there in the sunset watching me. I leaned out of the window. On his face I could read the expectations he had of me, and this put me in a solemn frame of mind; it was as if we were comrades-in-arms, and I was off to the front to fight to restore the fortunes of the family. However, I completely failed to fulfil those expectations. As time went by our ideas grew further and further apart, and after many disappointments his brotherly affection towards me cooled considerably.

My long-cherished dream materialized: I passed the entrance examination to Peking University. I was very happy and exicted, rather like a Christian must feel on entering a great cathedral. Peking University was a very different place from what it had been at the time of the May Fourth Movement. Ts'ai Yüan-p'ei had already resigned as president, and Ch'en Tu-hsiu had long since left Peking to devote himself to Communist Party work. Hu Shih was said to be at odds with those professors who were members of the Kuomintang, and had asked for extended leave, but there were still many other professors working at the university whom I looked up to. And then there was the library, which was stacked high with books I had never seen or even heard of before, and the porter's lodge, where many different sorts of publications were on sale. I was deeply impressed by the magnificence of China's highest educational institution, and as I drank in the air of learning and culture I felt that I was close to the vital pulse of the nation, the epoch, and the world. I think that this combination of reverence and exhilaration was felt by many of the young people who came to Peking from all over China in search of knowledge.

The political situation in Peking at that time was rather unstable, and was moving quickly to the left. As a result of the warlord Feng Yü-hsiang's change of allegiance, the confused war between the Fengtien and the Chihli warlords had come to an end; P'u-i, the last emperor of the Ch'ing dynasty, had been swept out of the Forbidden City in Peking; the political reverberations of the campaign launched by the Left after Sun Yat-sen's death could still be felt, and political life was in a state of lively ferment.[1] The May Thirtieth incident in

[1] On 15 September 1924, Chang Tso-lin (1875–1928), head of the Fengtien warlord clique, declared war on the Chihli warlords headed by Ts'ao K'un (1862–1938), then President of the Peking Government. This, the second Fengtien-Chihli war, was brought to an end within a month by the defection to the Chihli forces of one of the three top commanders, Feng Yü-hsiang (1880–1948). Having established secret contact with the Kuomintang, Feng called for the cessation of the war and moved his forces back to Peking, driving P'u-i (1906–67), the former emperor of the Ch'ing dynasty, out of the Forbidden City and inviting the Kuomintang

Shanghai, the world-famous Canton–Hong Kong general strike of
1925–6 and the Shakee shootings in Canton on 23 June[1] stimu-
lated and reinforced political developments among the intellectuals
in Peking. The Tuan Ch'i-jui regime in Peking was nothing more than
an empty shell propped up by a number of mutually hostile military
forces. Powerless to act by itself, it could not intervene in the process
of differentiation and regrouping taking place in the ideological and
political spheres.

The various cliques and factions of the northern warlords who at
that time controlled the Government in Peking lacked any conception of ideology. The politicians who were in their pay regularly published articles attacking the 'Red menace', but they were so absurdly
argued that people simply laughed at them. However, the warlord
Government did benefit indirectly from the activities of Liang
Ch'i-ch'ao's 'Study Clique' and Hu Shih's faction. Liang Ch'i-ch'ao's
advocacy of reform, rather than revolution, and Hu Shih's call for a
'government of good men' won some support among students, and
the negative tactics (such as the slogan of 'study for study's sake')
with which they opposed revolutionary activity had even more
influence. On the other hand, the Left in Peking was much stronger,
but had not yet clarified its ideas to the same extent as the Right.

At that time Peking was the publication centre of the whole of
China. Nearly every party, group, or tendency had its own paper or
magazine. According to statistics published in the *China Year Book*,
1925 (compiled by the English *Peking–Tientsin Times*), there were over
220 dailies and periodicals published in the city. But the two ideolog-

leader, Dr. Sun Yat-sen, to Peking. Tuan Ch'i-jui (1865–1936), leader of
the Anhui clique of northern warlords, came to Peking to be 'Provisional
Executive Chief of State'. Dr. Sun came to Peking with the aim of convoking
a national congress, but fell ill and died on 12 March 1925.

[1] In response to the May Thirtieth Incident in Shanghai, 250,000 Hong
Kong workers staged a general strike, beginning on 19 June 1925. They left
en masse for Canton. At the same time workers in Shameen, a settlement for
foreigners in Canton, also joined the strike. On 23 June, when the strikers
together with peasants, students, and soldiers, were marching along Shakee
(opposite Shameen), British and French marines entrenched behind barri-
cades in Shameen machine-gunned the demonstrators, killing 52 of them,
and badly wounding over 170. The Hong Kong–Canton general strike lasted
for over two years and played an important role in the Second Chinese
Revolution.

ical persuasions I have just mentioned were mainly represented by the newspapers Ch'en-pao (Morning Post) and Ching-pao (Peking News), and in particular by the supplements they published. Two popular weeklies, Hu Shih and Ch'en Hsi-ying's Hsien-tai p'ing-lun (Contemporary Review) and Lu Hsün and Chou Tso-jen's Yü Ssu (Thread of Talk), also more or less represented the two rival tendencies.

These supplements and periodicals were mainly literary in character, and rarely dealt with serious ideological or political questions. The disputes that broke out between them, such as the denunciations of Lu Hsün in Ch'en Hsi-ying's gossip column, and Lu Hsün's spirited counter-attacks, were often rather trivial and mostly revolved around personalities, but young people followed them as avidly as if they were affairs of state, and they were as influential as any weighty political controversy. It was in fact through these literary 'cold wars' that people learned to distinguish between new and old, progressive and reactionary, revolutionary and conservative. Together with a number of other literary publications like Mang-yüan (Deserted Plain) and Meng-chin (Forward), these periodicals succeeded in creating a renaissance of sorts in literature and art.

All these publications made a big impression on those of us who had just arrived in the capital. We eagerly awaited each new issue, and as soon as we got hold of a copy we would read it straight through from cover to cover, more assiduously than any university textbook. I think this was the highpoint of my love for literature. From being just an ardent reader of these publications I soon became a contributor to them, at first writing for Hsien-tai p'ing-lun, and then for Yü Ssu.

The Han Gardens and the Horse Spirit Temple area where the university was located could be compared in some ways to the Montmartre district of Paris. Apart from university students, all sorts of young intellectuals lived there. Most of them were very poor, interested in letters and disdainful of all conventions. The people one came across in the street were usually carrying weighty books under their arms or holding the latest issue of some periodical. They seldom bothered to comb their hair, and dressed untidily in long blue gowns and worn-out shoes or sandals. Only a few of them wore Western-style clothes. The hotels and cheap restaurants were full of every kind of aspiring scholar, artist, and rebel, chatting away in a mixture of dialects. For a long time I had been attracted by the romanticism of the Creation Society, and I had a weak spot for this sort of Bohemian existence. The world I now found myself in was in many ways an embodiment of my long-cherished dreams, and I was naturally very happy. I was eager to approach these young intellectuals, and soon made friends with some of them. Among those living in this 'Montmartre' of Peking were Feng Hsüeh-feng and P'an Hsün, two of the leading figures in the West Lake Poetry Society set up at Hangchow First Normal School. I got to know both of these men, especially P'an Hsün (later Mo Hua), with whom I was on the best terms.

Apart from the West Lake Poetry Society there were many other literary groups in this part of Peking. Some published journals, and others simply held discussions. I was interested in all these groups to some extent, but I never joined any of them. In my class I was closest to Wang Shih-wei, and on good terms with Chang Kuang-jen (later known as Hu Feng). By a strange coincidence, both these men later became victims of CCP literary policy.[1]

But my craze for literature and art did not last long, and my exhilaration at being a contributor to famous publications soon passed. Because of my financial plight, I was forced to write for those newspaper supplements which, unlike Yü Ssu and Contemporary Review, paid fees for the articles they published. I soon discovered that it was a real chore having to sell articles in this way, and the humiliation of hawking them around quickly dispelled all the feelings of vanity I had developed on becoming a writer.

An even more important reason why I did not continue as a writer was the fact that shortly after enrolling at the university I joined the then underground Communist Party. I became more and more involved in working for the revolution, and found that I no longer had any time left for dabbling in literature. My transformation from a Bohemian scribbler into a disciplined revolutionary brought about parallel changes in other spheres of my life, including my leisure-time interests and activities. After the winter vacation of 1926, I wrote hardly anything of a literary nature and did not even read any literature, despite the fact that I remained enrolled in the Department of Letters until I left Peking.

[1] Wang became famous for his article 'The Wild Lily' published in Yenan in 1942, for which he was bitterly criticized and later shot. Chang was arrested by the CCP authorities in the early fifties as the leader of a literary dissident group.

The tragic events of 18 March 1926,[1] which resulted in the death of
forty-seven young men and women and the wounding of a hundred
or so more, had a decisive influence on Peking and on me as well. It
would not be an exaggeration to say that March Eighteenth marked
the end of an era as far as the intellectual youth of Peking was concerned. From the May Fourth Movement right down to the eve of
March Eighteenth, the Peking student movement never appeared to
move beyond the limits of a revolution in ideology and literature.
Even though the May Fourth Movement was in one important sense
a political struggle, the political activities of the Peking students
lagged far behind Shanghai and Canton over the following five or six
years. Their social analysis lacked any real depth, and they confined
their activities to rallies in T'ien-an-men Square and petitions to the
Government. Even though the political atmosphere in the capital
livened up after Sun Yat-sen's visit to Peking and his death there in
1925, political life remained superficial. There was a festive spirit in
the air, and after the temporary reconciliation of the warring factions,
it was as if a national reunion was taking place. Feng Yü-hsiang's
clique (which held military power), the Anfu clique (which held
political power) and the leaders of the Kuomintang, the Study
Clique and the Communist Party seemed to be getting on so well
together that it was hard to imagine that there could be any irrecon-
cilable differences between them. Relations between the various
individuals involved were complex and ideological divisions blurred.
A few of the top-level leaders and most of the rank and file believed
that it was possible for the problems of the revolution to be solved
through personal contact and literary polemic, and that the revolution itself could achieve its aim through demonstrations and petitions. This was the honeymoon period of the revolution, its
romantic and literary phase. Periods of this sort are generally brought
to a close by bullets and bloodshed, and the tragic events of March
Eighteenth supplied these two missing ingredients. That day – called
by Lu Hsün the 'darkest day in the history of the Republic' – the
grief and indignation shown by Peking youth defied description in
its intensity, and in the university dormitories the general feeling was
that book-learning was absolutely useless. In the course of those days

[1] Peking students staged a huge demonstration to protest against
imperialist violation of Chinese sovereignty. They were beaten and fired on
by troops of the 'Provisional Executive' Tuan Ch'i-jui, thus ending the
more or less liberal interlude that had existed since the spring of 1925.

Lu Hsün wrote many excellent articles in which he gave voice to our feelings:

'All we have at present are a few poems and essays, a few more topics for conversation.'
'What use is that which is written with the pen?'
'I want no more petitions of this sort.'
'The legacy which those who have died have bequeathed to the future is ... to have taught those who continue the struggle to adopt other means.'
'A debt of blood must be repaid in the same currency.'

Three months later the revolutionary struggle which had started in the South, launched by the Kuomintang with CCP and Soviet support from Canton, began to spread like a prairie fire. Across the whole of south China the sky was ablaze. We watched from the darkness of the North, and were all the more deeply impressed by what we saw. We now had an additional reason to turn our backs on the sterile literary squabbles of the capital. We thirsted for action, and we desperately searched around for any revolutionary ideology or theory which could be linked to practice. It was then that many students wanted to join the Communist Party.

Contrary to what most people believed, there was only a handful of 'rebels' at Peking University in the period 1925 to 1926. When I first joined the Party, as a rank-and-file member, I had no means of knowing what the actual situation was, and it was not until I was brought into the leadership of the university branch that I discovered that of nearly two thousand students only twenty or thirty were Party members. I was told that there were more originally, but after the May Thirtieth Movement in Shanghai developments in the South called for more cadres, so that many comrades were either sent south or went there of their own accord. But at that time there was no need to worry about a shortage of members, since the tide was moving in our favour and many young people were very anxious to join. The Party did not open its doors widely, and had a very cautious recruitment policy in order to prevent an influx of careerists. As a result, there were many memorable figures in the Party's ranks at that time. As far as I know, none of the ones I knew in the early days in Peking were fortunate enough to survive and to find their way into the top echelons of the Party; many of them died a martyr's death. Among those whose memories are still dear to me are:

P'eng Shu-ch'ün, a brilliant student in the mathematics department, who was shot with Professor Kao Jen-shan in 1928; Tu Hung-yüan, another student of mathematics, murdered by Chiang Kai-shek; Chang Ching-ch'en, executed at Kunming in 1931; and Ch'en Ch'i-ch'ang, murdered in the headquarters of the Japanese gendarmes in Shanghai in 1943.

At first, branch activities were centred on the university, and our main aim was to extend our influence within the Students' Union. During that period our only rivals were the Kuomintang rightists who belonged to the Western Hills Conference faction,[1] but since they had no mass support, they were no real match for us. The Students' Union and the various bodies under it all came under our control. During the period in which I was politically active in the university, there were no great political storms to arouse the students, so we never had the chance to use the Students' Union as a weapon to carry on the struggle. Our main field of work in the university was education and training. We ran useful evening classes in which we taught members of the maintenance, cleaning, and service staff of the university, and poor people from the neighbourhood, to read and write. At the same time we organized and kept close contact with a great number of drinking-water vendors who worked in the vicinity of the university. During this period our most important task was to educate ourselves as revolutionaries and to win over the best of our fellow students to the Party. In the long term, this work was of crucial significance, since for a whole number of reasons Peking University had long since become one of the two most important sources of top-level cadres for the Communist Party. (Shanghai College, nominally under Kuomintang control but effectively run by the Communists, was the other.) The North China Bureau of the CCP, under Li Ta-chao, attached great importance to this work, and meetings for theoretical study were held frequently, but they were not very satisfactory. The member of the Peking committee responsible for branch education was Ch'en Wei-jen, who had returned from France after being sent there by the Society for Frugal

[1] The Western Hills Conference faction was a group of right-wing Kuomintang members with Tsou Lu (1885–1954) and Chang Chi (1882–1947) as their leaders, who met in the Western Hills outside Peking in May 1925 and for the first time voiced opposition within the Kuomintang to the policy of co-operation with the CCP.

Study.[1] We respected him as an individual: he knew how to suffer hardship, and was without the slightest trace of romanticism; his character was the precise opposite of us Han Garden Bohemians. He was our first glimpse of a professional revolutionary, and it was from him that we first heard such expressions as 'iron discipline' and 'absolute obedience'. We had never come across anyone like him before, and he made a deep initial impression on us. But before long it became obvious to us that his general learning and in particular his grasp of revolutionary theory was weak, and we were all very disappointed. He often used to give us lectures on questions of theory and on current political topics, but he was clearly only acting as a transmitter of other people's ideas. Worse still, he was only capable of reproducing about half of what he had heard elsewhere. Not only was he incapable of conveying these ideas to us, but he did not even understand them all himself. As a result, when we asked him about points which we did not grasp, he would answer evasively, or accuse us of asking too many questions. Liu Po-chuang, another member of the Peking committee, was a lot better than Ch'en Wei-jen, but he rarely came to speak to us. As for Li Ta-chao, he had long since gone underground as a security precaution, and I never once met him all the time I was in Peking.

We had taken the first step towards becoming activists, but we did not have even a rudimentary grasp of theory. This was a source of great worry to us members of the Party who were intellectuals. At that time, it was impossible to buy new books on social science in Peking. As far as I remember, all we had read by the end of 1926 was *A History of the Development of Society* edited by Ts'ai Ho-sen. There had been some Marxist writings in foreign languages in Peking University library, but because of the advance of the Northern Expedition and the Peking warlord Government's phobia about the 'Red menace' those books had been removed from the shelves and were no longer available for readers to borrow.

Depressed by my lack of theoretical training, bored by the monotony of the student movement in Peking compared with the heated struggles going on in the south of the country, and on the

---

[1] The Society for Frugal Study by Means of Labour was organized in 1915 by some anarcho-nationalists with the aim of helping poor students to study and work in France. By 1920 there were 11,200 such students, and a great many of them turned towards Communism and went to Russia. Ch'en Wei-jen was one of them.

verge of starvation as a result of my financial plight, I began to think of leaving Peking.

During my seventeen months or so in the capital, I was often very short of money. My elder brother kept his promise and did his best to supply me with adequate funds, but his own financial situation was bad, and he was not in a position to send me money every month; moreover, the money he did send was not always sufficient to meet my needs. I managed to supplement my income to a certain extent by writing, but the pay was pitifully low – the publishing houses themselves were extremely hard pressed. Even if a writer did manage to get two or three dollars for an article, the publisher would often pay part of the fee in postage stamps or in small change. On many occasions I did not even have the four dollars for a month's meals in the university refectory. Life dragged on in this way until the late autumn of 1926. I even had to pawn my winter gown, and did not have the money to redeem it. Since it was impossible for me to carry on in this way, I decided to give up my studies and ask the Party for permission to go to Canton.

I arrived in Canton by ship. At that time the Northern Expedition had already got as far as the Yangtse Valley. Wuhan had just fallen, and Chiang Kai-shek's main forces were massing around Nanch'ang. The Kuomintang Central Committee and the National Government had not yet moved north from Canton, which was nominally still the capital of the revolution. But it was already clear that Canton was in the process of losing its former status, and its main role was now that of rearguard of the revolution and its logistical centre. Politically, real power in the city had already fallen into the hands of General Li Chi-shen, who was then very close to Chiang Kai-shek and a member of the right wing of the Kuomintang. The forces of the Left, however, were still very strong; the Canton–Hong Kong general strike was still on and the strike committee could still insist on equal standing with the Nationalist Government in Canton.

The Canton I now saw was very different from the revolutionary Mecca I used to dream of when I was in north China, but it still aroused my enthusiasm and emotions. As soon as I got settled in I went on a tour of the bookstores. I was like a mole emerging into the sunlight: everywhere I looked there were all kinds of revolutionary newspapers, and the sight of them made me feel quite dizzy. I came across the communist New Youth for the first time, and I was pleasantly surprised to see *Guide Weekly*[1] displayed on the counter like any other magazine. Wherever one looked there were piles of books with words like 'Communism' and 'Marx' printed in bold characters on the covers. Ten days before, we only dared to mention such words in whispers behind closed doors. Almost without discriminating I bought up a great pile of literature, and came near to spending my last cent.

I was deeply impressed by *New Youth*, the current issue of which was entirely devoted to world revolution. Up to then I had never realized that there were so many or such profound theories about the revolution. All I had were a few general ideas, or rather simple convictions. I felt that it was impossible for people to go on living in the same old way, that darkness should not be allowed to hold sway any longer, and that imperialist oppression should no longer be tolerated; we should therefore make a revolution and as thoroughgoing a one as possible. The main reason we had joined the Communist Party was not because we had a deep understanding of things, but because it was the most consistent and the most revolutionary political organization we had ever come across. Some of the Party leaders in the North had even told us that there was actually no need for understanding, and that all that was necessary were these simple convictions, since revolution was first and foremost a question of action. Too much study, they told us, could turn people into 'academics', good only for spouting hot air. Even then we found this sort of attitude unconvincing, and we were dissatisfied with the 'pure activism' of Ch'en Wei-jen and others like him. We suspected that this was nothing more than a theoretical justification for their own lack of learning. We afterwards discovered that this was not just the isolated prejudice of one or two cadres in north China, but an important political tendency in the Party during the years 1925–27. For me, reading these issues of *New Youth* was like entering a completely new world, and I came into contact with many questions which I had never thought about before. For the first time such problems as the character of the revolution, the nature of Chinese society, the leadership of the revolution, and the relationships between the classes within the revolution and between the Chinese and the world revolution, began to invade my brain and

[1] The political organ of the CCP, founded in September 1922 and appearing until July 1927, mentioned at p. 6 above.

engage my intellect. These problems have been the main themes of my ideological life ever since.

Many of my old teachers and friends from Hangchow were then in Canton. Some of them had already joined the Kuomintang and were high or middle-level cadres in it or in the Government. They lived fairly well, and during the first few days after my arrival I was warmly received by my friends, so I had no problems in that respect. Through them I was able to get a clear picture of the internal functioning of the revolutionary institutions. I discovered that there was a world of difference between the cadres working for the Revolutionary Government in Canton and those of us who were working underground in north China. In my rather puritanical eyes, the revolutionaries I met in Canton did not entirely deserve that name. They were not sufficiently serious or vigilant, and they were not fired by great feelings of anger and sorrow. They appeared to spend their time enjoying themselves, and they lived a rather carefree life. For me the books and periodicals I bought in Canton were priceless treasures, but it seemed to me that there were very few people there who studied them seriously. Whenever young men got together they were much more interested in discussing women than in discussing politics. In Canton, Sun Yat-sen's famous slogan 'The revolution has not yet been achieved; comrades must still bend every effort' had been given a new twist: 'Love has not yet been achieved, comrades must still bend every effort.' No one ever discussed questions of revolutionary theory, and the main after-work activities of revolutionary cadres were eating out in restaurants or playing mahjong. Even though everyone admired the austerity of the Communist leader Yün Tai-ying, few followed his example. I found the situation more and more painful, since it presented such a stark contrast to the unrewarding labours of my comrades in the North. What distressed me most was the attitude towards revolutionary work which I found in Canton. It was considered as a means of entering the bureaucracy, and those people who wished to participate in the revolution were looked upon as job-seekers.

One of the reasons I had gone south in the first place had been my financial situation, but the main reason had been that I wanted to participate more directly, more whole-heartedly, and more effectively in the revolution. Now, when I arrived in Canton, everyone thought I had come looking for a job. My friends told me that they would try to find me a 'superior position' in the administration. The more kindness and sympathy they showed me, the more embarrassed they made me feel. As a matter of fact there were more people than jobs in Canton at that time, for although the revolutionary centre had moved north, all sorts of people – sincere revolutionaries and careerists, young and middle-aged alike – were still flooding in from all parts of China. It was not that there was no work in Canton, but that most people were after a 'better type of job', and these had generally been snatched up by early arrivals and those with good connections.

During my first fortnight in Canton I was absorbed in the books and periodicals I had bought, and, since I had no immediate worries about food and lodgings, I paid no attention to the problem of getting a position. A little later, I was offered a choice of three different jobs: one as editor of a paper published by a certain military organization; another as Kuomintang representative in an army unit; and, finally, the chance to return north and work underground. At that time many of the Communists who were working externally (i.e. in Kuomintang military or civilian organs) had been allotted their jobs through friends or contacts, and then had gone to the Party for confirmation. Of the three jobs I mentioned above, the first two were suggested to me by friends who were also members of the Party. I was keen to take the editing job, but since one of my friends also wanted it, and was more experienced than I was, I decided not to apply. The second job was with Commander Yen Chung's newly established Independent Division. One of my old teachers in Hangchow was now Yen Chung's secretary, and one of my old friends, Fan Chin-piao, was Kuomintang representative in one of the regiments in the division. These two men wanted me to take over as Kuomintang representative in another of the division's three regiments. I had received no military training, but neither had many of the other comrades in similar jobs. They urged me not to worry, and to take it anyway. For my part, I was quite attracted to the idea of trying something new, but after I had discussed the matter with leading members of the Communist Party, I changed my mind. They were not opposed to my joining the army, but they told me that if I really wanted to do something of value for the revolution, then I should go back to Peking and work underground behind enemy lines. I decided without hesitation to take this course.

My trip to Canton was by no means a wasted journey, despite what some of my friends said. I had seen the revolution with my own eyes, I had broadened my vision, I had increased my awareness, and I had dispelled some illusions: for all these reasons I was more confident than ever. Before I had gone south, the revolution was not exactly an abstract concept in my mind, but I was very hazy about its concrete form and its internal structure. I was completely ignorant about the internal contradictions that existed between the various wings of the revolutionary movement, and I was even so naïve as to think that no such contradictions existed. At this time the most important task of the Northern Bureau of the CCP, as I and my comrades in Peking had discovered from reports sent down from higher levels, had been to win over General Feng Yü-hsiang and oppose the Western Hills Faction. We had therefore been under the impression that, apart from a handful of old men around Tsou Lu and Chang Chi, the whole of the Kuomintang was on the side of the Revolution. Before I went south, I never heard a single word of criticism voiced against Chiang Kai-shek at branch meetings, but as soon as I arrived in Canton I discovered that reality was very different from what we had imagined. The forces of the Right were very strong, and real military power lay in their hands. Chiang Kai-shek's positions, far from being revolutionary, were similar to those of the Western Hills Faction. Chiang Kai-shek's combat organization in the Kuomintang at Canton was the influential Society for the Study of Sun Yat-sen's Thought, with the right-wing ideologue Tai Chi-t'ao as its moving spirit. The so-called left wing of the Kuomintang was made up of Communists working 'externally', who were on bad terms with Chiang Kai-shek: in fact there was no independent left wing. Those individuals who did hold left-wing positions were a tiny minority, and would never constitute a force to be reckoned with. When I first arrived in Canton, I often heard my friends expressing fears and anxieties about Chiang Kai-shek's increasingly obvious disloyalty, but I never came across anyone who had the slightest idea of how to forestall him or strike a blow against him. In Party speeches and publications even these fears and anxieties were not expressed. It was as if everyone was counting on the setting up and consolidation of a revolutionary government in Wuhan, and when Chiang was 'forced to agree' to the removal of the National Government to that city everyone heaved a sigh of relief, thinking that the right wing had been brought to heel.

The strike committee of the Canton–Hong Kong general strike, whose headquarters were in Canton, and its constituent bodies (the workers' tribunals and militia, the huge strikers' canteens, and so on), particularly impressed me. I had never seen anything of the sort before. By then the resources at the disposal of the strike committee had been depleted by the recruitment of workers to the Northern Expeditionary forces, but even so it was still a very impressive organization. On my second day in Canton I looked across the creek to the British concession on the island of Shameen, where I saw all the doors and windows of the Western-style houses sealed and shuttered. There was not a sign of life, and in the open spaces between the houses the grass was growing knee-high. The effects of the strike were to be seen everywhere. I had no opportunity to take an active part in that movement. All I saw were some of its external manifestations: I paid a visit to the communal canteen, which was capable of seating several hundred workers at a time, and I took part in lively mass meetings of the strikers. I remember vividly to this day the activities of the local strike-committee branches in Canton. In each branch there was a long table covered with red cloth, and on the walls were the pictures of revolutionary leaders framed in red. Sometimes there were groups of workers sitting around these tables discussing political issues of the day; at other times they would arbitrate on the disputes that arose between local workers and employers, and even put troublemakers (mainly hooligans) on trial. I was amazed to see how knowledgeable and capable the Canton workers were, but it was only after I got hold of some of the internal discussion documents on that period, published in Moscow in 1928, that I realized the true significance of what had happened: the strike committee was in fact rivalling the authority of the National Government in a situation of dual power, and had even taken the law into its own hands. This was the first time I understood what the theory of the hegemony of the working class meant in practice.

My stay in Canton also taught me that the Chinese and the Russian revolutions were intimately linked. This gave me much to think about. Questions such as that of Soviet aid to the revolution – a long-standing source of contention between the reactionary and the revolutionary parties – had played on my mind for a long time. Even before I joined the party, I had strongly resented the uproar that the papers of the Study Clique and the Young China Party[1]

[1] Young China Party. Also known as the 'Nationalist of the Awakening Lions'. Organized in Paris in 1923 by Tseng Chi (1892–1951) and others. Advocating nationalism, it fought not only against the CCP but also against the Kuomintang by aligning itself with various groups of Peiyang warlords.

raised when they called the Communists and even the Kuomintang 'rouble traitors'. I was angered not only because of my vague admiration for the October Revolution, but also because those people I knew who openly professed to being Communists, friends from my home town, were in my opinion entirely incorruptible. They would never have sold their souls for a few roubles. For that reason, I fervently hoped that all the talk about roubles would be proved untrue, so that there would no longer be any grounds for criticism on that score. By the time I arrived in Canton, my ideas had obviously matured a little, but I still could not help feeling uneasy at some of the things I saw: as my ship sailed into the Pearl River, a Soviet freighter passed the other way; when we anchored, I saw more freighters flying red flags anchored in mid-stream; after disembarking I frequently came across Westerners wearing Kuomintang military uniforms; and later, when I walked over to the Tung-shan area where all the foreigners and high officials used to live, I saw Russian advisers speeding by in motorcars, with pistol-toting Chinese bodyguards on the running-boards. It seemed to me that this was harmful to national honour and to the long-established Chinese concepts of frugality and integrity.

Fortunately it did not take long for me to shake off these remnants of nationalist thinking. After a few weeks I realized, through study and discussion, that the Chinese Revolution was part of the world revolution, and that it could only triumph in the context of the world revolution. From that moment on, I no longer had any doubts about Soviet aid. Whether or not this aid was used in the right way is, of course, another question, and one which at the time never occurred to me. It was only in 1928, after I had arrived in the Soviet Union, that I read about this question in internal CPSU (Communist Party of the Soviet Union) documents.

While I was in Canton I naturally learned more about the Russian revolution and the Soviet Union, but, because of the shortness of my stay and the lack of literature on the subject and of people qualified to talk about it with authority, what I learned was extremely limited and mostly inaccurate anyway. We got the impression that Borodin, the Russian political adviser in Canton, was more important than Lenin, and that General Galen (as Blücher was known when in China as chief Russian military adviser) eclipsed Trotsky as a military strategist. No one as much as mentioned the internal disputes that were going on within the Soviet Party.

In the winter of 1926, after my pilgrimage to the Mecca of the revolution, I returned to Peking University a more hardened and convinced revolutionary. I wrapped myself up in my lined gown against the bitter winter cold. The political climate in the ancient capital of China was equally bleak. The Fengtien warlords who controlled Peking were living on fear, caught unawares by the speed with which the revolutionary forces were advancing in the south. At first they panicked completely, but their confidence gradually returned when they realized that the revolutionary forces were not a unified bloc, and that the faction which controlled the army was in reality anti-Communist. After the conclusion of the Kiangsi campaign in November 1926, Chiang Kai-shek prepared to march on Nanking and Shanghai, while at the same time establishing secret links with Peking; as a result, the Fengtien clique launched a wave of frantic anti-Communist activity, with the covert support of the Japanese imperialists.

Japanese imperialism had become the main enemy of the Chinese Revolution after the advance guard of the Northern Expeditionary armies crossed the Yangtse from the British sphere of influence to the Japanese sphere of influence. In Peking, Japanese special agents actively co-operated with the local warlord Chang Tso-lin's police spies, and devoted all their efforts to dealing with the 'Red menace'. Since Peking University was well known as a Communist Party base, these agents made it their main target. Plain-clothes men lurked in every corner, especially in the restaurants and hostels of the Han Garden area, and it became more and more difficult for us to engage in any political activity. After my two months away I noticed that many changes had taken place in methods of Party work in the capital. In the past we had usually held our meetings in rooms in the university, but this was no longer possible. Some of the leading comrades of the university branch, who had previously lived like other students, now no longer dared to attend classes or to sleep in the student dormitories. Formerly we had been able to leave our mimeograph printing machine in the workers' night school which we had set up, and our work was semi-legal. Now we were forced to move it to a special place. Comrades were kidnapped while they were walking along the street by men who followed them in cars. We became more and more tense, and our communications more and more secretive. This was my first taste of both the fear and the excitement of real underground work.

After I had worked for a period in the leadership of the university branch the Party transferred me to the district committee, probably because of my experience in Canton. The work was nerve-racking and exhausting, with meetings and contact-work from early in the morning until late at night. As a result my studies came to a halt and I began my new life as a professional but unpaid revolutionary. We had to find our own means of livelihood. As far as I knew, only the members of the Peking city committee received payment from the Party. It was no longer possible for me to earn my living by writing articles, not only because I was too busy, but also because the publishing world was subject to more and more repression. One-time booming literary activities were now in sharp decline. For the first few months of 1927 my food was paid for by an old fellow student of mine from Hangchow, who was studying on an unofficial basis at the university.

Despite the fact that life was hard and I was overburdened with work, I still felt very happy. Finally purged of the decadent and romantic ideas of the Creation Society, I was seized by a new sort of optimism and filled with confidence. The history of China was leaping forward, and the old was being replaced by the new at a dramatic pace. It seemed to us that we could already look to the day when a rejuvenated China would become free and liberated from imperialist oppression, and even to the day when China would become Communist. Though we were still living under the muddle-headed and barbaric rule of the warlords and suffering daily persecution at the hands of spies and gendarmes, we knew quite clearly that the days of the regime were numbered, so we did not allow ourselves to be intimidated by such repressive measures, even learning to laugh at them. We joyfully got on with our underground work, and good-humouredly put up with the hardships of life. The revolution was in its ascendancy, and the honeymoon was not yet over. We revolutionaries who were working behind enemy lines were full of illusions – in our view the prospects were excellent.

Despite increasing repression, many young people were eagerly oining the Party. When I had joined it in the winter of 1925, the university branch only had twenty or thirty members, but by the early spring of 1926 membership had shot up to over two hundred. Most of the 'aspiring scholars' of the university quarter left their ivory towers to engage in the real struggle, and even after the arrest

and assassination of our leader Li Ta-chao this influx of new blood
into the Party continued.

But there were two things which worried me: the relations between
the Communist Party and the Kuomintang, and the general contempt
for theory in the Party. Among the revolutionaries actively working
underground in Peking at that time there was not a single real
member of the Kuomintang, which apart from a handful of right-
wing officials did not exist there as a separate organization. None of
the young students had any confidence in the Kuomintang or even
respected Sun Yat-sen, even though there was a flood of propaganda
after he died and he was described in the most reverent terms. We
found much of what we read in his lectures on the 'Three People's
Principles' – nationalism, democracy, and people's livelihood – too
laughable for words. Nevertheless we were forced to join the Kuomintang. When we were engaged in certain types of activity we had
to say that we were Kuomintang members and we were even forced
to set up phoney Kuomintang meetings. I remember that shortly
after I joined the Communist Party I was ordered to attend a meeting
of this sort. The first item on the agenda was to bow down in front
of a portrait of Sun Yat-sen and listen in respectful silence while his
political testament was read out. After that we listened to a number
of reports on the situation in the South. I later learned that of the
fifteen or twenty people at that meeting, only one was a real
Kuomintang member, and all the rest were Communists. I could not
for the life of me understand the necessity for such a charade, and I
found it even more ridiculous when the real Kuomintang members
we had invited failed to turn up, so that everyone at such a meeting
was really a member of the Party. The fact that we still bowed down
in front of Sun's portrait and read out his will made some of us
burst out laughing. When I mentioned my reservations to leading
comrades, they explained that this was necessary on account of the
united front. 'But there is no Kuomintang to unite with', I protested.
'The whole thing is a farce.' 'The situation is different in the South,
where the Kuomintang is a real force', they would reply. 'We have to
carry out the national line.'

In Peking, or at least in the branches under the district committee
for eastern Peking, there were only two books of a theoretical
character in circulation at that time. One was the first part of
Bukharin's *ABC of Communism*, and the other was Burkhardt's *The
Student's 'Capital'*. The first of these was very popular with Party

members because it was written in a style that was easy to understand, and we mimeographed several copies of it. But Burkhardt's
book was heavy going, and since we had no time to make a proper
study of it we read it without understanding it. So from an ideological point of view we were not qualified to be called Communists.
We were fighting for Communism, but none of us really understood
what Communism was. We were all very aware of this deficiency,
and hoped for more books to read and people to teach us; above all
we wanted the Party to set up a short training course. But, because of
the increasingly difficult situation and the negligence of higher-level
Party members, none of this was done.

There we were, working away in an almost light-heartedly optimistic frame of mind, under a regime of intensifying terror, inspired
by an ideology which we barely understood. Our goal was clear and
simple: opposition to imperialism and warlordism. Our task was
simply to expand the organization. It was only in April 1927, when
Li Ta-chao was arrested and killed, that our style of work, and more
particularly our state of mind, changed. Our easy-going mood gave
way to a profound sense of tragedy and anger.

As a middle-level cadre I did not know whether the Party had
taken any precautionary measures in advance of this incident, but it
seemed to me that the organization was aware that the authorities
had something planned. Several weeks before it happened, we were
all told to be especially careful in our movements. Two days before
the arrest, T'an Tsu-yao, who a few days later was to be hanged together with Li Ta-chao, told me that he was going to hide in a safe
place, the Legation Quarter, and urged me not to sleep in my lodgings. But we had no way of knowing that the enemy was to strike
precisely in that place which we usually considered safest. According
to the 1901 treaty forced on China after the Boxer Rebellion, the
Legation Quarter was not subject to Chinese sovereignty, but, with
Japanese help, the warlord Chang Tso-lin got permission from all the
signatories to the Treaty to send troops and police into the area on 6
April 1927. They openly violated the diplomatic immunity of the
Soviet Embassy and arrested the Communists who were in the
Chinese Eastern Bank adjacent to the Embassy building.

Many accounts have already been written of this incident. Future
historians, basing their conclusions on archive materials and eye-
witness reports, will undoubtedly write more detailed a ccounts of
the martyrdom of Li Ta-chao and his nineteen comrades. This is not

the place for me to write down my fragmentary recollections. But there is one point, which was widely talked about in Peking party organizations at the time, which I think should be raised. After the arrests there was a storm of protest, both at home and abroad, and considerable pressure from public opinion. Chang Tso-lin was therefore in a quandary: what was he to do with the Communists he had arrested? It was said that elements within his clique, in particular his leading adviser Chao Hsin-po, were speaking up for Li Ta-chao and the others, and urging that they should not be executed. Chang Shih-chao, one of Tuan Ch'i-jui's ex-ministers, also recommended strongly that the prisoners' lives be spared. As a result, Chang Tso-lin was said to be in favour of sending them to Mukden to sit out long prison sentences. But the 'Supreme Commander of the Revolutionary Armies', Chiang Kai-shek, urged Chang Tso-lin through secret channels to have them killed, thus helping Chang Tso-lin to reach his final decision. This information came from very reliable sources close to the Fengtien clique. The execution of Li Ta-chao and the others in Peking on 28 April came within days of Chiang Kai-shek's massacre of the Shanghai workers on 12 April, and the two incidents were clearly linked.

It was the start of a bloodbath. It had an enormous effect on the revolutionary camp, in particular on young revolutionaries like me, proving that revolution was not a game in which youthful romantics could indulge their imagination or get rid of surplus energy. Those of us with a more utilitarian outlook began to weigh up the advantages and disadvantages of continuing the fight. The merciless face of the class struggle revealed itself to everyone, acutely posing the question of whether or not to follow the revolution. We were all forced to make a decision, influenced by factors such as the background we came from, the depth of our understanding, and our strength of character. In other words, with the deepening and differentiation of the revolution, a differentiation also began to take place in the revolutionary ranks.

But, in Peking, the arrest of Li Ta-chao and the others did not immediately result in the collapse of the local party organization. Our work carried on as usual, and in the short term at least the bloody repression did not cause any wavering in our ranks. On the contrary, we became much more serious, and not a single comrade was driven out of the organization by fear. The warlord system was in its death agony, and was totally incapable of evoking panic. What shook Communists in the North more, and created uneasiness and confusion in our ranks, was the news of the savage purges that were taking place in the South as the leaders of the Kuomintang turned on all popular organizations. We were not prepared for this either ideologically or emotionally, and found it hard to believe that the leader of the revolutionary army could massacre the workers. The younger comrades were particularly embittered by the anti-Communist articles of the former radical Wu Chih-hui which were published in the Peking press, since we had always looked up to him as a progressive and admired his personality and lively literary style. We ran around commiserating with each other about the shocking news, and found it impossible to explain the sudden transformation in our former idol. Naturally enough, none of the people I was in contact with was in sympathy with Chiang Kai-shek or Wu Chih-hui: there was a widespread sense of regret and even betrayal, and a feeling that their actions could only benefit the enemy. We wanted an explanation for what had happened and instructions on what our attitude towards Chiang should be in the future. But the only explanation I could get from the Peking committee was that Chiang had capitulated to imperialism and the rightists and betrayed the revolution. I conveyed these remarks to the comrades in the branches. Shortly, however, we received the following consolation from the same source: 'Chiang's defection is not important; the Kuomintang still has a left wing, there is still Wang Ching-wei. They are our trusted allies. The centre of the revolution is now Wuhan'. This seemed to clear up our confusion. We resumed our work, and turned our eyes towards Wuhan. There was an immense amount of work to be done there, and not enough people to do it, so the Party asked the Peking committee to send some comrades south. It was decided to send those, myself included, most likely to be marked out for surveillance by the Peking police. There were ten of us in all, including P'eng Lien-ch'ing, the famous student leader of the Peking Women's Normal University, and Chang Ching-ch'en, chairman of the Peking University Students' Union. Early one morning in July 1927 we quietly slipped out of Peking. Thus ended my life as a university student.

CHAPTER 3

From Wuhan to Moscow

❂ ❂ ❂

Shanghai was blanketed in an atmosphere of terror and war. Checkpoints strengthened with sandbags and barbed wire were set up everywhere between the French Concession and Chinese territory. In the Old West Gate area in particular there was hardly a soul to be seen on the streets, and it was as if one could actually feel the fear and smell the blood which had recently been shed there. Attempts had been made to paint out the slogans on the walls, but it was still possible to make out the message they carried: 'Down with imperialism', 'Down with Chiang Kai-shek', 'Oppose the White terror'.

We had heard that it was dangerous to travel up the Yangtse from Shanghai to Wuhan, and people embarking for the trip were frequently arrested, but since there was no other way to get there we had to take the risk. We were all very nervous, and some of us had disguised ourselves so that we would not look like students, but when we boarded the steamer we found that things were not as bad as we expected. We had no trouble with the police. On arriving in Wuhan, we saw immediately that the situation in the city was quite unlike that in Shanghai. Even the weather was hotter, in line with the feverish political climate. Just as we got off the boat, a huge procession, with banners waving and slogans being shouted, came down the main road of what had been the British Concession until its recovery several months earlier, and the sight of it made our spirits soar. There were crowds everywhere, on the quayside and in the streets, all looking busy and excited. Red banners bearing slogans welcoming the convocation of the All-China Conference of the Confederation of Labour were strung across the streets, and fluttering proudly in the breeze. We were almost moved to tears. In Peking, it was dangerous to be in possession of a book with a red cover, but here there were slogans in huge characters painted on the walls of all the big buildings, with quotations from leaders of the Russian revolution such as Lenin and Zinoviev. The appearance of this revolutionary centre made us happy and excited, and we congratulated ourselves on being able to throw ourselves into real revolutionary work.

It was not long before we were disillusioned. After we had reported to Party headquarters, we found that the jobs we were assigned to were not as important as we had expected. There were too many people for the amount of work available. Some had been summoned from other areas and others had fled to Wuhan from the right-wing Kuomintang. Many had absolutely nothing to do. I was far more fortunate, and given an assignment at the Party headquarters of the Four Provinces Committee. This was an amalgamation of the four separate provincial committees, of Kiangsu, Anhui, Chekiang, and Kiangsi. Nominally of the Kuomintang Left, but largely staffed by Communists, it had been set up in Wuhan by leading comrades who had fled Chiang's purges. The original purpose of the head-quarters was to work out plans for underground activities in the four provinces, but in fact it functioned more as a refugee centre for dispersed comrades. Since I had practically nothing to do I could work up no enthusiasm for my assignment, although I at least had some-where to live and many interesting comrades to exchange stories with. What disappointed us most was to discover that political life in the city was rent by continuous conflicts. The 21 May Incident in Ch'angsha, provoked by Hsü K'o-hsiang, had already taken place; Hsia Tou-yin's rebellion had been crushed by the Wuhan Cadets' Army and the armed workers; and the Wuhan Army had defeated the Fengtien warlords in Honan province. Exaggerated reports of the victory in Honan appeared in all the newspapers, claiming that the revolutionary government had been further consolidated. But despite all this, fear and anxiety were increasing within Communist Party organizations. There were all sorts of rumours flying about: it was said that the attitude of General T'ang Sheng-chih, supreme com-mander of the Wuhan forces, was questionable, that the leading Kuomintang politician Wang Ching-wei was not to be relied on, and that Sun Fo, Sun Yat-sen's son, was secretly flirting with Chiang Kai-shek's rival government in Nanking. What should we do? This was the question uppermost in all our minds. It reminded us very much of the situation a year earlier: then we had all looked in vain to-wards Chiang Kai-shek, and despite his growing recalcitrance and his rapid shift to the Right we had been incapable of moving a finger to stop him. Now we were looking in the same way towards Wang Ching-wei and T'ang Sheng-chih. On the surface, at least, our relations with the so-called left wing of the Kuomintang were closer than they had been with Chiang Kai-shek. Wang Ching-wei seemed to be acting under the supervision of our forces, and the Wuhan government appeared to rely greatly on Soviet aid and the support of the Communist Party. But the situation was worsening, and even we lower-level cadres could clearly see that the revolution was reaching a crisis.

At that time I heard rumours that in April or May, after Chiang Kai-shek had openly broken with Wuhan, there was a dispute in the city about whether to march north against the warlord Chang Tso-lin or east against Chiang. Moscow was said to have favoured continuing the Northern Expedition, and as a result T'ang Sheng-chih moved his forces further up the Peking–Hankow railway. Many people were very unclear about the reasons for this decision, the most common explanation being that it was in order to link up with General Feng Yü-hsiang's army. According to the Comintern, Feng Yü-hsiang had been re-educated as a revolutionary in Moscow, and once the two armies linked up it would be easy to move against Chiang in Nanking. Originally I had been suspicious of Feng Yü-hsiang, but several months before, while I was in Peking, I had read his *Manifesto on Returning to China* ('I was born a worker's son'), which we had secretly mimeographed and distributed. I also heard that after the execution of Li Ta-chao and the others, Feng Yü-hsiang ordered all his armies to wear mourning and swore to avenge them as martyrs. Thus I too began to have hopes of him. A few days after we arrived in Wuhan, Feng Yü-hsiang and the leaders of the Wuhan Government met in Chengchow. Not all the decisions reached at this meeting were made public. Many people thought that Feng would come to Wuhan to discuss how to deal with Chiang Kai-shek, but he never came. From what I could see, the higher ranks of the Party were not at all encouraged by the outcome of the talks, and even the small handful of genuinely left-wing leaders in the Kuomintang appeared to be in low spirits. There were rumours that Feng Yü-hsiang wanted to 'arbitrate' in the conflict between Nanking and Wuhan. A few days later I met an old friend of mine from Peking, who a year earlier had gone to work in Feng's army. He told me that after the army had marched through the T'ung-kuan into Honan province, all the political workers had been packed off to Wuhan aboard a special train. I then realized that our hopes in Feng were completely misplaced, and that he had only been pretending to be a revolutionary in order to get weapons and ammunition from the Soviet Union; once his military position was firmly re-established, he had dropped this mask and revealed his true warlord features.

After the Chengchow conference the situation in Wuhan quickly deteriorated. The Communist Minister of Agriculture T'an P'ing-shan resigned on the pretext of illness, and Minister of Labour Su Chao-cheng soon followed suit. Wang Ching-wei and his supporters even more boldly attacked what they saw as the 'excesses' of the peasant movement in Hupeh and Honan, and loudly called on the Communist Party to curb the revolutionary activities of the Wuhan workers. The Party leadership appeared to retreat step by step, and *Guide Weekly* carried only a few timidly-worded protests at the attacks and some cautiously argued justifications of the revolutionary upsurge that was taking place among the workers and peasants. There was no political counter-offensive, and there was not even any intention of organizing one. The voice of the counter-revolutionaries was becoming louder and clearer, but we were at a loss for what to do. Irresolution and anxiety gripped the whole Party.

Normal Party activities had virtually ceased. Apart from occasional meetings with individual members of the Party leadership, I never attended a single branch meeting during the whole time that I was in Wuhan, and therefore had no real way of knowing what the attitude of the Party was on key questions. If I had doubts, it was very difficult to find anyone in a position of responsibility to discuss them with. I often used to meet and talk with comrades and friends, but they were just as much in the dark as I was. Everyone was very confused and in a state of near panic, so that hearsay took the place of regular internal reports, and guesswork that of informed analysis. Comrades working in top-level Kuomintang bodies became the sole source of reliable information, so that we knew what moves the enemy was making but were unaware of the tactical responses of our own Party.

One afternoon, while I was walking down a street in Hankou, I saw a large fleet of rickshaws stacked high with rifles and accompanied by a group of trade-union militiamen. The sight of them caused a stir in the street, and I heard someone say that the trade unions had volunteered to surrender their arms to Li P'in-hsien, commander of the local garrison. I asked what was going on. I was told that this move was necessary to avoid misunderstandings, and to convince the Government of our loyalty. Although I could not think of any

alternative I was dissatisfied with this answer. I understood instinct-
ively that it was impossible to further the revolution by making concessions of this sort.

At this time Hsü Chih-hsing, an old friend of mine from Hangchow and a member of the Communist Party, was confidential
secretary to the standing committee of the Central Committee of the
Kuomintang, and I frequently got my information from him. I went
to see him one Monday morning when all the headquarters staff
were at a Sun Yat-sen memorial meeting, and he suggested I should
go along with him to the great hall to take part in the meeting. By
chance this was the very morning when Wang Ching-wei made his
famous speech 'Our struggle against attacks from two sides', an
undisguised declaration of anti-Communism. I was shocked by the
arrogant way in which Wang Ching-wei spoke, the enthusiastic
response he got from most of those present and the frenzied cries for
revenge from the Hunanese landlords and Kuomintang party hacks
who got up to speak afterwards. I had never smelled the gunpowder
of the counter-revolution so clearly as I did then and my last
remaining illusions in the Kuomintang were dispelled. It was
obvious to me that the Communist Party was powerless to deal with
the situation, and this made me even more depressed. Hsü Chih-hsin
was completely disheartened by Wang's speech. After the meeting
was over, he invited me out for a meal. He suspected that he might be
killed at any time, and even went so far as to ask me to make arrangements for the disposal of his corpse. He had been wanting to leave
his post for some time now, but he told me that the Party would not
let him do so.

I knew that a long struggle had been going on within the Party on
the question of what strategy to adopt in the revolution, but none of
us ever found out what the content of this dispute was, and there was
not the slightest hint of it in the pages of Guide Weekly. We heard
rumours that the two main protagonists were Ch'ü Ch'iu-pai and
P'eng Shu-tse, but at the time we never saw any of the documents
relating to the discussion. It was only after the Wuhan Government
came out as openly anti-Communist that a pamphlet by Ch'ü
Ch'iu-pai entitled 'Against P'eng Shu-tse-ism' came into our hands.
We immediately read it through from cover to cover. Because our
theoretical level was shallow and because we could only follow
Ch'ü's side of the discussion, we accepted his thesis. He argued that
the completion of the agrarian revolution was an important guaran-

tee of victory in the Chinese Revolution as a whole, and that the revolution should be carried in one stage straight through to socialism; not in two stages, through democracy to socialism. But in fact Ch'ü's pamphlet did not succeed in dispelling all our doubts, in particular on questions such as relations between the Communist Party and Kuomintang, the arming of the workers, and the tactic of making use of the warlords. In terms of concrete alternatives, his position was no different from that of the official leadership, and was therefore incapable of showing a way forward. It was not until a year later, when we read of the arguments that had taken place within the Soviet Communist Party on the China question, that we really began to grasp the issues involved.

Having heard Wang Ching-wei's speech with my own ears, I had lost all my respect for that so-called left-wing leader of the revolution, but I could not help noticing that no criticism of him appeared in Party publications. Our basic attitude was still that we should support him, in order to ensure his leadership of the Revolution. I found it very difficult to understand the need for this policy, and frequently discussed my reservations with friends. It was my own belief that we should hit back. During my stay in Wuhan I used to write or translate occasional articles for a revolutionary newspaper. I thought, naïvely, that it would be a good idea to write an article attacking Wang Ching-wei, though I knew perfectly well that it could never be published. Half jokingly, I jotted down my ideas, and accused Wang of being a counter-revolutionary. When I went out later, I left the article lying on the table, where it was discovered by a Kuomintang 'left winger' who immediately informed on me.

The same night I was arrested and taken to the central public security station in Ho-chieh. Thus began the first of my four spells in prison. It was an old-style gaol with wooden bars, mud floors, a wall on three sides, and no windows. The sky could not be seen through the wooden grille, so there was no direct daylight, and although there was a low-volt electric light-bulb dangling outside the bars it was very gloomy inside the cage. Stepping through the gate, I saw twenty or thirty ghost-like prisoners, naked to the waist, huddled together in groups. The place stank appallingly, though I could not make out whether of sweat, putrefaction, or excrement. I was overcome by nausea. The floor was slippery and sticky, and when I bent down to take a closer look I saw that it was covered with urine. As a child I had heard people talking about the Buddhist hell and at middle school I had read Dante's Inferno, but never did I imagine that earthly prisons could be so terrible. Altogether I have spent an eighth of my life behind bars, but looking back I would say that for living conditions this was the worst prison I was ever sent to.

Because I was probably the first communist in Wuhan to go to gaol in this period, my spiritual torment was even more unbearable than my physical surroundings. It was not yet in fashion to imprison Communists in Wuhan, as the Government in charge of the prisons was still considered to be revolutionary. It was only my personal opinion that Wang Ching-wei was a counter-revolutionary. The Party had not yet come out openly against him, and the leaders of the Communist International still hoped to keep him on their side. The fact that I was still not quite sure, either emotionally or ideologically, that I had acted correctly in writing what I did about Wang Ching-wei, made prison even harder to bear. One's capacity for enduring hardship is not something absolute: it is decisively affected by such factors as the strength of one's individual convictions and the prevailing social climate. In certain periods, when the relationship of class forces and the social climate are such that many revolutionaries have to risk their freedom and even their lives for the realization of an ideal which is clearly within their grasp, they consider it an honour to go to prison, and even take positive pleasure in the sacrifice involved. At other times, however, imprisonment or execution are very hard to bear, not only for someone like myself, but even for a real hero. In Wuhan in July 1927 history was already demanding sacrifices for the Revolution, but because this process was being artificially retarded, here I was, a prisoner in advance of my time, in Wang Ching-wei's gaol.

After I had been in the cell for several hours, I discovered that my fellow prisoners were mostly landlords from Hunan awaiting sentence, or strike-breakers and small capitalists arrested by the Wuhan Confederation of Trade Unions. And there was I, their sworn enemy, a member of the Communist Party. Naturally I took care not to reveal my identity to anyone, and the other prisoners took it for granted that I was one of them, but the thought did cross my mind that other prisoners like myself might soon be taking their places.

Every day a number of my fellow prisoners were released, but I had no contact with the outside world or with the prison authorities for some time. On my fourth day in gaol my friend S. got permission to come and see me, and he told me that there was nothing to worry about, that all the comrades in the Four Provinces party headquarters, including the Kuomintang left wingers, were very angry about what had happened to me, and that I would soon be set free again. But it was not until ten days later that I was actually released. The comrades afterwards told me that the reason for the delay was because relations between the CCP and the Kuomintang had deteriorated considerably, and it would only have made things worse if they had interceded on my behalf. They had therefore requested Ching Heng-yi, former principal of Hangchow First Normal School and by this time Minister of Commerce in the Wuhan Government, to stand security for me.

I was released in about the middle of July. The situation in Wuhan had changed greatly during my imprisonment. The reactionaries were coming more and more out into the open, and there was growing panic in the revolutionary camp, some of whose members were already beginning to leave Wuhan. The economic situation was rapidly worsening, and the official paper currency of the Wuhan Government was losing value hourly. Ten dollars would no longer buy even an ice-cream, and everyone was desperately trying to get hold of silver dollars to pay for a passage out of the area. The Party leadership was in complete disarray, and some of its constituent bodies had already dissolved themselves. The masses were out on the streets demanding an eastern expedition against Chiang Kai-shek, and slogans supporting Madame Sun Yat-sen's proclamation (which called for continuing adherence to Sun Yat-sen's Three Great Policies of collaboration with the Soviet Union, collaboration with the CCP, and support for the workers and peasants) were to be seen everywhere. But none of this could disguise the fact that people were downcast and pessimistic. Unconfirmed rumours were flying round – for example, that a Comintern representative, M. N. Roy, had shown Wang Ching-wei the Comintern's proposals for arming the workers and peasants; that Ch'en Tu-hsiu had fled Wuhan; and that General T'ang Sheng-chih was collaborating with Chiang Kai-shek. Many of the younger comrades I knew were planning to enrol in the army of Ho Lung (who was soon to join the Communist Party) and go east, and I was thinking of joining them; but I was told during discussions with the Party leadership that I should go to Moscow to study military science instead.

Because the Revolution had suffered its first defeats on the periphery, most of the revolutionaries had fled to the 'centre', Wuhan, and, although there was never any formal estimate, the number of provincial cadres now living in the city must have bordered on ten thousand. Like me, most of these comrades had come there in high spirits, aiming to find work for themselves in the Revolution, or to get personal instructions from the Central Committee, and then either to return to where they had come from or to go elsewhere to carry out clandestine work for the Party. But they were soon disappointed, because the revolutionary centre was becoming a counter-revolutionary centre. Not only was there no work for them to do, but also more and more of those who did have jobs were being forced out of them. The central leadership, evidently no longer able to control the situation, simply left comrades to their own devices. Those of us who had come to Wuhan from Peking had never once been invited to discuss how things were in the old capital, despite the fact that we were the first group to go south after the death of Li Ta-chao. Later on the situation got much worse, and things became increasingly difficult for those Party members like myself who had gathered in Wuhan. They were in a quandary: most of them were on the wanted list in the places they had just come from, and they could not have returned even if they had wanted to. Since there was no longer any revolution in which to participate, many of them were forced to beg for their living on the streets and await arrest and execution. The main problem of the day was what to do with the scattered remnants of the revolutionary forces.

One solution to this problem was to send some of us to Moscow. As far as I know this was on Moscow's initiative, the aim being to give a group of us a short period of military training. Seven or eight hundred of us were selected to go. Workers and peasants were supposed to be given priority, but in practice over half of those chosen were students or intellectuals. Of the ten of us who had come down from Peking, five were to be sent. We were all very excited at the prospect of learning to use weapons. After the catastrophic defeat the Revolution had just suffered, the idea that armed force was the ultimately decisive factor in any situation was very appealing to us – we were in no position to make a deeper analysis of the causes of the defeat. The facts were only too clear: in less than six months we had watched one military man after another switch from leading the revolution to opposing it. In quick succession they had shamelessly and bloodily deceived us. We were like abandoned concubines, or pitiful and impotent old-fashioned scholars. It was natural that we should draw the conclusion that to achieve victory in the Revolution we ourselves should take up arms. Mao's idea that 'power grows out of the barrel of a gun' well expressed the mood of the Chinese Communists in Wuhan during this period. Not only was it natural, it was essentially correct. But we thought that things would be different from now on, that we would learn how to use arms, build our own army, and no longer have to look for suitable allies among the existing generals. I believe that this was a common sentiment among those of us who were about to go to Moscow.

Some time later I was on a boat out of Wuhan. By this time the counter-revolution was in full swing, and the local newspapers in Wuhan were beginning to publish advertisements in which former Communists announced their resignation from the Party. In Shanghai, where we stayed secretly in a small hotel, we heard the news of the Nanch'ang Uprising of 1 August. The Emergency Conference of the CCP at which Ch'en Tu-hsiu was removed from the leadership was just then being held in Wuhan, although we knew nothing of it. Several days later, we slipped aboard a Soviet freighter and sailed to Vladivostok. There were more than sixty passengers on board, among them Sun Yat-sen's widow, Soong Ch'ing-ling, and some members of the family of Eugene Ch'en, the former foreign minister of the Wuhan Government.

As soon as the ship had sailed out of the Huangp'u River, we crawled out from the hold and onto the deck. It was like being born again. The early autumn sun lifted our spirits, and we began to dance for joy and to sing the Internationale. We sailed further and further out to sea, gradually losing sight of the shores of the motherland. The water was like glass and our mood changed to one of meditation. We leant against the railings and gazed pensively into the distance, while thoughts flooded in. As individuals we were each beginning a new chapter in our lives, and it seemed to us as if the Chinese Revolution was also beginning a new chapter in which each word and each letter would be written in bullets and blood. In the struggles that lay ahead, the military training we were about to receive would have a decisive role to play. Seen in this light, the defeats, the terror, and the humiliations suffered over the last few months seemed to dwindle away completely.

One month before the tenth anniversary of the October Revolution, we arrived in Moscow.

CHAPTER 4

Chinese Students in Moscow

● ● ●

We stayed in Vladivostok for a couple of weeks, and the train journey to Moscow across Siberia took another thirteen days. During that time we got to know the Soviet Union better. Although we had never been so naïve as to think that the Russian Communists had already created a heaven on earth, we still had only the vaguest conceptions of what the country was like. Reality turned out to be very different from what we young Chinese Communists had imagined. For example, when we docked at Vladivostok, I was amazed to see raggedly-dressed Russians wandering around the wharf. On the evening of our third day my eyes were opened still wider. Two Chinese friends and I were strolling along the tramway on Lenin Road near the suburbs of the town when a man ran past us, threw a rotten tomato at one of my friends and disappeared up a side street, swearing furiously in a language we did not understand. From this small incident we learned for the first time that we were not universally welcome in the fatherland of the world proletariat, and that there were still people around who hated Communists, and foreign Communists in particular. We also learned that there was still a class struggle going on, and a very bitter one at that. It was only then that we really understood that a socialist revolution does not lead automatically to the successful construction of a socialist society, and that an ideal society cannot be built overnight The little revolutionary theory we had studied before was confined to such questions as how to make a revolution and lead it to victory. We had not the slightest idea about the sort of problems that might arise afterwards – the reorganization of the national economy on a new basis, class struggle under a workers' government, and so on. It was only after our arrival in Vladivostok that we realized that we had to study revolutionary theory not only for the sake of the revolution in China, but also in order to understand the problems of socialist construction in the Soviet Union.

We were received in Vladivostok by a German comrade, speaking in English. I was chosen to act as his interpreter. I learned that he had been a sailor, and had taken part in the German revolutions after the First World War before working for the Comintern. During my stay in Vladivostok I was also contacted by a Chinese called Liang Po-tai, who was a top-ranking official in the Far Eastern Province of the Soviet Union. The fact that Soviet officials were not all Russians struck us as a real illustration of the breakdown of narrow national barriers with the ending of racial discrimination. We had read about internationalism in books: it was a moving experience to see it with our own eyes.

An incident which took place during our train journey through Siberia burned deep into my memory. It is worth recording here, since it affected the later development of my thinking. We Chinese students occupied two sleeping compartments on the train. Each compartment had an orderly to look after and keep an eye on the passengers. Whenever we approached a bridge he would shout *most* ('bridge') and close all the windows in the compartment. No doubt these orderlies had connections with the security authorities. Ours was a middle-aged ex-Red Army man. He was agreeable and open towards us, and he looked after us very well. We became friends immediately, and he volunteered to teach us the Russian alphabet. We got on fine with him until one morning when we were sitting around in a circle, pencils in hand, practising the Russian alphabet. One of us traced out the word 'Stalin' in Russian. Our teacher took one look and turned away without saying anything. One of us gave him the thumbs-up sign and said: 'Stalin! Stalin! *Khorosho*! (good!)'. We were all grinning at our Russian friend, expecting him to react as enthusiastically as we did. To our astonishment, he stubbed out his cigarette, spat contemptuously and held up his little finger, saying '*Eto, eto!* (this one!),' red in the face with anger. Then he raised his thumb and said 'Trotsky! Trotsky! *Khorosho*!' After that he stormed out into the corridor, where we could hear him muttering away angrily in Russian.

At the time, we found the incident extremely perplexing. We knew very little about the internal struggles that were going on in the CPSU. In Wuhan we had been told that Lenin had been succeeded by Stalin, who was now the leader of the Communist movement both in Russia and in the world, whereas Trotsky was consumed by personal ambition, was a romantic, and was a militarist man of the Chiang Kai-shek type. The surprising reaction of our Red Army veteran was the first time we experienced a different assessment of the two men from that handed down by the leadership.

The incident I have just described took place about a third of the way through the journey. During the rest of the trip a marked change came over our Russian friend. He was still as kind and considerate as ever, but he was no longer as free and easy as before, and the Russian lessons came to an abrupt end. Looking back, it is obvious that he was afraid and regretted his emotional outburst. Knowing that all of us were Party members, he probably feared – unnecessarily – that we would inform on him.

The journey was an extremely happy one. I still remember the night our train passed Lake Baikal. It was the fifteenth day of the eighth month by the old Chinese calendar, the Mid-Autumn Festival – a holiday joyfully celebrated throughout China. Under the silvery light of the full moon the lake was beautiful beyond description. It took a whole night for our train to go round the southern shore. We sat at the windows from dusk to dawn, entranced by the beauty of it. The following morning we arrived at the lake-side city of Irkutsk, where we tasted the famous local smoked fish dishes.

Autumn must be the most beautiful season in Siberia. It was still too early for snow, but there was already something stern and for-bidding about the endless expanse of forest, which had turned from green to a yellowish colour. The air was so fresh and clear that we could smell the fragrance of the grass and trees through the train windows. The little stations and the communities built around them were particularly attractive and picturesque. All the houses were built of unpainted logs. Many of the stations were so well hidden in the forest that only when the train drew to a halt could you see that they were there. On the platforms there were often groups of young men wearing *rubashki* (traditional Russian shirts), playing the balalaika, singing and dancing. At every station country girls and old women sold boiled eggs, pickled cucumbers, and other food. The atmosphere was happy and peaceful. It was still several years before the Stalinist collectivization of agriculture reached its height, and the period when the centrists and rightists in the CPSU were making use of the rich peasants to attack the workers and their political representatives in the Left Opposition.[1] With Stalin's help, Bukharin

[1] Since the early twenties, especially after the death of Lenin in 1924, three factions emerged in the ranks of the CPSU: the Rightists, Centrists, and

was carrying out his policy of 'advancing towards socialism by enriching the peasants'. Needless to say, we had not the slightest idea at the time of the distant connection between these charming country girls selling us their surplus food and the downfall of Trotsky and his supporters.

We arrived in Moscow at the beginning of October, and moved into a building near Strastnaya Square. Other batches of Chinese students continued to arrive throughout the following weeks, and soon there were over six hundred of us living in the same hostel. It had been intended that we should all go on a six-month course at the military school attached to the Communist University for the Toilers of the East (KUTV). When we arrived in Moscow, however, the military school was not yet ready, probably because the defeat of the Chinese Revolution had taken everyone by surprise. We therefore had nothing to do for a few weeks, until it was decided to transfer a few dozen of us to the normal two-year course at KUTV. I was among those chosen, though I was not at all happy about the move. I considered that I had come to Moscow for military studies. At that time none of us really understood the crucial role of revolutionary theory, and as a result of our defeat we were obsessed to the exclusion of all else with what we took to be the decisive role of armed force. In any case, I still held the absurd view that to study seriously I would have to return to the National University in Peking. The last remaining traces of this prejudice only disappeared after I began a serious and systematic study of Marxism.

KUTV was a political university which specialized in training revolutionary cadres for the countries of the East. It recruited students from over seventy nationalities, including the minority nationalities of the eastern part of the Soviet Union and the oppressed nations of Africa and Asia. There were also some Japanese and black American students. We lived at Tverskaya Boulevard, in the same hostel that Ch'ü Ch'iu-pai and others had lived in during their stay in Moscow a few years earlier. In the early 1920s all

Leftists. The first faction of Left Opposition was formed by Leon Trotsky in 1923 with the aim of defending his and Lenin's views against the Centrist–Rightist bloc of Stalin–Zinoviev–Kamenev. Later it developed into an international organization called the International Communist League, which was the predecessor of the Fourth International.

Chinese students in Moscow studied at KUTV. After 1925, when the
Chinese Revolution was on the upsurge and more and more Chinese
came to Moscow to study, a new university named after Sun Yat-sen
was set up exclusively for them. Since Sun Yat-sen University was a
product of the period of collaboration between the Kuomintang and
the CCP it admitted not only members of the CCP and the Communist
Youth League, but also children of high-ranking Kuomintang
officials. Men and women who had been members of the CCP for a
longer time were still sent to study at KUTV.

In 1927, there was also an important political difference between
Sun Yat-sen University and KUTV. The president of the former was
Karl Radek, a prominent Trotskyist, whereas KUTV was run by Boris
Shumiatsky, an ardent supporter of Stalin. In order to further their
own interests, the faction in power in the CPSU Central Committee
bolstered KUTV in every way possible, and made sure that all the best
and most reliable students were sent there. By the time we arrived in
Moscow, however, the situation was beginning to change. The
Stalinists had won their struggle with the Trotskyists at Sun Yat-sen
University, and Pavel Mif had replaced Radek. The fate of Trotskyist
students at the university had also been settled: some had been
expelled from the CCP, and were awaiting transfer either to Siberia or
back to China, others had capitulated and renounced their views,
among them Chiang Ching-kuo, son of Chiang Kai-shek.

The moment we began our life as students we were drawn willy-
nilly into the factional struggle that was to decide the fate of the
CPSU, the Soviet Union, the CCP, and even the whole of humanity.
We were ignorant of the history of the Russian Revolution, and
knew next to nothing about the Soviet Union or the international
workers' movement. We were therefore completely at sea when
asked to take sides in the controversies of that period. Nevertheless,
we followed them with great interest, especially the controversy over
the Chinese Revolution. Although we lacked the necessary theoretical
background, we knew enough from our bitter experience to arrive
at our own conclusions. Even before we arrived in Moscow, many of
us had serious doubts about the course of events in China. Now that
we had begun to study and think, we concentrated single-mindedly
on the issues involved in the discussion, read the documents, and
attended meetings. By the tenth anniversary of the October Revolution, we had become more or less acquainted with the substance of
the controversy. Two months later, in December 1927, the Fifteenth

Congress of the CPSU was convened in Moscow. By that time I had in some ways begun to side with the Left Opposition. However, a deeper process of change was necessary before I could complete the transition to Trotskyism. At first we were prejudiced against the Left. The Party had successfully inculcated us with the habit of unconditional support for the majority and mindless obedience to the Central Committee. Although we had never read a single document and were ignorant of all the major issues in the controversy, we assumed that Stalin's side was right.

The first time my suspicions were aroused was at a plenary meeting of the Party members studying at KUTV, held shortly after our enrolment there. E. Yaroslavsky, the chairman of the Central Control Commission of the CPSU, gave a report to the meeting. Students from the different nationalities present sat together in groups to facilitate simultaneous interpretation into their own languages. The gist of the speech was that Trotsky was a Menshevik, and had consistently and deliberately opposed Lenin. His motives for participating in the October Revolution were bad, not to say treasonable, and history had shown that his participation had done more harm than good. We Chinese students accepted all this as gospel truth, since we knew nothing about the factional history of social democracy in Russia. Not so the other students, most of whom were Caucasians and Armenians. Yaroslavsky's remarks unleashed a storm of indignant protests among them. They booed and heckled during his speech. We could not understand a word of their interjections, but when we asked our interpreter to translate for us he refused and said: 'It's nonsense – just Trotskyists making trouble!' Some Chinese students who were in the year above us and already understood a little Russian whispered to us that they were shouting 'Shame!' and 'Liar!' We were flabbergasted, and not a little confused. After Yaroslavsky had finished his speech, a Russian student jumped up onto the stage to a chorus of hisses. He shouted angrily at the top of his voice. Then a section of the audience stormed the platform with the evident aim of dragging him off. Others sprang to his defence, and the meeting dissolved into chaos. Finally the chairman intervened to order him to stop speaking, and he was frog-marched off the stage, still shouting and struggling. By now things were threatening to get really out of hand, as each side squared up for a fight. We therefore withdrew from the meeting. We could not understand a word of what they were shouting at each other, but it was clear that a sizeable minority of the audience supported Trotsky. It was also clear that the struggle between the two factions had reached boiling-point.

What we had seen at the meeting fed our appetite for study. We devoured all the documents we could lay our hands on. But the more our interest grew, the more dissatisfied we became with the material available. The documents we saw were only excerpts from or résumés of the arguments of the Stalinist majority on the Central Committee. Since we had never seen a single document setting out the arguments of the Opposition, we asked the KUTV Party Committee to make some available to us, so that we could acquaint ourselves at first hand with the positions of the 'enemies' of the party. We were told in reply that the positions of the Opposition were explained in the documents issued by the Central Committee which contained many quotations from Oppositionist documents. We were not satisfied with this answer: the arguments attributed to the Opposition in this material were so obviously wrong that it was impossible for us to believe that prominent leaders of the revolution could ever have advanced them. One doubt gave rise to another, and we now began to question documents which we had hitherto accepted unconditionally. The leading members of the Party Committee obviously noticed our change in attitude, and took it as a bad sign. They showed us a translation into Chinese of a speech delivered by Trotsky at one of the sessions of the Central Committee, with many passages abridged or deleted. It was so badly hacked about as to be virtually unintelligible. The interjections and quips from Stalin, Bukharin and their friends were, however, recorded in minute detail, as was the enthusiastic acclaim with which Stalin's remarks were met, and the crude heckling to which Trotsky was subjected. But by reading between the lines it was possible to reconstruct the essence of the controversy. The three main issues in dispute were the Anglo-Soviet Trade Union Committee,[1] socialist construction in the Soviet

[1] The Anglo-Soviet Trade Union Committee was a link between the top bodies of the Soviet trade unions and the General Council of the British Trade Unions, created by Stalin and Bukharin before the British General Strike of May 1926 to win the support of British trade union leaders for the Soviet Union. Trotsky disagreed with this policy, arguing that it could only help the reformist leaders to cheat militant workers. On socialist construction in the Soviet Union, Trotsky and his friends then thought that priority should be given to heavy industry, while Stalin and his group wanted to develop light industry in order to humour the peasants.

Union, and the strategy and tactics applied in the Chinese Revolution. Because I was not clear about the reasoning behind the two positions I had still not formed an opinion on the latter. Like many other comrades I was not prepared to make a judgement, let alone take sides, until I had made a proper study of such subjects as the history of the international worker's movement, political economy, the history of the Russian Revolution, and the problems of economic construction in the Soviet Union. Naturally the Party Committee disapproved of our sceptical neutrality. In their view it was our duty as Communists to support the majority of the Central Committee unconditionally and unreservedly. For them, reading documents was simply a process through which such support could be given with greater awareness and therefore be firmer. There was no place in such a scheme of things for doubt or suspicion. In any case our 'party spirit' told us that it was a grave error to doubt the correctness of resolutions adopted by the Central Committee. The result was that we neither could nor would voice our doubts publicly. Formally we supported the resolutions unreservedly; but our sense of reason forced us to make mental reservations on a number of questions. Having raised our hands in support of the decisions of the Central Committee, we plunged all the more eagerly into the study of revolutionary theory, and in particular the theory of the Opposition.

One might almost say that my agreement with the Left Opposition on the controversial questions of the Chinese Revolution was instinctive. Should we have entered the Kuomintang? Should we have built and extended the organization of the Kuomintang? Had Chiang Kai-shek been a reliable ally of the proletariat in the Chinese Revolution? Were the Canton–Hong Kong strike committees a kind of soviet? Were we right not to mobilize and organize the peasants during the Northern Expedition? Had we been right to support another Kuomintang leader, Wang Ching-wei, in order to create a 'new revolutionary centre' after Chiang Kai-shek's betrayal? Had the tactic of a 'bloc of four classes' stood the test of events in China? As a result of my two years of first-hand experience of the struggle, I had my own answers to all these questions. Needless to say, my analysis was immature and incomplete. I knew next to nothing of classical Marxism, and had never read Lenin's theory of the role of the proletarian party and the tactics it should adopt in the bourgeois democratic revolution. But even during my time in north

China I and many other comrades had found it ridiculous that we were ordered to build and do mass work not for our own organization, but for the Kuomintang – a party which only existed at grassroots level through our own activities. I had also found it impossible to understand why we encouraged misplaced confidence in high-ranking Kuomintang generals and politicians, and why after being betrayed by one swindler we had switched our allegiance to another. Finally, I had found it difficult to explain why we had decided to hand over the weapons of the Wuhan workers to General Li P'in-hsien, and why we had denounced the struggles of the Hunan peasants as 'excesses' and helped to suppress them.

At first I had been bewildered by all these apparent inconsistencies. Later I was told that they had been mistakes committed by Ch'en Tu-hsiu in defiance of Comintern instructions. It was not until after my arrival in Moscow that the truth dawned on me. Despite the fact that the documents available to me were heavily censored, it emerged from a careful reading of them that it was not the Soviet adviser Borodin, or Ch'en Tu-hsiu, or the Comintern envoy Roy who had been responsible for these policies. They had simply been the executors of a policy formulated, adopted, and pushed through by the Central Committee of the CPSU, which ultimately meant by Stalin. I could see no difference in principle between his current policy and the policy he now maintained had been 'wrongly carried out' in China.

This was not so of the positions of the Opposition, which were clearly based on a strategy fundamentally different from the one we had been putting into practice in China. Nevertheless, none of us either dared or wanted to express support for the Opposition, which had after all been denounced as counter-revolutionary.

The KUTV party committee met several times a week to discuss the documents we had been given to study. We were very careful about what we said in the course of these discussions. It was only when the question of the Chinese Revolution came up that we had anything to say at all, and then we voiced some of our doubts by referring to our experiences in China. But more often than not we were immediately reduced to silence by the committee members, who quoted at us Marxist classics which we had never had the opportunity to read. Sometimes when we tried to generalize on our experiences and advance timid criticisms of certain points in the documents, they would adopt superior smiles and say in a quiet voice: 'Comrade,

your opinion would be welcomed by Trotsky (or Radek)'. Needless
to say, we Chinese revolutionaries were not cowards by nature. On
the contrary, most of us had considerable reserves of moral courage.
We only behaved in this way because words like 'Party', 'Central
Committee', and 'majority', had such a sacred and authoritative ring
about them that none of us either dared or were equipped to challenge them.

To that extent therefore, I was a 'Stalinist' at the time of the
celebrations to commemorate the tenth anniversary of the October
Revolution. On the day itself, a spectacular demonstration was staged
in Moscow. It was the first time in my life that I had seen anything of
this sort. It impressed me tremendously. We met at daybreak to
march in procession to the District Soviet, where we joined up with
other demonstrators. We reached Red Square at noon, and returned
home at about four o'clock. While we were marching past the Lenin
mausoleum we saw Stalin and other Party and State dignitaries for
the first time. They were standing on top of the monument, raising
their arms and waving their hands. As the various sections of the
march filed past, one of them was shouting slogans through a micro-
phone. We Chinese Communists received a particularly rousing
welcome, either because the Chinese Revolution was still fresh in
people's minds or else because Stalin wanted to show that it had not
been defeated, but on the contrary had entered an even higher stage
of development. No sooner had we turned the corner of the Kremlin
Wall and entered Red Square than we heard the thunderous shouting
of slogans: 'Long live the Chinese Revolution! Long live the Chinese
Communist Party! Long live the world revolution!' Each time the
masses cheered in response, as if to bring the sky down. The nearer
we got to the mausoleum, the more heated the atmosphere and the
louder the slogans. Countless red flags were fluttering and billowing
on every side of us, like a sea of fire. There were huge crowds everywhere. Alongside the mausoleum, guests of honour were packed
together on rostrums. On both sides of the procession tens of
thousands of people were formed up in columns, waving flags, hats,
and handkerchiefs in the air and shouting their heads off. They held
out their arms as if to embrace us, or to lift us onto their shoulders.
It was all unbelievably moving, so much so that we were all reduced
to tears. How proud we were to be Chinese! How fortunate we were
to be Chinese revolutionaries! How happy we were to have been
received by our Russian brothers on the tenth anniversary of their

revolution! The thunderous cheers accompanied us all the way across Red Square and continued until we reached the banks of the Moskva River. Looking back over my shoulder at that ancient and imposing parade-ground of the revolution, decked out in its brilliant colours, I was more than ever filled with respect and gratitude towards Stalin, the general of the assembled troops.

When we got back to the hostel, however, we learned that many people, most of them Russians, had experienced a very different reception. An old friend of mine, who had been living in Moscow for several years and was an interpreter at Sun Yat-sen University, told me that the Opposition had staged a counter-demonstration that morning, with placards demanding the fulfilment of Lenin's testament. They had taken part in the procession, but when they got to Red Square their placards were seized, clashes took place, and many of them were arrested. He also told me that someone had shot at the car in which Trotsky was travelling.

That same evening we saw a film about the October Revolution in the university common room. I did not notice at the time who the scriptwriter and director were, but I think it must have been V. I. Pudovkin's The Last Days of St. Petersburg. I afterwards learned that Sov-kino had decided to produce two films, one directed by Eisenstein, the other by Pudovkin, to celebrate the tenth anniversary of the October Revolution. Eisenstein based his film on John Reed's book Ten Days that Shook the World, and called it October. Both directors completed their films as scheduled, but because Eisenstein's October put Lenin and Trotsky on a par, it was not allowed to be screened. Pudovkin's The Last Days of St. Petersburg, however, was passed for showing to the public, and must therefore have been the film we saw. Although it had been approved by the Stalinist authorities, it did not depart too far from historical fact. After all, the internal struggle was still going on and the history of the revolution was still fresh in most people's minds. Therefore, Trotsky and other Oppositionists made frequent appearances during the course of the film, which soon turned into a sort of popularity contest. Every time Trotsky or Stalin appeared on the screen the audience erupted. Some clapped their hands and cheered, while others whistled and stamped their feet. Since the lights were out, there was little chance of detection. It was almost as safe as casting a vote in a secret ballot. In this battle of decibels, the support for Trotsky was at least as loud as, if not louder than, the support for Stalin. I remember at one point the film showed a series of close-ups of leaders of the revolution, and Trotsky's picture appeared straight after Lenin's. There was an immediate storm of cheers and clapping, and it seemed to go on for ages. The Stalinists started whistling and stamping their feet, but to no avail. The noise grew louder and louder until at last the lights went up.

For me and for most of the other Chinese, this film was our very first introduction to the events of 1917. It gave me a broad idea of the roles played by Trotsky and Stalin in the revolution. Despite the deliberate attempt to exaggerate Stalin's role and play down Trotsky's, the contrast between the two men – the one colourless and uninspiring, the other brilliant and outstanding – must have been clear to anyone not utterly blinkered by factional prejudice. My own admiration for Trotsky dated from the showing of that film.

The tenth anniversary of the October Revolution was important as a celebration of the victory of Stalinist reaction, a landmark on the road towards the degeneration of the Soviet Union. But it came at a time when the policies of the victorious Stalinist faction, whether in the Soviet Union itself, in Britain, or in China, had failed utterly. In order to consolidate its victory, the bureaucracy had to conceal its failure. This was the reason for the decision to celebrate the anniversary in such a solemn and spectacular way. The blood of the Chinese workers and peasants, the sufferings of the working class in Britain, and the persecution of the Soviet revolutionary vanguard were hidden away behind a wall of red flags and festivities. In this holiday atmosphere the Opposition could only appear as slanderers, troublemakers, and even traitors to the revolution.

After the holiday the factional struggle at the university became more heated. The Party cells continued to hold several meetings a week, but they became very different. Before the anniversary they had almost invariably centred on the documents we had received, with the aim of showing from a theoretical and political point of view how the Opposition was wrong. Now we were simply informed of the 'crimes' which the Opposition had committed. The gravest of these crimes was the staging of the 'counter-demonstration'. Other serious charges included the running of a secret printing press and the alleged links of the Opposition with a 'White Russian bandit'. We were simply informed of these charges, since there was clearly no basis for discussing them. Afterwards we would unanimously pass a resolution of censure, drafted and proposed by the Party Committee, despite our doubts. What worried me most was the charge of 'running a secret printing press'. How could it be a crime for prominent officials, some of them still at their posts, to keep a mimeograph or even a printing-press handy in order to publish their own views and those of people who thought like them? It worried me so much that when the question of the 'printing press plot' was raised at a meeting I asked how the law of the Soviet Union regulated the use and setting up of printing presses. The interpreter was rather taken aback by my question, but he translated it just the same. When he had heard me, the Russian who was addressing the meeting smiled mysteriously and gave me a meaningful look. Then he told me through the interpreter: 'In principle, the question is very simple. In our country, the means of printing are monopolized by the proletarian state. They can only be kept and used by the State. Counter-revolutionaries are not – absolutely not – allowed access to them.' 'But . . .' I opened my mouth to ask a supplementary question, but I was silenced by the interpreter, a Chinese Communist who had come to Moscow from Germany. 'But what?' he said, with a triumphant smile. 'Surely you're not going to deny that the Oppositionists are counter-revolutionaries?' All eyes in the room were on me. I became very embarrassed, and blurted out 'No . . .'. I felt someone tugging my jacket with the obvious intention of getting me to sit down again. 'No, of course not', I said, trying to sound convinced, and sat down. I turned quietly to the man who had tugged at my jacket and whispered: 'What's the matter?' He made no reply, but scribbled something like, 'Speak carefully, be patient', on a piece of paper, and immediately crossed it out again. He did the same thing several times.

One evening several days later, I went for a walk with this man along the Tverskaya Boulevard. We had a long talk, and he told me something about himself. His Chinese name was Lo Han. (For security reasons, every Chinese student in Moscow adopted a Russian name.) He had studied in France many years ago with Ch'en Yen-nien, Chou En-lai, and Li Li-san. He had given up his speciality of pottery manufacture to become a professional revolutionary, joining the party in Paris. After working for the party in Canton, he was made political commissar in a Kuomintang army unit. After the so-called Gunboat Chungshan incident of 20 March

1926[1], Chiang Kai-shek began to move against the CCP, and expelled all Communists, Lo among them, from the army. The Central Committee of the CCP sent them to Moscow to study Marxism. In seniority and qualifications Lo Han belonged to the first generation of the CCP. In his eyes I was a younger brother. Lo Han was always very kind in his dealings with other comrades, although he was by nature a reticent man. He told me many things about the Soviet Union and the internal struggle in the CPSU. He said that the views of the Oppositionists were not as ridiculous as they were made to appear in the official documents, and that it would be wrong to take sides in the dispute until further information was available. Finally he told me that all the members of the Party Committee in the university, Chinese and Russians alike, were time-serving bureaucrats who had not the slightest interest in the truth, so that it was pointless to open one's mouth at Party meetings. I asked him whether he had ever seen any of the documents of the Opposition. 'One or two,' he replied. He denied having any organizational links with the Opposition. This was true, as I later found out, for at that time there was no Oppositionist grouping among the Chinese students at KUTV. It was only because, alone among the Chinese contingent at KUTV, Lo Han and another student called Tuan had friends at Sun Yat-sen University who were in the Russian Opposition, that they occasionally got to see Oppositionist documents.

Lo Han did not convert me to the Opposition, but he made me increasingly sympathetic towards its aims. From that time on I was no longer a naïve and confused participant in the struggle. I had opinions of my own, and began to act with more prudence than before. I no longer voiced my doubts or objections at Party meetings, no matter what the subject of the discussion.

The persecution directed against the Opposition was now stepped up considerably. It no longer remained on the purely 'theoretical' level. Oppositionists were now dealt with by administrative means, harassed by the police and the GPU,[2] driven out of the party en masse,

[1] On 20 March 1926 Chiang Kai-shek carried out his first small-scale, pre-emptive coup against the Communists and Soviet military advisers working in the Kuomintang, on the pretext that the gunboat *Chungshan*, commanded by a Communist, had moved without his consent with the intention of opposing him.

[2] The predecessor of the KGB. GPU stands for the Russian initials of the State Political Board.

sacked from their jobs, and denied civil rights. We frequently heard of Oppositionists being physically beaten. At Sun Yat-sen University, a group of student Oppositionists were expelled from the party and some teachers sacked. Although nothing of this sort happened among the Chinese students at KUTV, a mood of anxiety and uneasiness grew up. Relations between fellow students became more and more strained. Everywhere there were spying eyes, and as newcomers we were singled out for special attention.

In early December the CPSU convened its fifteenth congress. There were no Oppositionists among the delegates: all of them had been purged before the congress met. As a congress it marked Stalin's final victory over Trotsky. All of the resolutions passed were simply a justification or confirmation of the measures that had been taken against the Oppositionists. The delegates endorsed the decision to expel all Oppositionists from the Party and hand them over to the secret police. Among the students at Sun Yat-sen University who were expelled and sent back to China were Ou Fang, Ch'en I-mou, Sung Feng-ch'un, and Shih T'ang. At KUTV many students from the minority nationalities of the Soviet Union were arrested, but since relations between students of the different nationalities had never been close we only heard of these arrests indirectly. None of the Chinese students at KUTV were arrested, and as far as we knew neither were any of the other foreign students. The only exception was a comrade from the Dutch East Indies, who was expelled and exiled to a place near the Finnish border. He was sent back home after the Sixth Congress of the Comintern in 1928, at the request of the Dutch East Indian delegates. He may have been Trang Malaca, who later became leader of a Trotskyist armed unit in the former Dutch East Indies during and after the Second World War, since according to bourgeois press reports Trang had studied in Moscow for a period.

News of the persecution of the Oppositionists filtered through to us with amazing speed. This was odd, since the persecution was carried out in conditions of strictest secrecy. There was not a word about the Oppositionists in the press. Nevertheless, whenever anything important happened, we nearly always got to know of it more or less on the same day. For example, news of the suicide on 16 November 1927 of the Soviet diplomat Joffe, the man who had signed the joint declaration with Sun Yat-sen, spread like wildfire. We heard of Trotsky's deportation the very same morning that it took place. Students gathered in small groups in the refectory, the corridors, and the lecture rooms of the university to swap news of the event. There was scarcely a happy face among them. For three months we had taken part in a virtually non-stop 'discussion' of the struggle between the Stalinists and the Trotskyists, and every day it had been hammered into us that the former were right and the latter wrong. We had voted for one resolution after another in support of the decisions of the Central Committee, and we had even put our hands up to approve of the expulsion of the Oppositionists from the Party. But now, when the expulsions were actually being carried out and the victims of the purge were being thrown into prison or exiled to some far-away place, we were saddened and began to feel some secret sympathy for those who had been defeated. It was partly a case of instinctive sympathy for the underdog but there was more to it than that: we were still not convinced that the Stalinists were right.

When the great struggle of the factions was finally over, a mood of discontent gripped the six hundred or more Chinese students at KUTV and the military school affiliated to it. Everyone seemed to be complaining all the time about nothing in particular. It was not our living conditions that we grumbled about. We were housed in a mansion which had formerly belonged to aristocrats, wearing Western clothes, eating European food, and had ten roubles every month as pocket money. Few if any of us had ever enjoyed such a secure and luxurious life. We slept on soft, warm mattresses covered with light and comfortable blankets. We could rub our hands against the walls hung with satin brocade, and admire the beautifully decorated ceilings and the huge crystal chandeliers. When we first moved in we felt like Cinderellas. But this did not last long. We soon got used to the new environment and our interest turned to other subjects. The depth of the defeat of the Chinese Revolution was becoming more and more apparent, and we soon realized that it was an illusion to think that after a few months' military training we could return to China and turn back the wheel of history. We were upset by the arbitrary and bureaucratic way in which the Stalinists conducted the inner-party struggle, and the suffocating atmosphere which this created. The gulf between what we thought and what we were allowed to say, between our sympathies and the demands of discipline, grew wider and wider. All six hundred of us had just left behind a revolution, and we were restless and full of energy. For young rebels like us, a life of peace and quiet was worse than death.

At last we found a target for our surplus energies in the shape of the handful of Chinese Communists who had worked with the KUTV Party Committee and had recently led the anti-Trotskyist campaign there. We referred to this group as 'the survivors', because they were all that remained of the Moscow branch of the Chinese Communist Party. They had long controlled Party work among the Chinese students, were on good terms with the university officials and the Eastern Department of the Comintern, and were without exception Stalinists and bureaucrats. It was on them that we vented all our complaints and grumbles. For most of the students this was simply a instinctive opposition to bureaucracy, but our dissatisfaction soon became caught up with the struggle for power at the top of the CCP, and was skilfully exploited by a rising faction. The struggle at KUTV was therefore part of a broader struggle for the leadership of the Chinese revolution being waged by factions within the CCP and the CPSU. It had an important, even decisive, effect on the development of the CCP in general and Chinese Trotskyism in particular. It is therefore worth explaining in more detail.

The Moscow branch of the CCP, which had flourished in the early 1920s, consisted exclusively of Chinese Communists resident in the Soviet Union. It had similar status to the former European branch of the CCP led by Chou En-lai in Paris. Organizations of this sort were not strictly in keeping with the organizational principles of the Comintern, by which every Communist Party had equal rights as a section of the International, and every Communist, regardless of nationality, had the right and duty to participate in the life of the Party organization in the country where he or she lived. The European and Moscow branches of the CCP originally came into existence because of the special nature of their membership. Most of the Chinese Communists in Europe and Moscow at that time were students, who had gone or been sent there to receive theoretical and organizational training related to the problems of China. The Moscow branch was nominally under the direct leadership of the Comintern, but in practice it was a part of the CPSU. Its status was therefore rather unclear and confused. Normally this was not a problem, but as the struggle among the Chinese students in Moscow became more heated it soon became one, as I shall explain later. The Moscow branch had been founded four or five years before we arrived, and was at first led by Liu Shao-ch'i, P'eng Shu-tse and others. Afterwards Yü Hsiu-sung became prominent in it, and by our time it was under the control of Wu Fu-ching. The power and influence of men like Wu was due to the fact that they had lived in Moscow for a comparatively long period of time, knew Russian well, and were known and trusted by the Soviet comrades. The way in which they ran the branch was chiefly aimed at maintaining their established position in Moscow and using it as a springboard for securing control of the CCP itself. They argued that it would be a waste of time for those Chinese students who arrived in Moscow after them to learn Russian, and they were against the study of theory on the grounds that it would turn us into useless academics.

The older members of the Moscow branch were about a dozen former students who had stayed on as Party officials, translators, and interpreters. They were the middlemen between the Chinese students and the Russian comrades, and their role in the Party was similar to that of the compradors in the treaty ports at home. They had translated a number of elementary textbooks of Communism and histories of the Communist Party of the Soviet Union and of the international workers' movement into Chinese. Whenever a new intake of Chinese students arrived in Moscow they would dole out these mimeographed textbooks, teach them a few rudiments that were supposed to be a 'must' for every Party member, and then pack them back off to China to 'take part in the real struggle'. Anyone who dared to challenge this system by learning Russian or studying more theory than was thought necessary was looked upon as an unreliable intruder. Such people would be severely criticized and even sent back to China ahead of schedule as a punishment.

There had already been one struggle against the branch before we arrived in Moscow, waged by a group of older comrades around Lo Han, among them Li Hsia-kung, Wu Chi-hsien, Chu Tan-chi, and others. These men had been politically active both inside and outside the Communist Party for many years. In their experience and learning they were head and shoulders above the leadership of the branch. It was out of the question that men of their calibre would accept the petty restrictions that the latter tried to impose on them. They demanded changes in the curriculum and insisted on more time for private study. After a brief clash, they won some slight concessions from the Party Committee: they were allowed more time for learning Russian; the number of cell meetings was reduced, which also implied a reduction in the number of harrowing criticism sessions; and the atmosphere became less hostile to the study of theoretical questions. Party power, however, remained firmly in the hands of the middlemen.

It was this group that we finally confronted and fought. They were heavily outnumbered, and their influence was much less than that of the Moscow branch in its heyday. It was only later that I realised why we had needed a bitter struggle in order to overthrow them. The entire administration of KUTV stood behind them, including the president, Boris Shumiatsky, an old Bolshevik and a staunch Stalinist, as well as the top officials of the Party Committee and the educational board of the university, who were all faithful Stalinists too. They were, almost without exception, loathsome bureaucrats. The head of the military training school affiliated to KUTV was a man called Maslov. He was the sort of officer who would have been more at home at a palace ball than in a revolution. He knew nothing about China and her revolution, and assumed an air of extreme arrogance. He imposed exacting discipline on his students, but was very perfunctory where his own teaching duties were concerned. The course in military training was only scheduled to last six months, which is probably why it was so elementary. Since the lectures were given in Russian and interpreted into Chinese, they appeared even more trivial than they actually were.

Many of the students at the school had studied military affairs before coming to Moscow, and even more had first-hand experience of war from their time in the army. Not surprisingly they were very dissatisfied with the way the course was run: they had not come to Russia to be taught trivia. But when they demanded an improvement, they were immediately rebuffed by the Chinese interpreters, who were time-servers, like the interpreters who used to work for the municipal council and the foreign firms in Shanghai, and who can still be found in Hong Kong. Above all they hated trouble, and they looked upon anyone who asked them to transmit a complaint as a trouble-maker. After trying and failing to deal with the military students' complaints themselves, they passed their demands to the Russian authorities, putting their own particular gloss on them. The Russian officials reacted in exactly the same way as their Chinese underlings, and flatly refused to consider them.

There was an eruption of anger as the students of the military school, backed by the KUTV students as a whole, declared war on the 'survivors' of the Moscow branch. Since nearly all the interpreters were 'survivors' it was only natural that the anger that was felt for Maslov should spill over onto the university's Party Committee. A delegation went to see Shumiatsky, who denounced their demands out of hand, thus adding fuel to the fire. The same day the students called an emergency general meeting and elected a new delegation. Yaroslavsky received them in person, and had a short talk with them, but nothing positive came of it. The next day, therefore, all the students from the military school marched in procession to the Comintern headquarters. Wildcat demonstrations of this sort had at one time been the vogue in China, but they had been strictly prohibited in the Soviet Union ever since Stalin's assumption of power. The sight of the Chinese students marching in procession through the main streets of Moscow caused quite a sensation, and was considered a very serious incident. Rumours were flying about that the students who had organized the demonstration would be severely punished, but nothing came of this threat. I later learned that this was because another faction in the Stalinist camp had attempted to turn the incident to its own advantage.

As soon as the two main CCP delegates to the Ninth Plenum of the Comintern's Executive Committee, Hsiang Chung-fa and Li Chen-ying, arrived in Moscow, they became involved in the struggle of the Chinese students. Hsiang Chung-fa, a boatman from the Yangtse River, was head of the labour federation in the Wuhan area and had stood out as a workers' leader during the revolution. He was an able and straightforward sort of person, but his weakness was that he was rather simple-minded. It was because he was a worker that he had been chosen as chief CCP delegate to the Comintern plenary session, as the predominance of intellectuals among the Party's leaders was then commonly regarded as the main cause of the defeat of the revolution. Hsiang had no personal relations with any members of the Moscow branch, whereas he did know a number of the KUTV students and had worked together with them in China. He therefore sided openly and unreservedly with the student rank and file as soon as he knew the situation. But this would not have sufficed to tip the balance our way. Our quick victory over the branch bureaucrats was due to the powerful forces behind Hsiang.

The two main figures behind Hsiang were Pavel Mif, the new head of Sun Yat-sen University who was later also to become head of the Eastern Department of the Comintern, and Wang Ming, a student

leader at the same university and Mif's chief lieutenant. Mif's initial
rise to fame was a result of his proficiency in Stalin-style 'Leninism'.
It was this that first brought him to Stalin's attention. He was then
made a lecturer at Sun Yat-sen University, where he taught a course
in 'Problems of Leninism' (the title of a book by Stalin). Wang
Ming was his favourite pupil. Before going to Moscow, Wang Ming
had been a middle-school student in Wuhan. When Wang Ming
arrived in Moscow he was not even a member of the Communist
Youth League. A shrewd, ambitious man with a strong will, he
was above all a master of flattery. Even in Radek's time as president
of the university, Wang Ming had already sensed Mif's bright future,
and deliberately played up to him by paying special attention to the
'Problems of Leninism' course. In the spring of 1927 the Comintern
sent Mif on a mission to China, and he took Wang Ming with him as
his interpreter. In Wuhan Mif urged the Central Committee of the
CCP to take on Wang as head of the Agit-Prop Department, but
Ch'en Tu-hsiu (then General Secretary of the Party) refused this and
assigned him to a trainee post in the department instead. Wang Ming
declined the job, and returned to Moscow with Mif. During the
struggle against the Oppositionists at Sun Yat-sen University Mif and
Wang Ming worked closely together and thereby cemented the
alliance on which their clique was based. It was as a result of his role
in this struggle that Mif gained promotion from lecturer to president
of the university and leading Comintern official. Wang Ming's rise to
power paralleled that of his teacher. He and his friends already
controlled the Party Committee at Sun Yat-sen University. Thus a
new Moscow branch of the CCP came into being, to rival and eventually eclipse the 'survivors' of the KUTV branch.

News of our struggle against the KUTV 'survivors' rekindled the
ambitions of the Mif/Wang Ming clique. Their aim was to gain
complete control over all the Chinese students in Moscow as a
spring-board for taking over the leadership of the CCP as a whole. A
crucial first step was to detach the six or seven hundred Chinese
students at KUTV from men like Shumiatsky, Maslov, and the
'survivors'. This is why from the very first they showed so much
interest in our struggle. The arrival of Hsiang Chung-fa and Li
Chen-ying in Moscow gave them the chance they were waiting for.
They put forward a three-point proposal for bringing an end to the
unrest at KUTV: 1, the 'survivors' should be sent back to China,
where they could correct their mistakes by participating in the real

struggle; 2, all the Chinese students at KUTV should be transferred to Sun Yat-sen University; 3, the military school (which had in fact just finished its scheduled six-month course) should be closed down and its students sent back to China, apart from a minority who should be transferred to Sun Yat-sen University, and an even smaller minority who should be sent to higher military academies for further training. These measures were pushed through quite easily, and we thought that we had emerged from the struggle as victors. But before long it became clear to us that the real victors were the Mif/Wang Ming clique. From then on the education and training of Chinese Communists in Moscow was entirely in their hands.

After this initial victory they proceeded to the second stage in their carefully prepared plan. When the other delegates returned to China after the meeting of the Comintern executive, they arranged for Hsiang Chung-fa to stay behind in Moscow for further training, so that they could use him as a tool in the inner-Party struggle. Six months later, at the Sixth Congress of the CCP in Moscow in June 1928, they succeeded in ousting Ch'ü Ch'iu-pai from the leadership and made Hsiang general secretary of the Party. In this way, they successfully laid the foundation for their subsequent influence in the Chinese Communist Party.

I was not neutral in the struggle I have just described, but neither was I particularly active. I did not like the 'survivors', mainly because of the way they behaved. They ingratiated themselves with their superiors and were arrogant towards ordinary students. As they themselves had never engaged in any serious study, they stopped others from doing so. The only thing they required of us was that we learn by heart the documents they handed round. I myself heartily despised them. But I could see no point in concentrating our efforts on struggling against the 'survivors' if this meant neglecting the much more central issues raised by the Russian Opposition.

I gradually became acquainted with the secret documents of the Trotskyists, and understood more clearly the problems at the heart of the Russian and Chinese revolutions. On one occasion I was selected to go on a delegation to see Yaroslavsky, chairman of the Central Control Commission of the CPSU. During the interview one of my fellow delegates sought to win the Russians' support by explaining at great length that we had nothing to do with the Trotskyists, and boasting how active we had been in the anti-Trotskyist struggle at KUTV. I was nauseated by this display. After that

I became less active in the struggle against the 'survivors', and decided to devote my time instead to improving my Russian, studying the basic theories of Marxism, and reading Opposition documents that I obtained from one of my old friends, Fan Chin-piao, with whom I had worked together several years before in Hangchow. We had met again a year later in Canton, where he joined the Northern Expeditionary Army as a political commissar in a regiment of the Independent Division commanded by the left-wing Kuomintang General Yen Chung. After General Yen Chung was stripped of his command by Chiang Kai-shek, Fan was also forced to quit the army, and shortly afterwards he returned to T'aichou county south of Hangchow, where he spread revolutionary propaganda among the peasants and began to organize them. He arrived in Moscow a month after me, and was assigned to study at Sun Yat-sen University. There he established contact with those underground Oppositionists who had been lucky enough to survive the purge, and he therefore became a Trotskyist before I did.

The first opposition document that I read was Zinoviev's *Theses on the Chinese Revolution*. A little later I read Trotsky's *The Chinese Revolution and the Theses of Comrade Stalin*, and after that the *Platform of the United Opposition of the CPSU*. They had an enormous impact on me, because of their unassailable logic and also their superb style. They were a real contrast to the lifeless and insipid documents of the Central Committee. The arguments and warnings of the Opposition, especially those concerned with the Chinese Revolution, were so obviously true and had been so often confirmed in practice, that I could not help nodding vigorously in agreement as I eagerly pored over them. I was also deeply moved by Zinoviev's writings. When I read these documents it was as if the scales fell from my eyes. I now realized that on all fundamental questions the CCP leaders had been acting on orders from the Stalin faction; that the ill-conceived policies which had led to the defeat of the Chinese Revolution were far from being Ch'en Tu-hsiu's mistakes; and that these mistakes had been warned against in advance, and could have been avoided. It was clear to me that on nearly all questions whether tactical or strategic concerning the Chinese Revolution, the Russian Opposition, and Trotsky in particular, had very different positions from those of the Stalinist Central Committee, and had given timely warnings about the consequences of the line Stalin was pursuing. It was only because of the stubborn refusal of the Stalin–Bukharin clique to acknowledge that the criticisms of the Opposition were correct that the leadership in China made so many disastrous mistakes, leading finally to the collapse of the Chinese Revolution.

I already knew something about the situation in Britain and the Soviet Union, and when I turned to the Oppositionist documents dealing with subjects such as the Anglo-Soviet Trade Union Committee and economic construction in the Soviet Union I again found myself in complete agreement with the criticisms raised.

From then on I became a 'Bolshevik–Leninist' (as the Oppositionists were called at that time). My ideological commitment soon became a practical one. This was towards the end of my second term at KUTV. By now the struggle against the 'survivors' of the branch was over, and most of the Chinese students, myself among them, were about to be transferred to Sun Yat-sen University.

CHAPTER 5

My Second Year in Moscow

⊙ ⊙ ⊙

In the summer of 1928 most of the students in Moscow were sent to the barracks for a month of military training. I and a few others were exempted on health grounds, and sent to a rest-house instead. We travelled there by train, and the journey took just over an hour. The rest-house was on a hill overlooking a river, and it commanded a splendid view. During my stay there I came into contact for the first time with ordinary Russian working people, and got the chance to find out about the life of Russian peasants. I also made my first contact with the various factions which had formed among the students at Sun Yat-sen University, and which were later to influence the factional struggles within the CCP.

Among my companions at the rest-house were students from both KUTV and Sun Yat-sen University. Later, after their period of military training was over, we were joined by the other Chinese students from Moscow for the remainder of the summer holidays. It was a carefree life, with five meals a day and time for a nap after lunch. We spent our time swimming, rowing, playing volley-ball, going for outings in the woods, listening to music (there were improvised concerts most evenings of the week), and making friends with members of the opposite sex. To the casual observer, everything was happy and tranquil. But beneath the surface it was a hot-house of political activities.

Both in China and in the Soviet Union the Communist movements were going through a difficult period and had reached important turning-points. The Ninth Plenum of the Comintern Executive had met in the February of that year; in June and July the CCP had held its Sixth Congress in Moscow; and while we were staying in the rest-house the Sixth Congress of the Comintern was in session. The two main items these three important meetings dealt with were the Chinese Revolution, and the Opposition within the CPSU. It was around these two questions that an important process of differentiation was taking place in the Chinese Party and in the International as a whole. At first factional and even personal interests seemed to play a greater role than political considerations in shaping the alignment of forces among the Chinese students in Moscow.

I showed earlier how the Mif/Wang Ming group used events at KUTV to get the 'survivors' of the Moscow branch sent back to China, and thus to win complete control over the training of Chinese students in the Soviet Union. I also explained how this clique intended to make use of Hsiang Chung-fa, chief delegate of the CCP to the Comintern Executive, in their bid for the leadership of the Party. This was quite a task of course, and in preparation for it Wang Ming and his friends staged a dress rehearsal at Sun Yat-sen University by starting up a campaign against what became known as the 'Kiangsu-Chekiang Provincial Association'.

Many of the older generation of Party members came from, or had connections with one or other of the five central and southern provinces of Kiangsu, Chekiang, Anhui, Hunan, and Kwangtung. This was entirely natural, given that the Chinese Communist movement originated in these areas. It is an elementary principle of Party life that Communists should never take into account regional loyalties or affiliations in their dealings with one another. But it was nonetheless inevitable that people who had been born in the same place or who had worked together in the same area would develop close personal ties. This is probably as true now as it was then, not only in China but also in Communist Parties elsewhere in the world. To admit that this is so is not to deny that such a state of affairs is a symptom of extreme backwardness. But the only sure way of eliminating abuses of this sort is to educate Party members thoroughly, and to make them politically more aware by plunging them into the fierce political struggles of the working class. Campaigns launched specifically against this sort of 'localism' are counter-productive, strengthening such relationships rather than weakening them. And this was precisely what happened when Wang Ming and his associates started up their campaign against the so-called 'Kiangsu–Chekiang Provincial Association' in the summer of 1927.

When Sun Yat-sen University was set up in the winter of 1925, many of its students were teachers or students from the Shanghai College, an institution set up by the Party in Shanghai to meet the ever-growing demand for trained and educated cadres. They were for the most part natives of Kiangsu and Chekiang provinces. There were also a number of worker Communists from factories in the Shanghai–

Wusih area of Kiangsu province. These facts explain how students from these two provinces made up the largest single regional grouping at the university. Among those from Shanghai were a number of fairly prominent intellectuals such as Tung I-hsiang, Ku Ku-i, and Yü Hsiu-sung, and it was only natural that these men should play an important role in the Party Committee at the university during the first period. The name 'Kiangsu-Chekiang Provincial Association', with its connotations of the regional clubhouses established by officials, merchants, and expatriates in general, was coined by a rival group of students, who aimed to seize power from Tung, Yü, and the others. Wang Ming and his group then used the name in their own attacks. But in reality there was no such 'Association', nor could there be. First, not all those accused of belonging came from Kiangsu or Chekiang, although quite a few of Wang Ming's supporters did, among them Wang Ming's right-hand man Ch'in Pang-hsien, who was born in Wusih, Kiangsu. Second, many interpreters like Chang Wen-t'ien, Shen Tse-min, Shen Chih-yüan, Wu Li-p'ing, and Chu T'ing-chang, accused of being members of the 'Association' because of where they were born, were in fact on very bad terms with Tung I-hsiang, Ku Ku-i, and other alleged leaders of the group.

By the time we were transferred to Sun Yat-sen University the attacks were over. The 'Anhui group' with Wang Ming, Wang Chia-hsiang, and others as its leaders stood at the head of the Party organization there. But the ill-fated name of 'Provincial Association' was still hovering around like a spectre in search of a new victim. When I first heard people using the term, I had no idea what they were talking about. I found it impossible to understand why they spent so much effort on exorcizing a devil which had never really existed. Later I realized that the whole affair was part of a plot by the Wang Ming group to smear Ch'ü Ch'iu-pai, Ch'en Tu-hsiu's successor as the Party's general secretary, who was soon to be replaced by Hsiang Chung-fa at the Sixth Congress of the CCP in Moscow. Wang Ming and his supporters used every opportunity to insinuate that Ch'ü Ch'iu-pai, who came from Changchow in Kiangsu province, was the real power behind this 'Association'.

The Sun Yat-sen University students I had met at the rest-house were among the main victims of the campaign against the 'Association'. My reason for getting in touch with them had nothing to do with the fact that I came from Chekiang. It was rather because they were by that time out of power. In the eyes of the Wang Ming group those of us who had studied at KUTV were alien and suspect elements anyway, and, since the 'Association' members had been driven out of power, they had nothing to lose by contacting us. Some of them were old friends of mine, and some were acquaintances. I was on very good terms with Tung I-hsiang, who was a bitter enemy of Wang Ming's, and was eventually to be murdered by him in Sinkiang in 1937. Tung, a learned man with mild and patient manners, had lectured at the Party's Shanghai College before coming to Moscow, and was an old friend of Ch'ü Ch'iu-pai. It was from him and his friends that I learned about the complicated relationships between the various student groups at Sun Yat-sen University.

I had disliked Wang Ming and his associates from the outset. I needed no encouragement from any fictitious 'Association' in my contempt for these mindless and arrogant young bureaucrats, who had never done a thing for the Chinese Revolution and who had only gained control of the Party organization at the university by toadying to their Comintern superiors. I based this judgement on something more than mere regional loyalty: I already had a political standpoint of my own. My first concern was therefore to enquire into the political differences that separated the 'Association' and Wang Ming's 'Anhui group'. To my disappointment I discovered that the 'Association's' attitude towards the Opposition was at least as uncompromising as that of the 'Anhui group', if not more so. At first I thought that this was to avoid laying themselves open to attack, but I soon found that I was mistaken. In private conversations Tung I-hsiang admitted to me that the Stalin–Bukharin leadership of the Comintern deserved some of the blame for the defeat of the Chinese Revolution, but he argued that in the main they had been right. He said that on most of the main questions, such as the entry of the CCP into the Kuomintang and the attempt to create a new revolutionary centre in Wuhan after Chiang Kai-shek's betrayal, Stalin and Bukharin had been acting in accordance with Leninist principles. On the question of the nature of Chinese society, they had some disagreements with the official view, and were inclined to accept the conclusion that capitalist relations predominated in China's economic life, but at the same time they were strictly opposed to calling for the dictatorship of the proletariat in China. They argued that the revolution in China would lead at most to the democratic dictatorship of the workers and peasants. In their assessment of the political situation in China at that time, they supported the resolutions passed at the Ninth Plenum of the International's Executive Committee even more unflinchingly than Wang Ming and his group.

I should explain at this point the controversies then raging on various questions relating to the Chinese Revolution. They were: the causes of the defeat of the revolution and the lessons to be drawn from it; the political situation in China and the tactics that should be adopted by the CCP; and the character of the future revolution.

The Ninth Plenum of the Comintern's Executive Committee was held following the defeat of the Canton insurrection. The Committee refused to acknowledge that the Chinese Revolution had been defeated. Instead, it put forward the well known formula that the revolution was passing through a short trough between two waves, and that a new rising wave was imminent. It therefore continued to uphold the policy of armed insurrection decided upon at the CCP's Emergency Party Conference of 7 August 1927.

The Sixth Congress of the CCP admitted the defeat of the revolution, but failed to point out its real causes. The Congress heaped all the blame for the mistakes made during the revolution on the shoulders of the 'opportunist' Ch'en Tu-hsiu. Apart from this the only other reason given for the defeat was that the imperialists had been too strong. They might just as well have said that the revolution in China was impossible as long as imperialist influence lasted. The Opposition's analysis, which located the real causes of the defeat in the wrong assessment of the role and character of the colonial bourgeoisie, the mistaken policy of CCP entry into the Kuomintang, the failure to substitute a coalition with the peasantry and the urban poor for the coalition with 'petty bourgeois' politicians, and the failure to understand the role of soviets and the need to organize them, was deliberately distorted and denounced in the Congress resolution, or else ignored. The Sixth Congress repeated the formulae laid down at the Ninth Plenum, although the word 'waves' was changed to 'tides'. Although the Congress formally condemned putschism, it still adopted a resolution endorsing a continuation of the policy of armed insurrection in China. While it argued the need for a democratic programme, it repudiated Trotsky's call for a national assembly. It therefore lacked a central political slogan with which to sum up and embrace all the other democratic demands. It predicted 'in accordance with Bolshevik tradition' that the coming revolution in China would be bourgeois–democratic in character, and that the revolutionary state would therefore be a 'democratic dictatorship of the workers and peasants', but it postponed the socialist revolution in China to the remote future.

The Russian Opposition had already expressed views on the events of 1925–7 in China. Its analysis of probable future developments there was to be found in the correspondence between Trotsky and his comrades in exile (particularly Preobrazhensky). All these views were repeated in a more precise and definitive way in Trotsky's *Critique of the Draft Programme of the Comintern*. Essentially the Opposition's line was as follows: after the autumn of 1927 there could be no further doubt that the Chinese Revolution had been defeated; that the main cause of the defeat was the opportunist policy adopted by the Stalin–Bukharin faction; and that the Chinese Communists should now recognize the reality of the defeat and investigate its causes, in order to decide upon a correct course for the future. If they insisted on closing their eyes to what had happened and on dressing up the defeat as a 'development of the revolution to a higher stage' they would lurch inevitably from opportunism into 'putschism', and thus prepare the way for an even worse defeat, squandering the forces of the revolution. Trotsky developed this line in his article 'The Problems of the Chinese Revolution after the Sixth Congress', in which he called for the setting-up of a national assembly in China.

Trotsky's own assessment of the situation in China was summed up in the following passage:

We are entering in China into a period of reflux, and consequently into a period in which the party deepens its theoretical roots, educates itself critically, creates and strengthens firm organizational links in all spheres of the working class movement, organizes rural nuclei, leads and unites partial, at first defensive and later offensive, battles of the workers and the peasant poor.

As for the contents and character of the coming revolution, he wrote:

It is not excluded that the first stage of the coming third revolution may reproduce in a very abridged and modified form the stages which have already passed. ... But this first stage will be sufficient only to give the Communist Party a chance to put forward and announce its 'April thesis', that is, its programme and tactics of the seizure of power.[1]

[1] 'Summary and Perspective of the Chinese Revolution', pp. 313–14 in *Leon Trotsky on China*, translated from the Russian by John Wright, Pathfinder Press, N.Y., 1970.

The position which the leaders of the 'Association' took up in this debate could be called 'centro-rightist'. In their view the main responsibility for the defeat of the revolution belonged to Ch'en Tu-hsiu, although Stalin and Bukharin shared some of the blame for it. As for the political situation in China, they too accused the Opposition of 'liquidationism' (as the Bolsheviks had done when the Mensheviks advocated exclusively legal activity after the failure of the 1905 Revolution in Russia), although they reluctantly admitted that the Chinese Revolution had indeed been defeated. As for the future of the revolution, they were more orthodoxly Leninist, in the peculiar sense that the word had by then acquired. They declared that there could be no question of establishing a dictatorship of the proletariat without first passing through a democratic dictatorship of the workers and peasants.

Since by then I had already accepted the analysis of the Opposition on these questions, I found myself in disagreement with the leaders of the 'Association' on these points. Through them, however, I did manage to get in touch with a group of Shanghai workers at the rest-house who had been under their influence. Among them was a former cotton-mill worker from Wusih in Kiangsu province called An Fu. He was the best-read and politically the most advanced of the group, and was already an Oppositionist or semi-Oppositionist. Since they were close to Tung I-hsiang and his friends, An Fu and the other workers were regarded by the Wang Ming factions as the rank and file of the 'Association'. During the factional struggle at Sun Yat-sen University, An Fu and the others had taken the side of the 'Association' and were therefore plunged into a deep depression after its defeat. The more simple-minded among them even went so far as to believe that since the Party was now dominated by such a mean and worthless man as Wang Ming, there was no longer any hope for the revolution in China. But after a period of frustration and disappointment, the more far-sighted among them realized that the factional struggle at the university had to be seen in terms of the titanic struggle which was going on within both the CPSU and the Communist International as a whole, between the two camps of Stalinism and Trotskyism. Their struggle ended up in the same way as ours at KUTV, but with one difference: whereas we had turned to the Russian Opposition after prevailing over our opponents, they had done so after suffering defeat on their campus.

*

In the winter of 1927 more than ten well-known Oppositionists, among them Ou Fang, had been expelled from the Party and sent back to China. Two of those expelled, however, Ch'en Ch'i and Wen Yüeh, were not allowed to leave the Soviet Union. Isolated from the rest of the students, they were kept behind on the campus, awaiting further punishment. No one dared to approach them, and they made no attempt to speak to their fellow-students. They just sat in the library all day reading, contemptuously ignored by the 'loyal elements' (i.e. the Stalinists of the Wang Ming group). They were regarded with curiosity by the uncommitted majority as museum specimens of the species 'Trotskyist'. While I was at KUTV and before I had any relations with the underground Trotskyist organization, this is precisely how the two men had struck me during my occasional visits to Sun Yat-sen University. They seemed set apart from the others, so that I gained the impression that apart from them there were no other Trotskyists among the Chinese students, or that if there were, they had been eliminated. In fact there were still quite a few secret Oppositionists among the teachers and the students at that time, and it was precisely these secret Oppositionists who won An Fu and others over to Trotskyism during the period leading up to the summer vacation of 1928. My old friend Fan Chin-piao also came under the influence of this group.

During the latter half of our stay in the rest-house we went through a period of extremely strenuous political thinking and activity. After we had been there just over a month we were joined by An Fu and his friends, who had by then completed their spell of military training. They brought with them to the rest-house tiny notebooks in which they had copied out the main Oppositionist documents, covering page after page with thousands of tiny Chinese characters. These notebooks were surreptitiously passed from hand to hand, and very soon they had influenced considerable numbers of Chinese students, especially those from KUTV, of whom there were over a hundred at the rest-house. A much greater number had been sent either back to China or on to higher military academies in Moscow and Leningrad at the end of the first school year. Most of the ex-KUTV students in the rest-house were incapable of putting up the slightest resistance to the ideological onslaught of the Opposition.

Within the ranks of the CPSU itself, a completely different mood prevailed. It was six months since the 'liquidation' of the Russian

Opposition, when all Oppositionists had been driven out of the Party and some had been exiled or imprisoned under Article 58 of the criminal code. To make things worse, Zinoviev and Kamenev, two prominent leaders of the United Opposition, had capitulated and renounced their views. A wave of capitulations followed. Every day *Pravda* was full of humiliating statements by former members of the Opposition, which was to all appearances in a state of demoralization and disintegration. But here were we Chinese Communists, stealthily and enthusiastically devouring these condemned and forbidden documents and turning *en masse* to the Opposition! On the surface, this seemed like a paradox. It certainly made a startling contrast with our frame of mind just after we had arrived in Moscow a year before. We were not really Stalinists then, but because of our ill-informed prejudices about the two factions in the CPSU we had supported Stalin in his struggle against Trotsky. During the discussions leading up to the Fifteenth Congress of the Russian Party some of us had doubted the correctness of the Comintern's policy in China, but few of us had thought the subject through to the end, or examined the arguments of the Opposition that emerged in fragmentary or distorted forms from the official Party documents. Most of us had believed that to do so would be disloyal to the Party and therefore to the revolution. It had been drummed into us from the very beginning that any form of opposition or factional activity was harmful to the Party and the revolution, if not downright counter-revolutionary. Without thinking, therefore, we had regarded the Opposition as something poisonous and threatening, to be avoided at all costs. During the factional struggle at KUTV both sides had refrained from smearing each other as 'Oppositionists', and both had been careful not to lay themselves open to such a charge, going out of their way to support the attacks on Trotsky. It was not that our support for Stalin had been insincere. In voting unanimously in favour of Stalin, we had been acting out of misconceived loyalty to the movement rather than from calculated obsequiousness to the leadership.

By the late summer of 1928 our attitude towards the defeated and 'liquidated' Opposition had changed. For those Chinese Communists at the rest-house emotional embrace preceded ideological acceptance. The Opposition no longer seemed poisonous or untouchable to us. There was an almost holy aura about it, wronged and persecuted as it clearly was, and it quickly gained our sympathy and admiration. Our view of loyalty and disloyalty to the Party was now quite the opposite of what it had been. At first I thought that this change was simply due to disillusion as a result of the factional struggles at the two universities, but there was more to it than that.

The main reason why most of the Chinese students in Moscow began to go over to the Opposition after the spring of 1928 was, as I soon realized, because the events of the last six months in China and the Soviet Union had confirmed the analysis of the Opposition with surprising speed. In China the Autumn Harvest uprising and the Canton insurrection in late 1927 demonstrated at terrible cost the failure of Stalin's policies. In the Soviet Union the fallacies of the Stalinists were just as mercilessly exposed. We had been repeatedly told that the Opposition was stirring up trouble amongst the Russian peasantry. We were also told that (thanks to the purging of the Opposition) the peasants had been mollified. In reality the opposite was true. The bread we ate was more and more often coarse and black. Emergency measures were introduced to ration food, and fruit had virtually disappeared from the market. After Trotsky's downfall, the kulaks went onto the offensive, forcing Stalin to launch a disorderly counter-attack of his own. It became obvious that the Opposition's warnings had been well-grounded. I learned later that during 1928, despite the wave of recantations by well-known Oppositionists, even larger numbers of rank-and-file members, especially young workers, joined or supported the underground organizations of the Opposition.

As autumn advanced the new term began, and all the Chinese students returned from the rest-house to Sun Yat-sen University. By this time one could say without exaggeration that nine-tenths of the former KUTV students had been won over to Trotskyism. An organization to unite them was urgently needed. One Sunday in late September or early October, a dozen or so of us travelled out of Moscow by tram in groups of two or three to have a picnic. We found somewhere quiet, and there we ate, laughed, and sang. As soon as there were no Russian holiday-makers within earshot, we got down to more serious business. We discussed and finally settled the problem of how to organize so many Trotskyists. Three of us – Fan Chin-piao, An Fu, and myself – were chosen from this conference of activists to form a leadership committee.

All this happened long ago, and I cannot remember all those who were present at this meeting. Lo Han had already returned to China.

One comrade whose presence I particularly recall was Chi Ta-ts'ai, a
memorable man of outstanding character. During the revolution Chi
Ta-ts'ai was chairman of the Federation of Labour in Chekiang province. He was a tough-looking individual, and his courage and loyalty
to the movement had won him enormous respect from the Hangchow workers. While he was in Moscow he showed himself to be a
good student, and made rapid progress in studying Marxist and
Leninist theory. Another comrade at the meeting who made a big
impression on me was a worker called Pien Fu-lin. He was a reticent
man who seldom spoke his mind, but when he did so he spoke well
and to the point. They were both later arrested and probably died in
Stalin's prisons.

After the establishment of our three-man committee, the influence
of the Opposition among the Chinese students in Moscow grew.
The existence of our organization was almost an open secret among
ex-KUTV students. Oppositionist documents were openly discussed,
even in the presence of students who had not yet become members of
the organization. It was at this time that we got hold of a mimeographed copy of Trotsky's *Critique of the Draft Programme of the Comintern*
that had been widely but secretly circulated among Russian Communists. Since most Chinese students were unable to read Russian, I
was assigned to translate the document into Chinese. I began to do
this in the KUTV library, where there were no longer any Chinese
students and where none of the other foreign students read Chinese.
I hid the document in a big volume of *Capital* and translated it while
pretending to take notes from Marx. At first I ran no risk of being
discovered. It was unlikely that any of the students of the other
nationalities would suspect me, since most of them knew who I was.
I explained to the librarian at KUTV, a very kind old lady, that I had
decided to come back to my old college to do my reading because I
enjoyed the quietness of her room. She welcomed me warmly. In
this way I managed to get most of the translation done. But then
Professor Ch'en Han-sheng, who had once taught modern history at
Peking University, also started to frequent the library, so I was forced
to stop going there for fear of detection.

The link-man between us and the Russian Trotskyists was a young
man called Poliakov, who had lectured at Sun Yat-sen University
when Radek was principal. During the struggle against the Opposition
he had been expelled from the Party and dismissed from his job.
Now he was a shop-floor worker in a Moscow factory. When he

heard that I could find nowhere safe to work on my translation, he invited me to use his home, a small room in an old-fashioned apartment block not far from the KUTV library. He had been married for about a year to a young woman who was still a student at Moscow University. The first day I arrived there Mrs. Poliakov was preparing a bottle for their baby, a little girl a few months old. She welcomed me warmly, and told me that my visit was very opportune, since she needed a baby-sitter that day. The baby was a beautiful child, lying asleep in her cot. 'If she cries when she wakes up,' my young hostess said to me, 'give her this bottle. She's a very good little girl, I don't expect she'll give you any trouble.' She gave me a cup of tea and a sandwich and left the flat with her husband, locking the door as she went. I then got down to work, pausing every now and then to feed the baby or change its nappy. I stayed there until the young woman returned home towards evening. This routine continued for nearly a fortnight until one morning, just as I was leaving college on my way to Poliakov's flat, I heard a voice calling out my name. I turned round to see a woman standing with her head and shoulders wrapped in a shawl, so that I did not recognize her at first. It was only when I walked up to her that I realized it was Mrs. Poliakov. She did not respond when I made to shake her hand, but beckoned me to follow her along the street. She was not her usual self: no joyous smile, no mischievous expression. Her eyes showed that she had been crying bitterly, and her face was pale with grief. We stopped at a corner of the street, where she told me that Poliakov had been arrested after leading a strike at his factory, and that she could no longer go back to university. She had no idea what to do next. Her only immediate plan was to return with the baby and her mother to her home town on the Volga. After that we both fell silent. I could think of nothing to say that would comfort her. Finally she handed me a book which I had left at her home: a volume of Lenin's *Collected Works* with my name on it in Chinese. 'You're lucky', she told me, 'the GPU men didn't see it. Otherwise you might have been involved as well.' I was grateful beyond words for her consideration. She dared not stay too long, so she shook hands with me, pulled her shawl back over her head again, and walked off, after we had wished each other good luck. This was the first time I had witnessed the persecution of a family of revolutionaries by the Stalinist secret police, and to this day I can clearly recall every detail of the scene. Since then I have heard nothing more of the fate of those

women of three generations. I hope that they really did have the
good luck that I wished them.

Poliakov was not the only one to be arrested. Along with him the
entire underground committee of the Moscow Opposition, of which
he was a member, had been rounded up by the GPU. Subsequently
even more people were implicated and taken off to prison. The fact
that nothing happened to us Chinese Trotskyists shows that not a
single one of those arrested betrayed our activities to the GPU.

Once again I was without a place to work, and at a time when the
demand for Chinese translations of Oppositionist literature was very
great. The exiled leaders of the Opposition were at that time scattered
all over the Asian part of the Soviet Union, from Central Asia and
Siberia to the Caspian Sea. It was almost as if the clock had been
turned back to the old Tsarist days. Here were these veteran revolutionaries, engaged in intense theoretical activity or political analysis
of the world situation from a small town along the north-western
border of China, a shabby hotel in Siberia or a ramshackle log-cabin
in the ice-sealed tundra. Stalin did not yet dare to prevent them from
putting their views in writing and circulating them among themselves. First among the questions they discussed was the Chinese
Revolution. The second was the Soviet economy, and the beginnings
of a Stalinist 'left turn' in economic policy. In these two discussions
there were sharp divergences among the leaders of the Opposition,
with Trotsky and Rakovsky on one side and Radek and
Preobrazhensky, who were later to capitulate to Stalin, on the other.
The letters and articles which this debate produced were typed out in
pamphlet form by underground Oppositionist groups and widely
circulated among the masses. We also got hold of some of these
publications, and naturally wanted to translate them into our own
language. Again, the problem was to find a safe place to work in.
Since we were foreigners, our only links in Russia were with the
Party, so that it was impossible for us to find a room outside the
university.

Much to our surprise we did find a place, and a very good one at
that, before long. But before telling that story, I want to mention
some other developments which took place during that period.

After the Sixth Congress of the CCP had taken place in Moscow in
1928, a few of the delegates stayed on for the Sixth Congress of the
Comintern. Among them were Ch'ü Ch'iu-pai, Chou En-lai, Chang

Kuo-t'ao, Wang Jo-fei, Kuan Hsiang-ying, and Lo Chang-lung. Ch'ü Ch'iu-pai had been stripped of the General Secretaryship of the Party at the Sixth Congress, and replaced, just as the Stalin/Mif/Wang-Ming group had wanted, by the worker Communist Hsiang Chung-fa. At the Sixth Congress of the Comintern, however, Ch'ü continued to act as chief spokesman for the CCP delegation, because of his proficiency in Russian and his relatively good grasp of Marxism. Officially Wang Ming's role at the Congress was that of interpreter, but in actual fact he and Mif began to play an important part in the Chinese delegation. They continued to edge Ch'ü Ch'iu-pai further away from the levers of power in the Party, and this angered and upset some of the other delegates. Having brought Hsiang Chung-fa into their orbit, Mif and Wang Ming set out to work on Chou En-lai. Since he was a brilliant organizer and administrator, they wanted to win him over to accept their political and ideological leadership. Chou was the member of the delegation most active among the Chinese students, and he received a particularly warm welcome from the Party Committee of the university, in other words the Wang-Ming/Mif group. Ch'ü Ch'iu-pai and Chang Kuo-t'ao were also invited to address us. But the manner in which the three meetings were arranged was very different. Ch'ü Ch'iu-pai's reception was much cooler than Chou En-lai's, and colder still was the reception given to Chang Kuo-t'ao.

Although Trotsky had submitted his *Critique of the Draft Programme of the Comintern* to its Sixth Congress, the presidium had decided that it should not be published or circulated. It was probably only after considerable pressure from some delegates that they decided to allow a few leading members of each delegation to see it, on condition that the document was returned after reading. But despite these restrictions, Trotsky's *Critique* had an important influence on the delegates. Nearly all those who read it were deeply impressed. Some of the delegations, for example the Americans and the Canadians, agreed with it immediately, smuggled a copy out of Russia and decided to struggle for its aims thenceforth.

As the member of the Chinese delegation who knew Russian, Ch'ü Ch'iu-Pai could read the document from beginning to end. The other delegates could only acquaint themselves with Trotsky's analysis at second-hand through a few quotations, mostly wrenched out of context, which Wang Ming and his friends had translated into Chinese.

I did not know Ch'ü Ch'iu-pai personally, nor did I have a chance to talk with him at that time. According to a friend of mine who was close to him, Ch'ü's first reaction to Trotsky's Critique was not entirely negative, and he said that some of the points it raised were worth considering. But when he spoke at the congress itself he sounded like a die-hard anti-Trotskyist, whole-heartedly supporting the official line of the Stalin–Bukharin leadership. Was Ch'ü being true to himself in making such a speech? My answer is both yes and no. Although Ch'ü is recorded in the history of the CCP as its leader in the period of armed putsches, he was both physically and spiritually a weak man. As was shown by his beháviour in later years, when he came under attack from his opponents in the Party, he succumbed to pressure relatively easily. It seems to me that this was why he sided with Stalin and Bukharin at the Congress, even though he might earlier have sympathized with some of Trotsky's positions. At the same time, however, the fact that he came out and denounced the Russian Opposition was not at all out of keeping with his beliefs, since on the question of the bourgeois–democratic revolution Ch'ü Ch'iu-pai was a Leninist of the pre-1917 vintage. Trotsky's ideas seemed to him to contradict what Lenin had written. In this respect, one could call him a Chinese Communist of the Russian 'Old Bolshevik' type. It is true that he had made a fairly systematic study of Lenin's works, but, like most Russian 'Old Bolsheviks', he failed to notice the change that had taken place in Lenin's thinking during and after the revolution of 1917. In my view this is the first reason why Ch'ü openly came out in support of a policy which had actually betrayed the Chinese Revolution. The second reason for his attitude was probably the fact that he had been influenced by the campaign Stalin and Zinoviev had been carrying on ever since 1923: a campaign which falsified Trotsky's ideas and misrepresented them as the absolute antithesis of Leninism.

But despite all this, Ch'ü Ch'iu-pai's Stalinism was not entirely to Stalin's liking. Ch'ü was a thinker, and he took up Stalin's policies in his own way and expressed them in his own words. He therefore became a target for personal attacks, and Mif and Wang Ming branded him a 'semi-Trotskyist'. In later years Ch'ü was very badly treated by the Party, and all those who had had links with him were cruelly persecuted. His younger brother Ch'ü Ching-pai was driven mad while still in Moscow, and died there.

Chou En-lai was a man who had never shown any interest in

revolutionary theory, but distinguished himself instead by his practical ability, his great energy, his shrewdness, his good looks (at this time he sported a long beard), and his eloquence. There is no denying that Chou was a revolutionary of sorts, but in the course of the ideological and political struggles that continuously rocked the inner life of the Party he was never once to be found on the losing side, upholding some remote and lofty ideal. That would have been completely out of keeping with his character. He was strong and wanted to be so, and in disputes he therefore invariably sided with the strongest party. He was born to be a kingmaker, rather than a king. Every aspiring leader in the Party always wanted to win over Chou and make use of his talents as an administrator. In the long history of intra-Party struggles in the Chinese Revolution the fact that Chou emerged so often on the winning side earned him the nickname of pu-tao-weng ('the old man who never falls down' – the name of a traditional Chinese toy). By comparison with Chou En-lai, Wang Ming was a mere dwarf. There was only one area where Wang Ming clearly excelled: in the tenacity with which he strove after the top place in the Party. He would stop at nothing to achieve his aim, and considered any tactics legitimate, however damaging to the revolution and however shameful.

The 1928 attempt to raise Chou En-lai's status at the expense of Ch'ü Ch'iu-pai was largely the work of Wang Ming. Considering his low status in the Party, it might seem that Wang still had a very long way to go before reaching his goal. But given his close links with the ruling group in the CPSU, he had every reason to make such preparations. In Wang Ming's timetable, the substitution of Hsiang Chung-fa for Ch'ü Ch'iu-pai was simply one step on the path towards the final seizure of power in the Party. Paying court to Chou En-lai was simply the modern equivalent of the second-century would-be emperor Liu Pei paying court to the brilliant administrator Chuko Liang. Chou En-lai was naturally pleased by the attentions being paid to him. He could not but have a poor opinion of Wang Ming, but he was full of admiration for Stalin, Mif, and others, whose faction had won control of the CPSU and the Comintern. Under such circumstances it was out of the question that Chou would consider seriously the theoretical and political arguments of the Russian Opposition.

Chang Kuo-t'ao, who lacked Ch'ü Ch'iu-pai's learning and Chou En-lai's talents, inspired not the slightest fear in Wang Ming and his friends, who made no attempt to court him, but ignored and even despised him. Chang was therefore the most lonely man in the Chinese delegation. I remember I once had a conversation with him in the room of an interpreter called Shih I-sheng. Since Shih and I were the only others present, Chang, who was usually a very reticent man, dropped his guard a little and began to talk more freely. He complained of the frustration he felt in Moscow. He told us: 'Lenin once said that people who cannot read stand outside politics. In Moscow, people who cannot read Russian stand outside politics.' The implication of his remark was obvious. I realized at once that he was dissatisfied with the Red compradors like Wang Ming. Shih responded to Chang's remark with an embarrassed smile, and I too smiled and said nothing. Chang seemed to sense that he had gone too far, so he suddenly changed the subject and began instead to talk about the one-eyed general Liu Po-ch'eng, who was at that time attending a military academy in Moscow, and the delicious Szechwanese food that Liu could cook. Knowing that Chang Kuo-t'ao was out of favour and dissatisfied with the faction in power, one Chinese comrade had tried to win him over to the Opposition. But it turned out that Chang was at least as unwilling as Chou En-lai to side with 'the truth in defeat'.

Some of the Chinese delegates, however, were sincerely interested in finding out about the view of the Russian Opposition. Among them were Wang Jo-fei, Kuan Hsiang-ying, and Lo Chang-lung. They came to the views of the Opposition without prejudice, and where they did not accept them were at least prepared to give them consideration. We gave all of them documents, which they read carefully and responded to rather favourably.

I have already described our difficulties in finding somewhere for me to do my translations after Poliakov's arrest. For about a fortnight after that I had found it impossible to do any work whatsoever. We searched high and low for a new place, and asked everyone we knew in Moscow. Then we were unexpectedly offered Wang Jo-fei's room in the smart Europa Hotel. After he had read the Oppositionist writings on the Chinese Revolution, Wang Jo-fei had been deeply impressed. His own experiences in China confirmed the truth of the Oppositionist arguments. On other issues in the dispute – economic construction in the Soviet Union, problems of the British and German revolutions and so forth – Wang was more doubtful:

because of his lack of theoretical training and his ignorance of world politics he found it impossible to say which side of the argument was right. On the current situation in China he did not accept completely the resolutions of the CCP Sixth Congress; but he did not agree with the criticisms Trotsky raised of the 'democratic dictatorship' slogan for China either. He had not formed any opinion of his own on the perspectives of the Chinese Revolution. Such was Wang Jo-fei's position at that time, and it is therefore not surprising that he took a sympathetic attitude towards us. As soon as he heard of my problem he made his room available to me during the day, while he was away at the office of the Comintern's Eastern Department. I would arrive at his room at about nine o'clock every morning, and he would leave shortly afterwards. I used to take a few slices of bread with me, so that I could work uninterruptedly until he returned in the afternoon. I worked in Wang Jo-fei's room for several days, just long enough to complete my translation of that part of the Critique which dealt with the Chinese Revolution. Wang Jo-fei was running something of a risk in helping us in this way, since his wife, Li P'ei-tse, a student at Sun Yat-sen University, was well known to be a staunch supporter of the Wang Ming group. Naturally Wang Jo-fei was well aware of his wife's political leanings, and was careful never to reveal his sympathies to her.

Wang Jo-fei died for the CCP in 1946, killed in an air-crash while flying back from Chungking to Yenan (others killed in the crash included General Yeh T'ing and Po Ku). I have decided to reveal this secret episode in Wang Jo-fei's life for two main reasons: first, he is dead anyway, and no harm can come to him for his 'error'; and second, the fact that he committed such an 'error' shows to my mind that he was not a time-server, but a revolutionary of character and integrity.

Wang Jo-fei and the other two delegates who had expressed sympathy for the Opposition (Kuan Hsiang-ying and Lo Chang-lung) returned to China one after the other. Once they plunged back into Party work, they lost all interest in the 'unpractical' disputes on theoretical principles which had disturbed their thinking for a while. They reverted once again to the 'blind activities' (wei-kan chu-i) at which they so excelled. They linked up with what was left of the Party apparatus after the defeats that had been suffered and threw themselves back into the struggle. Through hard work and effort they finally worked their way to the top of the Party hierarchy, and after that they never again re-established contact with the Chinese Trotskyist movement. Lo Chang-lung's political evolution was rather different from that of Wang and Kuan; he became the leader of a new faction in the Party, the so-called 'conciliationist' faction, as Wang Ming called those who opposed Li Li-san without whole-heartedly supporting himself. This grouping had no differences of principle with the ruling Stalinist faction, but in the recalcitrance they displayed towards the Wang Ming clique one could just catch a glimmer of the influences which their leader, Lo Chang-lung, had been exposed to in Moscow. Wang Ming and his friends attacked the 'conciliationists' in the most unscrupulous and treacherous way. Finally Chiang Kai-shek intervened to assure Wang Ming of victory in the struggle by arresting and executing all of the 'conciliationists' with the sole exception of Lo Chang-lung. Even after his narrow escape Lo refused to draw any lessons from his experience. He made no attempt to find a way to Trotskyism. Instead, utterly demoralized and disillusioned he opted for 'conciliation' with the Kuomintang.

In the winter of 1928 the Opposition rapidly expanded its organization among the Chinese students in Moscow. We had comrades everywhere: in the Lenin Institute, in the various military academies, and in particular at Sun Yat-sen University, where out of a total of four hundred students about one hundred and fifty were Trotskyists, either as members or as close sympathizers of the organization. By then copies of Trotsky's famous article 'Problems of the Chinese Revolution after the Sixth Congress' had already arrived in Moscow, provoking a heated debate, particularly among us Chinese students. Trotsky's arguments did not win unanimous or immediate support. We were particularly reluctant to accept his central slogan, the call for a constituent, or national, assembly (to which I shall return shortly). We were mere novices in revolutionary theory at that time, and we knew even less about revolutionary strategy and tactics and the need to apply them flexibly and in accordance with changing circumstances. What little theory we had been taught at university was abstract and schematic, and our grounding in the history of Bolshevism was extremely shallow. Moreover, the fact that we had just left behind a defeated revolution meant that we were embittered and enraged, and as such unconditional 'leftists', whether or not we were aware of being so. We were ready to accept any slogan or position which appeared to be leftist, 'pure socialist', or tending towards direct action. By the same token we found it very difficult to accept any tactic which could in any way be interpreted as 'rightist', moderate, or 'bourgeois' in character. Up to then we had considered Trotsky's positions consistently 'Left', but on reading his article, and in particular the section on the constituent assembly slogan, it seemed to us young fanatics as if he had suddenly leapt to the right of Stalin.

At the Sixth Congress of the CCP the call for establishing soviets in China was rejected as a slogan for direct action, but retained as a propaganda slogan to be acted upon when the next 'revolutionary wave' drew near. Thus the Sixth Congress left the CCP without a central political slogan, although nominally the call for soviets continued to play that role. This disastrous decision had come about because Stalin and Bukharin had failed to understand the new situation that had emerged in China after the defeat of the revolution. The result was that the CCP pursued counter-productive putschist policies for a number of years afterwards.

It was not until years later, particularly after the Sian Incident of December 1936, that I realized just how profound and far-sighted Trotsky's thinking on this question had been. If Trotsky's views on the Chinese Revolution were, without exception, the embodiment of his political genius, then his decision to put forward the slogan of the constituent assembly in the autumn of 1928 was his boldest and most flexible policy-stroke ever, if at the same time the most difficult for his followers to grasp. I sometimes thought that if the CCP had accepted this policy at that time, that is to say if they had adopted the slogan of a constituent assembly and fought for it as Trotsky proposed, instead of waiting for seven years until 1935 before coupling the slogan with offers of a shameful capitulation to the Chiang Kai-shek regime, then the lives of many tens of thousands of revolutionaries would have been spared, Chiang Kai-shek's reactionary rule would have ended much sooner than it did, the Japanese militarists would perhaps not have acted so recklessly, and the situation in China and Asia as a whole in the next two or three decades would have been quite different.

At the time, however, not only Stalinists but even those of us who accepted Trotsky's positions on every other fundamental question thought that he had made a grave mistake in putting forward such an 'opportunist' slogan. Among the Trotskyists in Moscow there was none who did not recognize that the counter-revolution had triumphed in China, and that its reign would last for some time.

However, none of us had gone on to ask what tactics we should adopt in our revolutionary work. We realized that in such a situation it was wrong to call for direct armed insurrection under the banner of soviets. Stalin and Ch'ü Ch'iu-pai knew it too, which was why they decided to withdraw it for the time being as a slogan for immediate action. But what slogan should we use? What slogan covered all the features of the new situation in which the counter-revolution had triumphed, in which all the democratic tasks remained unresolved, and yet in which the revolutionary forces, despite their severe defeat, had somehow managed to survive? We Trotskyists were just as incapable as Stalin and Ch'ü Ch'iu-pai of providing an answer to this question. It was Trotsky who came up with the correct formula: a revolutionary democratic programme, with the call for a constituent assembly as its central slogan. This was, of course, precisely what was needed to meet the circumstances, but Stalin, Ch'ü Ch'iu-pai, and others, rejected it as a 'liquidationist' or 'Social Democratic' deviation. Cowed by these attacks and influenced by our own immature prejudices, we dared not accept the slogan. We Chinese Trotskyists were so puzzled by it that we continued to argue and quarrel heatedly over it even after our return to China.

The first to accept this slogan was the veteran Communist Liu Jen-ching. However, his interpretation of it astonished us all: he pointed to the stability of the Chinese bourgeoisie, and argued that China could only develop politically through parliamentarianism. A new revolution would break out only *after* such a development, and its problems would be solved only 'at a higher historical stage'.

In the eyes of most Chinese Trotskyists, Liu was advocating the abandonment of the revolution. A few of our sympathizers were frightened away by Liu's ultra-rightist interpretation of Trotsky's policy. After long discussions, the majority of us accepted Trotsky's slogan, but we understood it to mean that our chief aim in a democratic struggle for a constituent assembly would be to re-establish contact with the masses during a period of counter-revolution, to rally the revolutionary forces against the military dictatorship, and to prepare the way for a new revolutionary upsurge. This interpretation, despite its imperfections, was leftist in orientation and was, in our opinion, much closer to the spirit of the slogan than that of Liu.

In this way the ideological confusion caused by the constituent assembly slogan was finally dispelled, and the organization of the Opposition among the Chinese students in Moscow continued to grow.

New names were added daily to our list of sympathizers. Despite its ambition of seizing the leadership of the whole of the Chinese Party, Wang Ming's university Party Committee neither led an ideological life of its own, nor allowed the students to lead theirs. It merely frittered away its time in trivialities. To take just one example: a girl student called Chu was cruelly rebuked and tormented for several nights in succession before a general meeting of all the students of the university just because she had fallen in love with two men at the same time. The overwhelming majority of the students found this sort of 'party work' nauseating. Not surprisingly, the more serious-minded among them turned towards the Opposition. We managed to keep our organization secret, and the existence of our three-man committee was known only to a very few people. Nevertheless, nearly everyone was aware of the functioning of the Opposition, and Oppositionist documents were easily obtainable. Of the ex-KUTV students, only a handful stayed outside the orbit of the Opposition: most of them either joined us, or sympathized with our aims. As far as I remember only two were worthless enough to turn towards the Wang Ming clique. One of these was nicknamed 'Old Widow' (lao kuafu), a pun on his adopted Russian name of Logov. 'Old Widow' was a native of Shensi province, and a former political commissar with General Feng Yü-hsiang's army. He was now playing the part of double-agent between us and the Wang Ming clique. It was he who a year or so later betrayed the whole of our Moscow organization to the GPU.

By the end of 1928 the Stalinist Party Committee at the university became more and more aware of a growing silent opposition to its rule on the campus. They took many measures to stave off the threat from the oppositionist forces. First they organized 'shock troops' to beat up suspected Oppositionists and intimidate 'undesirable elements'. This policy was carried out under the pretext of 'selecting and cultivating worker comrades', by grouping together strong but dull-witted worker comrades as 'Party activists'. Some of these comrades were natives of Shantung province who had been sent to work in France during the First World War and who had stayed on there after the Armistice, where they had been recruited by the CCP branch in Paris. Their main contribution to Party work in France was to defend the organization against attacks from thugs hired by the Chinese Nationalists. As comrades they were sincere enough, but they unfortunately completely lacked understanding. They believed in communism and the Party, and were willing to support anything that was done in the name of the Party and anyone who sat in the Party Committee offices. In their eyes, especially after they had been 'educated' by Wang Ming and his friends, anyone who had differenccs with the committee was as much an enemy as the Nationalists had been, to be dealt with in the same way. Apart from these men, Wang Ming's 'shock troops' also included a small number of workers from Shanghai, the two best-known of which were Li Chien-ju and Wang Yün-ch'eng. The 'shock troops' also served as Wang Ming's bodyguard. Wherever he went, his crack unit went with him. However, this display of force only made the Wang Ming clique even more abhorrent to the rank and file student body and helped the growth of the Opposition.

The second main measure used against those suspected of belonging to the Opposition was the so-called 'transference of Party membership'. The aim of this manoeuvre was to purge Oppositionists from the Party without resorting to formal expulsion. In accordance with the principle of internationalism, members of one section of the world Communist movement automatically became members of another section when they passed from one country to another. In this way, CCP members studying in the Soviet Union for any length of time had till now been automatically considered to be members of the CPSU, and so far no one had thought of questioning the procedure. All of a sudden Wang Ming and his friends discovered that this was wrong, since in their view membership of the CCP could not be put on a par with membership of the CPSU. They argued that a Chinese Communist in Moscow had fewer rights than a Russian Communist, and if he wanted to live, study, and work in Russia as a Communist, he should have to apply to the CPSU for membership and be subjected to a careful examination. This process was called 'transference of Party membership'. General meetings of the whole student body were convened, at which those students who had applied for transfer were called to the platform and asked to give a report on their own background and personal history. They were then subjected to criticism from the 'masses' (i.e., the Party Committee), and were made to answer questions. If the 'masses' were satisfied with an applicant's report and with his answers to the questions and criticisms raised, his application for transfer was granted and he was thereafter regarded as a 'first-class Party member'. But if doubts were raised, his application was most unlikely to be accepted. In such cases some of the unsuccessful applicants were allowed to retain their 'second-class' membership (i.e. of the CCP), but others were stripped even of that. Needless to say, this was precisely why the 'transfer meetings' were held. However, the fact that Wang Ming and his friends were prepared to admit openly that the CPSU enjoyed a higher status than our own Party clearly exposed their servility. It also showed how evil-intentioned they were, driving people into hell under the pretext of sending them on to heaven. They held several general meetings of this sort, and each one provoked more and more people to anger. Finally we decided to boycott such sessions and to refrain from applying for transfer. Nine out of ten students supported this boycott, and the Party Committee was forced to abandon the transfer ceremony.

The frustration of this plot did not mean of course that Wang Ming and his friends gave up persecuting and oppressing their opponents on the campus. On the contrary, they continued to do so with redoubled efforts after the spring of 1929, but the methods that they adopted were no longer the same.

I mentioned earlier that by this time the influence of the Opposition in the Soviet Union was growing rapidly. As a result of the deepening crisis in the country, Stalin was forced to adopt some of the ideas of the Left Opposition, and to break with his right-wing Bukharinite allies. Trotsky's warnings against the danger from the Right, denounced as 'slanders against the Party' just a year ago, were suddenly 'confirmed'. These were now taken up by Stalin himself, who urged all Party members to be ready to fight against a threat the existence of which he had denied right up to that very moment. Trotsky's prestige was therefore restored with surprising speed. The Russian people were more ready than ever to listen to what the Opposition had to say, and Trotsky's secretly-circulated articles were in great demand. A similar shift of mood and sympathy also took place among the Chinese students in Moscow. Those who a year ago had half-heartedly supported Stalin began to turn towards Trotsky.

Clandestine Trotskyist organizations in Moscow were repeatedly raided, but new ones immediately sprang up to replace them Trotsky himself was exiled to Alma Ata, a remote city in Soviet Central Asia near China's western border. He lived there under close surveillance, and his correspondence with friends was both censored and otherwise interfered with. But, despite this, his articles were invariably in wide circulation within a month of being written. Trotsky had supporters and sympathizers everywhere, and even some of the secret police agents detailed to keep watch on him used to give him covert help on occasions. Since the struggle for power between the various factions had not yet finally been settled, some professional bureaucrats were continuing to hedge their bets in case of a sudden reversal of fortunes in the final round.

Every year the Chinese students in Moscow had to spend a certain part of their time in productive work. Some of them were sent to work in the Moscow factories, while a smaller number, usually those who had lost their membership of the Party, were sent out to factories or gold-mines in the provinces. When they got back to Moscow they brought with them information about the local situation and the mood of the workers. We learned from these sources that Russian workers were becoming more and more sympathetic to the Trotskyists, and were so dissatisfied with the Government that the smallest incident would often provoke a strike.

Naturally Stalin was very worried by these developments. And yet he dared not put Trotsky in gaol, let alone kill him. At first he tried to silence his opponent by ordering him, in the name of the Central Committee, to put a stop to his political activities; but Trotsky refused to do so. Stalin therefore decided to deport him from the Soviet Union, a decision which was carried out in January 1929. The preparations for Trotsky's deportation were made in strict secrecy. We already knew that Stalin and the Central Committee would place harsher and harsher constraints on Trotsky's activities, and we fully expected that the persecution of the Opposition would increase. However, none of us imagined that they would go so far as to deport him. Naturally the news was a great shock to the Oppositionists, but publicly people did not seem to be very much concerned by it. The report of the deportation was tucked away in an obscure corner of *Pravda* and we did not notice any particularly emotional reactions to it among any sections of the community. But a fortnight or so later something very different happened. We were on our way to the university one morning when we noticed clusters of people standing around news stands reading, talking, and even arguing. Realizing that something important must have happened, I bought a paper and found a piece by Yaroslavsky on the front page with the banner headline 'MR TROTSKY'S FIRST STEP ABROAD'. Alongside the article was a photographic reproduction of the front page of the London *Daily Express*, featuring an article by Trotsky. Without even revealing anything of the content of the article, Yaroslavsky claimed that no sooner was Trotsky out of the country than he was fighting against the Soviet Union and was in collusion with the imperialists.

Yaroslavsky's attack was a real blow below the belt. After ten years of outright hostility between the Soviet Union and the imperialist countries there was a widespread misconception, especially among young people, that under no circumstances should a revolutionary make use of the bourgeois press. This misconception had been further strengthened by the fact that in the Soviet Union the press was controlled by the Communist Party. People were either unaware or had forgotten that revolutionaries under bourgeois regimes were sometimes compelled to make use of the bourgeois press, publish books through bourgeois publishing houses, and issue statements through the 'mass media'. Taking advantage of this ignorance, Yaroslavsky and Stalin used the fact that Trotsky had granted an interview to a *Daily Express* correspondent and had contributed an article to the paper, to launch a smear-campaign against him. The trick worked. The report caused a sensation, arousing suspicion not only among ordinary Russians but also among us Chinese Trotsky-ists. We regretted that Trotsky had committed a blunder, which in our view could only play into the hands of his enemies.

Trotsky had not yet been deprived of his citizenship and was living in the Soviet consulate in Constantinople. He was well-informed about what was going on in Russia. As soon as he heard what had happened, he wrote an article entitled 'An Open Letter to the Soviet Workers' in which he exposed the hypocrisy of Yaroslavsky and Stalin, accusing them of persecuting him in collusion with a reactionary foreign government, and protested against Stalin's criminal decision to deport one of the founders of the Soviet Union from his own country. He then went on to give examples from Lenin's life to show that it was common practice and entirely permissible for revolutionaries to grant interviews to bourgeois correspondents and write articles for the bourgeois press. His open letter was widely circulated among the masses, and was warmly received as it was brilliantly written and full of passion. I translated it into Chinese, and although it lost much of its original fire and beauty in the process, it still greatly charmed and moved our Chinese comrades, some of whom began to cry as they read it. It is a pity that neither the original nor the translation was ever sent to China. I remember it as one of the most moving things that Trotsky ever wrote, matched only by the article 'Son, Friend, and Fighter', which he wrote after the mysterious death of his son, Leon Sedov, in a Paris hospital in 1938.

However, Trotsky's deportation and Stalin's campaign against him could not prevent the further growth of the Opposition in the Soviet Union. By this time the split between Stalin and Bukharin was an open secret. Bukharin wrote an article criticizing Stalin's policy towards the peasants, and we were told that he had made secret contacts with Kamenev, his former opponent and now a capitulator to Stalin. Before long we saw Stalin striking heavy blows at the rightist opposition. The quarrels between the Stalinists and the Bukharinites did much to open the eyes of the masses to the reality of the 'Leninist solidarity of the Central Committee of the Party'. Up to that time there had been a feeling among the masses (in part created and encouraged by the bureaucracy) to the effect that although Trotsky was an outstanding leader and a great hero, he was by nature an uncooperative trouble-maker. Some people therefore saw it as a regrettable necessity to get rid of him in order to maintain the 'Leninist' solidarity of the Central Committee and permit it to function as an efficient collective. Demagogic talk about the need for a collective leadership was one of Stalin's main weapons against Trotsky, and it was in the name of precisely such a 'collective leadership' by 'ordinary folk' that he denounced the Trotskyists for engaging in hero worship and the cult of personality.

After the spring of 1929, however, naïve misconceptions and deliberate smears of this sort were refuted by events. The reason why a 'great hero' had been driven out of the country by 'ordinary folk' was by now clear: a thoroughly ordinary individual was himself anxious to lay claim to 'genius'. Although not everyone saw this immediately, they could hardly miss the fact that only a month or so after the deportation of the 'trouble-maker' Trotsky there was still no solidarity in the Central Committee: the differences between the various leaders were if anything more unprincipled than they had ever been. Lenin's 'faithful disciples' were behaving in a way unworthy of the name, fighting against each other at one moment and recanting and capitulating the next. The result was that the common people began to think more and more sympathetically of Trotsky. The deeper one went among the masses, the more often one would hear remarks such as: 'He alone was a real man'. This was particularly the case among those who had personally experienced the revolution, and among ex-Red Army men who had fought under him. Although the few contacts I had in Moscow were for the most part Party members, I also heard several remarks of this sort.

It was at about this time that we began to exchange correspondence with those Chinese Trotskyists who had been expelled and sent back to China a year before. From their letters we learned that they had succeeded in organizing Oppositionist nuclei in Shanghai, Hong Kong, and Peking. In Shanghai they had established a connection with a book company called New Universe, through which they were preparing to publish a few Oppositionist pamphlets. We were told that our Hong Kong friends were working in the docks, while those who had gone to Peking were active among students, and had published a national magazine called Our Word. I sent the Chinese translations of the Oppositionist documents to Shih T'ang, who was at that time responsible for the Shanghai organization, through the New Universe Book Company.

A number of students were due to be sent back to China in May or June of that year. Some of them had been chosen by the Party Committee, while others were going of their own accord. The majority were either secret members of, or sympathizers with, the Opposition. We were faced with two questions: how we should work once we got back to China; and how we should go about setting up an all-China Trotskyist organization. These questions were the two items on the agenda of a conference we convened at the campus of the Artillery School in Moscow. Besides the three leading members of the Oppositionist organization at Sun Yat-sen University, representatives of Oppositionist groups at the various military schools also attended, together with Liu Jen-ching. We arrived at the following conclusions:

1. When we returned to China we should stay in the CCP and thereby prove ourselves to be good Communists. We reasoned that it was only by establishing our reputation as brave fighters, and by winning the respect and confidence of our fellow Party members through our part in the actual revolutionary struggle, that we could earn the right to put forward our views and win support for them. But in order to remain within the Party we would have to hide the fact that we were Trotskyists, since the Party rules forbade the existence of factions. We therefore decided that in our actions we would abide by party discipline and obey the decisions of the majority, while in

ideological or political discussions we would criticize the wrong tactical and strategic decisions adopted by the Sixth Congress of the CCP in such a way as would not immediately reveal us as Oppositionists.

2. Since we still considered ourselves to be a faction of the CCP, and saw our task as rectifying the mistakes in the Party caused by the dominant influence of Stalinism, we did not intend to form a new political party. If we were expelled (which was sooner or later inevitable, whether or not we abided by democratic centralist principles), we would not make any attempt to set up a new Oppositionist organization, but would continue our revolutionary activities within the framework of the organization already established by the Trotskyists who had returned to China before us.

With the sole exception of Liu Jen-ching, who declared that he had no intention of wasting time and energy on working in the CCP and would devote himself entirely to Oppositionist work once he got back to China, all those present at the meeting accepted these decisions and agreed to abide by them. Liu, who had only contempt for the 'callow youths' who were working for the Opposition in China, declared that it was impossible for him to say in advance whether he could work with them once he returned to China, or precisely what form his work for the Opposition would take. He could not be bound by any decision in this respect. We were very dissatisfied both with his attitude towards the CCP, which was in contradiction with that of the rest of the Opposition, and also with his arrogant attitude towards the Oppositionists who had returned to China before us. After a long discussion and considerable criticism, Liu finally agreed to submit to the majority, though his actions when he got back to China belied his apparent submission. He returned from the Soviet Union via Europe, and stopped off en route to pay a visit to Trotsky in Prinkipo. He spent some days with the Old Man, who took advantage of the occasion to write the 'Draft Programme of the Chinese Bolshevik–Leninists', which Liu Jen-ching afterwards brought back to China with him.

Most of us Chinese students in Moscow were very keen to get back to China as quickly as possible, so that we could put the political line of the Opposition into practice. We reasoned that as we were first and foremost Chinese revolutionaries, our proper battlefield was China. If we stayed on in Moscow we would undoubtedly increase our academic understanding of Marxism, but there would be less and less work for us to do there. Our activities were of necessity confined to the Chinese student body, whose numbers had dropped by the summer of 1929 from almost a thousand to only four or five hundred. Of that number, nearly a third had already been won over to our side. We believed that returning to China was the only way in which we could prove the correctness of the platform of the Opposition and win new forces to it. True, it would be safer and more comfortable to remain in Moscow, since China was at that time in the grip of the White terror and revolutionaries were losing their lives every day and every hour. But only the sort of cowards who belonged to the Wang Ming clique would tremble at the idea of returning home, or would attempt to intimidate those they disliked by threatening to send them back. We despised them for their attitude, and the overwhelming majority of underground Oppositionists among the Chinese student body wanted to return to China as soon as the second academic year was over.

As our desire to return became more and more apparent, the members of the clique in charge of the Party Committee changed their attitude accordingly. If their aim had simply been to seize power at the university, as it had been eighteen months earlier, then they could easily have disposed of the problem by shunting all undesirable and 'unreliable' elements back home. But now their ambitions had swollen, and they looked upon the whole of the Chinese Party as their 'sphere of influence'. The methods they used to deal with their opponents, Trotskyists and non-Trotskyists alike, changed correspondingly. They would no longer just send us back, without regard for what we might get up to in the Party in China. They preferred to keep us in Moscow, where they could keep an eye on us and if necessary have us liquidated with the help of Stalin's secret police. It was therefore no easy matter for us to be sent home, especially for those of us considered by the Party Committee to be 'suspect' but politically able, and unlikely to quit the Party or go over to the reactionary camp once we got back to China. Those of us who were in this category would scarcely be allowed to return unless we managed in some way to win the confidence of the Wang Ming group.

Here I would like to relate two incidents which concern myself. My health had never been good and while I was in Moscow I used to go to see the university doctor once or twice a month. I was rarely seriously sick: most of my ailments were of a minor sort, such as colds and high temperatures brought on by fatigue, so I had never applied to go to a rest-home or a sanatorium. However, one day in the spring of 1929 I was unexpectedly informed by the head of the university hospital that I had been granted permission to go to a health resort on the Black Sea. It was like a gift from heaven! My destination was a place near the beautiful town of Feodosiya on the Crimean Peninsula, where I stayed for a month. It was a very picturesque little place, and most of the people taking cures there were high-ranking officials from factories and Party or government offices in Moscow and Leningrad. The only other Chinese there apart from me was an active supporter of the Wang Ming group. Obviously to be sent to a resort such as this was a very different matter from being sent to a rest-home in a Moscow suburb, and was in fact a privilege reserved for the higher ranks. So why was it that I was sent there, and even before the summer holidays had begun? Lying there on the sandy beach soaking up the warm Crimean sun, I could not help asking myself this question. It was obvious that the Party Committee must have spoken up on my behalf, or I would never have been so lucky. But my relations with the Party Committee were cool, not to say hostile. I had no personal contact with Wang Ming. We did not even acknowledge one another when we met on the street. I heartily despised him, and for his part he clearly had no reason to like me. He could not yet know for certain that I was a member of the Opposition, but he must have realized that I was not an active supporter of the Party Committee. The number two man in the hierarchy of the Wang Ming faction was Ho Tzu-shu; he and I were in the same class together at Sun Yat-sen University and we were on fairly good terms with one another. Nevertheless, one could hardly call our relationship a close one, since he was a top member of the Party Committee while I was a 'non-activist'. Shortly before I was notified of my selection for a health-cure, however, I noticed that he began to warm towards me, constantly asking after my health and chiding me for not looking after myself properly. It was therefore not very difficult for me to guess who I had to thank for my stroke of good luck. Then I realized that this unasked-for favour was actually part of a plan to win me over to the side of the Wang Ming group, and thus to strike a blow at the dissident camp among the Chinese students in Moscow, which they feared might provide the nucleus for a Chinese Trotskyist Opposition.

The second incident was even more unexpected than the first. One evening towards the end of July, not long after I had returned from the Crimea, I was called to the office of the Party Committee and told that I had been assigned to participate in a big anti-war and anti-imperialist demonstration in Leningrad on 1 August, as the CCP representative in a delegation that included several members of the Comintern and that was to be led by Ernst Thaelmann, leader of the Communist Party of Germany. There was also a number of other well-known German leaders of the delegation, including Remmele, who was killed by Stalin a few years later. I was very surprised to find myself in such distinguished company; but even more so by the fact that the Party Committee had chosen me to represent them. After all, an assignment of this sort was far too good for someone who was not even a member of the Wang Ming clique. Members of such delegations would be entertained and cheered wherever they went, they would watch the demonstration from a special rostrum, and be expected to make short speeches at meetings and to pay visits to factories and other institutions. So how was it that I, a rank-and-file student who had no special links with the Party Committee, suddenly found myself singled out for such an honour? Was it because I knew a little Russian? But there were other followers of Wang Ming whose Russian was better than mine. In terms of seniority and work record, my qualifications were rather meagre. So what, then, was the real cause of my sudden promotion? Without doubt, it was just one more step by the Wang Ming faction in their long-term strategy for fighting the Opposition. Nevertheless, it gave me a chance to see at close range something of the privileges which the Soviet bureaucrats enjoyed, at a time when the system of privileges in general had not yet fully developed. In addition to this, I also got the chance to visit the scene of the October Revolution.

Thaelmann and others had just attended the Tenth Plenary Session of the Comintern Executive. This meeting was a landmark in the history of the Comintern, and represented an abrupt lurch to the left. It was at this plenum that the Communist International officially announced that the world revolution had entered its 'third period', during which world capitalism would collapse on all fronts and the revolution would go into a general offensive. Stalin also performed an important organizational manoeuvre at this session, officially removing Bukharin from the position as head of the Comintern to which he had been elected at its Sixth Congress. Perhaps it was as a reward for the services he rendered in this operation that Thaelmann was chosen to officiate at the Leningrad demonstration on his way back to Germany. Two Italian students from the Communist University for the Toilers of the West (KUTZ) and I were added to the German delegation to give it a more international look.

On·the night of 30 July we travelled to Leningrad by train. I shared a compartment with an Italian comrade called Nicolo, who taught me how to sing *Avanti popolo!* (a song I can still sing even now). It was daybreak when we arrived in Leningrad. Outside the railway station there were some cars waiting to take us to the Smolny Institute, where the headquarters of the October Revolution had been. I felt as if I were on a pilgrimage. Only a few months before I had read John Reed's *Ten Days that Shook the World*, and I was therefore familiar with the role that the building had played during the revolution. I had a fresh impression in my mind of the corridors milling with workers and soldiers, and the rooms where Lenin, Trotsky, and the other Bolshevik leaders had worked. Now I had the chance to see with my own eyes what I had so far only read in books. It was a fascinating experience, but at the same time it set me thinking: the two giants who had planned and directed the revolution from this place were now gone; one dead and the other deported.

Nicolo and I, together with another German comrade, were put up for the night in the 'Peasants' Home' in Smolny. It was a quiet place, ideal for resting in, which before the revolution had been a dormitory for senior nuns. Thaelmann and the other VIPs stayed in a luxury hotel.

On the day that we arrived in Leningrad, a meeting of Party activists was held in the Uritsky Palace to celebrate the approaching 1 August Anti-War Day. We were seated on the platform as part of the presidium. Kirov, who became famous a few years later after his assassination, officiated at the meeting, and Thaelmann delivered the main address. There was no doubt about Thaelmann's talents as a speaker. Unlike most communist leaders in recent years, he did not read from a long prepared text, but spoke fluently and impromptu, with a lively style. He had a resounding voice, and gave an impression of real strength to his audience. What was more, he spoke briefly and to the point, which must have been a pleasant surprise for his listeners, for whom set speeches were generally a torture.

That afternoon or the next (the exact date escapes me), there was a demonstration of tens of thousands of workers through Leningrad. We were again invited to mount the rostrum, where we stood alongside all the dignitaries. We reviewed the procession, and received the cheers of the demonstrators. This was the last time I was to play such a role. Those of us on the rostrum were expected to acknowledge the cheering crowds by waving back at them and keeping fixed smiles on our faces for what seemed an interminable period. Of all the Stalinist ceremonial formalities, this was perhaps the commonest, and to review such a demonstration was regarded as a matter of the highest honour, by reviewers and reviewed alike. I saw things rather differently, however: in my opinion the role was a painful one to play, and the performance as a whole quite meaningless. This is not to say, of course, that the demonstration itself was meaningless. But it does seem to me that once something becomes a mere formality, a pre-arranged ceremony in which every last detail is prescribed by some bureaucrat, it inevitably loses all its revolutionary significance. Worse still, this whole ridiculous performance could only serve a reactionary and counter-revolutionary purpose. It was precisely in rituals of this sort that the ugliness of the 'personality cult' and the ambitions of some leaders revealed themselves most clearly. As I write these lines in the autumn of 1956, the leaders of the CCP are busy expressing their opposition to Stalin's 'personality cult'. But the most fanatical and dramatic expression of that cult, the march past the reviewing stand, has been plagiarized to the letter in China on an even more massive and intimidating scale. One is forced to conclude that the CCP has yet to take the first step on the road to opposing the 'personality cult'.

On the day after we had reviewed the demonstration, we were taken on a visit to Tsarskoe Selo ('Tsar's Village') and a number of factories, including the Putilov steel works, which had played such an important part in the October Revolution. The afternoon was free of official engagements, and we were allowed to go wherever we liked. I went to see a friend I had got to know during my stay in the Crimea, a leading trade unionist at the Red October Confectionery factory. He spent the whole afternoon showing me round Leningrad. First of all he took me to the Viborg district, which had provided the main forces for the revolution in 1917. Then we went for a walk along the Neva River and the Nevsky Prospect. He also took me to the world-famous Hermitage Museum. In the evening he invited me to his home to have dinner with some members of his family and with some other men and women I had met in the Crimea. His wife did the cooking, and it was the first and only time during my stay in the Soviet Union that I ate with a Russian family. Their kindness and hospitality, typical of all Russians, overwhelmed me. But it was clear from the way they behaved and talked that they were supporters of the 'Thermidor'.[1] I compared them with the few Russians I knew in Moscow, and found the differences striking. My Russian friends in Moscow were mostly Oppositionists. They too were young, but most of them had been in the Party for a long time. Nearly all had taken part in the revolution or the civil war, had suffered much, and had been tempered by their experiences. Naturally they held firmly to revolutionary principles, knew more about politics, had a broader outlook, and paid less attention to the material pleasures of life. They had made friends with us Chinese Communists chiefly, even exclusively, because of our common position towards the revolution. It was quite different, of course, with my Leningrad friends, who were very contented with their lot and hardly ever bothered to think about political questions. In fact all of them, men and women alike, were much more interested in the latest fashions in clothes than they were in politics. They were good workers and activists in their various fields, but the main reason they worked so hard was because they wanted to improve their living standards. Nearly all of them were members of the Party or the Komsomol, but they knew little of the world and even less of China. Indeed, one pretty young girl, a Komsomol member and a clerk at the confectionery factory, asked me whether there was electric light in China and whether Chinese could live together with monkeys. My Leningrad friends were more typical of the new generation of Soviet youth than the Russians I knew in Moscow. Seeing them, it became clearer to me why Stalin had beaten Trotsky in the Party struggle. Obviously Trotsky's theory of permanent revolution was neither to the liking nor in the interests of these young men and women.

We stayed in Leningrad for another four or five days, and spent much of our time travelling round the barracks on the outskirts of the city, making speeches to the soldiers. We visited several places a day, and once we even went as far as the Finnish border. Wherever we went we were invariably welcomed by thousands of soldiers, whom we usually addressed very briefly from a makeshift platform in the barrack yard. What we said was rather commonplace, but need-

[1] Stalin's right turn in the mid-1920s was often compared with the right turn in France after the fall of Robespierre and the left-wing Jacobins in the month of Thermidor of Year II by the revolutionary calendar (July 1794).

less to say in the spirit of Stalin's new left turn: we spoke of the
imminence of war and the need for the solidarity of workers all over
the world. The soldiers responded enthusiastically, and, after we had
delivered our speeches, it was usually impossible to break through
the encirclement of the young Red Army men, who attacked us from
all sides, captured us, tossed us repeatedly into the air amid great
cheers, and finally carried each of us shoulder high across the parade
ground. I remember that on one occasion Thaelmann, who was a
large and rather stout man, was spared this treatment, but only after a
considerable amount of begging and pleading on his part. These
displays of enthusiasm by the Red Army men were quite genuine,
and there was no question of their being stage-managed by the
officers. After all, the October Revolution was still only eleven years
old, and despite the fact that Stalin's theory of 'socialism in one
country' was beginning to have an effect in Russia, the internationalist ideas propagated during the revolutionary years before Lenin's
death had captured the imagination of the ordinary Soviet people.
They therefore still regarded us foreign Communists as comrades
closely connected with their own life-and-death struggles. It was not
until after 1935 that the bureaucracy began to regard every foreigner
as a spy and every foreign Communist as a 'running dog' to be
patted or kicked, favoured or put down at will.

I only attended one official dinner in Leningrad, and it was not
particularly luxurious, quite unlike the unbelievably sumptuous
feasts that the Stalinist bureaucrats in the Kremlin started to give in
the late 1930s. But even at that early date it was obvious that the top
bureaucrats lived far better than the ordinary Soviet people. Take my
case, for example. As an ordinary student I usually got ten roubles a
month, but while I was on the Leningrad delegation I got that
amount each day, supposedly to spend on food – which I was mostly
given free anyway. By the time I got back to Moscow I was therefore
quite a rich man, with enough money in my pocket to treat my
friends to Chinese meals.

On my return to Moscow, Ho Tzu-shu was even more friendly
towards me than before: he congratulated me on the success of my
mission to Leningrad, and told me that he hoped that from now on I
would be more active and take on more assignments from the Party
Committee at the university. It was by then obvious that they were
putting pressure on me to join the Wang Ming faction. I was quite
familiar with their carrot-and-stick tactics: first a polite invitation,

and then, should it prove necessary, crude harassment. They had extended their invitation: the next step was up to me. I raised the matter at a meeting of the clandestine committee of the Opposition, and it was unanimously agreed that it was no longer possible for me to stay on in Moscow. Certainly the Party Committee would no longer be prepared to tolerate my apparent inactivity. It was therefore decided that I should go back to China as soon as possible. Once the Party Committee had abandoned the carrot and taken up the stick, that would be the end of my hopes of returning home. But on what grounds should I apply to return? It was obvious that Wang Ming and his friends suspected that I might have something to do with the Opposition in the university, and it might well be that they would not allow me to leave.

Once again the summer vacation came round, and this time the students were to be sent to the Crimea for their holidays. Since I had only just got back from there, I asked to be allowed to stay on in Moscow, and my request was granted. Apart from me there were another dozen or so other students who had been allowed to stay behind in the capital, on the grounds that they were about to return to China. Some of them were Oppositionists, others Wang Ming supporters. Among them was a girl comrade called Yeh whom I had married several months before, so I grasped the opportunity and asked to be sent back to China with her. It was a reasonable-sounding request, and since all the Chinese members of the Party Committee had left for the Crimea, I was able to apply directly to a Russian comrade for permission to return. He consulted the Eastern Department of the Comintern, and it was granted. For the second time in my life I set off on the Trans-Siberian Railway, thus bringing to an end my two-year stay in the Soviet capital.

Just before the holidays began we had carried out a reorganization of the Chinese Opposition in Moscow. In view of my decision to leave Russia, another conference of activists was convened at which a new member, Chao Yen-ch'ing, was chosen to replace me on the leading committee of the organization. Chao, former principal of the First Normal School of Hupeh province, was much older than most of us and was a kind and popular man. Those of us who knew him were therefore dismayed as well as surprised to learn six months or so later that he was responsible for the smashing of the entire Moscow organization, numbering some two to three hundred Chinese Trotskyists. This is a subject to which I shall return.

CHAPTER 6

Working under Chou En-lai

❂ ❂ ❂

As I remember, there were eighteen of us, including five married couples, who returned from Moscow to China together. Among the married couples were Li Ts'ai-lien and her husband Lu. Li Ts'ai-lien later won great respect in Opposition circles, remaining a loyal member of the movement until her death. Two years after our return to China her husband went over to the Kuomintang, betraying both his wife and his Communist ideals. Two others in the group, P'u Teh-tse and Chao Chi, remained faithful to the Trotskyist cause and are at present in China, although I am not sure what has become of them. Another, Hsieh Ying, gave up active politics twenty years ago, but continued to sympathize with the Trotskyists and as a result was sentenced by the CCP to twelve years' hard labour. The two comrades Yün Yü-t'ang and Chin Kuan-chen were shot by the Kuomintang. Li Ts'ai-lien's husband and another man called Huang drifted with the wind, working for whichever government happened to be in power, and ended up by collaborating with the enemy during the Sino-Japanese war. As for the rest of the group, most of them continued for longer or shorter periods of time to work for the Communist Party or the Opposition, but none proved strong enough to withstand the rigours of life as a revolutionary. One by one they abandoned politics to become 'law-abiding citizens' (among them my first wife Yeh). One of them, Kao Li-wen, later made a career for himself in politics as an influential member of Chiang Ching-kuo's entourage. But as for myself, I am still proud to call myself a Communist of the Trotskyist tendency.

Disguised as overseas Chinese, we slipped back into Shanghai via Korea, then a Japanese colony. On our journey we had heard from many sources that the police in Shanghai harbour were making careful searches of everyone entering the country. While still in Moscow I had read in a Japanese newspaper that one group of students returning from the Soviet Union had been arrested even before they disembarked in Shanghai, and had been taken ashore by detectives working for the Shanghai–Woosung Garrison Headquarters. Some comrades with access to private funds (among them Liu Jen-ching, Wu Chi-hsien and Wu Liang-p'ing) applied for permission to return to China via Europe; but we took our hearts in our hands and boarded a ship in Vladivostok. As it turned out the rumours were exaggerated, and we arrived back safely in the motherland. This is not to say, of course, that there was no terror in Shanghai at that time. Chiang Kai-shek's repressive apparatus had its tentacles everywhere and was hunting down revolutionaries with the same ferocity as it had during the purges of 1927; but it was to be some years before it was rearranged on a 'scientific' basis, with a 'mass organization', combining professional detectives and part-time agents and modelled on Stalin's GPU. In his struggle against the Communist Party Chiang Kai-shek had to rely on the *pao-ta-t'ing* or spies of the International Settlement, who were notorious for their corruption, ineptitude, brutality, and stupidity, but whose ruthlessness rarely yielded results.

In the autumn of 1929 the Kuomintang had just defeated the rival Kwangsi clique of warlords in a large-scale civil war, and its power appeared to have stabilized a little. At the same time, the revolutionary forces also appeared to be undergoing something of a revival. They had recovered from the *débâcle* of 1927 and the losses suffered during the putschist uprisings of the following year. The new Central Committee, which was in the process of developing underground activities throughout China, was based in Shanghai. Chiang Kai-shek therefore concentrated his White terror on that city, hoping to destroy the party in its nerve-centre.

On arrival in Shanghai, we at once reported to the Party's Central Committee, in accordance with the decisions reached at the Moscow meeting of the Chinese Trotskyist Opposition. Liu Jen-ching had arrived back several days before us, but ignored the Moscow decisions and obstinately clung to his original view that, as there was no point in working within the Party, we should immediately devote all our energies to independent activities of our own. It was only on our insistence that he grudgingly wrote to the Central Committee announcing his return, but at the same time making a full disclosure of his Trotskyist affiliations. Needless to say, the Party severed all links with him. Since it was not yet our view that the Communist Party as a whole was beyond redemption, Liu Jen-ching's frankness could only be seen as a pretext for opting out of the struggle to win over the Party rank and file to our policies. For our part, we decided to persevere with the decision agreed in Moscow to conceal our Trotskyist views from the leadership.

After we had reported to Party headquarters, Chou En-lai, then head of the organization department, arranged to meet about a dozen of us in the Chen-hua Hotel on Foochow Street. The meeting spread over two afternoons, during which Chou made a general analysis of the situation in China. A few days later we got together for a course in a three-storey European-style building at the end of Hsin-cha Road, secretly rented by the Party as an activities centre. Apart from those of us who had returned to China through Siberia, there were several others who had come back via Europe, making more than twenty of us altogether. The main aim of the course was to prepare us for underground work in China. All of us had been away from the country for at least two years, so that we knew little about the situation, and even less about clandestine work. The course lasted for nearly a fortnight, and we listened to reports from Chou En-lai, Yün Tai-ying, Hsiang Chung-fa, Hsiang Ying, Lo I-yüan, and Ku Shun-chang. Li Li-san, head of the propaganda department, was regarded as the Party's top theoretician, but he never put in an appearance.

The main speaker was Chou En-lai, who spent several days discussing the political situation with us. I have already explained that this was the so-called 'Third Period' of the Third International, when the whole world was supposed to be heading for a revolutionary upsurge. It was also the time when Stalin was in the process of defeating Bukharin's challenge to his leadership of the CPSU. The Chinese Communist Party was in a dilemma, having carried out a disastrous adventurist policy from late 1927 until the spring of 1928 under the leadership of Ch'ü Ch'iu-pai and on the direct instructions of Stalin. At the Sixth Congress of the CCP in July 1928 this putschist line was severely criticized, and even though the Congress still failed to adopt correct policies it at least admitted that the Revolution had suffered a defeat. During this period the most effective revolutionary strategy in China would have been Trotsky's revolutionary-democratic programme, centred around the call for a constituent assembly. The Stalinists were not prepared to adopt such a line, but since they had also abandoned the demand for immediate soviets, they were left without a central slogan to unify all their separate political demands. Had they been considering the problem from the point of view of China alone, they would probably have come round sooner or later to something like the strategy that Trotsky was advocating, which would have enabled the revolutionary forces to regroup while awaiting a favourable opportunity to take the offensive. But unfortunately this was the period in which Stalin, for reasons connected with the internal situation in the Soviet Union and the renewed crisis of European capitalism, put forward his 'Third Period' theory, which like all Stalin's theories was mechanically presented as a universal truth. Since the whole world was in the throes of a revolutionary upheaval, how could China be an exception? Within less than a year the apparent retreat from a crudely putschist line was abruptly reversed, and a new line was promulgated. In the same meeting of the Executive Committee of the Comintern at which Bukharin was removed from the leadership, it was decided that the Chinese Revolution was on the point of a new 'high tide', and the CCP was once again launched on a putschist line even more extreme than that of Ch'ü Ch'iu-pai. Naturally the tragic consequences of this policy became evident when the attempt to stage a nation-wide uprising in 1930 failed, causing heavy losses to the Party and its allies. After the full extent of the disaster became apparent, Stalin put the whole blame on Li Li-san, just as he had previously blamed Ch'ü Ch'iu-pai. Li Li-san was formally ousted in 1931, and Chou En-lai, Ch'ü Ch'iu-pai, and virtually the whole of the old leadership of the Party were bitterly criticized or removed. The person responsible for carrying out this 'great exploit' for Stalin was Wang Ming, who took the opportunity to promote himself from Party boss at Sun Yat-sen University in Moscow to leader of the CCP. He held on to power for four years, and under his leadership, according to Liu Shao-ch'i's report at the Party's Eighth Congress in 1945, the revolutionary forces lost over ninety per cent of their membership. But all this happened later, and I will come back to it in due course.

I would now like to return to our discussions with Chou En-lai at the educational course. The Central Committee had just been informed of the Moscow resolution forecasting the imminence of a new 'revolutionary high tide'.[1] Since I have no access to the relevant

[1] In this connection, the reader would do well to look at Mao Tse-tung's *A Single Spark can Start a Prairie Fire*, written in January 1930, in which the author quotes part of a letter which he had written several months before to the Central Committee in Shanghai. In this letter he criticizes the directives of the Central Committee for their passivity, and offers the following interpretation of the phrase 'there will soon be a high tide of revolution': 'It is

materials, it is not possible for me to reproduce the exact wording of the original resolution, but I remember its general drift quite clearly. After the contents of the resolution were made known to the Central Committee of the Chinese Party, the leadership was thrown into confusion, first because the memory of the putschist period was still fresh in their minds, and second because the subsequent attacks on this line were still ringing in their ears. Did the claimed imminence of a new 'revolutionary high tide' mean that armed insurrection was once more on the immediate agenda? And just how high was the 'high tide'? What exactly did the term mean? In particular, the interpretation of the word 'imminent' created problems for many comrades, as Mao pointed out in his article. At first the majority of the Central Committee inclined towards a cautious interpretation of this directive from the International. They were afraid that if they gave too leftist an interpretation to the phrase, they might end up cracking their heads against the wall again. While Chou was discussing the text of the resolution with us, he was very hesitant about how precisely to take it. We returned again and again to the words 'high tide', and even studied the Russian text. Since the original Russian word (*pod'em*) had the connotation of both 'high tide' and 'on the rise', Chou En-lai finally decided to translate it as 'rising tide' (in Chinese *kao-chang*), explaining that the translation 'high tide' ran the risk of being misinterpreted as 'climax' and could easily lead to a repetition of the old putschist line. As far as I remember we decided that the word 'imminent' was to be understood in the sense of 'still quite a long way off'. Before long, however, as a result of the Comintern stepping up its 'Third Period' activities and the abrupt left turn of the Stalinist parties worldwide, together with the echoing of this line by comrades within the Chinese Party (in particular those in the Kiangsi soviet area), the Central Committee began to interpret the phrase 'imminent high

like a ship far out at sea whose masthead can already be seen from the shore; it is like the morning sun in the east whose shimmering rays are visible from a high mountain top; it is like a child about to be born moving restlessly in its mother's womb'. (See *Selected Works of Mao Tse-tung, Vol. 1*.) If we take 1946 as the actual date of the arrival of the 'high tide' of the Chinese Revolution, then Mao's 'ship' took sixteen years to reach its port, his 'morning sun' took sixteen years to rise, and his 'restless child' remained for sixteen years in its mother's womb.

tide' in a more and more leftist way. The result was the so-called
'Li Li-san line'.

   Apart from Chou En-lai's outline of the overall political situation,
other leading comrades delivered reports on their specific fields of
work. The person we most enjoyed listening to was Yün Tai-ying, an
excellent speaker and a man of great practical experience. What he
had to tell us could never have been found in books. Lo I-yüan gave a
lecture on the peasant movement, but made a poor impression on
us. He clearly knew a lot about his subject, but was incapable of
putting it across well. He looked like a merchant, and it seemed
quite out of character that such a man should have led a peasant
movement in his younger days. Two years later I was to meet him
again in the prison of the Lung-hua Garrison Headquarters in
Shanghai. In his hour of mortal danger he behaved shamelessly and
presented a pitiful appearance, betraying his comrades in the hope of
saving his own skin, but ending up in front of the same firing-squad.

   Ku Shun-chang, who was in charge of the Party's special service
department, lectured us on how to work underground. Before joining
the Revolution he had been involved with the Shanghai underworld,
and although a member of the party for many years he still had
many gangster traits, knowing nothing about ideological questions.
Although he came from a working-class background and was very
vigilant, it was nevertheless a mistake to give responsibility for
undercover work to a man like him, and some of the blame for his
subsequent defection should be given to those comrades who first
promoted him to such an important post. People like Ku Shun-
chang are indispensable to any revolutionary movement and it is
impossible to carry out a mass uprising if they are refused admission
to the Party, but it is also essential to understand that the negative
role of the 'lumpenproletariat' in the Revolution far outweighs the
positive one (a theme on which Marx and Lenin both had much to
say). The leadership of the Party never learned this lesson, so that
over the years they suffered countless betrayals at the hands of such
people. When Ku Shun-chang gave away the entire structure of the
Party to the Kuomintang in 1931, delivering it its most damaging
blow, it was simply one of many such betrayals.

   After the course, I was assigned to work as an aide to Chou En-lai
in the organization department of the Central Committee. Apart
from Chou's second-in-command Lo Teng-hsien, there were four
aides altogether: Yün Tai-ying, Ch'en T'an-ch'iu, Wu Fu-ching, and

myself. Wu Fu-ching was one of the leading 'survivors' of the Moscow branch whose regime we had overthrown eighteen months earlier at KUTV. All my colleagues in the organization department were nine or ten years older than I, and belonged to the first generation of the Party. I was a young man of twenty-three, and naturally had less experience. Yün Tai-ying in particular had been an idol of mine ever since my middle-school days, and now I was to have the opportunity of working with him. Of course the prospect excited me, and I resolved not only to work very hard, but also to learn from the experience of these older comrades. They were very kind to me. True, the leadership of the Chinese Party had already become involved with the internal struggles of the CPSU, and sided with Stalin against Trotsky; yet most of the membership cared little or nothing about what was happening in the Soviet Party. Some comrades were completely at a loss to understand the issues at stake in the Stalin–Trotsky dispute, and others felt that it was essentially an internal Soviet quarrel. Their whole attitude was limited to Chinese questions, and more particularly the day-to-day activities of the Party. They were not interested in which faction one had belonged to in Moscow, but would judge one solely by the extent to which one devoted oneself to the Chinese Revolution and its Party. No doubt Moscow informed the Chinese leadership that the majority of the group sent back to China were suspected of being Trotskyists, and at the very least they must have known that we were not all orthodox, but Chou En-lai treated us exactly the same as everyone else, and never once brought up the 'errors' of Trotskyism during the discussions we had with him. What is more, despite the fact that the Party branch at Sun Yat-sen University had viewed me with suspicion, I was assigned to a position of some importance in the leadership.

This tolerant attitude towards the Opposition lasted for several months, until the Central Committee of the CCP received a telegram, shortly after the wholesale arrest of the Oppositionists in Moscow, ordering it to expel all those not prepared to give up their Trotskyist convictions. The telegram caused quite a stir in the Central Committee, and only then did the faction in power begin to adopt a more severe attitude, both towards us, and particularly towards Ch'en Tu-hsiu and the group around him, who had been moving closer to Trotskyist positions. Even so, the older members of the party were far less hostile towards the 'Trotsky–Ch'en faction' than the Stalin faction in Russia was towards the Left Opposition. This was because the real threat to their power came not from the 'Trotsky–Ch'en faction', but from the Mif–Wang Ming clique, who were the direct representatives of Stalin in China. Mao Tse-tung, Liu Shao-ch'i, Li Li-san, Chou En-lai, and others, had been under sustained attack from the inner circle of the Stalinist grouping for some time, whereas they had never engaged in any serious struggle with the 'Trotsky–Ch'en faction'. This is not to say that Mao, Liu, Chou, and the rest, sympathized with Ch'en Tu-hsiu and the Trotskyists. They were supporters of Stalin, not only for reasons of Realpolitik, but also because they shared a similar ideology and style of work. Stalin had the powerful resources of the Soviet Union at his disposal, and was in a position to lend essential aid to his supporters in other countries. After the defeat of 1927, the Chinese Communist movement depended for its very existence on Soviet aid. This was the practical reason why Mao and other leading Chinese communists supported Stalin. From another point of view, however, the ideology of Stalinism, with its narrow-minded pragmatic outlook, its bureaucratic hierarchy, and its personality cult, was very much to the taste of China's would-be emperors. Although they were never taken into Stalin's confidence and were under constant harassment from his henchmen such as Wang Ming, they continued to support him, however guardedly. The attitude of the top leadership of the CCP towards the Chinese Trotskyists partly reflected their relationship with Stalin. They treated us as enemies and did their best to stamp out our influence, but not always with equal vigour: on the contrary, they sometimes adopted an almost conciliatory approach towards us, depending both on the state of the factional struggle in the CCP leadership and their individual personalities. Later I will give some examples of this.

The work in the organization department was very hard. Because the local Party organization in Shanghai was under the direct control of the Central Committee, our department was responsible for the various districts of the municipality. At that time no one in the Comintern or the Chinese Party, not even Mao Tse-tung in Kiangsi, would have thought of moving our main activities from town to countryside, or of basing the party on the peasantry rather than the urban proletariat. It seemed natural to focus our activities on Shanghai. The Party concentrated most of its forces on rebuilding and expanding its organization in the working-class districts of the city, with the aim of leading the struggle in the various sectors.

More than two-thirds of the organization department's time was devoted to Shanghai work, and only a small part to directing work in the rest of China. Shanghai was divided into five districts: north, south, east, west, and centre. The four aides in the organization department, together with the vice-head, each took responsibility for one of these districts. I was assigned responsibility for central Shanghai. The most important of the five districts were east and west Shanghai, since it was here that the big factories were concentrated. However, central Shanghai was where all the shops were, and most of the Party members in that district were clerks or shop assistants. Their role in production and economic life was not so important as that of the industrial workers, but since they worked in the centre of town, all their activities had considerable impact, and we therefore set great store by their struggles. At that time the workers in the second-hand clothes shops in that part of Shanghai were particularly militant. The workers in the department stores along the Nanking Road were also renowned for their militancy, having fought hard for a number of years, and had become one of the main pillars of the Shanghai trade union movement. When I took over the leadership of this district, the general strike of the workers in the second-hand clothes shops in the Fukien Road area was not long over, and there were still occasional flare-ups between workers and employers. In the smaller shops, relationships between boss and worker were very different from those in the big factories and the big commercial firms. Many of the employees got their jobs through family ties or because they came from the boss's town or village, and once a strike broke out the hatred and hostility between the two sides was particularly intense. It was not just a question of wages and conditions – all sorts of other emotions flooded to the surface. These struggles often involved unusual violence and cruelty, and the scenes I witnessed during that strike were like a dress rehearsal for the bitter clashes which took place during the Five Antis movement against corruption[1] and the Campaign for the Socialization of

[1] A campaign launched at the beginning of 1952 by the Peking government against those industrialists and merchants who were alleged to have committed any of the following five crimes: bribery of Party and government officials, tax-dodging, misappropriation of state property, dishonesty in carrying out government contracts, and stealing government economic information.

Capitalist Industry and Commerce in the 1950s. In relation to capitalism as a whole, small firms of this sort are an anachronism: in order to survive they have to transfer their own unbearable burden onto the shoulders of their employees, but, by the same token, they are vulnerable to the slightest attack from their opponents in the class struggle. As Communists we naturally had to develop the combativity of these groups of workers in order to heighten their class-consciousness, but struggles often ended in tragedy for both sides. Unfortunately, small-scale commercial enterprises occupied a very important place in the urban economy of China, so that the question of how to lead struggles of this sort was to become an important point of controversy in the CCP. From the Canton and Wuhan periods right through to the late 1920s, the right wing of the Party tended to favour mediating between boss and worker, whereas the left wing wanted to encourage class struggle. After several months' practical experience of the problem I shared the assessment of the left wing, but it was obvious to me that, outside an economic and political struggle on a national scale, such struggles were bound to fail.

The fact that the shop workers could not be the mainstay of the working class did not mean, of course, that we should abstain from leading them, or that we should only begin to pay attention to them once the factory proletariat had started to move. I did not hold this view at the time, and it was never the position of the Chinese Trotskyists. All along we actively participated in and led the struggles of this section of workers. They were extremely volatile and often acted as a catalyst for the broader movement. At that time, in order to co-ordinate and if possible hasten the 'imminent nation-wide high tide of revolution', we frantically searched everywhere for the slightest sign of a struggle. Sometimes top-level conferences would be called, with members of the Central Committee, the District Committee, and the Kiangsu Provincial Committee (this latter represented by Wang K'o-ch'üan), to discuss some trifling altercation between shop-owner and employees. These meetings would often carry on into the early hours of the morning. It was like taking a sledge-hammer to crack a nut. From early morning to late at night we searched high and low for 'the spark to light a prairie fire', keeping ourselves in a state of artificially induced tension. Our aim was to transform the central district of Shanghai, China's first city, into a beacon for the rest of the country.

All this took place some thirty years ago, but I still vividly remember those months, during which I worked harder than at any other time in my life. We would get up at the crack of dawn and hurry down to talk to the shopworkers before business started. Then we would hold a meeting, rush around making contacts, hold another meeting, make more contacts, and so on until the early hours of the following morning. Besides working in my own district, I also had regular meetings of the organization department, as well as talking to comrades who arrived in Shanghai from other areas (I was responsible for receiving comrades from Indochina, Anhui province, and Yünnan province). Although I was overworked, my load was lighter than that of the other four aides, so I was given more to do. When I got home at night I had to work on a translation of Lenin's *On Organization*. I was not at all put out by all this work. As I disagreed with the 'high tide' theory and did not believe that it would be possible to create such a tide solely by our own efforts I was in no danger of disillusionment on this point. The reason I was happy to work so hard for a policy I disagreed with was that events were clearly showing that the line of the Opposition was correct; that I had discovered that some of the more sincere comrades, unhappy about the way things were going, were gradually coming to realize that the line of the Sixth Congress was wrong; and that it gave me practical experience of underground work.

During that period the person I was closest to was Yün Tai-ying, and before and after meetings we always got together for a short chat. He had tuberculosis, and was physically very weak. It was sheer will-power and devotion to the Revolution that enabled him to work so strenuously. During breaks he would collapse, totally exhausted, and sometimes he even dropped off to sleep during meetings. He was renowned as a man of action, and could put up with any amount of hardship. Whenever he came up against a problem, he was always ready with an immediate solution, and as a born optimist he never allowed anything to get him down. If he had one weakness it was his contempt not just for pedantry but for learning itself, despite the fact that he himself had been an intellectual before he became a revolutionary. During the later period of our work together, however, he told me more than once that he was looking forward to a chance to do some theoretical study. We never had time to discuss any question in depth, and because of pressure of work we had no chance to develop a personal friendship or hold a non-political conversation of any length. But I remember how once, when the organization department was about to hold a meeting in my room, Tai-ying came a little early and lay down on my bed for a nap. He woke up after a while, and, seeing that none of the other comrades had yet arrived, began to flick through some of Lenin's pamphlets on my desk that the Party had given me to translate. I commented that he needed a rest, and suggested that he ask the Party to send him to Moscow for a period of study. His brief, dismissive reply spoke volumes. Most of the older generation of Party activists were contemptuous of those comrades who returned to China after studying in Moscow, and even more of people like Wang Ming, who only joined the Party after leaving China and who, despite their total lack of practical experience and Communist moral qualities, took on all the airs of a 'foreign revolutionary', fluently mouthing all the latest 'Marxist' jargon. Most of the latter quickly capitulated to the forces of the reactionary movement on returning to China. The best that could be expected of them was that they would retire quietly without betraying their comrades. The general contempt in which these 'returned students' were held was therefore richly deserved. In another sense, however, this attitude towards foreign study was an expression of the traditional backwardness of the Chinese Communist Party, its over-emphasis on practical questions and its inability to grasp the principle that practice must be guided by theory. This contempt for theory was ultimately responsible for the bungling of many revolutionary opportunities, and for the tendency of the leadership to follow the Stalinist line blindly and to resort to frequently unprincipled tactical manoeuvres. It can also be seen as one of the root causes of the Party's decline into bureaucratic dictatorship.

Yün Tai-ying provides a good example of the mixed feelings with which the older generation of CCP cadres viewed studying abroad or even any theoretical study at all. Many of them, like Lin Po-ch'ü, Wu Yü-chang, Hsü T'e-li, Tung Pi-wu, Yeh Chien-ying, and Hsieh Chüeh-tsai, had themselves studied in the Soviet Union, but were originally sent there for special reasons. Until 1927 they had been working in the so-called 'external affairs' section as leading members of the Kuomintang, so that when the Party was forced underground after the defeat of the Revolution, they had found it difficult to adapt to the new conditions of work and had become prime targets for the Kuomintang secret service. They had remained loyal to the Communist Party, however; and, since there was no work that they could do and no secure hiding place for them, the only solution had been to send them to Moscow to study. Yün Tai-ying naturally resisted this arrangement. He did not want to be looked upon as one of the 'old men' of the Party, and as a matter of fact he was not. Even though he had worked for a period of years in the top hierarchy of the Kuomintang as a military and political activist, he was just as good if not better in his new role of underground revolutionary. But it was quite apparent that, apart from his physical ailments, Tai-ying suffered from a sort of melancholia. He never talked openly about it to me, and even less did he voice doubts about the official Party line, but he constantly betrayed signs of anxiety, like a man trying to boil a pot of water with only a handful of straw.

During the course of our conversation he complained about the faint-heartedness of some of the worker comrades in east Shanghai, and told me that some Party sympathizers were afraid of him visiting them because of the danger of detection. I seized the chance to ask him whether he thought that the present situation in China was more analogous to that of Russia after the defeat of the 1905 Revolution, or on the eve of the revolutionary high tide of 1917. He thought for a while, and then said bitterly:

'I've never made a serious study of the Russian Revolution. I'll have to try and find a chance to read up on it.'

Our conversation ended here. The other comrades were beginning to trickle in, and the meeting soon started. The discussion centred, as usual, on only one problem: how to speed up and prepare for the 'imminent revolutionary high tide'.

A year or so later Yün Tai-ying was arrested while handing out leaflets in the factory district of east Shanghai. (By this time I had been expelled from the Party.) He was taken for an ordinary rank-and-file Communist, and sentenced to two years' imprisonment in Nanking gaol. Shortly afterwards Ku Shun-chang, who was in charge of the Party's special service section, went over to the Kuomintang and informed them of Yün Tai-ying's identity, whereupon the latter was taken out and shot, on Chiang Kai-shek's direct orders. The real responsibility for his death, however, should be placed at the door of Stalin's theory of the 'Third Period'. Yün Tai-ying was only one of many tens of thousands of Communists who lost their lives as a result of this policy.

The situation in the Far East at this time was very unstable. The Japanese imperialists were vigorously pursuing an aggressive policy towards China, with the aim of swallowing first the three north-eastern provinces, and then the rest of the country. Under Japanese pressure the Chinese bourgeoisie and their American financiers were moving towards a close alliance. Although crises were developing everywhere, the Revolution was still some way off. With the aid and encouragement of American imperialism, Chiang Kai-shek's counter-revolutionary regime was strengthening itself. Against the background of a world economic crisis, the Chinese bourgeoisie was experiencing a freak economic revival (which could actually only deepen the process of colonization). Whereas the capitalists were full of self-confidence, the working class, after severe defeats, was only just beginning to re-group its forces as a result of the economic revival. These forces were fragile, faint-hearted, anxious to be left in peace, and fearful of con-tact with revolutionaries, so it is not surprising that despite almost super-human efforts we were unable to bring the pot of cold, or at best lukewarm, water to the boil, and that even the Party's toughest activists became depressed.

During the latter period of my work in the organization depart-ment the already frantic pace was stepped up still further, and it was then that the practice that Trotsky ridiculed as 'directing the revolu-tion with a revolutionary calendar' was introduced. The party decided that it would hold a demonstration on each of the anniversaries of the international workers' movement. In order to get maximum publicity, the demonstrations were always held in the Nanking Road in my area of the city. In one sense these demonstra-tions were pure farce, but for the revolutionaries themselves the joke often turned out very sour. Having decided on a time and place, we would mobilize as many Party members as we could – never more than a few hundred – and gather furtively on either side of the Nanking Road. At a pre-arranged signal, a handful of comrades would rush out into the middle of the street, shout a few slogans and scatter some leaflets around. If the red-painted lorries of the Inter-national Settlement police had still failed to turn up, the rest of us would gather round to swell the numbers and march raggedly down the road for a hundred yards or so shouting slogans until the police arrived, when we scattered in all directions and pretended to be ordinary passers-by. Some of the less fortunate ones would be arrested and dragged into the red lorries, and afterwards handed over to the Kuomintang to be imprisoned or shot. The demonstration was over, and yet another 'high tide' had come and gone. The organizers of these demonstrations were anxious and confused about what role they were supposed to play, and those who were mobilized to take part in them were very bitter. For Party members, the term 'commemorating an anniversary' became synonymous with pointless activity.

During the several months I spent working in the organization department the Party achieved hardly any real success, despite the amount of energy that was put into developing the class struggle among the Shanghai workers. The harder we worked, the further our 'imminent high tide' receded. The more active we were, the more the workers seemed to fear us. The Shanghai workers' movement, like the whole of the Chinese labour movement, had reached a low ebb. In the May Thirtieth movement of 1925 it had entered the arena of the class struggle for the first time, and during the spring of 1927 it reached its highest point of development in the three famous Shanghai insurrections, only to be bloodily suppressed by Chiang Kai-shek's forces on 12 April. This was its first defeat, but it remained resilient. In the autumn of 1927 the Revolution was defeated on a national scale, and the counter-revolutionary bourgeois regime intensified its repression of the Shanghai workers. In 1928, however, the tramcar workers, post and telecommunications employees, and others, counter-attacked heroically, thus providing a justification for the putschist policies of the Ch'ü Ch'iu-pai leadership of the Party. But the workers' struggles of that era (like the peasant movements in Hunan and Hupeh) were not a 'permanent ascent of the Revolution' (as Ch'ü Ch'iu-pai and the Comintern described them), but were the dying flicker of the Revolution of 1925–7. From 1929 onwards, as a result of the oppression by the Kuomintang armed forces and the 'yellow' trade unions, the Shanghai working class fell into a passive mood. After the Japanese invasion of the north-eastern provinces in 1931 and the Shanghai war of January 1932, there arose a broadly-based national democratic movement composed mainly of students, but throughout this period the workers' movement never got off the ground again or played a conspicuous role in any of these campaigns. Nor did the workers play an independent role in the War of Resistance against Japan, fought from 1937 to 1945. During the eight years of rule by the Japanese and their puppets the position of the Shanghai working class deteriorated even further. It showed no sign of revival until the defeat of the Japanese in 1945.

Thus another fifteen years were to elapse before the 'high tide' which we were so fervently awaiting actually arrived, and meanwhile the Chinese Communist Party paid a very high price for Stalin's mistaken prophecy. The Shanghai working class was abandoned by the Party, whose Central Committee withdrew completely from the city around 1933, at first because of the pressure of circumstances and then as a result of a conscious and deliberate choice. Only the Trotskyists stayed behind to share the fate of the working class, but we were unable to provide the workers with a durable and broadly-based organization. Right up until the Japanese capitulation there was no revolutionary trade union organization in Shanghai.

To return to 1929, and the internal life of the party in Shanghai: in late autumn the organization department began to talk of 'internal troubles' in the Party, indicating that some branches in east Shanghai and Chapei were composed exclusively of Ch'en Tu-hsiu supporters. Until then our department had confined itself purely to organizational questions, methods of struggle, and the assignment of comrades to the various areas of work. We had rarely discussed theoretical questions. I remember on one occasion Wu Fu-ching, who was responsible for the Chapei area, reported that some Ch'en Tu-hsiu supporters had asked him why the leadership claimed that the Chinese Revolution was still bourgeois in character. Although Wu Fu-ching had always despised theory, he had an excellent memory, and instead of answering the question he simply reeled off the resolutions of the Sixth Congress at them. Naturally the Ch'en Tu-hsiu supporters were not satisfied with his reply. They quoted back at him from the Marxist classics, which left him dumb-founded. He told us what had happened and asked Wu Hao (Chou En-lai's party name at the time) for some guidance on how to deal with them. Yün Tai-ying, who was then in charge of east Shanghai, also gave a report on the problems he had had with Ch'en Tu-hsiu supporters and on the general situation in the branches in his area, claiming that the Ch'en-ites were about to join with the Trotskyists.

Chou En-lai did not take the question very seriously, and apart from rehearsing the old arguments about the bourgeois nature of the Revolution, told us that the Ch'en Tu-hsiu problem was being dealt with by the Standing Committee of the Politbureau. At the time it was not clear what he meant by this, but I afterwards learned from Trotskyist sources that the Comintern representative in Shanghai had tried to persuade Ch'en to go to Moscow for discussions and to take up a post in the Comintern. Ch'en Tu-hsiu had no hesitation in turning down this proposal.

After the Emergency Conference of the Central Committee in Wuhan on 7 August 1929 had formally removed him from his position as General Secretary, Ch'en Tu-hsiu had returned secretly to Shanghai, where he lived in the eastern area of the city. Since the responsibility for the defeat of the Revolution had been laid mainly at his door and he had been denounced as an opportunist, his state of mind can readily be imagined. I have no idea how he managed to live during the period immediately following his return to Shanghai; and afterwards, when Ch'en and I lived together in the same house, we never had time to discuss such questions. By then they belonged to the remote past. According to what Wang Meng-tsou, who was one of Ch'en's best non-political friends, told me, he was lonely and unhappy, like a lion returned to his lair to lick his wounds. I think this must be a fairly accurate description. Whatever his weaknesses, Ch'en was certainly a lion. If Ch'en had been the usual spineless sort of politician he would have agreed to take all the blame onto his own shoulders, thus enabling Stalin to ride out the storm of criticism from the Trotskyists. Had Ch'en chosen this course, he would have retained his status in the Comintern and would probably have been able to climb to the top again in the Chinese Party.

But although Ch'en Tu-hsiu was a man of integrity, he lacked the theoretical framework to hit back effectively against the Stalinist slanders. He knew little about the disputes which were raging in the Soviet Party, and his grasp of revolutionary theory was limited, so that without outside help he would never have succeeded in clarifying the issues involved. He was very indignant about the campaign of vilification being waged against him, but he was unable to say precisely why and how he was being wronged. All he could do was withdraw into a corner and ponder fruitlessly for over a year. His political activities during this were confined to writing two letters to the Central Committee of the CCP criticizing the Canton Insurrection. He also turned down an invitation to go to Moscow to attend the Sixth Congress of the Party. Just as his letters consisted more of passive advice than of active criticism, so his refusal to go to Moscow was a petulant response to his earlier humiliation, rather than a confident and determined counter-attack. In 1929, after fighting broke out between Chinese and Soviet troops for control of the Chinese Eastern Railway, a line that ran through Chinese territory and had formerly been owned by the Tsarist authorities, Ch'en wrote to the Central Committee disagreeing with the Party's slogan of 'armed defence of the Soviet Union'. But it was only when the Li Li-san leadership totally distorted and attacked his views that the old Ch'en Tu-hsiu sprang to life and leapt back into the fray. Although he did not yet have any contacts with the Trotskyist movement, we sympathized with the opinions he expressed. As a means of exposing Chiang Kai-shek's plans to attack the Soviet Union under the cover of an appeal for the defence of national sovereignty, his slogan 'Oppose Kuomintang mismanagement of the nation' was not as ridiculous as the CCP leaders claimed, at least as a tactical ploy. But Li Li-san's propaganda machine launched a fanatical attack against him, accusing him of plunging headlong into the quagmire of 'bourgeois patriotism'. Ch'en immediately took up the challenge and a number of veteran cadres gradually started to gather around him, among them P'eng Shu-tse, Cheng Ch'ao-lin, Ho Tzu-shen, Yin K'uan, Li Chi, Ma Yü-fu and others. Thus a new ideological current began to form in the Party ranks.

It was while I was working in the Central Committee after my return from Moscow that the Ch'en Tu-hsiu faction began to make the turn towards Trotskyism. They managed to get hold of the documents of the Russian Opposition, first from some of the students who had returned from Moscow and afterwards from Liu Jen-ching, and immediately accepted its positions on the historical problems of the Chinese Revolution. For Ch'en Tu-hsiu this was undoubtedly a great discovery. He learned for the first time that Stalin himself had all along been the supporter or originator of the very proposals for which he, Ch'en, was afterwards so fiercely denounced, and that the Russian Opposition had consistently pointed out the errors of these policies long before these were revealed in practice. Of course, Ch'en himself had expressed his disagreement with some of these policies at the time, and had carried them out only reluctantly, although he had accepted others in the firm belief that they were a true expression of 'Bolshevism'. After the 1927 débâcle, Stalin had done his best to clear himself of responsibility for the defeat, both by denying having issued certain key directives to the Chinese Party and by accusing his emissaries, Roy and Borodin, of distorting them. When all else failed, he put the blame on Ch'en Tu-hsiu. Ch'en was at a loss to defend himself. He knew very little about the actual source of the directives, apart from the fact that they were from the Comintern, or about how they were argued over and arrived at, and at first he was stunned by the suddenness of the defeat and the intensity of the campaign Stalin and Ch'ü Ch'iu-pai launched against him. But the documents of the Russian Opposition helped him to understand his own role in the defeat of the revolution, and to make a more realistic assessment of his share of the responsibility for its failure, as he later explained in his famous 'Open Letter to All Comrades'. He also agreed with Trotsky's views on the current situation in China, and only hesitated over the nature of the forthcoming third Chinese Revolution. He still considered that it would be bourgeois–democratic in character.

When the news of Ch'en Tu-hsiu's move towards Trotskyism first reached the Party, Chou En-lai responded contemptuously: 'Very well, let the old opportunists see if they can find a way out by joining the Trotskyists'. But the news caused quite a sensation among the older generation of cadres. It also alarmed Moscow, since Stalin naturally feared the possible repercussions in the international Communist movement of so important a figure as Ch'en going over to the Opposition. The Central Committee was forced to deal with the question more seriously, and a representative of the International was sent to see Ch'en and lure him to Moscow. When Ch'en Tu-hsiu spurned this offer and attached himself even more openly to the Opposition, the Central Committee and the International started up a campaign, in China and in Moscow simultaneously, against the 'Trotsky–Ch'en liquidationist centre'.

Ch'en Tu-hsiu was officially expelled from the Party on 15 November 1929, and responded on 10 December by issuing his 'Open Letter to All Comrades'. Five days later a collective document entitled 'Our Political Platform' was put out over the signatures of 81 veteran Communists who either had held or continued to hold top positions in the Party. Besides these signatories, there were many other Party members who wavered between the two positions, upset by the division in the Party and unable to make up their minds whether to follow the Old Man or stick with the new Central Committee. Since I was still working in the Central Committee, I was able to see what was going on with my own eyes. To take just one example, a comrade called Huang, in charge of technical work such as printing in the organization department, who held Ch'en in great respect, having worked under him for a long time, showed clear signs of stress during the campaign against 'liquidationism'.

Another comrade, Ho Po-ch'eng, who had worked as a liaison officer in the department for many years, also respected Ch'en greatly. The last time we met, after it was discovered that I was a Trotskyist, he sighed and told me that he had a big family to support, implying that otherwise he would have joined us.

This might seem incredible to some, so to clarify the point I will say a few words about the conditions under which members of the Party lived during that period. It is only natural, of course, that people who worked full time for the Party should expect to get their living expenses paid from Party funds, and this is so in all political parties. According to Lenin, who made a special study of the question, a political Party of the proletariat will never achieve its goal unless it first develops a body of professional revolutionaries who devote their whole time and energy to the theory and practice of the Revolution. Lenin was especially contemptuous of those amateur 'revolutionaries' who sacrifice only evenings and weekends to strike terror into high-society ladies. People of this sort cannot and will not overthrow capitalism. One of the main reasons why the Bolsheviks succeeded for the first time in history in carrying out the proletarian revolution was because they created such a cadre of professional revolutionaries. In itself Lenin's analysis is irrefutable. The creation of such a cadre was a precondition for the success of the Chinese Revolution also.

But in the CCP's anti-Trotskyist campaign, Lenin's thesis produced many harmful side-effects. After the defeat of the Revolution in 1927, the reconstructed Party apparatus contained many professional revolutionaries, who in the cities even outnumbered ordinary rank-and-file members. According to Party regulations, those rank-and-file members with jobs were expected to hand over dues each month to support the revolutionaries. But because there were so few Party members with jobs there was never enough money to go round, and the enormous deficit had to be made up by financial aid from the Soviet Union. Chou En-lai told me that the bulk of Party expenses were met by the dues paid in by the CPSU membership in Leningrad. We saw this as a graphic illustration of proletarian internationalism at work: the Leningrad workers had every right to give their money and the CCP every right to take it – only an arch-reactionary would complain about such a thing. Comrades working for the Central Committee earned twenty-five dollars a month, and members of District Committees nineteen, which was roughly the average worker's wage. Comrades with special needs, such as medical expenses, or dependants living in the secret Party offices, were given extra.

No one had joined the Party to make money, so how was it that financial considerations prevented some comrades from joining the Opposition? One reason was that although no revolutionary would put money before his revolutionary beliefs, the situation changed somewhat when it was a question of choosing between two different factions within the same Party, as Stalinism and Trotskyism were at that stage. Although many people in the Soviet Union sacrificed high state or Party rank to follow Trotsky, even more renounced the Opposition in order to cling to their privileged positions. The situation in the CCP could not be compared with that in the Soviet Party, where the choice between the two factions might be between the Kremlin or Siberia; but even in China it was an unpleasant experience to be an Oppositionist. We had no funds of our own and no external source of finance. As if earning a living was not hard enough, we had to put money aside regularly to finance the work of our organization. Chang Kuo-t'ao, who afterwards deserted the CCP, once said to P'eng Shu-tse, 'You can get by on translation work, but how could I earn a living if I left the Party?' This remark exemplified the dilemma facing many members. Comrades could be heard lamenting the fact that they were professional revolutionaries rather than revolutionary professionals, so that they had no job to fall back on should they disagree with the official line and want to distance themselves from the Party apparatus. The scarcity of employment under the old regime in China thus helped Stalin to defeat the Trotskyists.

Even so, Ch'en Tu-hsiu's conversion to Trotskyism provoked a serious crisis in the ranks of the Party. Adherents of the liquidationist line were found everywhere – in the Central Committee, the Provincial Committees, the Party branches, the Communist Youth League, and in the mass organizations. A systematic purge was carried out at all levels of the movement, and every week the Party journal, *Red Flag*, published lists of the names of those who had been expelled.

The stir caused both inside and outside the party as a result of Ch'en's expulsion took Stalin and his Chinese supporters by surprise. They found that, despite the ferocious attacks levelled against him, he still enjoyed great authority among Chinese Communists. Recognizing their mistake, they sent Ch'en a ridiculous telegram through the

Central Committee of the CCP inviting him to go to Russia 'specially to discuss the question of his expulsion' with the Executive Committee of the Comintern – the same Ch'en whom they had expelled three months earlier as a liquidationist and a traitor. Ch'en contemptuously turned down this invitation, and immediately wrote a vehement and brilliantly-worded reply, thus bringing to an end his relations with the Party he had created.

During the early stages of the anti-Ch'en campaign I myself never came under attack, either because Chou En-lai did not suspect me, or simply because he was giving me a chance to change my political allegiance quietly. I continued as usual, working as hard as I could for the Party and saying as little as possible, in line with the policy of our group at that time.

At the meetings of the organization department, nine-tenths of the talking was done by Chou En-lai, who was a brilliant administrator and a first-rate speaker. After I had been working with him closely for some time, however, I began to notice his idiosyncrasies. Once he started speaking he could never stop. He spoke in logical order, but was incapable of bringing out the main points of what he had to say. Also, though he got everything in the right sequence he continually repeated himself. Despite the fact that his audience consisted of his most intimate colleagues (the five aides of the organization department, and occasionally his wife Teng Ying-ch'ao), he would spell things out as if addressing a class of primary-school children, chasing one analysis or explanation with another. He could spin out a report for seven or eight hours, often sending us to sleep in the process. Like Mao Tse-tung, Ch'en Tu-hsiu was a better writer than a speaker; but even though they both spoke badly they always managed to keep to the point. In this respect Chou En-lai could never match them. But for me Chou's long-windedness had the advantage of distracting attention from my deliberate silence. Even more articulate comrades like Yün Tai-ying and Lo Teng-hsien kept fairly quiet at such meetings, and it was only during meals that they could express their own opinions. Of my own rare contributions to discussions, I only remember one clearly. The views of the Kiangsi comrades on the land revolution in the Kiangsi Soviet area had been conveyed to us by Chang Kuo-shu (the younger brother of Chang Kuo-t'ao, later to be shot by Chiang Kai-shek). Although they felt it was necessary to oppose the rich peasants in order to mobilize all the forces of the Revolution, they were concerned that this might mean defying the resolution of the Sixth Congress of the Party, which had defined the Revolution as bourgeois–democratic in nature.

The apparent contradiction gave some of our comrades quite a headache. Chou En-lai talked at great length, but was unable to resolve the basic dilemma: should one develop theory on the basis of the objective facts of the situation, or hold back the struggle in the interests of a preconceived strategy? Since this problem touched on one of the central issues in the Stalin–Trotsky dispute, I was unable to hold myself back. 'If the needs of the struggle require us to oppose the rich peasants', I said, 'then we should do so, irrespective of the bourgeois nature of the Revolution.' Although my outburst did not reveal me as a Trotskyist, it created something of a stir at the meeting. Wu Fu-ching, who was particularly sensitive to such questions because of his experience in the anti-Trotskyist struggle in Moscow, hinted that what I had said could lead to dangerous conclusions, and I immediately resumed my silence.

By keeping my views secret I was able to continue working in the Central Committee until the early spring of 1930, when I was taken dangerously ill and hospitalized. However, I still remained a member of the Party until our underground network in Moscow was betrayed by an informer.

The Oppositionist organization among the Chinese Communists in Moscow had grown even bigger after my return to China. Since there had been over two hundred of us in 1929, we must eventually have come to account for at least half of the five hundred or more Chinese students there. I have already described how the Party branch under Wang Ming at Sun Yat-sen University came to suspect that there was a secret Trotskyist cell among the Chinese students and took precautions against it. But they never realized how strong we were, and thought that after the campaign of late 1927 there were no real Trotskyists left in the Party. Naturally, Wang Ming and his friends had no way of knowing about the rapid developments of the Opposition in the Soviet Party around 1928, since Russian officials kept them completely in the dark about it. They thought that at worst there might be a few Trotskyist infiltrators among the students transferred from KUTV to Sun Yat-sen University, but they reckoned that the overwhelming majority of them would remain passive and would prefer to rest on their past records as veteran members of the Party. They did not, therefore, consider former KUTV students as enemies, although they frequently discriminated against them and treated them with contempt. In my opinion, the reason why this changed so abruptly was because of the activities of the Shanghai Trotskyists and in particular Ch'en Tu-hsiu's defection to the Opposition, after which the university authorities suddenly threw all their resources into rounding up Trotskyists, undoubtedly on the orders of the Comintern; that is, Stalin. I received the account of what happened at Sun Yat-sen University from two Chinese Trotskyists who escaped from Siberia and got back to China.

At the end of 1929 the Sun Yat-sen University authorities launched yet another campaign against the Trotskyists. On wall-newspapers and in the Party branches all the old issues were revived, and Trotsky's 'harmful' policies for the Chinese Revolution were fiercely denounced. Until then, few non-Oppositionists had even heard of Trotsky's views, and it was only now that they got to know of them (albeit in caricatured form). Trotsky's proposals were denounced as 'liquidationist', and his supporters in China were said to be working hand in glove with the Ch'en Tu-hsiu 'born opportunists'. Trotskyist students in Moscow were aware that this campaign was a reaction to our activities in China, but since they anticipated a wave of repression their elation was mingled with apprehension. Ch'en Ch'i and Wen Yüeh, who had been kept on in Moscow as 'specimens' of Trotskyism, were reportedly sent into exile near the Persian border: one of them was shot dead by a border patrol and the other captured and sent back to a Moscow gaol while they were trying to escape across the frontier. All former KUTV students were automatically suspect, and carefully selected agents were ordered to mix with them and infiltrate the Opposition. Among them was the former KUTV student with the Russian name of Logov, nicknamed 'Old Widow'. He was on very good terms with 'Mamashkin' (Chao Yen-ch'ing), who had taken over from me as one of the leaders of the Trotskyist organization in Moscow. Even though their politics were not the same, they were the best of friends and used to talk quite freely together. The Old Widow knew that Mama was a Trotskyist, and worked hard to get him to confess, bringing all sorts of pressure to bear. Mama was not very sophisticated, and he lacked a strong will. After a period of painful vacillation, he finally handed over a complete list of the Trotskyists he had come into contact with. The Party apparatus took immediate action, and that very night an armed detachment of GPU men arrived at the Chinese students' dormitory, dragging some two hundred men and women from their beds and driving them away in prison vans. Mama was the only one not to be arrested. The Old Widow and his friends tried to console him, saying that the Party would richly reward him for his 'glorious deed'. Before the next day dawned Mama hanged himself above the empty beds of his comrades.

Discovering that half the Chinese students in Moscow were Trotskyists must have shocked Stalin even more than the defection of Ch'en Tu-hsiu. He now saw that Sun Yat-sen University had failed in its original purpose, and therefore decided to close it down. Most non-Trotskyist students were sent back to China, although some were transferred to other educational institutions or assigned to serve in Soviet government or Party posts. Of those arrested, a few gave in under interrogation, and after making full confessions were imprisoned for a while, expelled from the Party, and later sent back to China. Others also renounced their beliefs, but because the Party feared that they were still capable of playing a role in the Opposition and might rejoin the organization once back in China, they were not allowed to return home, and sent instead to labour camps in the Arctic Circle. Many comrades, however, stood firm, among them my old friend Fan Chin-piao, who reportedly lost the sight of both eyes shortly after being sent to gaol. Since they refused to admit that they had done anything wrong, they suffered unbearable treatment at the hands of their gaolers and were sent to serve long sentences in Siberian labour camps and prisons. The only news we ever heard of these comrades was from a Yugoslav Communist by the name of Anton Ciliga, who had been one of the Yugoslav representatives on the Executive Committee of the Comintern and who had been imprisoned for several years for offending Stalin. According to Ciliga's articles about his prison experiences, Communists with yellow skins received far worse treatment than their white fellow-prisoners. Of more than two hundred Trotskyists arrested, less than ten made a complete recantation and were afterwards sent back to China. Another two comrades managed to escape back to China from Siberia. There is no record of what happened to the rest, but many undoubtedly died in Stalin's prisons or in front of a GPU firing squad.

From the confessions of those who had been arrested the Party was able to build up a complete dossier on us, revealing that more than thirty Trotskyists had already returned to China. Moscow immediately transmitted a coded message to Shanghai informing the Central Committee of this. I was lying ill in hospital at the time, and

when Chou En-lai saw my name among those on the list he came to
visit me there. His attitude was very friendly. He told me that he was
satisfied with my work over the last few months. He hoped that I
would think of my 'future as a revolutionary', and issue a written
statement denouncing Trotskyism, to be published in *Red Flag*, the
Party's political organ. If I did as he suggested, he guaranteed that I
would be allowed to keep my membership. I did not argue, but
simply agreed to write a statement, which a liaison officer came to
fetch the next day. What I wrote was not at all what had been hoped
for. Instead I had taken the opportunity to express my disagreement
with the resolution passed at the Party's Sixth Congress on the reasons
for the defeat of the Revolution, the present situation and tasks, and
future perspectives for development. I also pointed out that my work
over the past few months clearly showed that I was prepared to abide
by the decisions of the majority, even when I disagreed with them. I
declared that I would continue to uphold my different point of view,
but was still prepared to serve the Revolution within a democratic–
centralist framework. I therefore requested the Party to respect
Leninist organizational principles and allow me to continue working
in its ranks.

After I had handed over my statement, I knew what to expect. I
was not so naïve as to believe that Chou En-lai, Li Li-san, and the
others would show the same tolerance towards opposition as Lenin
had done, and knew that even if they had been inclined to do so,
Stalin would never let them. I was aware that the Party would sever
all relations with me, and that I could no longer expect to have my
medical expenses paid. A short statement would simply be published
in *Red Flag* announcing my expulsion. I therefore discharged myself
from hospital the same day, and found a small room to rent. I did
not remove a single stick of furniture from my secret 'office' in
central Shanghai, but simply sent the Party a letter telling them to go
and fetch the chairs and tables they had given me. A few days later the
announcement of my expulsion appeared in *Red Flag* alongside that of
Wu Chi-hsien, editor of the Party's theoretical organ *Bolshevik* right up
to the moment of his expulsion. Wu Chi-hsien was at that time an
aide to Li Li-san, head of the propaganda department, just as I was
aide to Chou En-lai.

Thus ended almost five years of work with the Chinese Communist Party. We refused to accept the legitimacy of our expulsion, however, on the grounds that the Party was acting in violation of the

Leninist norms of organization. We continued to view ourselves as a faction of the CCP until the founding of the Communist League of China (CLC) in 1934.

For my wife and myself the most immediate problem was how to find enough money to pay for food, rent, and medical treatment. The Party had managed to get my wife a job in the Workers' Hospital in West Shanghai, but she had been forced to give it up because she was pregnant and about to go into labour. I had still not recovered from my operation, and was confined to bed. The situation was desperate, and our only chance of making some money was from my writing. As luck would have it, an Oppositionist in Shanghai had recently opened a small bookshop called Hu-pin Books, with the aim of publishing a series of social science classics. I dictated a translation of Plekhanov's *From Idealism to Materialism* to my wife, who sat by my sick-bed and transcribed it. To our surprise we were paid 120 dollars for the translation, which was equal to five months' Party allowance. This tided us over our first crisis after my expulsion from the Party.

CHAPTER 7

Unification of the Four Groups

Although I had devoted myself full time to work for the Chinese Communist Party during the short period between my return to China and my expulsion from the Party, I had kept up regular contact with my fellow Oppositionists, and met the *Our Word* comrades about once a fortnight to exchange information. Like Shih T'ang, Chang T'e, and the other comrades responsible at that time for the *Our Word* group in Shanghai, I recoiled from the idea that Ch'en Tu-hsiu was moving towards Trotskyism. We saw him as an inveterate opportunist trying to find his way out of a blind alley. Hence our attitude and tactics towards the Ch'en group: we would do all we could to expose the base motives of its opportunist leadership, while trying to win over the rank and file under its control. Although this approach was totally misconceived, we clung stubbornly to it until Trotsky himself intervened in January 1931.

Some of the Oppositionists who had returned with me from Moscow, like Liu Jen-ching, Chao Chi, and Liu Yin, had absolutely refused to participate in Communist Party work from the start. I have already mentioned that on his return Liu Jen-ching simply sent the Central Committee a statement declaring his allegiance to Trotskyism. Liu Yin and Chao Chi had turned up at the educational course held shortly after our arrival in Shanghai, but later found pretexts for not taking up their assignments in Shanghai, where they had been apprenticed to the district and sub-district committees, and thus had made their exit from the Party. Together with Liu Jen-ching, they spent all their time discussing how to organize a new Trotskyist movement with Ch'en Tu-hsiu and his friends. This implied, of course, that they did not recognize the *Our Word* group, despite the fact that it had already been active for a year or two, particularly in north and south China. Instead they wanted to set up a new organization, run not by 'childish amateurs' but by 'experienced politicians'. The supporters of the *Our Word* group viewed them with the same suspicion as we did Ch'en Tu-hsiu. I felt the same way as the other comrades, not only because of my assessment of Ch'en Tu-hsiu's group, but also because it seemed to me that Liu Jen-ching in particular had violated our Moscow agreement in starting up a new organization, rather than joining Our Word, the existing Oppositionist group in China. In fact Liu Yin himself had never actually joined the Opposition in Moscow; his relationship with us there had been more social than political, so his posing as a veteran Trotskyist made him even more odious in my eyes.

Such was the state of the Opposition shortly before my expulsion from the Party. After I had been expelled and had recovered from my illness, the situation looked very different. Liu Jen-ching had broken with Ch'en Tu-hsiu's group. Disputes had also broken out within the Our Word group, and the leaders of the north China, Shanghai, and south China groups eventually split on issues which I did not properly understand at the time and have long since forgotten. The north China Trotskyists, under Sung Feng-ch'un and Tung Tzu-ch'eng, linked up with Liu Jen-ching against both the Ch'en Tu-hsiu group and the Shanghai-based part of the Our Word group under Ou Fang and Chang T'e. In order to justify the separate existence of his group, Liu Jen-ching drafted a political criticism of what he called the 'remnants of Ch'en Tu-hsiu's opportunism'. Liu Yin and Chao Chi also broke from Ch'en, although I am not quite sure on what grounds. They attracted a number of people to them and set up yet another group.

I learnt of all these splits and regroupings from comrades who came to visit me on my sick-bed, and the news depressed me immensely. Because of the prejudices I felt towards the Ch'en group, I wanted nothing to do with them, not even with those who were old friends or acquaintances. I considered myself a member of the Our Word group, but unfortunately lost contact with them when Shih T'ang, my only acquaintance in the group, was imprisoned in the Shanghai International Settlement. The people I knew best were Liu Yin and Chao Chi, but I had a very low opinion of Liu both from a political and a personal point of view. During my years as a revolutionary I have seen many careerists drift in and out of the movement, but never such a self-seeking petty bourgeois as Liu Yin. At the time of the Northern Expedition, he had been a leader of the Wuhan student movement. He was a very good speaker and brilliant agitator, but more than anything else wanted to be a leader. He was very weak ideologically and lacked the spirit of self-sacrifice which marks a real revolutionary. It was therefore quite natural that he should go over to Chiang Kai-shek and become his hired intellectual stooge. While in Moscow he had called on the Opposition to 'unite' with him – over two hundred men unite with one! – but what he really meant was that, if we invited him to become our leader, he would consider the offer. His suggestion made him the laughing stock of the Moscow Oppositionists, and infuriated Fan Chin-piao. I could not join an organization led by someone like that, and thus the only group I could and would get into contact with was the one set up by Liu Jen-ching and Sung Feng-ch'ün. Sung had been one of the first to join the Opposition during his Moscow days. He had been expelled by the Party in the winter of 1927, and had been sent back to China together with Ou Fang and others. He had made his way to Peking, with Ko Ch'ung-o and Hsiao Ch'ang-pin, where they met up with Lo Han, at that time a member of the Peking District Committee of the CCP. They had immediately started to work among students, until Lo Han was arrested and Sung Feng-ch'un left for Shanghai, where he arrived some time towards the end of 1929. Sung had originally been the driving force in the *Our Word* group, but because of his unhappiness about the growing conflict between Ou Fang and Chang T'e, he went to work as a labourer in a cotton mill. He was an excellent revolutionary, and an extremely modest man who could put up with every kind of hardship. Later he was arrested with me and sent to Shanghai gaol, but released about a year afterwards when influential friends of his family interceded on his behalf. A few days after his release he was re-arrested together with Ch'en Tu-hsiu. This was too much for him; he lost his faith in the Revolution and left our ranks.

In the early summer of 1930 Sung was the person I was closest to in the movement. He and other comrades from north China had joined with Liu Jen-ching to draft a collective political programme as a basis for uniting all the Oppositionists. When I came to read the programme, which was actually written by Liu Jen-ching, under the title 'An Open Letter to all Trotskyist Comrades'. I found that Liu's line on the subject of the constituent assembly had not changed since his Moscow days, and that he still proposed limiting the aims of the struggle to the establishment of a parliamentary system in China. He quoted at length from Marx's *The Eighteenth Brumaire of Louis Bonaparte* to show that such a system would be qualitatively superior to Chiang Kai-shek's military dictatorship. I disagreed profoundly with his analysis, and although he was usually intolerant of other people's views he responded to my criticisms by proposing that I rewrite the part devoted to the question of the constituent assembly and submit it to the others for discussion. Urged on by Sung Feng-ch'un and others, my line was as follows: that as the counter-revolution had triumphed and the democratic tasks of the Revolution had not yet been completed, so the only correct slogan was the call for a constituent assembly. This would make it possible to re-organize the scattered forces of the working class, bring together the separate struggles of the peasantry and the urban petty bourgeoisie, and clear the way for the CCP to re-enter the political arena – all with the ultimate aim of hastening the arrival of a new revolutionary storm. Whether or not it would prove possible in the course of such a struggle for a parliamentary system to come into being and establish itself was, of course, another question entirely, and one which could only be answered by events. The main reason for raising the slogan of a constituent assembly was to help the revolution mature in a period of counter-revolution, and to hasten the proletarian revolution.

The exact interpretation of this call for a constituent assembly was to remain a major controversy in Chinese Oppositionist ranks for many years. My own approach to the problem may not have been perfect, but in my opinion it was much closer to the spirit of Trotskyism than Liu Jen-ching's purely social-democratic interpretation. Sung Feng-ch'un and the others agreed with my draft, and Liu Jen-ching only put up token resistance before agreeing to substitute it for his own. My criticisms accepted, I added my name to the Open Letter together with those of the other comrades. As far as I can remember there were nineteen signatories in all, including Li Ts'ai-lien, a brilliant woman comrade. The north China Oppositionists also gave their support to the Open Letter as soon as they got hold of a copy, although they did not formally add their signatures to it. Liu Jen-ching and I then started up a journal which we called *October*, and we were soon dubbed 'Octobrists' by the other Trotskyist groups.

By the summer of 1930 four mutually hostile Oppositionist groups had emerged: the Octobrists; the Ch'en Tu-hsiu group, which issued a journal called *The Proletarian* and went under the name of The Proletarian Society; the *Our Word* group, which continued to publish a periodical of that name; and finally Liu Yin and Chao Chi, who with a handful of other comrades brought out one issue of a journal called *The Militant*, and therefore went under the name of The Militant Group.

It seems to me in retrospect that the 'struggle' between these four groups was waged over trivial and petty issues with exaggerated intensity. As is not unusual in a political or ideological movement in its early stages of development, personal ambition and factional prejudice become entangled with genuine differences of opinion, and the best and the worst motives often become indissolubly mingled. When political activities are restricted to writing and discussion, it is difficult for any organization to test the real strengths and weaknesses of its membership.

People's motives for becoming Trotskyists in the first place varied enormously. Some joined because they found it difficult to realize their ambitions within the Party, and thought that the best thing would be to branch out in a new direction; others were intimidated by the intensity of the White terror, and used the Opposition as a stage in their retreat from the Revolution; and still others took advantage of the left-wing reputation of the Trotskyist movement to retreat into a world of 'revolutionary' mouthings, with no practical consequences. But although many sorry types were coming over to our side, the overwhelming majority of Opposition supporters in China at that time were sincere revolutionaries driven by the best of motives, who firmly supported Trotsky's proposals for the Chinese Revolution and considered them far better suited to the conditions of China than those of Stalin. It was for this reason that they gave up their established positions in the Party and devoted themselves wholeheartedly to the Oppositionist cause.

The problems I have just mentioned were more or less common to all four groups. During the period when fighting between factions was at its most intense, the pace was set by people driven by egotism and personal ambition, who gave little thought to the overall needs of the movement. Afterwards, under the pressure of the majority and more particularly as a result of the personal intervention of Trotsky himself, the unification campaign began, giving the signal for the genuine revolutionaries in our ranks to pull down the 'mountain-strongholds' erected by the leaders of the four groups. The campaign soon succeeded in isolating the sectarians, so that they either left the movement to become inactive or defected to the reactionary camp.

The period in which the four factions each had their own separate existence lasted for just over a year, from early 1930 to 1 May 1931.

This period can be subdivided into two: before January 1931, when the differences between the factions were exaggerated and inflated; after 8 January, when a letter arrived from Trotsky urging us to unify our forces, and a period of 'negotiations' began. At first the controversies centred on questions such as the slogan of a constituent assembly, the Chinese Red Army, the nature of the coming Revolution, and the lessons of the defeat of the 1925–7 Revolution. There is no need to go into any detail about these old controversies, and I will restrict myself to pointing out that we deliberately exaggerated our differences in order to justify the existence of our various factions. Liu Jen-ching, for example, deliberately and wilfully exaggerated the differences that separated us. At first he enthusiastically welcomed Ch'en Tu-hsiu's conversion to Trotskyism, but when he failed to get what he was after, which was control of the propaganda department, he wrote an article in which he quoted the ancient Greek philosopher's remark 'I love my teacher, but I love the truth even more', implying that he had had to break with Ch'en as a matter of principle. Afterwards, when he split from the Octobrists, he suddenly discovered that he could love both his teacher and the truth. People like Liu Jen-ching, however, were in a minority, so that when the different factions came into more frequent contact with one another, these differences dwindled away.

During those years controversy raged around the call for a constituent assembly more than any other issue, but, as Trotsky later pointed out, such discussions were for the most part purely hypothetical. For example, there was the question of whether a constituent assembly could ever actually be brought into being, and if so, whether it would ever be able to solve any of the problems facing the country. Then there was the question of the relationship between a constituent assembly and the soviets. Of course it was pointless, not to say ludicrous, to raise questions of this sort, which could only really be answered by events themselves. Anyway, there was broad agreement between all the Oppositionists except Liu Jen-ching on this question.

Questions such as the Chinese Red Army and the lessons to be drawn from the defeat of the 1925–7 Revolution were raised only to discredit Ch'en Tu-hsiu. In The Proletarian Ch'en wrote an article on the future prospects for the Red Army, arguing that, unless the peasant struggle was led by the urban proletariat, the Revolution would either degenerate or be destroyed. If Ch'en Tu-hsiu was wrong on this point, then Marx, Engels, and Trotsky were wrong too. At the time, however, we did not realize the wider implications of this question, and all of us (myself included) attacked what we saw as Ch'en's slander of the Red Army. We seized on imperfections in the way in which he had worked his article and his one-sided slanting of the issue. In reality we were simply swelling the Stalinist anti-Ch'en chorus.

The question of the lessons to be learnt from the defeat of the 1925–7 Revolution was also raised to discredit Ch'en Tu-hsiu, and was essentially a demand that Ch'en admit his share of the blame for the policy of the Stalinists. Many comrades felt that for Ch'en to admit to having been the executor of Stalin's policies was not only not enough, but was positively dishonest. In our view Ch'en had been a *conscious* tool of Stalin. I am still convinced that our interpretation of his behaviour was not unreasonable. Ch'en Tu-hsiu was no puppet, but a revolutionary with a mind and a will of his own. We have Ch'en's own word for it that although he carried out some of the Comintern directives and resolutions between 1923 and 1927 unwillingly, to others he gave his full assent and agreement. In my opinion it would have been a much more effective rebuttal of Stalinism and an important contribution to the historiography of modern China if Ch'en had distinguished between these two categories and compiled a detailed record of what happened, but unfortunately he never did so. However, it was completely wrong of us to demand that he should go down on his knees to confess his guilt to us as 'orthodox Trotskyists', since this only delayed the unification of our forces.

The dispute on the nature of the coming Revolution was at first over whether to struggle for a 'dictatorship of the proletariat' or a 'dictatorship of the proletariat and the poor peasantry'. Later the crux of the argument was whether or not the third revolution would be socialist in character from the very outset. Ch'en Tu-hsiu had argued in *Our Political Platform* that a successful third revolution would inevitably lead to the establishment of a dictatorship of the proletariat and the poor peasantry. Trotsky always talked of the 'dictatorship of the proletariat' or the 'dictatorship of the proletariat at the head of the poor peasantry'; but Ch'en Tu-hsiu's formula appeared to give equal weight to both forces, and therefore to be making a concession to the outdated old Bolshevik slogan of the 'democratic dictatorship of the workers and the peasants'. (This problem is discussed fully in

Trotsky's *The Permanent Revolution*.) This difference was first seized on by Liu Jen-ching, and was subsequently picked up by all the other Trotskyists outside the Ch'en camp. Liu accused Ch'en of attempting to smuggle the poison of the 'democratic dictatorship' into the ranks of the Opposition, and dismissed Ch'en's article as a 'pitiful and hypocritical document'. Although, unlike Liu Jen-ching, we had not originally intended to make this the sole basis for our attack on Ch'en's so-called left turn, we were influenced by Liu's criticisms. We felt that that Ch'en's formula was close to the 'democratic dictatorship', and in fundamental contradiction to the 'dictatorship of the proletariat' slogan. Trotsky, however, on reading Ch'en Tu-hsiu's document, declared that it was simply a popularization and amplification of the 'dictatorship of the proletariat' formula, and that in his view there was no contradiction between the two. Liu Jen-ching was left dumbfounded by Trotsky's intervention, but for the rest of us it was as if the scales had suddenly fallen from our eyes.

The last of the four differences that separated the various factions involved the nature of the coming (third) Chinese revolution. It was Trotsky himself who originally forecast that this revolution would be socialist in character from the very outset, and not one of us disagreed with his analysis. Where the disagreement arose, however, was over an interpretation of it advanced in an article I wrote after the unification campaign was already under way, to which I will return later.

In brief, the squabbles and disputes of this period did not, as Trotsky pointed out, involve any differences of principle, but were more often than not blown up for purely factional reasons. After he had studied the various documents we had sent him, Trotsky wrote a long letter to us on 8 January 1931 proposing that we should immediately unify our forces. His tone was very pressing and earnest: 'Dear friends, merge your organizations and your papers today! Don't delay too much in preparing for unification. Otherwise, you will unconsciously create artificial differences between yourselves.' His prestige among us was so high that even the most diehard sectarian could find no further excuse for delaying unification; and shortly after receiving his letter the four factions decided to set up a 'Committee to Negotiate Unifications', which would draw up documents and unify on a common platform.

As I said earlier, this unification campaign was very beneficial for our movement, strengthening and concentrating us numerically, and at the same time involving a process of purification and selection. The small minority of comrades who could not accept the loss of their 'mountain strongholds' left the unified Opposition of their own accord, unable to reconcile themselves to the idea of working in a broader and numerically stronger organization. To clarify what went on during this period of regroupment, I would now like to say something about some of the individuals involved in the different organizations, beginning with the October group of which I myself was a member.

The natural leader of the Octobrists was Liü Jen-ching. He was older than the rest of us, and had better credentials. He had been one of the original twelve delegates at the First Congress of the CCP in 1921, and had also been General Secretary of the Chinese Communist Youth League. He had visited Trotsky at Prinkipo in Turkey, and even used to brag that Trotsky had chosen his pen-name, Niel Shih, for him. In Moscow I had had my differences with Liu, but I had always respected him as a veteran of the movement. On returning to China, when we got together with other comrades to publish *October* and organize our group, I continued to hold him in fairly high regard, but as soon as I and the other comrades began to work closely with him we discovered that he had many faults. As a theoretician, he was one-sided and unstable. Of Lenin's 'three component parts of Marxism', he was versed in only one – the history of the modern European revolutionary movement. He knew nothing of political economy and had only an elementary knowledge of philosophy. His instability in ideology enabled him to change his views according to his own ever-changing needs. However, what made us split from him after no more than a few months of co-operation was his way of working, which was entirely different from ours. He was obsessed with cultivating the famous, and he held himself aloof from the working class. He left our organization after only two issues of *October* had appeared. After the split we continued to publish under the new name of *The Road to October*. Liu Jen-ching brought out two issues of a one-man paper called *Tomorrow*. Later, he lapsed into inactivity after failing to win a place in the leadership when the four factions united. In 1934 he was hired by Harold Isaacs to translate material for his book *The Tragedy of the Chinese Revolution*. He was later arrested in Peking, but let out of prison after a period of 'reflection'. In 1938 he joined General Hu Tsung-nan's Anti-Communist League. When the Communist Party took power in

1949 the first thing he did was to write a statement denouncing Trotskyism.

Fortunately people like Liu Jen-ching were in a tiny minority in the movement, and of the eighty or more members of the October group in Shanghai and north China only one other, a man called Lu, went over to the counter-revolution. Among these eighty there were many truly heroic figures, such as Ko Ch'ung-o, Li Ts'ai-lien, and Lo Han, all of them utterly dedicated.

The group which continued under the name of Our Word after 1930 was in effect confined to Shanghai and Hong Kong. Its leadership was made up of the first generation of Moscow Trotskyists, Sun Yat-sen University students sent back to China in 1927. They had already been working for a few years in the country, and in Hong Kong had established a particularly strong base after Ou Fang, Ch'en I-mou, and others went to work in the T'aiku dockyards. In Shanghai, where Shih T'ang and Lu I-yüan were in overall charge of the activities of the Our Word group, there were fewer successes, but some contacts were established among workers and intellectuals.

Twenty-seven years later, at the time of writing, it is possible to look back on the events of those days dispassionately and to weigh up the merits of the various groups. It seems to me that the Our Word group was the healthiest of the four factions, more militant than the Ch'en Tu-hsiu group and with a broader base than either the Octobrists or the Militant group. It had some outstanding leaders, among them Ou Fang, who was resilient, modest, optimistic by nature, and both a man of action and a thinker. He dressed just like a labourer and was a brilliant writer and speaker. Tragically, Ou Fang was arrested together with Ko Ch'ung-o of the October group before unification could be carried out, and both comrades died at the hands of the Kuomintang in Shanghai gaol. Then there was Ch'en I-mou, who, although not as good a thinker or writer as Ou Fang, had at least as much capacity to endure pain. Ch'en also died in gaol. Sung Ching-hsiu, another outstanding and determined revolutionary, was the leader of the workers' section of the Our Word group in Shanghai. He died in the same prison as Ou Fang and Ch'en I-mou. This is how the Revolution always treats the people who take part in it, physically destroying the strong and the loyal, and spiritually destroying the weak and the bad. Other leaders of the Our Word group such as Shih T'ang, Lu I-yüan, Chang T'e, and Liang Kan-ch'iao belonged to the latter category. Shih T'ang and Lu I-yüan were weak, and later dropped out of politics altogether, but Chang T'e and Liang Kan-ch'iao actively went over to the counter-revolution, becoming 'specialists' in anti-communism for the Kuomintang.

The Proletarian Society was made up of over eighty high- and middle-ranking cadres trained during the early period of the CCP, all of them experienced and able activists. They would have been a powerful asset to any ideological movement, especially with a man of Ch'en Tu-hsiu's calibre at their head. Whatever his mistakes, Ch'en was still the symbol of China's progressive and revolutionary movement, both at home and abroad. The Proletarian Society might therefore have been expected to play an important role in the formation and development of the Chinese Trotskyist movement. But this never happened, the reason being that most of these old comrades were by now too apathetic. During the long period of CCP–Kuomintang co-operation many of them had adopted the style and attitudes of a bureaucrat or a member of the gentry, and having got used to working within a ready-made organizational apparatus found it hard to come to terms with the problems of building a new movement from scratch. As events were later to show, only a small minority of this organization of officers and general staff were as capable of fighting in the ranks once unification had been achieved.

For a long period the Militant group had only four members. Apart from Liu Yin and Chao Chi, the other two members were called Wang and Hsü. Wang and Hsü went over to the Kuomintang with Liu Yin shortly after unification, and only Chao Chi continued to work alongside the other Oppositionists. While the unification campaign was gathering strength, a member of the Communist Party called Ming Yin-ch'ang, who was responsible for the workers' section of the CCP in North Shanghai, was recruited to the Militant group by Chao Chi. Twenty or so other worker Communists joined with him, so that the Militant group could boast a couple of dozen members by the time of the unification congress in 1931. But of all the groups in existence at that time the Militant group was without doubt the smallest.

The first concern of the more sectarian-minded comrades in the various groups was how to secure for themselves the best possible representation on the committee set up to negotiate unification. Should the various groups be represented on a proportional basis, which would work out to the advantage of the bigger organizations, or should the groups be represented equally, which would favour the smaller ones? After some preliminary discussions the decision was made to allot each organization – regardless of size – two delegates. Originally Ou Fang and Shih T'ang, who had just been released from the International Settlement prison in Shanghai, were chosen to represent the Our Word group; Wu Chi-hsien and Ma Yü-fu the Proletarian Society; Liu Yin and Chao Chi, the Militant group; and Sung Feng-ch'un and myself, the Octobrists. Shortly afterwards the Our Word group's delegation was changed to Liang Kan-ch'iao and Ch'en I-mou, after the arrest of Ou Fang and the desertion of Shih T'ang, who secretly left Shanghai for his home town. The first few sessions of the unification negotiations committee were marred by quarrelling, and at meeting after meeting old issues were revived and old disputes re-enacted. These so-called negotiations (altercations would be a better word) dragged on for about two months, to the disappointment of many of the delegates and all the genuine Oppositionists in the four groups. The committee had originally set itself two tasks: to draw up a series of documents for voting on at a subsequent unification conference, and to organize such a conference. Both tasks were to prove difficult to achieve.

I was chosen to draw up the platform of the Chinese Left Opposition – not a particularly exacting task, since all it entailed was making a few editorial changes to the draft platform Trotsky had already sent us – on the Nature of the Coming Chinese Revolution. Trotsky had written in his draft: 'Our strategic general line is directed towards the seizure of state power. . . . The dictatorship of the proletariat in China will without doubt make of the Chinese revolution a part of the world socialist revolution'. As it seemed to me that this formulation was not complete, I drew on a passage from Trotsky's *The Summary and Perspectives of the Chinese Revolution*: 'The third Chinese revolution . . . will be forced from the very outset to effect the most decisive shake-up and abolition of bourgeois property in city and village'. On the basis of this I wrote, 'the coming Chinese revolution will be socialist in character from the very outset'.

To my surprise, this sentence raised a storm of protest, and Liu Jen-ching rose to denounce it as mechanical and ultra-leftist; he had himself long maintained that the Chinese revolution would inevitably go through a Kerensky stage. After this, *Our Word* and *The Proletarian* published articles both for and against my formulation. I have forgotten the details of the argument, but I do remember that the majority of the Our Word group supported me, whereas the majority of the Proletarian Society opposed me. My most uncompromising opponent was P'eng Shu-tse, and my firmest supporter in the Proletarian Society was Cheng Ch'ao-lin, while Ch'en Tu-hsiu wrote an article which fell between the two camps. Other theoretical problems of rather less importance were also argued over in the negotiating committee. Here too everyone refused to move from their positions, so it took a long time to draw up the documents to be voted on.

Organizing the unification conference proved to be an even thornier problem. First, it was very difficult to work out just how many members there were in each group. On this point Liang Kan-ch'iao's attitude was particularly obstructive. Liang Kan-ch'iao, a soldier who had been through the Whampoa Military Academy, showed not the slightest interest in theoretical questions, but as soon as the discussion switched to questions which concerned the future control of any unified organization that might be set up, he would immediately spring to life and devote his undivided attention to what was going on around him. For him, everything that anyone else might say was always part of a plot, and he therefore had no scruples about carrying out any cynical organizational manoeuvre. To ensure himself a dominant position in any future elections, he approached us Octobrists with proposals for an anti-Ch'en alliance; but when we turned him down he decided to adopt another tack, hugely exaggerating the strength of 'his' group and claiming without so much as a blush that its membership was equal to the rest of the three groups put together.

The general tone of the negotiations angered many of those present, and caused great anxiety to the more genuine comrades. Wu Chi-hsien and Ma Yü-fu, the representatives of the Proletarian Society, were the first to lose their enthusiasm, and they decided to waste no more time attending the meetings. It seemed like the beginning of the end for the negotiations. At first we thought that Wu and Ma were simply impatient at the lack of progress being made, but I afterwards learned that internal problems within the Proletarian Society probably also influenced their decision to resign. Trotsky's letter of 8 January 1931 had in fact changed the relationship of forces between the different Trotskyist groups. Before it, the Ch'en group had neither prestige nor status, and the other three factions (in particular the Our Word group) all prided themselves on their orthodoxy. Time and time again Ch'en and his friends expressed their readiness to engage in joint activities and even to put their forces into the existing organization, but their advances were turned down out of hand, and they were subjected to a ferocious political battering. But it was not long before Trotsky read Ch'en's document, praised it, and stretched out his hand to the former leader of the CCP in comradeship, at the same time strongly urging the other Chinese Trotskyists to unite with him immediately. After this, the situation was reversed. The other three groups accepted Trotsky's advice with extreme reluctance and not a little embarrassment. Ch'en's Proletarian Society entered the negotiations as victors, turning the tables on the rest of us, pretending that they were the only orthodox Trotskyists, and trying to give the impression that they were above our 'childish nonsense'. Needless to say, none of them dared to express his feelings openly, but they wore superior smiles and turned up their noses at others. They had no confidence in the negotiations, and it was with little enthusiasm that they sent their representatives along. After weeks of unceasing bickering the prospect of unification receded further and further. Their delegates would have liked nothing better than to withdraw from the negotiating committee, and they began to display their arrogance and superiority more and more openly. Worst of all was P'eng Shu-tse, who argued that it was pointless to continue talking about unification, and that the groups should go back to working by themselves; any other Oppositionists who were sincere about working for the Revolution could join the Proletarian Society. These proposals found some support among the veteran cadres, especially Wu Chi-hsien and Ma Yü-fu, but many others in the Proletarian Society, in particular Cheng Ch'ao-lin and Yin K'uan, opposed them. The negotiations temporarily broke down, and whether or not the unification movement would continue depended largely on the attitude of Ch'en Tu-hsiu.

One day in March Ch'en Ch'i-ch'ang, an old friend of mine from Peking University and a member of the Ch'en Tu-hsiu group, paid me a visit and told me that Ch'en Tu-hsiu would like to see me for a talk at the home of Yin K'uan. This was the first time I had ever met Ch'en Tu-hsiu, and although I was no longer as hostile to him as I had been several months earlier, I was still critical of him. As soon as I set eyes on him, however, I gained a most favourable impression. This middle-aged man in his early fifties, with his sincere and unassuming ways, swept all remaining traces of factional prejudice from me. We talked all afternoon, allowing our conversation to follow its own course, but dwelling chiefly on my own personal history, from the time I was at Peking University down to when I worked under Chou En-lai in the organization department. He asked many questions and said little himself, but once a subject captured his interest he would join in with relish. I was particularly impressed by his straightforwardness – there was not the slightest trace of ceremony or pretentiousness about him. But, for all his frankness, I saw no signs of his notorious hot temper. On the contrary, it seemed to me that he was extremely considerate and modest in his attitude towards others. Finally we got around to talking about the question of unification. He asked me my opinion, and I gave it to him without hesitation. I explained how I had at first been opposed to co-operating with his group, but had afterwards changed my mind and was now looking forward to unification. He seemed pleased, and said that in his view it was absolutely imperative for the Chinese Trotskyist movement to unify its forces, as otherwise there would be no future for any of the groups. He added that this applied equally to the Proletarian Society, since it was mostly made up of 'old men', and the tasks confronting the Opposition in China could only be carried out by young people. After we had finished our conversation, we left separately. It was dusk by now, and as I walked home I was filled with rare emotions. I felt as though a big change had come over me. I had got to know a great figure in the history of revolutionary thought in modern China. The enormous respect I developed for Ch'en Tu-hsiu remains with me to this day.

The following morning Ch'en Ch'i-ch'ang came back to see me, and told me what Ch'en Tu-hsiu's impressions of the conversation had been. I was pleased to hear that Ch'en Tu-hsiu had told him that I was 'the complete opposite of Liang Kan-ch'iao', whom he had invited over for a similar talk the previous day. This was hardly surprising, as Liang was to defect to the Kuomintang only a few weeks later and take over as head of Chiang's secret police: how could comparison of a revolutionary with a man like that even be considered? Ch'en Ch'i-ch'ang also told me that the Proletarian Society had decided to replace its representatives on the negotiating committee with Ch'en Tu-hsiu and Yin K'uan, hoping in this way to speed up progress towards unification.

There was a dramatic change once Ch'en Tu-hsiu arrived at the negotiations. The squabbling stopped, and the determination to achieve unity infected all those present. Differences on theoretical questions were now resolved without the interminable disputes which used to accompany them, and exaggeration and hair-splitting frowned upon. It was decided that the documents should be re-written. Ch'en Tu-hsiu was to write the political platform and the agrarian programme. I was chosen to draw up some theses on the question of the constituent assembly; if I remember rightly Liang Kan-ch'iao was assigned to write the organizational resolution, and Yin K'uan a resolution on the workers' movement. The resolutions were written and submitted in record time, and after a frank and good-natured discussion they were quickly voted on and passed. As for the controversial question of the nature of the third Chinese revolution, Ch'en Tu-hsiu's draft reverted to Trotsky's original form-ulation, arguing that it would result from the very outset in a decisive shake-up of private property in both town and country. The platform was unanimously accepted.

After the political preparations for unification had been com-pleted, the only problem outstanding was the election of delegates for the forthcoming unification conference. A sub-committee con-sisting of Yin K'uan, Chao Chi, Liang Kan-ch'iao, and myself was set up to deal with this. The simplest thing would have been to allocate delegates proportionately, according to the strength of the various groups, but the difficulty was that Liang Kan-ch'iao had exaggerated the size of his group. As for the other three groups, there had originally been eighty signatories to the collective platform of the Proletarian Society, but during the last few months they had gained some adherents both in Hong Kong and north China, which had boosted their membership to over a hundred. The October group had originally collected nineteen signatures in Shanghai alone for its platform, and afterwards it won over a dozen or so new supporters in addition to the fifty or so members of the *Our Word* group in north China who came over to them, making about eighty in all. The *Militant* group had at most thirty members, all of them in Shanghai. The *Our Word* group had a similar membership there. In Hong Kong their organization was stronger, consisting of some seventy or eighty comrades. But Liang Kan-ch'iao was insisting that their total membership was over three hundred. We asked him to supply a membership list, but he refused on the grounds that this would be dangerous. When Yin K'uan proposed sending someone to make an on-the-spot investigation he replied that this was impossible, since the comrades were scattered throughout the East River area and Chungshan county in Kwangtung province. After several days of haggling we at last succeeded in making a deal with him, agreeing to grant the Our Word group representation on the basis of 120 to 140 members. One delegate was allowed for every twenty members, so the Our Word group got six or seven. The Proletarian Society had five delegates, the Octobrists four, and the Militant group two.

The problems of finance and venue were left to the Proletarian Society. I afterwards learnt that the money was provided by Li Chung-san, a friend of the famous Kuomintang general Yang Hu-ch'eng, who pawned his fur coat to raise it, while Ho Tzu-shen rented a house for the conference in the Dairen Bay Road area of east Shanghai. None of us knew in advance the exact location of the house.

The various factions soon elected their representatives to the conference. Ch'en Tu-hsiu, Cheng Ch'ao-lin, Chiang Ch'ang-shih, Wu Chi-hsien, and the veteran railway worker Wang Chih-huai or Ho Tzu-shen, were chosen to represent the Proletarian Society. The Our Word group was represented by Liang Kan-ch'iao, Ch'en I-mou, Lou Kuo-hua, who was unable to attend for other reasons and whose place was taken by Sung Ching-hsiu, Chang Chiu, a worker from Hong Kong, and two or three other Hong Kong comrades. The Octobrists decided to send Lo Han, who had just got out of gaol in Peking, and represented the north China comrades, Sung Feng-ch'un, P'u Teh-chih, and myself. The Militant group sent Chao Chi and Lai Yen-t'ang.

The Unification Conference of the Chinese Left Opposition was called for 1 May 1931 and met for three days. The first two days were taken up with discussion and amendment of the various documents submitted by the negotiating committee, and on the third and final day a new leadership was elected. Ch'en Tu-hsiu inaugurated the conference and delivered a short political report. During the subsequent debate the only issue which caused any real controversy was whether or not the national unification of China could be achieved under Chiang Kai-shek. No one argued that none of the democratic tasks could be achieved except under the dictatorship of the proletariat, and Ch'en Tu-hsiu's report did not exclude the possibility of at least the *appearance* of national unification under the existing regime, even though he agreed with our fundamental postulate. Most of the delegates, myself included, opposed this formulation, and so Ch'en allowed it to be struck out from his political report when it came to voting. All the other documents were approved unanimously.

The Unification Conference put an end to the rivalry between the four factions, and the atmosphere afterwards was one of harmony, solidarity, and hope. It was as if all of those present in that small room saw a bright future for the Chinese Bolshevik–Leninists (as Trotskyists throughout the world continued to call themselves at that time) and were convinced they would play a decisive role in the coming Chinese revolution. The only exception to this general mood of unity was Liang Kan-ch'iao, who was so narrow-mindedly factionalist in his attitude that the very idea of a unified movement was distasteful to him. After the documents had been voted on, elections followed. All the delegates ignored previous factional demarcations and cast their votes regardless of old factional ties. The following comrades were elected to the formal leadership body of the new unified organization: Ch'en Tu-hsiu, Lo Han, Sung Feng-ch'un, Ch'en I-mou, Cheng Ch'ao-lin, Chao Chi, and myself. Others were elected as alternate members. (Whether P'eng Shu-tse was elected as a full or alternate member I can no longer say with certainty.) The most striking feature of these results was that the 'heroes' of the aimless factional skirmishing of the last year or so, men like Liang Kan-ch'iao, Liu Jen-ching, Liu Yin, and Ma Yü-fu, who had bent all their efforts towards securing themselves positions of dominance in the movement, failed without exception to gain election to the new leadership body. The fact that manoeuvres got them nowhere confirms my earlier statement that unification was a process of natural selection, a remorseless and unerring process of purification. Less than a month after the conference Liang Kan-ch'iao made his way to Nanking to seek out Chiang Kai-shek, who had been head of the Whampoa Military Academy when Liang was trained there, and issued a statement declaring that 'communism is not in harmony with the Chinese natural character.' Liu Jen-ching lapsed into complete apathy. Liu Yin bided his time, waiting for the highest bidder to buy him out of the movement. Ma Yü-fu immediately defected to the Woosung–Shanghai Garrison Headquarters of the Kuomintang to join their special agents.

Now that unification had been achieved, the Left Opposition of the Chinese Communist Party made great progress in several fields. The new Central Committee made Ch'en Tu-hsiu General Secretary; Cheng Ch'ao-lin was put in charge of propaganda; Ch'en I-mou was given responsibility for organizational work; Lo Han was made secretary of the Central Committee; and I was put in charge of our theoretical organ. At the first plenary session of the Central Committee Lo Han drafted a telegram to Trotsky joyfully announcing that the Chinese comrades had taken a step of great significance, and that the banner of the Chinese Bolshevik–Leninists would soon be fluttering from one end of China to the other. The tone of this message reflected our boundless confidence. At that time the Kuomintang were toying with a provisional constitution, and a struggle for democracy was beginning at all levels of society, just as Trotsky had forecast. We therefore decided to launch a nationwide campaign for a genuine constituent assembly.

Our unification also came at a very opportune moment from the point of view of the internal struggle in the CCP. But before I go into that question in more detail, I want to take another look at the doings of our old friend Wang Ming, who had returned to China only a few months after us. By early 1930 he was back in Shanghai, together with the other members of the so-called 'Twenty-eight Bolsheviks' (or 'Returned Students') faction. Among these twenty-eight were Ho Tzu-shu, Ch'in Pang-hsien (alias Po Ku), Ch'en Ch'ang-hao, Ch'en Wei-ming, and Sun Chi-ming. I was very familiar with all these men, most of whom (with the sole exception of Ho Tzu-shu) were very shallow-minded. When they first got back they were treated just as we had been several months before, and despite the fact that Wang Ming was in favour with Stalin and had excellent relations with Hsiang Chung-fa, then General Secretary of the CCP, he was assigned to a very lowly position in the propaganda department under Li Li-san. However, a man of his ambition was not going to settle for such a humble situation.

At that time Li Li-san was still leader of the Party, having imitated Stalin's 'Third Period' line with his theory of a 'new revolutionary high tide', and achieved an initial success for the Revolution 'in one or several provinces'. In Shanghai he tried to occupy the streets by mounting adventurist demonstrations along the Nanking Road; and nationally he aimed at occupying Ch'angsha and even Wuhan with the help of the Hunan and Hupeh Red Armies. As defeat followed defeat many comrades came to question the Li Li-san (or rather the Stalin) line. By September 1930, after the failure of the Red Army's second attack on Ch'angsha, the failure of Li Li-san's policy was plain for all to see. At the Third Plenary Session of the Sixth Central Committee in the same month, a group of CCP leaders headed by Ch'ü Ch'iu-pai put an end to the Li Li-san era. By this time, of course, we Trotskyists had been expelled from the Party, so I have no clear idea of what role Wang Ming and his group played in the overthrow of Li Li-san. But judging from the factional changes in the leadership of the CCP over the previous year or two, Ch'ü Ch'iu-pai, who had been removed as General Secretary at the Sixth Congress in Moscow in 1928, was hardly in a position to carry out such a coup without backing from elsewhere.

It seems to me that Wang Ming must have played a role behind the scenes through his protégé, the General Secretary Hsiang Chung-fa, and with the help of both the Comintern representative in Shanghai and of Moscow. Less than four months later, at the Fourth Plenary Session of the Sixth Central Committee held in January 1931, Wang Ming and his supporters emerged from the wings, overthrew Ch'ü Ch'iu-pai, just as Li Li-san had been overthrown shortly before, and, with the active support of Hsiang Chung-fa and the connivance of Chou En-lai, snatched the leadership for themselves. Wang Ming, 'hero' of the battle against the Trotskyists at Sun Yat-sen University in 1927, victor over the 'Kiangsu–Chekiang Provincial Association' and the 'survivors' of the Moscow Branch of the CCP, the man who amalgamated KUTV into Sun Yat-sen University and unified the leadership of the Chinese students in the Soviet Union into his own hands – this same Wang Ming had now won his biggest battle, the battle for the leadership of the whole Party. From start to finish it had only taken him four years, during which time this ambitious non-entity, this total outsider to the Chinese Revolution, had manoeuvred his way into the Politbureau of the CCP. It was an amazing record. But for anyone at all familiar with the reality of Stalinism, the para-dox is only too easy to explain. Wang Ming's rapid rise to power had less to do with natural ability, which played only a very minor role in the whole enterprise, than the fact that his ambitions fitted in very well with Stalin's needs.

After his victories over Trotsky and Bukharin, Stalin immediately set about Stalinizing all the other Communist Parties in the Third International. The first to fall were the supporters of the Left Opposition, soon followed by all genuine Communists with minds of their own. It was during this campaign that Stalin raised the slogan in the Comintern of 'Bolshevization', but what he meant by

'Bolsheviks' were only the docile and spineless supporters of his own factional interests. The best example of such a 'Bolshevik' was Wang Ming himself. Of the early leaders of the CCP, Ch'en Tu-hsiu was definitely not a 'Bolshevik' of this sort, and Ch'ü Ch'iu-pai was far too fond of expressing his own opinion. Chou En-lai came a little closer to the mark, but he had no direct relations with the Stalinists, and in any case was far too able for Stalin to trust. Hsiang Chung-fa was certainly qualified in one way to receive the appellation, but he had absolutely no talent at all and as far as theory went he was illiterate. Mao Tse-tung, of course, was less qualified than any of these last three for such a title.

Stalin, and his immediate entourage including Mif, had long intended to cultivate a loyal agent among the Chinese students in Moscow. Wang Ming's nomination as Stalin's Chinese puppet emperor had already been decided on by late 1927 and his performance at the Fourth Plenum of the Sixth Central Committee was stage-managed by Stalin through Mif, then the Comintern agent in Shanghai. It was about this time that Wang Ming wrote his pamphlet *The Struggle for Bolshevization of the CCP.* In his pamphlet Wang Ming launched an attack on Li Li-san's 'ultra-left line' and raised the new charge of 'conciliationism' against Ch'ü Ch'iu-pai. The result was that both men were kicked out of the leadership and made to confess their 'mistakes'. Chou En-lai, also, was ordered to make a self-examination. Li Li-san was sent to Moscow to 'study'. Ch'ü Ch'iu-pai's fate was different. It was almost as if he had been expelled from the Party completely: he lived in Shanghai at the house of a non-Party friend called Hsieh Tan-ju and engaged in left-wing literary activities.

Despite the fact that Wang Ming and his friends had never been elected to the Central Committee, they manipulated it at will. They were co-opted straight onto the Politbureau and given posts of high responsibility. The most authoritative Maoist document available, ('Resolution on Certain Questions in the History of our Party') had the following to say on the coup carried out by Wang Ming and his friends in the guise of 'Bolshevization':

. . . This new 'Left' line [was carried out] under Comrade Ch'en Shao-yü's [Wang Ming's] leadership. . . . Organizationally, the exponents of this new 'Left' line violated discipline, refused the work assigned them by the Party, committed the error of joining with a number of other comrades in factional activities against the central leadership, wrongly called upon the Party membership to set up a provisional leading body and demanded that 'fighting cadres' who 'actively support and pursue' their 'Left' line should be used to 'reform and strengthen the leading bodies at all levels'; they thereby created a serious crisis in the Party. Hence, generally speaking, the new 'Left' line was more determined, more 'theoretical', more domineering and more fully articulated in its 'Leftism' than the Li Li-san line, even though it did not call for organizing insurrection in the key cities and, for a time, did not call for concentrating the Red Army to attack those cities.

In January 1931 the Fourth Plenary Session of the Sixth Central Committee of the Party was convened under circumstances in which pressure was being applied from all directions by the 'Left' dogmatist and sectarian elements headed by Comrade Ch'en Shao-yü and in which some comrades in the central leading body who had committed empiricist errors were compromising with these elements and supporting them. The convening of this session played no positive or constructive role; the outcome was the acceptance of the new 'Left' line, its triumph in the central leading body and the beginning of the domination of a 'Left' line in the Party for the third time during the period of the Agrarian Revolutionary War. . . . Under this programme the Fourth Plenary Session and the subsequent central leadership promoted the 'Left' dogmatist and sectarian comrades to responsible positions in the central leading body on the one hand; on the other, they excessively attacked those comrades headed by Ch'ü Ch'iu-pai who were alleged to have committed the 'error of the line of conciliation', and immediately after the session the Central Committee wrongly attacked the great majority of the so-called 'Rightist' comrades. . . .[1]

Although most of what is said about Wang Ming in the piece I have just quoted is true, the really important things are left unsaid. Since it deliberately avoids naming the main instigator of these crimes, dressing up a mere pickpocket as a big-time criminal, it cannot therefore draw the correct lessons from the historical events which it attempts to describe. Wang Ming's coup was not the mistaken action of an isolated individual, but part of a more general process of Stalinization which was affecting all sections of the Comintern. When Lenin and Trotsky were in power, the Comintern was the supreme organ of power in the world Communist movement. The cPSU was simply a subordinate section of the International, to which it looked for leadership, as did the whole Soviet Union, the state which it had created and which it controlled. All fraternal Parties enjoyed equal status within the Comintern. As headquarters of

[1] *Selected Works of Mao Tse-tung*, Vol. 3, 1965, pp. 187–8. Note that this resolution was omitted from later editions of the *Selected Works* because of its favourable references to Liu Shao-ch'i, Ch'ü Ch'iu-pai, and others.

the world revolution, the Comintern was made up of the most authoritative and talented revolutionaries, who had won the respect of the masses in their own countries. If Lenin played a leading role in the International, this was due to his superior talents and his unique experience, not to his position as leader of the Soviet state. From time to time certain leaders were expelled from the International because they fell short of the standards required of them, but this was only after proper discussion and consultation and with the aim of advancing rather than harming the interests of the revolution. Gradually, however, the Soviet Union began to degenerate and the theory of 'socialism in one country' became an official tenet of the CPSU. The first thing that happened was that a change came about in the relationship between the CPSU and the Comintern, which, from being a headquarters of the world revolution, changed into an arm of Soviet diplomacy. At the same time, the trend towards degeneration which was becoming more and more apparent in the CPSU was paralleled in the Comintern and in the Parties affiliated to it. But the Soviet bureaucrats could only really control the Comintern if the leaders of the various foreign sections submitted completely to their will. The old generation of Communists, who had inherited a revolutionary socialist tradition going back for almost a century and who had been tempered in the struggles of the immediate post-War period, were hardly likely to change into yes-men overnight. The subjugation of the foreign Parties required a long process of so-called 'Bolshevization'. Stalin spared no effort to achieve this aim, working at it for months and even years, and not hesitating wherever necessary to sabotage any revolutions which were not under his immediate control. At the same time he murdered countless thousands of foreign revolutionaries, either in the prison camps of Siberia or in the Lubianka gaol in Moscow (where, for example, the entire central committee of the Polish Communist Party were imprisoned), so that by the early 1930s, Communist Parties throughout the world were dominated exclusively by 'Bolsheviks' of the Wang Ming type.

I am not suggesting that Mao himself was unaware of who Wang Ming's patrons were, or of the true implications of the 'Bolshevization' campaign. There were two main reasons why Mao put all the blame on Wang Ming: first, he was at the time of writing anxious not to impair Sino-Soviet friendship; and second, Mao Tse-tung was himself a Stalinist – ideologically, if not in terms of faction.

The Unification Conference of the Chinese Trotskyist movement took place three months after the CCP's Fourth Plenary Session. The CCP was still reeling from the after-effects of Wang Ming's *coup*. The tragic fate of the so-called 'conciliationist' or 'rightist' faction particularly saddened the middle and lower cadres of the Party. I will briefly explain what happened. Lo Chang-lung, Ho Meng-hsiung, Lin Yü-nan, Li Ch'iu-shih, and the group of Communists under them were all veteran cadres of the Party, most of them members of the Provincial Committee of Kiangsu province and some of them long-standing activists in the trade union movement. These men were outstanding professional revolutionaries and pillars of the workers' movement, down-to-earth, hard-working, and indissolubly linked to the proletariat. Even though none of them was an outstanding theoretician or could match Wang Ming in his manipulation of quotations from the 'classics', the fact that they lived like true revolutionaries and shared the day-to-day fate of the working class meant that they had a genuine feeling for the movement and were receptive to the smallest change in its mood. This was completely unlike the members of the central committee of the Party, who took as their starting point the telegrams and resolutions they received from Moscow. As early as 1928, when Stalin sent his 'prodigy' Lominadze to China to direct Ch'ü Ch'iu-pai in a new putschist wave, the 'conciliationists' had voiced a number of correct and sharply-worded criticisms. Their resolution of May of that year was quoted at length by Trotsky in his article 'The Chinese Question after the Sixth Congress', where he called it 'a remarkable document on the policy and the regime of the Communist International'. Independently and on the basis of their own experience, the 'conciliationists' of the Kiangsu Provincial Committee had reached similar conclusions to those which the Left Opposition had deduced from its broad theoretical analysis.

After the CCP Sixth Congress, some of these individuals became more interested in Trotskyist ideas, but their empiricism, or else their lack of courage, prevented them from breaking altogether with Stalinism. When the Stalinists came out with their 'Third Period' theory immediately after the Sixth Congress – a theory which in China was embodied in the 'Li Li-san Line' – they once again began to express deep dissatisfaction, and when the Li Li-san Line came under fire at the Third Plenum, the Kiangsu Committee supported Ch'ü

Ch'iu-pai. Afterwards, when Wang Ming began a more thorough-going purge of Li Li-san and his handful of supporters and moved to topple Ch'ü Ch'iu-pai, they gave Wang their tacit support. But as soon as Wang Ming and his friends took over the leadership, their even more absurdly 'leftist' line and domineering ways alienated their Kiangsu supporters. Wang Ming therefore counter-attacked, relying on Comintern support and his newly-acquired position in the CCP leadership to launch a ferocious onslaught on the 'conciliationists', or 'rightists'. All the odds were on Wang Ming's side. But the 'rightists' showed considerable mettle, and refused to surrender. Even though they realized that their cause was hopeless, they fought back heroically, and were even prepared at one point to organize a new Communist Party as a vehicle for their ideas. But before they could realize their plans, tragedy struck. While all the main leaders of the Kiangsu group were attending a meeting in the Eastern Hotel just behind the Sincere Department Store in Shanghai, they were surprised by agents from the Woosung–Shanghai Garrison Headquarters and arrested. Despite attempts to bribe and intimidate them, not one capitulated to the Kuomintang, and they were all taken out and shot. Among the twenty-five martyrs were Ho Meng-hsiung, Lin Yü-nan, Li Ch'iu-shih, my old friend Chao P'ing-fu, and Yün Yü-t'ang, who had come back from Moscow with me. The novelist Hu Yeh-p'in, husband of the writer Ting Ling, was also among the martyrs.

The death of these comrades caused grief and anger in the Party's ranks. There were rumours that Wang Ming was responsible for this incident, and had informed the police of their whereabouts as a way of getting rid of them. Such treachery was the normal practice of the Stalin/Wang Ming school, but there is no proof that it actually happened. It is undeniable, however, that their martyrdom was linked at least indirectly to the inner-Party struggle, and that it had a demoralizing and depressing effect on the Party rank and file. Despite the crisis, Wang Ming and his friends did not let up for a moment in their campaign to seize control of the Chinese Party, ruthlessly persecuting, dismissing, and even expelling all those old cadres who proved 'uncooperative' or who fell foul of them in any way.

The Chinese Oppositionists presented a complete contrast to this picture of disarray. After May Day, 1931, we were united in one organization, and led by the founder of the Chinese Communist movement, Ch'en Tu-hsiu. The main reason why we did not make our influence felt more was that Chiang Kai-shek, with the help of the traitor Ma Yü-fu, unexpectedly came to Wang Ming's aid. Our newly elected leaders had been at their posts scarcely a month when almost all of them were arrested during a police raid on the night of 21 May, after Ma Yü-fu had tipped off the Kuomintang. Apart from Ch'en Tu-hsiu and Lo Han, the entire Standing Committee of the organization was arrested, including Cheng Ch'ao-lin and his wife Wu Ching-chen, Ho Tzu-shen and his wife Chang I-sen, Sung Feng-ch'un, Ch'en I-mou, Lou Kuo-hua, Chiang Shang-shih, P'u Teh-chih, Wang Chih-huai, and myself. This crushing blow brought the activities of the newly unified Opposition to a temporary standstill. As for myself, I was about to enter a new chapter in my life – a chapter mainly made up of long periods of imprisonment. But before I go on to describe those experiences, I would like to say a few things about the literary activities of the Oppositionists, which is how many of us earned our living during that period.

In the history of revolutionary movements, revolutionary ideologies have generally tended to precede the actual implementation of revolution. China in the 1920s was an apparent exception to this rule. It is true that the May Thirtieth Movement of 1925 was a natural development of the May Fourth Movement of 1919, and represented a transformation from bourgeois-democratic ideology to socialist consciousness – a transformation clearly embodied both in the person of Ch'en Tu-hsiu, the most important ideologist of the period, and in the New Youth magazine which he edited. In this sense, the Second Chinese Revolution, which started up at roughly the same time as the May Thirtieth movement, could be said to have been preceded by an ideological upsurge. But in fact the pace of events during the Chinese Revolution rapidly outstripped the range of previous revolutionary thinking.

After the end of the European War in 1918, and especially as a result of the October Revolution of 1917, socialist thinking found its way to China. It became the 'most fashionable decoration on the soul' of China's intellectuals. All sorts of Western ideologies were seized upon, some of them going back a hundred years or more, so long as they bore the label 'socialist'. It mattered little whether they were scientific, utopian, revolutionary, reformist, or even reactionary. So long as they fulfilled this minimum condition, they were translated into Chinese, published in all sorts of magazines, chatted about in bourgeois drawing-rooms, and even lectured on in the academies by young men anxious to make a name for themselves as progressives or simply to make money. As soon as they had been published and politely chatted about, they were immediately forgotten, and our 'socialist' heroes would go off to rejoin their warlord friends; or even, like Chiang K'ang-hu, the founder of the Chinese Social Democratic Party, to visit the former Emperor in the Forbidden City.

Of course, not all intellectuals with socialist leanings were like this. The group around Ch'en Tu-hsiu and Li Ta-chao quickly opted for scientific socialism in its most modern form – Bolshevism. They set up the Chinese Communist Party, and began to establish contacts with China's newly-emerging social force, the proletariat. But, because the Chinese Revolution developed so quickly, the first generation of socialist revolutionaries had no conception of how to lead the class struggle; in fact they could not even recognize the struggle when they came face to face with it. In Russia, the complete opposite had been the case. There, revolutionary intellectuals had investigated and thoroughly discussed all the fundamental problems of the Revolution some ten or twenty years before its actual outbreak. They already had both a strategic and a tactical programme, and a fighting organization unifying all the most deteimined revolutionaries in its ranks, so that, when the Revolution actually arrived, it developed almost as if according to plan for Lenin, Trotsky and others, although not without the most bitter struggles. In China, things turned out differently. During the revolutionary years 1925 to 1927, most of the leaders of the CCP had only the sketchiest understanding of theory, culled from largely undigested foreign sources, and were incapable of adapting it to Chinese realities. The result was that Moscow did their thinking for them. As an internationalist, I consider that it is entirely permissible for national revolutions to receive direction from a world revolutionary headquarters. But unfortunately those doing the thinking were no longer Lenin and Trotsky, who had brought the revolution to fruition, but Stalin, who had betrayed it. Although Trotsky and his fellow-thinkers had a strategy which could have led the Chinese Revolution to victory, their views were suppressed by the Stalinists, who advanced what amounted to a Menshevik line for China. None of the leaders of the CCP was capable of distinguishing between these two positions and carried out this line more or less blindly, with the inevitable tragic results.

Wielding the big hammer of the counter-revolution, Chiang Kai-shek broke and bloodied a great number of revolutionary heads, but at the same time awakened many of those who were lucky enough to survive the bloodbath to the need for theory. During the darkest days of the defeat many revolutionaries became profoundly aware that in the past they had acted blindly. Because of their lack of theoretical understanding they had been forced to drift wherever the wind took them, like boats without rudders. It is a tragic fact that the Chinese socialists only went out in search of socialist theory after the defeat of the Revolution. But the socialist cultural movement which started in Shanghai in 1929 was nevertheless of great historical significance, and the important role played in it by the Chinese Trotskyists is also worthy of note. It was not a movement consciously set in motion by any individual or group, but a reflex reaction by hundreds of revolutionaries to the defeat. Moreover, as a result of the defeat many revolutionary intellectuals had been forced back to their studies, thus giving an added impetus to the cultural movement.

After 1929 small publishing houses sprang up everywhere in Shanghai, which had long been the main publishing centre of the country. All of them specialized in social science publications. The men who provided the capital for these publishers came from many different walks of life: former bureaucrats and military men out-numbered ordinary merchants. These people had for one reason or another fallen out of favour with Chiang Kai-shek, and therefore come to form a sort of opposition to the Nanking Government. During their enforced idleness many of them entrusted a small part of their accumulated wealth to friends or acquaintances to set up 'cultural enterprises'. Their real aim was to build a reputation for themselves on which they could capitalize during any future attempt at a political comeback. The friends and acquaintances to whom they entrusted their money were for the most part former subordinates – men who could deal only in bureaucratic niceties and who were completely ignorant of the new cultural movement. These latter therefore sought out the help of people with some experience of the publishing world to do their editing and writing for them. Naturally, the majority of such people were intellectuals who had emerged from the revolutionary movement.

The largest of the new publishing houses was the Shen-chou Kuo-kuang Company. The funds for it were put up by General Ch'en Ming-shu, leader of the famous Nineteenth Route Army which in 1932 waged a heroic resistance against the Japanese around Shanghai. Actual responsibility for the day-to-day running of the company was in the hands of Wang Li-hsi. I am not sure what Wang's background was, but he liked to think of himself as a classical poet. He knew nothing about publishing and the social sciences, but he was an honest enough man, and because he knew very little about politics he had few preconceptions. As long as you were a 'left-wing personality' or could trot out a few social science terms he would immediately snatch you up to work for his firm. He liked to think of himself as a second Ts'ai Yüan-p'ei (the liberal Chancellor of Peking University during and after the May Fourth Movement), and employed writers from right across the political spectrum, including the pro-Kuomintang rightist T'ao Hsi-sheng, members of the Stalinist faction, and even Trotskyists. During the early part of 1930 his links with the Left Opposition were particularly close, and Liu Jen-ching, Li Chi, Wang Tu-ch'ing, P'eng Shu-tse, Tu Wei-chih, P'eng Kuei-ch'iu, and Wu Chi-hsien were among those who worked for him. Through Liu Jen-ching I received a commission from Wang Li-hsi to edit and translate material for an illustrated history of the Russian Revolution. I was paid by the month at a rate of three dollars per thousand Chinese characters, which worked out on average at some sixty dollars a month, over twice what my monthly Party allowance had been. The history was based on Comintern-produced material and John Reed's *Ten Days that Shook the World*. After it was completed, Wang Li-hsi sent the manuscript to the propaganda department of the Kuomintang Central Committee in Nanking for submission to the censors, where unfortunately it was confiscated. Up until my arrest in May 1931 this was my sole source of income.

All the other leading Oppositionists with any literary talent also earned their living by writing or translating social science books. We were expected not only to keep ourselves and our families, but also to provide the necessary funds for the running of the organization and for feeding and clothing those who worked full-time for it. No wonder, therefore, that the Opposition was renowned for its poverty. Nevertheless, our 'rice-bowl' literary activities during that period played no small part in popularizing and deepening socialist thinking in China. Apart from the Shen-chou Kuo-kuang company, the Hu-pin, 'New Universe', Ch'un-ch'iu, and 'Oriental' publishing houses had links with the Oppositionists. (The Oriental Book Company had a special relationship with the Left Opposition, which I will return to later.) We also made use of other publishing houses, such as the 'New Life' company, run by T'ao Hsi-sheng and Fan

Chung-yün. Our literary activities were not organized according to any plan, but separately decided on in discussions with the publishers themselves. However, we managed to bring out a varied collection of Marxist classics, including works by Marx, Engels, and Lenin. Trotsky's *My Life* was published simultaneously in no less than three different translations, all by Oppositionists. (This was before unification, of course.) We also translated many histories of the European revolutionary movement, including works by Kropotkin, Trotsky, and others. During the same period the Proletarian Society brought out an influential periodical called *Tung-li* (*Motive Force*), which popularized Trotskyism and more general social science.

The CCP in Shanghai launched their own left-wing cultural movement, but they lagged a long way behind us in their publishing. Most of the officials of the CCP-sponsored movement were men of letters, and their main focus was therefore 'proletarian literature'. They achieved nothing of note, just like similar 'proletarian literature' movements elsewhere in the world, and it was not until after 1933, when Ch'ü Ch'iu-pai joined them, that their cultural movement began to show any real sign of life. By that time, however, all the main Trotskyist writers were in gaol, and those claiming to represent Trotskyism in the famous debate on the nature of Chinese society in the pages of *Tu-shu tsa-chih* (*Study Magazine*) were either pseudo-Trotskyists or former members of the movement.

CHAPTER 8

Prison Life

The Kuomintang repression of its political opponents can be divided into four stages. There was first the 'party purification' campaign and its direct aftermath, which lasted roughly from 1927 to 1930, when anyone seized by security forces could expect summary execution. In this early stage, the Kuomintang's repressive apparatus had not yet been centralized, and the fate of those arrested depended solely on the personal whims of local officials. The Kuomintang police agents had close links with underworld gangster organizations, who were given a free hand to attack anyone they liked. These gangs killed indiscriminately, using the opportunity to blackmail, kidnap, and settle private scores. No one felt safe from attack, and even a section of the bourgeoisie itself began to express disquiet. After this came the second or 'democratic' period, when the Kuomintang declared that any Communists arrested would be tried according to 'due processes' of law. This period was very short-lived and meant nothing in practice. None of the genuine Communists who were arrested enjoyed any sort of legal protection, and many were shot on the spot. The third period began after the proclamation of the emergency laws early in 1931, which stated that all revolutionaries arrested were to be handed over and dealt with by military tribunal. In the late spring of that year the Kuomintang Government launched a fierce offensive against the forces of the Revolution. In Kiangsi it carried out two encirclement campaigns against the Red Army, and throughout China it made use of its new emergency laws to persecute revolutionaries. During the fourth period which began in 1934 or thereabouts and extended right up until the final collapse of the Kuomintang in 1949 the Ch'en brothers and the fascist Blueshirt clique, the two rival factions in the Kuomintang's repressive apparatus, took charge of anti-Communist activities, each of them controlling organizations modelled on Hitler's Gestapo and Stalin's GPU.

The arrest of the Oppositionists came at the start of the third of these four periods. We were arrested in the British-Controlled

International Settlement in Shanghai and by rights should have
enjoyed the protection of extraterritoriality, but where revolutionaries were concerned British imperialists usually worked hand in
glove with Chiang Kai-shek. After spending one night in the police
station at T'i-lan-ch'iao, we were formally tried in the International
Settlement court and extradited to Chiang Kai-shek's Investigation
Corps. We then spent two or three days in the Pai-yün Temple
headquarters, where we were interrogated several times, and were
finally transferred to the Woosung–Shanghai Garrison Headquarters
in the Lung-hwa district of Shanghai.

Ch'en Tu-hsiu, the main target of the raid in which we were
arrested, managed to escape the dragnet. As only the smaller fish were
landed, the informer Ma Yü-fu and the police lost much of their
interest in their catch, and soon after we arrived at the gaol the
urgency which had surrounded our case was dispelled. After our
transfer to Lung-hwa the authorities seemed to forget our existence,
and we were totally ignored for six months. It was not until the
early autumn of 1931 that we were put on trial and formally
sentenced. Our trials were unremarkable. After the sentencing, we
were transferred to Ts'ao-ho-ching Prison to serve out our terms.

Our experiences in Lung-hwa Gaol were an eye-opener to what
was happening in the CCP. There were three cell blocks in the
Woosung–Shanghai Garrison Headquarters, each containing twenty
cells, and the gaol normally held some five to six hundred prisoners.
Within each block the cells were opened in the morning and locked
again at night, and during the daytime only the main door of the
block remained locked. Detainees therefore had a certain freedom of
movement, and the prison developed a sort of social life of its own.
Although a few prisoners were being held on suspicion of robbery or
kidnapping, most were there for political reasons. This created a
special atmosphere in the prison, one which I was sensitive to because of my previous experience in Wuhan gaol. The police cell in
Wuhan had only been for short-term detention and the prison
population was never static, but despite this a whole power structure
had grown up among the inmates, with a boss and a swarm of underlings who would blackmail newcomers or force them to sleep next
to the night-soil bucket. There were also other forms of maltreatment
which prisoners without relatives outside or valuable possessions
(such as clothes) to buy off their tormentors were forced to suffer.
At Lung-hwa practices of this sort had been totally eliminated by the

political prisoners, and a new system introduced whereby new-comers, whether in gaol for political or criminal offences, were automatically taken care of by old hands, who made sure that they received proper treatment. In this way people who had suddenly lost their freedom could settle down less painfully. This scheme worked so well that even hardened criminals and gangsters gave up their bullying and adapted themselves to the new regime.

In the cell blocks at Lung-hwa I came across many old friends, most of them victims of the 'Li Li-san line' and some of them arrested while acting as 'raw material' for the artificial 'new high tide'. There were also many who had been arrested as an indirect result of Wang Ming's coup, including several of the 'conciliation-ists' who had escaped execution. Among my acquaintances were Kuan Hsiang-ying and a number of other higher-level CCP cadres. Since the police did not know who they were, they had avoided transfer to Nanking, where almost certain death would have awaited them. Instead they were being kept on in Lung-hwa as hostages.

At that time, CCP members arrested in Shanghai were dealt with in one of three ways. There were first the top leaders, who were executed immediately. Most of them were handed over to the Kuomintang by the foreign authorities in the International Settle-ments, kept in a guardroom where a judge was brought in to 'identify' them, and then taken out to the airport or the prison yard to be shot. This was the fate of men such as P'eng P'ai, Hsiang Chung-fa, and Yang P'ao-an. The second category included both the so-called second-rank leaders and the very senior leaders whose cases had to be dealt with by the supreme authority, Chiang Kai-shek. Such people were detained for one or two days in the guardroom before being transferred to Nanking. The third category consisted of lower cadres, and any top leaders who had managed to escape recognition by the police or prison authorities. These people were left to be dealt with by the military tribunal of the Garrison Head-quarters. Their presence in gaol was welcomed by the Kuomintang military and police authorities, who saw them as an excellent source of ransom money. (Hence the Lung-hwa prison's nickname, the 'Kidnappers' den'.) The so-called investigation was in fact a bargain-ing process, after which one could expect either to be released or else to be sentenced to death or imprisonment.

The commander of the local garrison was General Hsiung Shih-hui. The head of the detention centre was, like him, from

Kiangsi, and was an old hand at ransom negotiations. He was not at all shamefaced about his dealings, and detainees could even take the initiative in asking him for an interview to discuss terms. He would also act as a middleman between detainees and the military judges, and would even allow relatives of the 'kidnap victims' to be present in his office while negotiations were taking place. Some prisoners were unaware of the secret dealings that went on, but if anyone had a visit from a relative who looked wealthy the chief warder would immediately instruct one of his men to go down to the cells and inform the visitor of the procedure for release. As a result, the so-called investigation period always dragged on for at least six months, and only when all attempts at negotiation had failed was the prisoner formally tried and sentenced.

Since the officials were running a big risk in parleying with the prisoners, the ransoms were high, and few of us were in a position to pay. Most of us came from poor families, and, even when prisoners did have rich relatives, they had usually long since broken off relations with them. In my experience every one of the prisoners ransomed from the gaol was close to the group in power in the Party, which raised the ransom-money on their behalf. Among those released in this way were Kuan Hsiang-ying, Ch'en Wei-jen, and Hsiang Chung-fa's secretary. The most striking case was that of Wang Ming's friend Ch'en Wei-ming (alias Sakov, one of the so-called Twenty-Eight Bolsheviks), whose release was arranged after only two or three days in prison. But there were other Communists who, although they belonged to the 'most important' category, were on bad terms with the Wang Ming leadership and were not ransomed for that very reason. Among this group was Li Chen-ying, a veteran revolutionary leader of the workers' movement in north China, a member of the Central Committee of the Party and a CCP delegate (together with Hsiang Chung-fa) to the Ninth Plenum of the Executive Committee of the Comintern held in Moscow in 1928. Li should have been among the first to be ransomed, but because he had sided with Ho Meng-hsiung and the others in the struggle against Wang Ming he was looked upon as a 'dissident', and was left to rot in gaol by the leadership. At this time there was a Comintern-sponsored body called the International Association for Aiding Revolutionaries, which specialized in aiding left-wing political prisoners throughout the world, Communists and non-Communists alike; but the Wang Ming leadership saw to it that Li Chen-ying did not get assistance even from this quarter. Instead he had to get by with the vegetables and other everyday necessities which we Trotskyists gave him. We also arranged somewhere for him to go when he got out of prison, to save him the humiliation of having to beg for his food, but despite our efforts he still had to spend several nights sleeping out on the pavement. Afterwards Li Chen-ying dropped out of politics altogether, returning to Tientsin where he worked under an assumed name as a shop-assistant, and I have no idea what happened to him after that. He was one of many such cases.

There was not the slightest trace of hostility between Party members and Oppositionists among the prison inmates. On the contrary, relations between the two groups were extremely friendly, and in conversations we held nothing back from each other. Cheng Ch'ao-lin in particular, with his modest ways and his great learning, won the love and respect of all the young Party members, at whose request he gave lessons every day in Communist theory and the history of the CCP. Even veteran leaders of the party like Kuan Hsiang-ying used to come along to listen to him. I too was very close to these young Communists, and often used to hold discussions with them. This was the first time I became aware of the extent of Wang Ming's influence within the Party. New arrivals at the prison would talk with great admiration of their leader 'Wang Ming, alias Ch'en Shao-yü' and quote in hushed tones from the great man's 'classic' work The Two Lines. It was saddening to hear these sincere young comrades naïvely voicing the praises of their new leader, as it was clear from what they said that, with the help of Stalin and Mif, Wang Ming's ambition had finally been achieved: he had become supreme leader in the Party. I was surprised that Wang Ming had realized his ambitions so quickly and I saw his success as a tragedy for the CCP and the Chinese Revolution. The Wang Ming cell was a cancerous growth in the Soviet bureaucracy, transmitted abroad to poison foreign revolutions; but here were these naïve young revolutionaries praising them as 'brilliant and far-seeing leaders'. I did not have the heart to destroy their illusions, since for many fresh recruits the leadership and the Revolution itself are one and the same thing, and in the purgatory of the counter-revolution, disillusionment with the former can easily lead to disillusionment with the revolutionary cause as a whole. But all this convinced me all the more of the need for a Trotskyist movement in China.

*

Three months after the date of our arrest Ch'en Tu-hsiu had got to-gether a handful of activists from among the remnants of the old Central Committee, including P'eng Shu-tse, and comrades like Sung Ching-hsiu from the rank and file of the movement, to set up a new provisional leadership. But then misfortune struck again. One day in the late summer of 1931 Yin K'uan, Sung Ching-hsiu, Chiang Chen-tung, and three or four other comrades, were arrested and brought to the 'kidnappers' den'. We were still being held in custody together at Lung-hwa when the Japanese Army began their seizure of northern China on 18 September 1931. A stormy anti-imperialist movement sprang up, and the whole political scene changed in favour of the Revolution. On hearing that the comrades under Ch'en Tu-hsiu had played a significant role in the new move-ment, our spirits rose, and we longed for release so that we could take our rightful part in it. Needless to say, neither our relatives nor the organization itself had been able to arrange a ransom for us, so our only hope of getting out of gaol remained a change in the political situation.

In October our cases came up for the first time before the military tribunal, but in practice our trial amounted to no more than a repeat of the interrogation we had been submitted to in the Investigation Corps Headquarters straight after our arrest. Immediately after the hearing we were all chained together at the ankles with heavy fetters. Our friends among the other inmates were very alarmed when they saw what was happening, since this was normally the prelude to an execution. It soon became clear that it was in fact an ultimatum from the 'kidnappers' – pay up or be shot. We Trotskyists were penniless and quite unable to raise the sort of sums asked, so there was nothing for it but to resign ourselves to our fate. Each of us remained calm in spirit. Our fellow prisoners, all of them so-called Stalinists, were extremely sympathetic towards us, and even ordered us some pork cooked in soy sauce and honey, the only delicacy available from the prison kitchen. Soon after this we learned from our families that the only ones whose lives were in real danger were Cheng Ch'ao-lin and Ho Tzu-shen. They responded to the news magnificently, showing not the slightest sign of fear. Cheng Ch'ao-lin in particular was like a Buddhist priest who had attained the Way, and who knew before-hand the date of his own achievement of nirvana. He carried on with his lectures, and continued to play chess and to chat and joke with other prisoners. His behaviour deeply moved the 'Stalinist' prisoners.

At the time of writing these lines, Cheng Ch'ao-lin and Ho Tzu-shen are back in prison under their old 'friend' Mao Tse-tung, together with many other Trotskyist comrades. (In late 1927 Ho Tzu-shen had been head of the organization department and Mao secretary of the Hunan provincial committee of the CCP.) I say prison, but they may have suffered a worse fate at the hands of Mao's security forces. The Revolution is truly a 'devourer of men', and leaves no room for human warmth and friendship. I am bringing up these points not for sentimental reasons, but because in my opinion it is vital to testify at every possible opportunity that these precious Communists are absolutely not guilty of the charge of 'counter-revolutionary activities', and to show them as loyal champions of the proletariat and the socialist cause.

To return to 1931, we were kept in suspense about our fate for more than a month, until in November we were finally sentenced and transferred from the detention centre to a proper prison. It was only then we learned that Cheng Ch'ao-lin and Ho Tzu-shen were not to be shot after all. This cheered us up enormously. Just before we were transferred, our sentences were read out to us. Cheng Ch'ao-lin was given fifteen years, Ho Tzu-shen ten, Sung Feng-ch'un, Ch'en I-mou, Chiang Shang-shih, Lou Kuo-hua (who had in fact been sentenced a few weeks earlier), and myself six, and P'u Teh-chih two and a half. There were two reasons for P'u's relatively light sentence; first, his family managed to raise a little money towards his ransom, and second, Hsü Shih-ying, Kuomintang Ambassador to Tokyo, interceded on P'u's behalf at his brother's request.

First we were taken to the Second Kiangsu Model Prison at Ts'ao-ho-ching, where we spent only two months. On 28 January 1932, large-scale fighting against Japanese armed aggression broke out in the Woosung–Shanghai area, and we were all transferred to Hangchow, and from there to Soochow. My experiences at Ts'ao-ho-ching horrified me. I do not intend to waste much ink on the matter: it should be enough to point out that nine-tenths of the prisoners who had been transferred to Ts'ao-ho-ching from the Garrison Headquarters a year before perished in the prison sick-bay. Thanks to the chance intervention of Japanese imperialism our stay there was a short one and we were lucky enough to leave the prison alive; but if it had not been for this I would certainly have died within six months. Even before two months were out our comrade Ch'en I-mou fell sick and died, and by the time we were transferred to Hangchow

I was so ill that I could barely stand. To be sent to this prison was to be sentenced to death by a form of execution which differed from the firing squad only in being slightly more drawn out.

The Soochow Military Prison outside the city's P'an Gate was a paradise by comparison. The food consisted of unhulled rice, but unlike the rice in Ts'ao-ho-ching, which was a mixture of grit, gravel, and coal dust, it was edible. You could eat as much as you wanted, and there was real cabbage soup to go with it. But all this was of minor importance – the main thing was that in Soochow our morale was much better. When we first got there the prison authorities were relatively liberal and enlightened: the prisoners were allowed to have all kinds of books and magazines sent in, and the warders were more lenient than in Ts'ao-ho-ching. Prisoners were even allowed to communicate with each other between the different cells. All of us prepared study-plans, and wrote out long lists of books which we then asked friends and relatives to buy for us.

Altogether there were four hundred or so 'criminals' in the Military Prison, eight out of ten were political offenders, and only a small proportion military or criminal offenders in the usual sense of the words. There were a number of CCP members who had already been there for some time, some for a year or two and others for as much as three years. They had been divorced from the Party and from real political life for many months. The 'Li Li-san line', the 'Conciliationist faction', and the Trotsky–Stalin struggle were unknown to most of them. They therefore welcomed us Trotskyists without the slightest hesitation. To a limited extent they had succeeded in organizing the prison, and had led a number of struggles for better conditions. They had also established contact with the outside world, and even provided some of the comrades with the everyday necessities of life. As soon as they found out that we were Trotskyist Communists, their leader asked us to write an objective account of the reasons for the split and a summary of the arguments on either side, so that they could discuss them among themselves. We happily agreed to do as they asked, and I was chosen to write some of this material. I crouched down in a corner of the cell and wrote out an introduction to Trotskyism, while the Stalinist comrades kept watch for me at the cell door. After I had finished writing it, it was delivered to the next cell by means of the 'telephone wire', a small hole high in the wall through which a single light-bulb illuminated the cells on either side. In this way my document was read by all the political prisoners, and even though there were no sudden conversions, it created a good impression generally. Although there was contact between prisoners, we were still very isolated from one another, and it was impossible to have a full exchange of opinions. Needless to say, men who had paid the price of freedom for the sake of the Party were hardly likely to start doubting the correctness of their leadership after hearing only one side of the argument. But even if they were not willing to come over to us, they were not prepared to look upon us as heretics and even less so to join in the chorus denouncing us as counter-revolutionaries. In short, all the other political prisoners were extremely friendly towards us and showed not the slightest sign of hostility either before or after reading the document I had written, despite the fact that from beginning to end only a handful of them actually came over to our side.

We had been in Soochow only a few months when suddenly a large batch of prisoners was transferred to the First Military Prison in Nanking, among them Cheng Ch'ao-lin and Ho Tzu-shen. Lou Kuo-hua and I stayed behind. Once again our group had been split up. Earlier Chiang Shang-shih and Sung Feng-ch'un had been sent back to Ts'ao-ho-ching prison near Shanghai, but some months later Sung's relatives managed to secure his release.

In the late autumn of 1932, we received news from outside the prison that the entire Opposition leadership, headed by Ch'en Tu-hsiu, had been arrested during a raid. Apart from Ch'en himself, those seized included P'eng Shu-tse and his younger brother Tao-tse, Lo Shih-fan, and P'u Teh-chih and Sung Feng-ch'un, both of whom had been imprisoned along with us in 1931, and released only shortly before their re-arrest. This was another heavy blow for us, destroying the comparatively influential Trotskyist movement which had been built up in the wake of the Woosung–Shanghai fighting against Japan. It was to be several years before we succeeded in putting the pieces together again.

Altogether, Lou Kuo-hua and I spent four years in Soochow and were then released on parole having served two-thirds of our sentence. Those four years were marked by a monotonous regularity. It is true, of course, that life goes on everywhere. Even in a prison cell measuring ten feet by ten, with walls so high that it was like living at the bottom of a well, life continued to unfold.

Prisons have always been the universities of revolutionaries, and naturally we did not waste our four years in Soochow. Although I had had the good fortune to spend four years at university before going to prison, two of them in Peking and two of them in Moscow, my true university was gaol. Either because of lack of funds or because I was too busy doing other things I had never really got down to any systematic study in Peking or Moscow. It was not until I got to Soochow that I began to study economics and western classical philosophy in real earnest. However, I achieved no significant results in my studies, mainly because of the shortage of books. The prison regime was constantly changing, and the arrival of a new prison governor frequently meant the removal of all our literature.

Towards the end of 1934 I was released from gaol. Lou Kuo-hua was released a few months later. Years of physical and mental maltreatment had taken their toll of us, but as if that were not enough a still worse blow awaited us in the world outside: both our wives had found new partners while we were in gaol, and had kept the news from us until our release.

In the life of a revolutionary incidents of this sort are not uncommon and cannot be considered as tragedies, but this does nothing to lessen the impact of the blow on the person immediately concerned. I fell sick, and Lou Kuo-hua, who was in better physical shape than I, lived like a hermit for six months on a farm near Shanghai, licking his wounds.

When I returned to Shanghai at the end of 1934, the comrade mainly responsible for the running of the organization was Ch'en Ch'i-ch'ang. In conversation with him I discovered that but for him the organization would long ago have ceased to function. At first Liu Po-chuang and some other veteran comrades had tried to keep things going after the arrest of Ch'en Tu-hsiu and the others, but before long they had followed one another to Peking to take up posts as professors or lecturers at the university, after which the whole weight of the movement had fallen on the shoulders of Ch'en Ch'i-ch'ang.

Some time in 1933 or early 1934 two foreign journalists had come into contact with the Opposition in Shanghai. One of them, a veteran South African Communist with the adopted Chinese name of Li Fu-jen, had come over to Trotskyism at the end of the 1920s. The other was the American journalist Harold Isaacs, who had originally been a Stalinist sympathizer. Isaacs had started bringing out a left-wing English language periodical in Shanghai called China Forum, and in 1932 the CCP tried to get him to write an article attacking the recently-imprisoned Ch'en Tu-hsiu. They supplied him with false information defaming the Trotskyists, but the result was quite the opposite of what they had intended, and their squalid manoeuvres merely succeeded in driving him into our camp. After his conversion to Trotskyism, Isaacs had the idea of writing a history of the Chinese Revolution. He wound up his publishing enterprise, donated his printing press to the Opposition, and moved to Peking, where he employed Liu Jen-ching to translate Chinese materials for him. The two men soon settled down and gathered an active group of Peking students around them: three of them, Liu Chia-liang, Ssu Ch'ao-sheng, and Wang Shu-pen, later became relatively well known in the organization. When I got out of gaol Liu, Ssu, Wang, and another comrade called Hu (I never got to know his full name) had already moved from Peking to Shanghai and had set up a provisional Oppositionist organization, together with Li Fu-jen. These young comrades had received their theoretical training from Liu Jen-ching, and it is therefore not surprising that as soon as they got into the leadership they moved to settle accounts with Ch'en Tu-hsiu. Once again they brought up the whole catalogue of Ch'en's alleged crimes ('opportunism', 'slandering the Red Army', etc.) from which Trotsky had already exonerated him, and passed a resolution demanding that he either confess his guilt or be expelled. When Ch'en Ch'i-ch'ang, Yin K'uan (who had just left prison), and others heard of this they were appalled and protested vigorously, whereupon they too were 'expelled' from the organization.

The arrogance of these young comrades had something in common with that of the Wang Ming clique, since both groups had their international patrons. Of course, both Li Fu-jen and Isaacs were sincere revolutionaries (Li Fu-jen has remained a Trotskyist to this day, although Isaacs has reverted to being a bourgeois democrat), but they were unfamiliar with the Chinese Opposition, and therefore fell foul of Liu Jen-ching's demagogy. Isaacs even helped the latter to write a pamphlet in English (it was never published) called Five Years of the Chinese Left Opposition, which portrayed Liu Jen-ching as the Lenin or Trotsky of the Chinese Opposition: the text later formed the basis of Ssu Ch'ao-sheng's and Liu Chia-liang's political programme. In August 1933, Isaacs went to Norway and showed this document to Trotsky. The two men discussed it together, and Isaacs sent a transcript of the conversation back to China, where we published it as an appendix to the Chinese-language version of Trotsky's *Problems of the Chinese Revolution*. Many of Trotsky's criticisms were extraordinarily perceptive. For example, Isaacs recorded: 'He [Trotsky] found it laughable that Liu Jen-ching equates what he himself thinks with what the masses think'. Trotsky also expressed his impatience at some of the more trivial criticisms which Liu Jen-ching raised in his document, and, shaking his head in disagreement, said: 'To let future problems stand in the way of our first step towards activity – absurd, absurd!' As for the expulsion of Ch'en Tu-hsiu and the other comrades, Trotsky considered it absolutely impermissible.

The whole tragi-comedy stemmed from Liu Jen-ching's attempt to manipulate the naïvety of two foreign comrades and the vanity of a handful of younger ones as a means of avenging himself for what he saw as years of 'unfair treatment'. But the drama was to have a very short run. In the early summer of 1935, Ssu Ch'ao-sheng and three other comrades were arrested in Shanghai and Liu himself was arrested in Peking, after the organization had been infiltrated by a public utility worker who was a Kuomintang agent.

A series of important developments took place in the Communist movement throughout the world during the period of my imprisonment, in particular a change in status of the Trotskyist movement. As I described above, international Trotskyism at first looked upon itself as a faction within the world Communist movement, but now it took up an independent position outside the Comintern. The turning point was Hitler's accession to power in Germany. This provided decisive proof of the irreversible corruption of both the German Communist Party and international Communism as a whole, which shamefully surrendered without a fight in the face of the fascist onslaught. This was an event of historic importance, matched only by the capitulation of the Second International to imperialism in 1913. Trotsky declared that the Comintern was no longer reformable, and that a new start would have to be made. When I arrived back in Shanghai at the end of 1934, the movement to build a new International had already started up there, but, for various reasons of which I was not fully aware at the time, it did not get far. The official birth of the Communist League of China (to replace the Left

Opposition of the CCP) had to be postponed until the beginning of 1936.

After spending only a few days in Shanghai, I stayed for six months in a village near my home town recuperating from my illness, not returning to Shanghai until the summer of 1935. By this time Liu Jen-ching, Liu Chia-liang, and others had been arrested, and the Provisional Central Committee had ceased to function. Isaacs had left China for Europe, and although Li Fu-jen was still around the organization had no leading body. In the whole of Shanghai there were no more than thirty Oppositionists, but all were anxious to revive the organization. Ch'en Tu-hsiu smuggled a message out of prison proposing that a triumvirate of Ch'en Ch'i-ch'ang, Chao Chi, and myself should be set up, to sort out the affairs of the movement and to start up some sort of activity.

By this time Li Fu-jen, who was also keen to see the organization revived, was once again on good terms with Ch'en Ch'i-ch'ang and Yin K'uan, and they saw each other frequently. The main obstacle to the restoration of the Trotskyist group was Ch'en Tu-hsiu's burning hatred for Li Fu-jen, and Ch'en wrote letter after letter urging us never again to co-operate with the *Mao-tzu* ('Hairy Ones' – originally a nickname for the Russians, but afterwards applied indiscriminately to all foreigners). Ch'en Tu-hsiu's attitude was based on his experiences with foreign Communists over the previous ten years and more, since their role in the Chinese Revolution was more often than not a negative one. China also had her imitation 'hairies', most notably Wang Ming. They acted like houseboys for the colonialists, basking in their borrowed authority and ordering their Chinese comrades around. Ch'en Tu-hsiu had always hated behaviour of this sort, and for this reason had never really got on with the Comintern representatives in China. After the defeat of the Revolution in 1927, when Stalin – the greatest 'hairy one' of them all – took all the credit for himself and heaped all the blame on the shoulders of yesterday's collaborator, Ch'en could stomach no more, and from then on could not bear even the word 'foreigner'. To cap it all, these two new 'hairies', Li and Isaacs had suddenly turned up from nowhere and joined forces with a handful of youngsters barely out of school to make a long list of all his mistakes, demand a recantation, and – when this failed – pass a resolution expelling him from the organization!

After the collapse of the anti-Ch'en Provisional Central Committee in early 1935, Li Fu-jen, by now better informed about the Chinese Opposition, repeatedly asked Ch'en Ch'i-ch'ang to arrange for him to visit Ch'en in Nanking Gaol, but the latter categorically refused. After my own return to Shanghai from the countryside, Li Fu-jen contacted me through the woman comrade Li Ts'ai-lien and requested a meeting. At first I was reluctant, since from what I had already been told of the events of the past six months, I was hostile towards Li Fu-jen, but Ch'en Ch'i-ch'ang persuaded me to relent and the two of us met for a talk. The result was that I formed a very good impression of him. I asked straight out whether he had come to Shanghai as a representative of the International Secretariat of the Left Opposition. The question startled him, and he told me that he had come to China in the course of his work as a journalist and had never claimed to be a representative of the International Secretariat. He said that he had contacted the organization because he felt that it was his duty as a Trotskyist to do so, and asked me to convey this information to Ch'en Tu-hsiu. When I told Li that Liu Jen-ching had claimed that he had come to China in such a capacity, he was very indignant. With this problem out of the way we swapped news about the movement both in China and internationally, and freely voiced our opinions. I discovered that he was an honest and sincere comrade, and was neither a bureaucrat, as I had previously suspected, nor an adventurer, of which there were many in Shanghai at that time. His sole aim was to participate in the work of the organization and to use his time in China to give us whatever help he could. The sad thing was that his enthusiasm had been exploited by Liu Jen-ching in pursuit of Liu's own personal ambitions.

After our conversation I decided to work as hard as possible for the restoration of the organization. We soon managed to organize a conference of representatives of those comrades still living in Shanghai, and elected a provisional Central Committee consisting of Ch'en Ch'i-ch'ang, Yin K'uan, Chiang Chen-tung, Li Fu-jen, and myself, with Li Fu-jen as the secretary-treasurer. After repeated explanations by Ch'en Ch'i-ch'ang, Chao Chi, and myself, Ch'en Tu-hsiu finally gave his approval to our collaboration with the Mao-tzu.

CHAPTER 9

The Founding of Struggle and the Darkest Days of my Life

●●●

The Provisional Central Committee formed in late 1935 occupied an important position in the history of the Chinese Trotskyist movement. It was the most enduring and productive of all the bodies we established, reviving and expanding the organization, both in Shanghai and nationally. We began publishing a series of writings by international Oppositionists, and even more important, we started bringing out a monthly political organ called *Struggle* (Tou-cheng) and a theoretical organ called *Spark* (Huo-hua). Between spring 1936 and late 1942 these two periodicals were published almost without interruption.

The first task of the new leading body was to set up its own print-shop. When Harold Isaacs left Shanghai for Peking he had handed over a small printing press to the organization, but it had been sold to cover running expenses when Ssu Ch'ao-sheng and his three young comrades took over the leadership in 1934. We were not in a position to buy a new press, so some comrades who were printing workers rigged up a primitive wooden frame in which we inserted lead type: the latter was in fact our sole outlay. With this contraption we could turn out a reasonable-looking page of print in two colours. Our publications were so good, in fact, that Lu Hsün accused us of receiving 'dirty money', implying that we were financed by the Japanese. At first our print-shop was looked after by two comrades who were printing workers, but when one of them defected he tried to steal the printing press from us. We therefore staged a raid. Li Fu-jen, the foreign comrade, dressed up as an Inspector of the International Settlement police, and with two other Chinese comrades, disguised as detectives, burst into the defector's home and retrieved the press. For a long time after that, comrades Lin Huan-hua and Mao Hung-chien were in charge of printing.

The second task of the new leading body was to put the organization in order. In the Shanghai area we still had many contacts, and once the organization was on its feet again it was a relatively easy matter to start up activities. We then began to turn our attention to Hong Kong, which had been one of the Opposition's earliest bases. Many workers there had been part of the organization, but over the years most of them had lost contact with the centre, as a result of the repeated arrest of the leading members in Shanghai and elsewhere. So in May 1936 it was decided that I should go south to re-establish contact with them. I stayed a month in the colony, and worked with Comrade Lo, a former member of the Proletarian Society, and Comrade Ch'en Chung-hsi, who later died at the head of a Trotskyist guerrilla unit during the War of Resistance against Japan. We re-united a dozen or so cadres, set up a local organization and, following the example of Shanghai, built a primitive printing press with which we began to publish a paper called *Sparkle* (Huo-hsing). Earlier, after we had lost contact with Hong Kong, certain comrades there had ill-advisedly got mixed up with Chang Po-chün's Third Party. It was my first job therefore to draw the line clearly between ourselves and them and to put an end to the attempts of some comrades to straddle the two parties. Reviving the tradition of the two Trotskyist martyrs, Ou Fang and Ch'en I-mou, the comrades immediately turned their efforts towards the industrial proletariat. Li Fu-jen, who had gone with me to Hong Kong, made use of his special status as a foreigner to bring our south China friends large quantities of Oppositionist literature. It was the first time for many years that they had had a chance to read publications of this sort.

At the same time our organization was unexpectedly reinforced by an influx of young comrades in Kwangsi, a province in which our leadership had never made any special efforts. Chang T'e, who as I mentioned abandoned Trotskyism after the unification of the four groups in 1931, had returned to Kwangsi, where Huang Kung-tu, a powerful associate of the leading local warlords, cultivated him. Although Huang had studied in Moscow, he had never had any links with the Opposition, and as far as I know did not even join the Communist Party, but despite this he made Chang T'e his confidant after his return to Kwangsi. When the Kwangsi warlords came out in open opposition to Chiang Kai-shek, putting on a left 'face' for the occasion, many Communists who had either left the Party or kept up their membership secretly were summoned to Kwangsi to rally support for the local authorities. At the same time a power struggle was going on inside the Kwangsi clique between Huang Kung-tu's group and another faction within the local bureaucracy. To strengthen his hand Huang Kung-tu managed to summon a number of ex-Trotskyists to Kwangsi with the help of Chang T'e. None of those who accepted Chang T'e's invitation was still a member of the Opposition at that time. Most of them were assigned to work as teachers at Kwangsi middle schools or universities, and among them was Shih T'ang. Shih T'ang had earlier left the movement but, as the saying has it, 'even when the lotus root breaks the fibres hold together'. In his contacts with students he continued to propagate his old beliefs, and as a result won many over to Trotskyism. By the time that we had set up the Provisional Central Committee, the Kwangsi group had already established direct links with us in Shanghai, and before long they sent representatives to Shanghai for discussions. The two comrades mentioned above, Lin Huan-hua and Mao Hung-chien, were among the members of the delegation, and as I recall, the third member was a comrade called Mo Chün-ch'i.

There was no organization of ours functioning in north China at this time. When the four factions had unified in 1931, the former Octobrist and Proletarian groups had been quite strong in north China, especially in Peking. I had heard while in prison that after the arrest of Ch'en Tu-hsiu and others big campaigns to free Ch'en had been launched in Peking. In many universities students supporting Ch'en and Stalinist students who opposed him had demonstrated in equal strength at a number of rallies. But around 1934, after Shih Ch'ao-sheng and others went south to Shanghai and Liu Jen-ching was arrested and thrown in gaol, the activities of the organization in Peking had come to a halt. In Shantung, a group of comrades kept up political work and succeeded in building a base in many counties of the area. After the establishment of the Provisional Central Committee – I think it was in the summer of 1936 – they sent a delegation to Shanghai to re-establish links with the centre. Among the delegates was Comrade L., one of the few comrades who has survived and remained loyal to the cause to this day.

Trotskyist activities in Wenchow, the ancient city in south-east Chekiang province, were still only in their infancy during this period. The comrades there did not establish contact with us until some time later. Events in the Wenchow area had taken a similar course to those in Kwangsi, and it was almost as if a group of young Trotskyists had sprung up spontaneously from nowhere. The seeds of Trotskyism had in fact been planted in Wenchow by a man called

Tseng Meng, who like Shih T'ang in Kwangsi, had earlier left the movement. Tseng Meng had become a Trotskyist while in Moscow and had been arrested together with Ch'en Tu-hsiu and the others, but he had soon been released when his family used contacts he had made during his days at the Whampoa Military Academy. Before leaving gaol he was made to sign a document denouncing Trotskyism, and naturally took steps to avoid meeting us; he returned instead to Wenchow, his home town, where he lived like a recluse. Eventually he joined up with a group of young people, and explained the ideas of Trotskyism to them. Although he did not mean to spread propaganda on our behalf, many Wenchow Middle School students came over to our side as a result of their contact with him. Together with Chungshan county in Kwangtung province, Kwangsi, and Shantung, Wenchow was later to become one of the four main areas from which the Chinese Trotskyist movement recruited its second and third generations of cadres.

Although it is not uncommon in the history of revolutionary parties for people to leave the organization, either voluntarily or under pressure, in order to protect themselves and their families, they often secretly or unconsciously despise themselves for abandoning the cause. As reactionary political governments grow more and more corrupt, incompetent, and unpopular, their schizophrenia deepens. No matter how rich or successful the renegades become in their new professions, many find it impossible to shake off their earlier convictions. They often continue to sympathize with the aims of the Revolution, maintain old friendships and, under certain conditions, even appear to make partial amends for their past weakness by making new recruits to the movement, as did Shih T'ang and Tseng Meng. When the Revolution once again enters a period of upsurge and the revolutionary party grows in influence, people of this sort more often than not return to the ranks and resume the struggle. It is true, of course, that careerism and human weakness can also play a part in this, and that such 'conversions' can be an important factor in speeding up the degeneration of the revolution. But the phenomenon of the return of the 'revolutionary prodigals' has its roots in the depths of society and human nature, and if the Party is to be built there is, generally, nothing for it but to accept such people at face value.

When the leaders of the newly-unified Chinese Opposition were rounded up, those members of the four organizations who had not by then been brought into the new structure often drifted off and lost all contact. Many of them were worthless, but some of these comrades were schizophrenics of the sort I have just mentioned. We were often approached by young people who had found their way to Trotskyism by involved and circuitous routes, and when we asked who had first introduced them to Trotskyist ideas they would mention some name which we only vaguely remembered from the distant past, or in some cases had never heard before.

By the time our organization had reunited, Hitler had already been in power for over a year, and Germany was advancing towards militarism, thus hastening the outbreak of the Second World War. The Japanese imperialists had already invaded Manchuria and parts of the Yellow River valley, and central China was clearly their next target.

Stalin responded to the military threats from Germany and Japan by raising the 'popular front' slogan at the Seventh Congress of the Comintern in August 1935. Now he was willing to collaborate not only with the social democrats, whom only yesterday he had derided as 'social fascists', but with all kinds of democrats, including 'democratic' imperialists, in the name of anti-fascism. Meanwhile, at home he was stepping up his persecution of revolutionaries and had begun to carry out his policy of killing off the entire generation of old Bolsheviks.

The Kuomintang Government, still pursuing its policy of 'internal pacification before resistance to the invader', made repeated concessions to the Japanese imperialists in order to concentrate all its forces against the Communist armies in Kiangsi province. In late 1934 it scored a decisive military victory, forcing the Red Army to set out on its famous Long March to the north.

In January 1935, at a meeting of the CCP Central Committee's Politbureau at Tsunyi in Kweichow province, during the Long March, Mao Tse-tung took over from Wang Ming as the real leader of the Party. This represented a victory of 'indigenous' Communists over Stalin's representatives in China. On 1 August of the same year, in line with Moscow's new 'popular front' policy, the CCP issued a manifesto calling for an end to the Civil War and unity with the Kuomintang against Japan, an abandonment of the class struggle, and the drawing up of a programme for resistance. In October the

Communist armies established a new base in north Shensi province.

It was in this political climate that *Struggle* was born. Since I have lost all my records, I have no way of checking exactly when the first issue came out, but it was some time in the spring of 1936. The first article – which I wrote – was an open letter to the CCP, attacking the Party's new 'popular front' line.

The publication of *Struggle* fulfilled a very urgent political need, and could not have come at a better time. Both at home and abroad a period of rapid change had begun. With each turn of events people were becoming more and more confused. Everyone was keen to understand the situation and eager to get involved in some practical political activity. In a limited way, *Struggle* was the answer some of them were looking for. As far as we Trotskyists were concerned, this period had a special significance, since it confirmed in every detail the analysis of the future path of the Chinese Revolution which Trotsky had made in 1929. For the previous four or five years the Stalinists had been calling us the 'Trotsky–Ch'en liquidationist faction'. We had argued that there was no longer even a revolutionary situation after the autumn of 1927, let alone the actual conditions for a revolutionary uprising; that the most one could hope for was a struggle along democratic or national lines; and that the Chinese proletariat and its Party should put forward a revolutionary demo-cratic programme calling for an all-powerful constituent assembly, so that they could then lead such democratic struggles and prepare the way for a new socialist revolution. The Stalinists were fundament-ally opposed to this approach, and for five long years had carried out their so-called 'leftist' line on the mistaken premise that a 'new high tide of revolution was imminent', so that in the towns the CCP organization was completely smashed, and in the countryside their armed forces were on the brink of annihilation.

Meanwhile, as a result of continuous Japanese aggression against China and the creeping capitulation to it of the Kuomintang, an upsurge of anti-Japanese and anti-Kuomintang feeling was taking place in the cities, particularly among the petty bourgeoisie. This nationalist awakening was exploited by bourgeois politicians active in the National Salvation Association, a patriotic body formed in 1935, and by other organizations. Such developments were a com-plete vindication of what we in the Chinese Trotskyist movement had been arguing for years, and pointed clearly to the need for a revolutionary-democratic programme along the lines that we had been proposing. But when Stalin announced his change of policy, members of the CCP were transformed overnight from out and out 'leftists' into out and out rightists. For years they had constantly misrepresented and caricatured our democratic programme, but suddenly they took up positions identical with all the worst features of the caricatures they had made of us. For years they had been accusing us of 'liquidationism', and now they themselves were pursuing an active liquidationist line, disguised as a struggle for democracy. Only yesterday they had condemned any call for a constituent assembly as treason to the Revolution. Now they not only demanded a constituent assembly (devoid, of course, of any revolutionary content), but were even prepared to drop the class struggle, reorganize the Red Army, and swear allegiance to Sun Yat-sen's Three People's Principles (nationalism, livelihood, and demo-cracy), all in order to get the Kuomintang to join in a popular front with them. The change was so dramatic and so sudden that not only people outside the Party but even Party members themselves were left dazed. Mao Tse-tung himself was taken aback. In *Thirty Years of the Chinese Communist Party* the orthodox Maoist historian Hu Ch'iao-mu described these events as follows:

At that time there was a pressing need to make a correct analysis of the situation in the country following on the Japanese invasion, to decide on Party policy and to rectify the prevailing current of 'left' closed-door sectarianism in the Party. The Party Central Committee had proved in-capable of completing these tasks during the years 1931 to 1934, and Comrade Mao Tse-tung was also unable to complete them in the course of the Long March of 1935. It was only with the help of the Comintern's correct policy of the anti-fascist united front that this need could be met.[1]

From this extremely guarded passage it is possible to discern that it was not Mao who 'completed' the new liquidationist policy to-wards the Kuomintang, but the Comintern (i.e. Stalin), and that the new line in China simply followed the one adopted by Communist Parties throughout the world.

We were the only group capable of expressing a critical view of the Party line – in the pages of our organ *Struggle*. The tragedy was that our equipment was primitive and our 'productive forces' un-developed, so the best we could bring out was a four-page monthly

[1] *Thirty Years of the Chinese Communist Party*, first published in Peking, June 1951, and reprinted by the People's Publishers, Canton, July 1951.

with a run of 200 copies. But because *Struggle* appeared regularly over a period of years, it steadily grew in influence.

I would now like to recount an episode connected with the new turn taken by the CCP: the correspondence between Ch'en Ch'i-ch'ang and Lu Hsün on the question of the anti-Japanese united front. At the time there were two different attitudes to the CCP's new turn among left-wing writers and intellectuals in Shanghai. Although I never had the chance to read all the relevant material on this debate, in essence it revolved around the problem of whether literature should encourage struggle or collaboration between classes. The main proponent of class struggle was Lu Hsün, who was rather more insistent on the original position of the League of Left-Wing Writers.[1] The main advocates of class collaboration were Hsü Mao-yung and Chou Ch'i-ying (better known as Chou Yang), who unconditionally supported the CCP's new line on literature. Seen in its broader context, this struggle was simply a manifestation of the transition in Stalinist thinking from the 'Third Period' phase to the Popular Front. Lu Hsün was unhappy with the new slogan of 'a literature of national defence' proposed by Hsü Mao-yung and Chou Yang, and proposed instead the slogan 'a literature of the masses for revolutionary war'. In our view the old 'Third Period' philosophy and the new Popular Front line were equally disastrous, but we admired Lu Hsün as a great writer who had sympathized all along with the struggle of the oppressed and downtrodden, and who had never capitulated to nationalism in any of its forms. Although never a Marxist he had advocated 'proletarian literature' for many years and fought fiercely against both the Kuomintang hack writers and the advocates of a 'Third Line',[2] so it was not surprising that he bitterly resented the sudden change of front. When we heard about the dispute Ch'en Ch'i-ch'ang became very excited and wrote Lu Hsün a letter, enclosing some back issues of *Struggle* and some Chinese translations of

[1] The League of Left-Wing Writers was inaugurated in March 1930 in Shanghai, and consisted of most of the pro-Communist writers of that time, including Lu Hsün.

[2] These were a group of writers in the mid-1930s in Shanghai, mainly represented by the magazine *Hsien-tai* (*Contemporary Magazine*). They rejected both Kuomintang nationalism and 'proletarian literature'. Their leader was the poet Tai Wang-shu.

pamphlets by Trotsky. These were sent to the Uchiyama Book Company in Shanghai, a shop Lu Hsün frequented. Lu Hsün's reply was first published in the magazine *Reality* (*Hsien-shih*). The gist of his letter was that he was amazed to see how well *Struggle* was produced, and suspected that it was financed by the Japanese.

I was in Hong Kong when Ch'en Ch'i-ch'ang wrote his letter. Since he had not discussed its contents with any of the other members before sending it, he came in for heavy criticism from the rest of us. Ch'en Tu-hsiu in particular, who was still in Nanking gaol at the time, flew into a rage when he heard the news, and demanded to know how we came to have illusions about Lu Hsün. In his opinion the relationship between Lu Hsün and the Communist Party was the same as that between Wu Chih-hui and the Kuomintang: both of them were flattered by the attentions paid to them, eager to show their gratitude, and totally incapable of pursuing the truth for its own sake, without regard for the consequences. Ch'en Ch'i-ch'ang, who idolized Lu Hsün, felt very bitter when he read his reply, not so much because of the slanderous assertions it made against him personally, as because of the discovery that even a man of 'unbending morality' could end up parroting the Party line and stooping to the sort of tactics he had hitherto despised, by hinting that we took Japanese money. Ch'en Ch'i-ch'ang wrote another letter to Lu Hsün, but received no reply. Shortly after this Lu Hsün died, and six years later Ch'en Ch'i-ch'ang was murdered by the Japanese in Shanghai. At the time I also thought that Ch'en Ch'i-ch'ang had acted rather rashly in writing the letter, but since the correspondence was included in Lu Hsün's *Collected Works* and readers can decide for themselves who was right, perhaps it was not such a bad thing to have done after all.

In their struggle against Trotskyism the Chinese Stalinists never once met us on the theoretical plane, but gaoled or executed our supporters in the areas they controlled; and, in areas they did not control, spread rumours and slanders about us, in particular the accusation that we took money from the enemy. To put the record straight, I will outline our financial situation when we were publishing *Struggle*. Our expenses totalled just over fifty dollars a month: thirteen for the rent of our print-shop in a small detached house in the French Concession in Shanghai; thirty to support the two printer comrades; and about ten for items such as newsprint and ink. We had no other expenses, since all our cadres were expected not only to earn their own living but also to give ten per cent of what they earned in party dues. Those of us in the leadership who earned our living through literary activities of one sort or another were often very poorly paid, and our meagre dues came nowhere near meeting organizational costs. Our expenses were therefore almost always met by the foreign comrade, Li Fu-jen. But where did Li Fu-jen get his money from? Was his money dirty? When he first came to Shanghai, Li Fu-jen had been a reporter on the *Shanghai Evening Post* and then on the *Shanghai Times*. During his last three years in Shanghai, he was the assistant editor of the *China Weekly Review*, with a monthly salary of some three hundred dollars. It was as a Communist and a member of our organization that Li Fu-jen helped to finance our activities in China.

In August 1936 Moscow staged the notorious trial of the so-called 'anti-Soviet Trotsky centre'. Sixteen members of the Bolshevik Old Guard, headed by Lenin's comrade-in-arms Zinoviev and the top Party theoretician Kamenev, were accused of organizing a 'conspiracy to overthrow the Soviet Government in order to restore capitalism in Russia', in collusion with Trotsky, then living abroad in Norway. If the charges were absurd, even more absurd was the way in which these old revolutionaries stepped forward one after another to plead guilty. As a result, all of them were sentenced to be shot. Apart from the religious Inquisition of the Middle Ages, the world had never seen such a spectacle. What was happening in Moscow, and how could it be accounted for? People all over the world were shocked at the news of the trials, and questions such as these plagued friends and foes alike of the Soviet Union. It was only natural, therefore, that *Struggle* should devote itself more and more to coverage of this issue. With what little knowledge of the situation we had, we advanced various explanations of the tragedy then unfolding in Moscow, and translated and published all that Trotsky himself wrote on the subject.

At this point I want to introduce Wang Meng-tsou, owner of the Oriental Book Company, into my story. Wang Meng-tsou was a most remarkable man. His book company was in existence for over fifty years, from the late 1890s to 1952, but he was much too far ahead of his time to make any money. If a new ideological current was being persecuted and the authors associated with it could not find a publisher, then he would publish them. But by the time such ideas had become the vogue, he would already have moved on, so that the books which yesterday nobody had wanted to buy but which today were best sellers made fortunes not for him but for other companies. In the meantime Wang Meng-tsou would be busy publishing some new item of *avant-garde* literature. Time passed and there were many changes, but Wang Meng-tsou's way of life stayed much the same, with the result that he always found himself in the company of the persecuted, and generally speaking shared their fate.

Wang Meng-tsou was a lifelong friend of Ch'en Tu-hsiu, and I got to know him through Ch'en. I had just been released from Soochow Gaol, and was completely destitute. Wang Meng-tsou was planning to bring out a series entitled *Lives of Bourgeois-Democratic Revolutionaries*, and hoped to get his old friend Ch'en Tu-hsiu, who at the time was still in Nanking Gaol, to be its chief editor. Ch'en Tu-hsiu asked me to stand in for him, and to edit the series jointly with Dr. T'ao Hsing-chih, one of Chiang Kai-shek's political opponents and later a leader of the anti-Japanese National Salvation Society. In fact the project never got off the ground, but Wang Meng-tsou and I became friends for life, and for a long period I depended on him for my livelihood, working as an 'editor' for his book company at a monthly salary of twenty dollars. During all that time I never once edited a single volume for him, since he was very short of the necessary capital for new projects. But in the autumn of 1936, after the Moscow trials had shaken world opinion, old Wang suddenly got very excited and decided that, whatever the cost, he must reveal the truth about what was going on in Stalinist Russia. We discussed the matter, and decided as a first step to bring out two small books, *The Moscow Trials and World Public Opinion* and *The Truth about the Moscow Trials*. They were to consist partly of original material, which I was to write, and partly of translations from the European and American left-wing press. The first book did not take long to produce, and I had already got some way through the second when I was once again arrested by Kuomintang special agents and taken off to gaol. Fortunately Ch'en Ch'i-ch'ang took over from where I had left off, and the second volume appeared soon afterwards. Ch'en Ch'i-ch'ang also translated for Wang Meng-tsou Trotsky's famous speech I *stake my life*, and parts of the Dewey Commission report on the Moscow trials, which had found that the whole affair was a massive frame-up and exonerated Trotsky and his son Sedov completely.

*

As far as I remember, only two issues of our theoretical organ *Spark* came out before I was arrested for the third time. The most important articles in them concerned the preparations for the Fourth International and Trotsky's criticisms of both the 'Popular Front' and the new Soviet Constitution. Apart from these, I should also mention Ch'en Tu-hsiu's thesis on democracy, which signalled an important change in his thinking, in effect representing a retreat on his part after two decades of uninterrupted advance. After his imprisonment and his enforced separation from the struggle, Ch'en Tu-hsiu's thinking began to show signs of retrogression. At first he voiced doubts on the nature of the Soviet Union, which in his view was no longer either a workers' state, or even, as Trotsky analysed it, a degenerate workers' state. He argued that once the working class had been driven out of the state machinery it could by definition no longer be called a proletarian state, and therefore characterized the Soviet Union under Stalin as a bureaucratic state. This was an emotional and instinctive response to the Moscow trials, rather than a thoroughly thought-out piece of historical and sociological research. Later he made a serious study of the historical evolution of democracy, in which he concluded that the history of mankind was essentially the history of the development of democracy, and that, from the time when slave society had destroyed the democracy of primitive communism down to the present, the replacement of one social form by another had invariably signified a qualitative development and extension of democracy – even though historical development did not follow a linear path. This led him to his second conclusion; namely that democracy, apart from being the most reliable indicator of whether a given society is progressive or reactionary, was completely devoid of all class character, and certainly not specific to the bourgeoisie. It was reactionary for socialists to reject democracy on the grounds that it pertained to a class other than the proletariat, since a workers' state would by definition be much more democratic than a capitalist state.

Not one of us agreed with these views of his. We thought that by raising democracy above class as a historical factor he had reduced it to an abstraction. As I followed Lenin's line on democracy, it was decided that I should write a reply to Ch'en's article, to be published alongside it in *Spark*. At the time I was in the middle of reading Trotsky's *Communism and Terrorism*, which contains many excellent arguments refuting Kautsky's ideas on democracy, so I translated a

number of passages from the book and sent them to Ch'en Tu-hsiu
for him to read. They had no effect on him, however, and he stuck to
his guns. After the signing of the Hitler–Stalin pact in 1939, he even
began to urge support for the democratic powers against the Soviet
Union, thus completing his ideological break from Trotskyism.
Some of his writings from this period were afterwards published in
Shanghai by his pupil Ho Tzu-shen.

Between 1936 and 1937 the Kuomintang carried out a number of
important improvements to its machinery of repression, entering
what I earlier called the 'fourth period' – the period of 'scientific
repression'. Shortly after the new Provisional Central Committee of
our organization came into being, Yin K'uan suddenly disappeared,
and many weeks later we learned that he was being held in the secret
prison of the Kuomintang special service. At about the same time
Han Chün happened to be released from another prison, so he took
Yin K'uan's place on the Central Committee. Han Chün told us that
special agents were everywhere, and were extremely interested in our
group. He warned us to improve our security, but even he did not
really know just how the special agents operated and what methods
of surveillance they were using, so we were unable to take effective
precautions against spying and infiltration. In March or April 1937 a
worker who had been arrested together with Yin K'uan and later
freed bumped into Ch'en Ch'i-ch'ang and had a quiet conversation
with him, explaining how he had been arrested, forced to recant his
ideas, and subsequently released from prison. He warned Ch'en that
we could not continue working in the old way, as we were already
under close scrutiny from the special agents, who could finish us off
whenever they chose. He told Ch'en that he wanted to wash his hands
of the movement, and said he was only telling him all this for the
sake of past friendship.

Ch'en immediately became very excited and rushed over to my
place to tell me the news. We realized that the situation was serious,
but suspected that the man who had given the warning might have
become a special agent himself, and might therefore have been
deliberately exaggerating the danger. We agreed that we had to be
more vigilant, but that there could be no question of abandoning our
old way of working. Shortly afterwards, Ch'en Ch'i-ch'ang was on
his way to visit Han Chün one afternoon when he spotted two men
in workmen's overalls behaving suspiciously outside the front door

of Han's house. He abruptly turned round and started walking back the way he had come, with the two agents closely shadowing him. After several hours he managed to shake them off, and hurried back to Han Chün's place to warn him of the danger. Han Chün had no time to pack any of his belongings: if he had hesitated for a moment, he would almost certainly have been re-arrested. All the other comrades who might have been in danger of arrest were ordered to leave their homes immediately. Thus we successfully weathered yet another storm.

The situation was indeed extremely serious. The CCP underground organization in Shanghai had been defunct for many years, partly as a result of Kuomintang repression and partly following the Party's decision to withdraw to their bases in the countryside. Now the Kuomintang clearly intended to uproot our organization as well, fearing that we might benefit from the anti-imperialist mass movement growing up as a result of Japanese aggression in north China. We were very aware of the imminent danger, but there was little we could do. Calling a halt to our activities was obviously out of the question. Should we then follow the example of the CCP and leave the cities? But we had no bases to retreat to, and in any case our orientation towards the working class would not allow us to leave Shanghai. There was no alternative but to carry on and take the consequences. In May 1937, the inevitable happened and I was arrested by Kuomintang special agents, exactly a year after I had married for the second time, and a few weeks after the birth of my daughter.

In a way, I profited from the disaster of my arrest, for I got to know a great deal about the new 'scientific' police techniques which the Kuomintang had learned from Stalin and Hitler. Today Hitler and Stalin are dead, but their 'science' lives on in ever more parts of the world, and many of my close friends are even now suffering as a result. That is why I intend to devote rather more space to my experience of such methods than my own importance warrants. Any bitterness I might feel is secondary; my real aim is to denounce the system in all its barbarity and inhumanity.

I was arrested in the French Concession of Shanghai by two plain-clothes agents. They acted in complete disregard for all legal procedures, simply pointing a pistol at me, dragging me into a car parked nearby, and speeding off to the Special Service headquarters in the Chinese area of the city. Immediately on arrival I was dragged off to the interrogation chamber, and subjected to non-stop 'hot and cold' treatment for over forty hours. At first I was 'welcomed' by a young man speaking with a Shensi accent, who said he was an old friend of mine and asked me if I recognized him. This was of course a lie, but it was clear that at one time or another he had been a member of the Communist Party. After some polite remarks, he produced pen and paper and told me to make a voluntary confession, adding that we were not in a prison but in a centre for making voluntary confessions. I told him that if I was not under arrest I did not have to do so and that by rights I should be free to go. He then said that he would dispense with the confession; all I had to do was give him the addresses of a few comrades. He would invite them to come and make voluntary confessions, and I myself would be set free. I replied that as all my friends were non-political there was no point in bringing them there. Just then two burly thugs rushed in from the next room shouting at the young man that there was no need to be polite with me. One of them grabbed me by the shoulders, while the other smashed a thick piece of wood on the back of my head. Everything turned black, and I fell unconscious. After a while I came to. I had a splitting headache. Several ferocious men were looking down at me, arms akimbo. They were just about to start on me again when two other men – these with kind, smiling faces – intervened to push them aside. They offered me a cup of tea and feigned 'concern' at the wound on the back of my head. One of them, who seemed to be the leader, even pretended to upbraid the others for beating me. Ordering them to leave the room, he sat down opposite me and 'sincerely apologized' for what had happened.

I was disgusted by the whole spectacle. Every one of them was an atrocious actor, but they were not in the least concerned with audience reaction, staging the same performance over and over again. Finally they reduced their demands to only one: I should tell them the addresses of three comrades, and then I would be free to go. By this time I could see there was no point in shamming ignorance or giving them misleading answers, so I told them directly that, do what they would, they would never get a single address out of me. The same afternoon, after seven or eight hours of the 'hot and cold' routine, the little drama reached its climax. I was dragged off into a special room by a gang of thugs. One of them gagged me and threw me down on the floor. I lay there flat on my face, with my legs tied tightly together, while men on either side of me jerked up my arms, and two others clubbed me on the back of the thighs and on the ankles. I am not sure how long this went on, for I lost consciousness after about thirty blows. By the time I came to, I was lying in an armchair in another room.

Once again it was time for the 'warm spell'. My 'old friend' asked me if I was hungry. I did not answer, but he went ahead and ordered me a meal of fried rice. I had eaten nothing all day, but I did not touch it, since I had completely lost my appetite. He then told me that I should 'look after my health', and think of my wife and daughter. Once again he asked me to hand over the addresses, but I ignored him. The gentle approach having seemingly reached stalemate, the strong-arm men made another entrance, but the 'gentlemen' motioned them out again. I was now left alone in the room with just one man, who stood there looking at me. The atmosphere was very tense. The men in the next room were pretending to have an argument, just loud enough for me to catch the drift of it. The man who stayed behind with me pretended to be sympathetic, and said: 'Why go through it all again? You'll have to give in eventually, everyone does once they get in here. Use your brains. What's the point in resisting?' I was inwardly composed, having had ample experience by now of their torture, and knowing exactly what to expect. The worst they could do was kill me. The torturers came in again, and I braced myself for the onslaught. Two ordered me to get up and go with them. I could not stand, so each grabbed an arm and I was frog-marched out of the room. I thought I was in for another beating, but to my surprise I was deposited in a bare cell with wooden bars. They told me to get some rest. I lay down on the ground, my whole body racked with pain and bleeding from the head and ankles, but far too tired to feel depressed and wanting only to sleep. I closed my eyes, but within five minutes a group of men rushed into the cell and dragged me out. By now I was completely incapable of supporting myself, and they had to carry me.

To my astonishment I found a group of scholarly-looking gentlemen waiting for me. There were several armchairs in the room, grouped around a small circular table, on which were tea and cigarettes. I was told to help myself. As I was carried into the room the 'scholars' stood up and helped me to an armchair, with expressions of sympathy on their faces. After that one of them began to speak, saying that he wanted to exchange opinions with me and discuss a few questions: that they were entirely without any preconceived ideas and that all they were interested in was the truth. He also told me that if I managed to persuade them of my ideas they would join me, but if as a result of our discussion I decided that they were right, then they hoped I would follow their example of open-mindedness and go over to their side. After he had outlined the aim of the meeting, another one of the 'scholars' suggested that we should discuss the 'nature of the Chinese Revolution'. Despite the horror of it all I could see the humour in the situation and felt like laughing, but this impulse was immediately submerged by a wave of anger. The discussion continued, and one after another the 'scholars' stepped forward with 'brilliant arguments' in the service of the 'truth'. Gradually my anger and hatred dissipated, and I began to see them as pathetic. The fact that such shameless cynics could exist on this earth made me want to weep. They spoke as if they had been wound up like gramophones beforehand, and what they called a 'discussion' was in fact the same old record played over and over again: all they had to do was open their mouths, and out it came. The argument went as follows: the Chinese Revolution was bourgeois in character – Lenin, Stalin, Trotsky, all were unanimous on this point – and, as 'scholars', they agreed with this view. It was therefore only natural that Generalissimo Chiang Kai-shek should lead the Revolution. Like Mao Tse-tung, we Trotskyists committed one absolutely unforgivable error: while we admitted that the Revolution was bourgeois in character, we refused to recognize that Chiang Kai-shek, the Kuomintang, and the bourgeoisie were the leaders of the Revolution. As a result, we did nothing but cause trouble and disruption, thus preventing Chiang from completing the Revolution. Not only were we acting contrary to the needs of the Revolution, but we were violating the instructions of Lenin and Trotsky. Therefore, they concluded, if I wanted to be a true Marxist–Leninist, I should put my trust in the Kuomintang.

At first I said nothing in reply, but when they pressed me I told them that I was ignorant of theoretical questions. Finally I could stand it no longer, and said that if they really wanted a discussion with me they should first restore my freedom, since between prisoner and gaoler no discussion was possible. At this point some 'experts' of the other sort took over and ordered me to my feet, but by now I was incapable of standing. They again ordered me to get up, saying that I could rest against the table if I needed to. When I collapsed they told me for a third time to get up, and one of them fired a single question at me: 'Where does Ch'en Ch'i-ch'ang live?' All I had to do was answer that one question and I could go back to my cell and sleep. If they actually managed to catch him as a result of my tip-off, they would set me free immediately. I said nothing, and they started screaming at me like frenzied animals: 'Where does Ch'en Ch'i-ch'ang live? Where does Ch'en Ch'i-ch'ang live? Answer! Answer! Are you going to tell us?' They asked me the same question over and over again with monotonous regularity. Sometimes they shouted at the tops of their voices, sometimes they adopted a less aggressive tone. At the same time other men kept on walking round me in a circle, rolling up their sleeves in a threatening way, glowering at me and swearing constantly. Every now and then a 'friend' would intervene on my behalf and push them out of the way, at the same time earnestly advising me to co-operate. After a while the exercise became pointless, and they once again changed tactics. Someone came in from the next room and whispered to the apparent leader of the team of interrogators, loud enough for me to hear: 'Do you want me to bring Ch'en Ch'i-ch'ang in now?' The man pretended to think for a while, and then shook his head. Turning to me, he said: 'We have already got Ch'en Ch'i-ch'ang here. We picked him up a long time ago. We were only asking you to tell us his address to give you a chance to prove that you're sincere about confessing.' It was a crude trick, which a child could have seen through. And so it went on, minute after minute and hour after hour, for almost two days and nights, during which time the only respite I got apart from a few visits to the toilet was the two or three hours I spent in my cell.

By the second night I was half dead, lying in a daze on the floor of my cell. The thugs returned once again to drag me out, and my 'old friend' with the Shensi accent was waiting for me. He told me that I was a great disappointment to them, and that they had wasted a lot of time trying to save me from the pit into which I had fallen. There was nothing more they could do except send me to Nanking. Just before I was to leave he came up to give me some more 'friendly' advice, telling me that the new method of dealing with political offenders was to destroy them either politically or physically. The old days were now over, and I should harbour no illusions on that score. It was no longer a question of sitting out one's sentence at public expense, while studying in preparation for the day when one would return to the fight.

What he told me was true. The days of 'bourgeois democracy' were well and truly over, and the 'scientific' policing techniques perfected by Stalin and Hitler and adopted by Chiang Kai-shek were becoming more and more widely used. Any revolutionary arrested under such conditions had to be clear on this point, and face up to the stark choice between political and physical annihilation. Shortly before my arrest I had pondered at length on the strange behaviour of the old Bolsheviks at the Moscow trials, little realizing that I would very soon find the key to this apparent riddle in my own experience. Lying there in my cell, I suddenly remembered that Trotsky had once said: 'Even Bolsheviks are made of flesh and blood'. I shuddered involuntarily, resolving to increase my vigilance from then on.

I was put on the Shanghai–Nanking night-train by two special agents. I fell asleep as soon as I got on the train, and only awoke when we drew into Hsia-kuan railway station in Nanking. My first stop in Nanking was a secret service centre housed in a luxury mansion surrounded by a big garden. I was led off to a beautifully furnished and decorated room where I flopped into an armchair, absolutely exhausted and racked with pain from the maltreatment I had suffered. The guards left me completely alone, so I managed to snatch a few hours' sleep. Later on, in the afternoon, a man dressed in the khaki uniform of a Kuomintang officer came in to inspect me. I braced myself for yet another bout of torture, but he simply asked my name and place of birth, and then left. After a while another man came in, also in officer's uniform. This time it really was an old friend of mine, an ex-Trotskyist I knew from Moscow. I prepared to resist his attempts to cajole me into surrender, but to my surprise all he did was offer me a cigarette and order the guards not to maltreat me. He then told me that if I wanted anything, I should send him a message, and left. Finally, a man in a Sun Yat-sen jacket came rushing in with a file of documents in his hand, saying that he had just finished reading the secret service reports on me from Shanghai and that in his opinion I had a 'feudal' sense of morality. 'Actually', he went on, 'it would be much more moral of you to tell us your friend's address, so that he can start a new life.' He told me that I should think about what he had to say. When I said that I knew of no addresses, he smiled knowingly and sighed. As he left the room I could hear him saying, 'Such a pity, such a pity!'

After that two guards and a special agent dragged me off into a car and drove me out through the Nanking city gates and along a country road. I was sitting on the back seat, with a guard on one side and the special agent, who was holding a revolver, on the other. My hands were handcuffed together. No one said a word, and all three of my escorts had grim looks. The fields were absolutely deserted. We were racing along at high speed. I expected that at any moment the car would screech to a halt, and I would be pushed out and shot in the back of the head. The idea almost cheered me up, since at least it would have meant an end to the torture, and I was inwardly very composed.

My expectations proved to be unfounded. After an hour's drive we arrived at a small town, where I was taken out of the car and into another secret service detention centre next to the Nanking Metropolitan Reformatory.

Inside the detention centre there was a small courtyard. The atmosphere was quiet and almost peaceful. Around the courtyard there were ten newly-built one-man cells, so tiny that there was only room in them for a bed and a bucket. The distance from wall to wall was less than an arm's breadth, and from the door to the back wall less than five paces. The walls and the ceiling were whitewashed, so that after a few hours one's eyes began to ache. The bed was a bare wooden board. In other gaols the authorities would issue blankets or cotton-padded military overcoats, but here prisoners had to rely for warmth on the clothes they happened to be wearing at the time of their arrest, whatever the weather and whatever the time of day or night. It was early summer when I first got to the prison. Summer and autumn passed and winter set in, but throughout this whole period all I had to cover me was my thin western-style jacket.

I was totally cut off from all contact with the outside world, so there was no chance of getting my family to bring me in the things I needed. I was simply left to rot. I asked the gaoler for a cotton-padded uniform, but was told: 'You can have whatever you want; all you have to do is to comply with the demands of the authorities'. In other words, I would have to betray my comrades. Clearly their 'scientific' methods knew no limits: they were even prepared to exploit the changing seasons in their campaign of persecution. Here, unlike in normal prisons, there was no regular supervision of the cells every few minutes or so. The only time we ever saw the warders was when they came into the yard to make a quick inspection at the beginning of each new watch, but they always left again immediately. The chief gaoler would then lock the outer gates and post a guard outside. This was all part of their 'scientific' method, intended to prevent prisoners from fraternizing with the guards, so that there was none of the smuggling out of secret messages which had been a common feature of normal prison life.

For a long time I never saw a soul, not even the grim faces of the prison guards. Although the other nine cells were occupied, contact was impossible, and any attempt at establishing it would have been extremely dangerous, since one could never be sure whether the man in the cell next door was a genuine prisoner or not. Not only did I never see anyone, but I never heard a single sound either. The court-yard was absolutely silent and deserted. How I longed for some sign of life! Anyone who has never lived through such an experience could not possibly imagine the extent to which loneliness and isola-tion can eat into the soul. It is impossible to sleep all the time – for long periods of the day and night you must be awake, and once awake, you cannot keep your eyes closed, however much you try. But all the time you have them open, you are forced to look at that dazzling sheet of whiteness, at once menacing and monotonous. The bleak emptiness of it eventually makes you colour-blind, and even drives you mad. When awake it is also impossible not to think. But since you are without books to read, paper to write on, or contact with people or things, your thoughts wander aimlessly, like a small boat which has lost both rudder and sail. This seeming loneliness and isolation is in fact fraught with danger, for at any moment torturers may arrive to put an end to that terrible quiet. To die is not in itself a difficult thing – what is difficult to endure is the permanent threat of torture hanging over your head. There is a limit to the physical pain which torture can cause; but the idea that the solitude may suddenly be interrupted by yet another bout of agony is enough to shatter your nerves.

I asked the prison authorities for a book to read – any book, on any subject. 'You shouldn't be reading', the guard answered politely, with just the trace of a smile. 'You should be doing some serious thinking. When you've thought matters through to a con-clusion, you may request an interview with the prison authorities.'

I had been in the 'experimental' prison for over a month when I was summoned from my cell for the first time. Two armed guards escorted me along the corridor, and I was taken into an interrogation chamber. Inside there were several agents in civilian clothes waiting for me. Some were standing up, others were seated. Each looked at me in a different way: some glared, others were smiling, some appeared to be totally indifferent, and some affected to show concern for me. My escort ordered me to sit down and wait, and told me that the chief interrogator had not yet arrived. I sat on the edge of my seat, bracing myself for the possibility of torture. After half an hour or so, a high-ranking official came into the room. The atmosphere became even more tense, and all the agents in the room seemed to be busy making preparations for some sort of sacrificial ceremony. The official sat down, and I was asked to sit down in front of him. Pretending to leaf through a file of documents, he proceeded to check my name, age, and place of birth against the report he had received from Shanghai. He asked me if I had anything new to say. I told him no. He then adjourned the sitting, ordering the guards to escort me back to my cell for 'another think'. It was not at all clear to me whether this little episode, which had started out so menacingly only to fizzle out, was a sign of the inefficiency of the secret service or part of a carefully conceived plan to break my will.

After an interval of two months, during which time I was ignored, another high-ranking officer of the secret service came to make an inspection of the courtyard. When he arrived at the door of my cell I seized the opportunity to demand either to be handed over to the judiciary or to be transferred to the military police headquarters in Nanking for a proper trial. He politely asked me my name, getting one of his aides to note it down for him, and then told me that I would receive an answer very soon. The same afternoon I was summoned from my cell and escorted to a room bare of all furniture. Two agents ripped off my coat, and while one of them held me by the arm, the other beat me on the back with a rubber truncheon until my shirt was in shreds and my blood was pouring down me. For days after this incident I had to lie on my stomach because of the wounds. This was their way of answering my demand.

The next stage in the war of nerves against me was to move me into a bigger cell with two other men. One of them, called K'ung, had been chief of staff to General Wang Teh-lin, one of the commanders of guerrilla forces fighting the Japanese in Manchuria. K'ung told me that he had been sent to Nanking by his commander to receive instructions from the central Government. Unaware of the antagonisms between the various factions in the capital, he had fallen foul of the Ch'en brothers by making contact with their rivals the Blueshirts, for which he had been arrested and thrown in gaol. By the time I met him he had been there for several months, during which time he had never once been contacted by the prison authorities.

Our other companion was a martial arts practitioner of the Shao-lin School from Honan province. I later learned that he had been the bodyguard of one of the leaders of the 'Central Statistical Bureau' of the Kuomintang intelligence services, and had been imprisoned as a punishment for some minor misdemeanour.

I had no idea why my conditions had suddenly improved, but after spending such a long time in solitary confinement I was glad of any human company. K'ung was a pious Christian, and getting on in years. He was very sentimental and emotional, always worrying about his wife and family who were hiding out with the guerrillas on the wooded slopes of the Ch'angpai Mountains in north-east China. He was deeply embittered, and during his months of isolation his one way of finding solace was through prayer. He prayed several times a day, but saved his longest and most moving prayers for the evening, just before going to bed. Sitting there in the darkness of the cell, he would invariably add a short prayer for his fellows in misfortune. Then he would break down, sobbing and choking with emotion. After he had said his final Amen, we would lie there in complete silence. I am a convinced atheist, and normally detest all forms of wallowing in emotion, but I must admit that his prayers disturbed my peace of mind.

At first I suspected that K'ung was a plant, and that his prayers were all part of the 'scientific' war of nerves against me, but I soon realized that he really was a leader of the North-East Volunteer Army and that his prayers were from the heart. The Shao-lin boxer, on the other hand, was a plant. Every day he was summoned out of the cell for an hour or two. Finally, in a bout of conscience, he confessed that he had been ordered by the authorities to spy on us, and told that he would be released from prison early if he found out the addresses of some of my comrades in Shanghai.

The tactic of improving my treatment had failed, and I was taken back to solitary confinement. It was like returning to the bleakness of the desert, with the never-ending isolation gnawing at the soul. And so it went on, day in, day out, until after the outbreak of hostilities in Shanghai on 13 August 1937. Even then it was not until the Chinese forces had suffered repeated defeats that any change came about. During that period the monotonous silence of the courtyard was broken only twice.

The first time was one midnight, when I heard the heavy tramp of jack-boots coming along the corridor, getting louder and louder.

The heavy iron gate was clanked open, and a file of men marched into the courtyard. This was most unusual, since normally the change-over of sentries was a much more relaxed affair. I sat up and braced myself for the worst, but to my relief the men marched past the door of my own cell and stopped at another at the end of the row. I heard them opening the lock and withdrawing the iron bolt, and a voice ordering the prisoner to come out. This command was issued in a quiet but menacing voice. A terrible silence followed, and I could see in my mind's eye the tense confrontation that was taking place. I heard a distraught voice asking 'What for?' Once again the command was repeated. 'I'm not coming,' answered the prisoner, terror and anger in his voice. 'Come out, nothing's going to happen to you, we just want to move you somewhere else.' They were obviously trying to coax him out. Another terrible silence followed. Then there was the sound of a struggle as the man was beaten and dragged from his cell. Once more I heard the feet tramping past my cell door, marching out through the iron gate and disappearing along the corridor. Then the blanket of silence returned.

The second incident also took place at night. I suddenly heard noises coming from the cell to the left of me, where someone was hammering wildly on the cell door, screaming and crying at the top of his voice. The guards immediately rushed into the courtyard. First of all they shouted at him to be quiet, and when this failed, threatened and finally beat him. Despite everything they did, the man continued to cry and shout. He had evidently gone mad. After all else failed the guards tied him up and left him to calm down. He kept on shouting out a woman's name. At first his voice was clear and loud, but later became very hoarse and began to crack and falter. He carried on like this until the afternoon of the next day, when the poor fellow was carried out, trussed up like a dead pig. Once again the silence returned.

I knew nothing of the outbreak of the war with Japan until the middle of August, when I saw three aircraft flying overhead and heard the sound of nearby anti-aircraft guns. Naturally I was unaware of what precisely was happening, but it was obvious that the Japanese had declared war on China. I became very excited, since whatever happened in the real war, at least the war of nerves against me would almost certainly be called off. I would either end up being shot as a victim of Kuomintang frustration in the case of a defeat, or else be released unharmed.

After the aerial battles over Nanking started, the atmosphere in the courtyard changed. At first, the guards became less stern than usual, and sometimes even exchanged a few words with me. Previously, prisoners had been strictly forbidden to make contact with each other, but now the guards would occasionally open two cells at a time when bringing round food or taking away the night-soil buckets, and would allow us to chat together. After they had left the courtyard, we would even hold shouted conversations through the little holes in our cell doors.

I now learned for the first time that my neighbour to the right was no less than Wang Shao-ao, a leading member of the Democratic National Reconstruction Association, who became Vice-Minister of Finance in the People's Government after the liberation. He had managed to keep his spirits up during his imprisonment, despite being an old man of nearly sixty. He used to practise shadow-boxing in his cell to while away the time, and through our 'telephone' conversations we got on very well together. When he was eventually released around the end of August he delivered a letter to my wife for me, and we kept up our friendship long after our release from gaol. I have met many of the leaders of the small so-called democratic parties that emerged after the Japanese surrender. Most of them were political careerists with talents more appropriate to an official than to a revolutionary, but Wang Shao-ao was different. He was a man of backbone who always insisted on sticking to his own opinions, despite the fact that his politics were extremely confused, and he thought that the programme of the Chinese Revolution could be confined to demanding the right to education and the right to work.

One afternoon something very strange happened. We heard the sound of slogans being shouted from the Nanking Reformatory next door. One man took the lead and the others immediately echoed him, so that we could hear the words very clearly. 'Long live Generalissimo (or Chairman?) Chiang', 'Long live the Three People's Principles', 'Long live the Kuomintang'. I could not imagine for the life of me what was happening. I also heard the same high-pitched voice that had been leading the shouting, delivering some sort of speech. This went on for several hours, and when the sentries came round the courtyard I asked them what was happening. They told me that the man making the speeches was the Communist representative Chou En-lai, and that he had come to explain the CCP's new united front policy to the men working in the Reformatory, all of whom were members of the Party. I listened again, and sure enough it was the high-pitched voice of my old friend. I already knew that the CCP had changed its line and realized from my long experience as a revolutionary that tactical manoeuvres were often necessary and permissible; but to a 'dogmatic' revolutionary like myself, this display was both absurd and incredible, and I could hardly believe what I had heard.

Shortly afterwards all the prisoners in the Reformatory were released, and even those of us locked up in the little courtyard were being set free one by one, so that I too expected that a change would come about in my own situation. Towards the end of August, the authorities finally remembered my existence and sent two high-ranking officials down to talk with me. They told me that I could go free if I agreed to issue a statement supporting Chiang and the Kuomintang, but I refused. I was prepared to declare my firm support for the War of Resistance to Japan under the leadership of the Kuomintang, but not to give up my own approach to the various other questions involved. Our talk went on for several hours, and was rather like a haggling session in the market-place, but no deal was struck. Just before I was escorted back to my cell one of the officials said to me: 'You can't blame us for keeping you here, you know. It's your own fault. You obviously don't want to be let out.'

September and October passed, and half-way through November I was still sitting there in my solitary cell. Other prisoners came and went, although as the months went by their political complexion gradually changed from anti- to pro-Japanese; but I, who 'didn't want to be let out' stayed behind bars throughout. It was clear from the growing number of Japanese aircraft over Nanking, where they enjoyed unchallenged supremacy, that the War was going very badly for China. I think Yentzuchi (which was where the gaol was) must have been on the Japanese warplanes' route to Nanking, because we always heard them flying overhead just before the bombs fell on the city. At first the Kuomintang had regularly sent up a few planes to intercept the invaders and engage them in dogfights in the air-space above us, but after a while they stopped coming, and the Japanese were free to come and go as they pleased, circling the city continuously from morning to night. Although splinters sometimes fell in the courtyard, and the prison was rocked by explosions, we were never allowed to go down into the air-raid shelters. As soon as the sirens sounded the guards would lock the iron gates and hurry off to the shelters, leaving us to the mercies of the enemy aircraft. At first I was scared by the attacks, but I soon got used to them. Since there was nothing I could do about them anyway, I used to climb up to the cell window and watch the patterns traced out against the sky by the Japanese bombs and the anti-aircraft fire.

By late November the repercussions of the disintegration of the Nanking Government could be felt even in our little courtyard, where none of the normal regulations seemed to apply any longer. Sometimes guards would not turn up for sentry duty, and many of them had deserted their posts to escape the coming holocaust. Two days before I was finally released I and another man called Chin, who had been arrested on suspicion of collaborating with the Japanese, were the only two prisoners left in the entire camp. We used to get our food sent in from a neighbouring village, since the prison kitchen had by then stopped functioning. There were no longer many aircraft around and the rumble of artillery fire was getting louder and louder, indicating that the Japanese armies were by now very close to Nanking. The next day the collaborator was released, and I was the only one left in the courtyard. The day after that (I remember it was 28 November 1937, twelve days before Nanking officially fell to the Japanese) I finally gained my freedom. The only remaining guard, a man called Wang Shun-lin, unlocked my cell door and said: 'Everyone else has gone. I want to go too. I want to get out before the Japanese get here. You're free to go now.' I told him that when I arrived at the prison a watch and a few dollars had been taken from me and locked up in the office, and asked him if he would go and get them for me. He smiled and told me that I was a 'frog at the bottom of the well', implying that I obviously knew nothing of the world outside. 'You must be mad if you think they're still there,' he said. 'All the staff have fled already, and they've taken everything worth taking. Run for your life!' But that was easier said than done. I was friendless and penniless, the weather was freezing and all I had on was a ragged cotton shirt and a western-style jacket. If I didn't starve I would certainly freeze to death. To his credit, the guard put his hand in his pocket and gave me two dollars, so that I was able to make my way to Nanking, where a friend of mine was living.

This was the last I saw of that 'scientific' hell. I was now about to start out on a new stage in my life.

*

But before I finish this chapter there is one more thing that I would like to mention. I learned later from friends that Yeh Chien-ying, then CCP representative in Nanking, spent two days scouring the capital trying to secure my release, apparently sometime in late September or early October. By then all the other Trotskyists had been freed, Ch'en Tu-hsiu and P'eng Shu-tse from civilian prison, and Cheng Ch'ao-lin, Ho Tzu-shen, and others from military prison. I was the only member of the organization still imprisoned, and no one knew where I was. Ch'en Tu-hsiu asked some of his friends in the Government to make enquiries about me at the secret police headquarters, but they were told that there was no record of anyone of my name. Lo Han, who was at that time a pottery teacher in Ihsing county, also went to Nanking, and on hearing the news decided to ask for Yeh Chien-ying's help. This was typical of Lo Han's naïvety, but to everyone's amazement Yeh Chien-ying agreed to his request. The two of them then got into a car and drove round all the semi-secret special service sections in Nanking for two days, but received the same reply wherever they went: 'Never heard of him.' My comrades therefore concluded that I was dead, murdered by the secret police.

I am not trying to suggest that Yeh Chien-ying spent so much of his time trying to track me down because I was in any way a 'big fish'. I am telling this story only to show once again that the attitude of CCP members towards us was neither consistently nor uniformly hostile. As Stalinists they all opposed Trotskyism, but only a handful of them were clear about the issues involved and positively supported Stalin; and of these only Wang Ming and his friends used opposition to Trotskyism to bolster their own political position. Most people attached no importance to the struggle between the two factions, considering it an internal affair of the Soviet Party. The majority of the older generation of Party members could never really take seriously the wild allegations levelled against us, and continued to look upon us as fellow-revolutionaries. The fact that Yeh Chien-ying continued to treat Lo Han as an old friend and went to such lengths to help him gain my release can have no other possible explanation.

CHAPTER 10

Ch'en Tu-hsiu, the Chinese Trotskyists, and the War of Resistance

◑ ◑ ◑

I walked all the way from Yentzuchi to Nanking, where luckily I managed to borrow another twenty dollars from a friend of Lou Kuo-hua. The whole area was devastated by war, and the weather freezing. Transport and communications had almost broken down completely. The story of how I got from Nanking to Wuhan via Hsüchow and Chengchow on my twenty-two dollars is a very moving one. For the first time I experienced what it is like to be a beggar and a refugee. What I heard and saw in the course of my two week journey completely revealed the reactionary way in which the Kuomintang was leading the War of Resistance, and the tragic consequences that followed. Although such things are not without importance, this is not the place to talk about them, and in any case, others with better qualifications to do so have already told the story of those tragic times.

When I arrived in Wuhan after an absence of ten long years it was already mid-December. Soon after getting there I read in the Wuhan press how General T'ang Sheng-chih had abandoned Nanking after swearing that he would 'stand or fall' with it, and how Japanese soldiers had brutally put the city to the sword. Naturally these terrible events attracted my attention, but my most immediate problem was how to keep body and soul together. Even though I knew a number of my friends were living in Wuhan, I had no way of finding out their addresses. I walked the streets and hung around the ferry wharf in the hope that I might bump into someone I knew, but all to no avail. I slept two nights at the Ta-chih-men railway station in Hankow, without even the money for a crust of bread. On the morning of the third day I sold my only remaining possession, a tooth-mug, to a stall-holder near the railway station. The sale brought me a few cents, which I used to pay for the ferry across the Yangtse to Lanka Hill in Wuch'ang. There I hoped to borrow some money from a professor at Wuhan University whom I knew from when we were

at school together, although I would never have even thought of
going to see him had I not been on the point of starving and freezing
to death. After getting off the ferry I went into a small restaurant to
buy some noodles. Imagine my relief when in the restaurant I
bumped into my old friend Li Chung-san! Not only did he spare me
the embarrassment of begging from someone I could not stand, but
he brought my entire eight-month nightmare to a close – a period
which I can describe without hesitation as the most difficult in my
life.

After treating me to a hearty meal, Li Chung-san bought me a
cotton-padded jacket and some other clothes. In the afternoon he
took me to Ch'en Tu-hsiu's home, where I stayed for nearly a fortnight. We talked together about many questions, some of which are
worth recording in detail.

Ch'en Tu-hsiu had been freed from gaol three months earlier than
I had. Just before his release he had drafted some papers on the
Anti-Japanese War.[1] After being set free, he had sent them to the
comrades in Shanghai, who found that they did not completely
agree with them. It was about this time that Lo Han arrived in
Nanking. As soon as he read Ch'en's papers he gave them his whole-
hearted support; he even argued that we should use them as a
platform for gathering together a broadly-based movement encompas-
sing both Trotskyists and others opposed to Japan and the Kuomintang.
The first step would be to propose to the CCP that they co-operate
with us. Ch'en Tu-hsiu knew of Lo Han's scheme, but did not
encourage him in it. Lo Han, however, decided to take things into
his own hands. He told Yeh Chien-ying of his proposals, who
encouraged him to go to Yenan to talk with Mao Tse-tung in person.
Lo Han therefore left Nanking for Sian, where he stayed at the house
of Lin Po-ch'ü, also an old friend of his and the CCP representative in
that city. Lin Po-ch'ü immediately transmitted Ch'en's papers and Lo
Han's proposals for co-operation to Mao in Yenan by special
messenger. Several days later Mao's reply came through, saying that
if Ch'en Tu-hsiu admitted his past mistakes and renounced Trotskyism, he could then work together with the CCP. Naïve though dear
old Lo Han was, he was never so naïve as to think that Ch'en Tu-hsiu
would agree to such conditions. His hopes dashed, he left Sian. His
actions not only angered Ch'en Tu-hsiu but were roundly criticized

[1] Since I no longer have these documents to hand, I cannot describe
them in any detail.

by the provisional leadership of the Trotskyist movement in Shanghai, and he quietly returned to Ihsing county to resume teaching pottery.

At the time Ch'en Tu-hsiu was extremely dissatisfied with the Trotskyist leadership in Shanghai. Feeling that their narrow sectarian approach would never get anywhere, he had decided not to go east but to move on to Wuhan instead. After the main battles in the Shanghai area had been fought and lost and the Kuomintang armies along the Nanking–Shanghai railway had collapsed in disarray, Wuhan had temporarily become the political and military centre of China and the new hotbed of the mass movement. All the social forces and political groupings stirred into being by the War of Resistance had converged on that city. Although Ch'en Tu-hsiu had no organized force to back him up, he still enjoyed great prestige among the masses, and none of the existing political groupings could afford to ignore this old man of the Revolution. Before I arrived in Wuhan, Ch'en had been invited to give two public lectures at the YMCA headquarters, where he attracted capacity audiences. In his speech he made it clear that in giving his views on the future of the resistance he was speaking only for himself and not for the Trotskyist movement as a whole. The contents of his speech were more or less the same as the papers he had drawn up earlier in Nanking gaol.

He let me read his papers and the text of his speech the day after I went to stay with him. The first day of my visit he kept off more serious topics, to give me a chance to get over my recent experiences. We chatted about prison life in Nanking, and that evening he even took the unusual step of getting his wife to cook some special dishes for me. This unexpectedly conventional gesture from so unconventional a man as Ch'en was a sign of his joy at meeting me again after the gap of six long years.

At that time Ch'en was living in an old-fashioned, single-storeyed house with a garden, owned by a Kwangsi officer who would only accept a nominal rent from his famous tenant. Ch'en was in excellent health, and used to get up very early in the morning. While in prison he had got into the habit of pacing up and down his cell, and even after his release he would still walk round and round his garden every morning. On the second day of my visit I joined him in this exercise, and it was then that we began our more 'formal' discussions. He immediately launched into a fierce tirade against the Trotskyist leadership in Shanghai. (The new provisional leadership had been chosen at a conference of activists shortly after P'eng Shu-tse and other comrades had arrived back in Shanghai from Nanking. Apart from Ch'en Ch'i-ch'ang, Han Chün, and Lou Kuo-hua, all three of whom were survivors from the old provisional leadership, the only newcomers to have been co-opted on to the Committee were P'eng Shu-tse and Liu Chia-liang.) He told me that in his view they were capable of nothing more than reciting Trotsky's old articles, and were useless when it came to real political struggles. He even went so far as to say that he no longer considered himself a member of any political party, and that from now on Ch'en Tu-hsiu would represent Ch'en Tu-hsiu and no one else. The question of who were his friends and who his enemies would have to be decided afresh in the course of the new struggles. I was at a loss to know what to say in answer to his attacks and complaints, having been separated from the movement for so many months and knowing little of the various points of view involved. I told him that I wanted to study both sides before giving my own opinion. He then took me back to his study, and gave me a copy of his papers on the War of Resistance and the texts of his two speeches. He told me that the Shanghai friends had sent him letters explaining their own point of view, but that he had not kept them – it occurred to me that he had probably thrown them into the waste-paper basket in a fit of rage. I read through what he had written, but did not agree with it completely. It seemed to me that apart from a general expression of support for the War of Resistance, he had entirely failed to mention our own distinctive position as Trotskyists. However, we postponed further discussions until I had had a chance to acquaint myself with the views of the other comrades. That same morning I asked him what he thought of the idea of starting up a journal in Wuhan. He rejected it out of hand, saying that it was not only impossible but unnecessary, and went on to argue that it was time to reject our old ways; if we really wanted to play a role in the political struggles of the day, we should adopt new methods.

After that we spent every morning strolling around his untidy little garden, chatting freely about everything under the sun. We talked about his linguistic studies, Trotsky's History of the Russian Revolution (the only book in the English language which he ever bothered to take with him on his travels from one town to another), prison life in Nanking and the Moscow trials, the Chinese Trotskyist movement and the Fourth International, the future of the War of

Resistance and the coming World War, and many other things besides. Rather than argue, we simply expressed our respective points of view; in most cases I did no more than listen to what he had to say. In this way I gradually became acquainted with his opinions on the various fundamental questions of the day. Ch'en poured scorn on what he saw as the naïve notion that the War of Resistance could give birth to a revolution: 'if there was no skin, how could there be hairs?' He went on to point out that, because of the defeats suffered so far, the industrial cities had fallen to the enemy and the proletariat had been dispersed. Should the War be prolonged, a new industrial centre might grow up with American support in the south-western provinces. He therefore saw no chance of any revolution during the War of Resistance, let alone one along the lines that we imagined. It was true, of course, that the War would bring increasing suffering to the masses, especially the peasant masses, and this suffering could well give rise to riots and disturbances. But as long as the Kuomintang continued to resist the Japanese invasion, there was no possibility of that unrest growing into a revolution against the regime. In future years many things would change, and discontent would grow both in the towns and in the villages. But the question was, who could lead these movements? Only those groups and parties which stood for democracy and freedom, and which at the same time commanded their own armed forces. It was therefore necessary to abandon the old idea of organizing workers and winning them over to the revolution simply by publishing newspapers and journals. The only feasible method to adopt was first to unite all political tendencies independent both of the Kuomintang and the CCP on the basis of a broad programme of freedom and democracy, and second to infiltrate the armed forces active in the resistance and thus create a means through which future developments in the situation could be exploited in favour of the revolution.

Ch'en Tu-hsiu's dissatisfaction with the Shanghai organization had two main causes. First, he bore a personal grudge against some of the individuals in the leadership, in particular P'eng Shu-tse – relations between Ch'en and P'eng had been very bad while they were in Nanking gaol together. Second, and more important, the comrades in Shanghai were in his view incapable of seeing what he had seen. In my opinion, the positions he was advancing had not yet reached the stage of a fundamental break with Trotskyism, and were even less in opposition to Lenin's ideas. On the contrary, Ch'en constantly talked about Lenin during this period of his life, arguing that the latter's greatness lay precisely in his refusal to be bound by ready-made Marxist formulae and in his courageous insistence on adopting new political slogans and methods of struggle to meet changing times and circumstances. His differences with the Shanghai comrades therefore involved questions of policy and tactics rather than fundamental beliefs of the socialist revolution. What particularly angered him was their refusal to engage in the slightest way in real practical activity, let alone plung headlong into the political and military struggles of the day. Instead, they simply sat in their rented rooms in the International Settlement, commenting from the side-lines on the course of the war. Whatever the times and whatever the conditions, their conception of revolutionary work was invariably reduced to the production of a rather pathetic Party paper. It was no wonder that Ch'en reacted so negatively when I suggested starting up a journal in Wuhan.

While I did not completely approve of Ch'en's arguments and criticisms, I felt that his proposals for practical activity were well worth considering. As Trotsky himself said (in a letter to the Chinese Oppositionists), Ch'en Tu-hsiu was an 'astute observer' and could grasp political struggles in a concrete way – a quality he amply displayed in his conversations with me at that time. Even before Ch'en Tu-hsiu had informed me of his views I felt that, in the swelling tide of resistance to Japan, it was out of the question to confine our-selves to reciting old dogmas and necessary to find ways of playing an active and positive role in the struggle. But I disagreed with his proposal to reduce our programme to the 'struggle for freedom and democracy', with his plans for an alliance with various so-called 'democratic groupings' and with his pessimistic assessment of the chances of a revolution developing during the War of Resistance. Although I thought he was right to stress the need for new methods of struggle, I also considered that we needed a paper as a rallying point for the formation of the Party. Since he himself was so fond of quoting Lenin, I reminded him that Lenin had called the party organ the 'organizer of the party,' and went on to argue that without a party all our political and military work would be like a kite without a string. Our insignificant forces would be swallowed up without trace in the vast ocean of the resistance.

After several days of discussion, we got round to the question of how to start work in Wuhan. We tacitly agreed to leave on one side for the time being our fundamental disagreements on questions such as the relationship between the dictatorship of the proletariat and democracy (which we had already debated several years earlier in the pages of our theoretical journal *Huo-hua*). Ch'en carefully avoided raising issues of this sort, but whenever our discussion drifted in that direction it seemed to me that he had returned to a more classically Leninist stance. He maintained this position right up to the Hitler–Stalin pact of August 1939. When Ch'en Ch'i-ch'ang went to visit the Old Man in Chiangchin in Szechwan some time in the second half of 1938, he had still not publicly come out in opposition to any of the main postulates of Marxism or Leninism. As he himself later put it, he was still 'deeply pondering' his basic ideas. The point of view expressed in the formal statement which he asked Ch'en Ch'i-ch'ang to send on to Trotsky in Mexico was the same as that which he had discussed with me in December 1937: that the Chinese Trotskyists should bend all their efforts to playing a real part in the resistance, and that outside such a framework it was pointless to talk of revolutionary activity. It was the Hitler–Stalin pact which precipitated the final change in Ch'en Tu-hsiu's thinking, what one might broadly define as his retreat from Bolshevism to Kautskyism. But all this happened at a later date and I will therefore return to it in the following chapter.

After I had been living in Ch'en's house for about a fortnight, P'u Teh-chih arrived in Wuhan from Anch'ing in Anhui province. The last time we had seen each other was in the Shanghai–Woosung Garrison Headquarters at Lung-hwa in 1931. During the six intervening years we had both been in and out of prison twice. The second time he had been arrested and released together with Ch'en Tu-hsiu, and for four long years the two men had lived close to one another. I found that he had changed little during the six years of our separation, and still retained all his youthfulness. As a boy he had ˙been to Japan, where he had developed a love for the theatre, and he was a long-standing member of the famous Nan-kuo Dramatic Society that had been formed in the 1920s to spread new, Western styles of drama. He had what one might call an artistic temperament, and sometimes gave the impression of being rather flighty and superficial; but, on meeting him this time, I found that he had gained in depth, probably as a result of Ch'en Tu-hsiu's influence. After his release from gaol in August, he had gone home to Anch'ing to recuperate, but as soon as his health had recovered went straight to

Wuhan to rejoin his old friend. Ch'en Tu-hsiu was overjoyed to see him. His arrival added sparkle to our conversations, and put Ch'en Tu-hsiu in an even better mood than usual. P'u Teh-chih and I moved out of Ch'en's house and went to live in the home of an old friend of mine called Wu. Since Wu lived by himself, we could behave more freely than in Ch'en Tu-hsiu's home. But we continued to spend most of the daylight hours together with Ch'en, and if for any reason we failed to visit him, he would come round to see us. Sometimes we would eat out together at a small restaurant, or go for a stroll along the Yangtse river. We no longer talked about the more basic questions, where we continued to differ, but concentrated instead on how to penetrate the military forces of the resistance and how to make contact with other political groupings. On the fundamental questions P'u Teh-chih's positions were close to mine; he was rather dissatisfied with Ch'en's proposal to reduce our programme to the struggle for 'freedom and democracy'.[1] He called Ch'en's two speeches at the Wuhan YMCA 'shamelessly grey' (a term used to describe people who concealed their radical views and made concessions to bourgeois public opinion). But, like me, he was also deeply influenced by Ch'en's 'activist' approach to methods of work.

Ch'en Tu-hsiu was not the sort of man given to empty talk. Using his many connections, he soon began to take steps towards putting his plan into action. At that time there was a general named Ho Chi-feng convalescing in Wuhan from wounds he had received somewhere in north China. This same man had headed the brigade stationed at the Marco Polo Bridge outside Peking when, in July 1937, the famous Incident[2] took place which was to lead directly to the full-scale Japanese invasion of north China; Chi Hsing-wen, who was known throughout the country as the heroic commander of the regiment which fired the first shot in the resistance, was in fact under the direct command of General Ho; and Ho himself was under the command of General Sung Che-yüan. By the time that we came into contact with Ho, he had already been promoted to the post of commander of the 179th Division of the Twenty-Ninth Army. He

[1] P'u's differences with Ch'en, written under the pen-name of Hsi Liu, can be found in the Chinese edition of Ch'en Tu-hsiu's Last Articles and Letters.

[2] On 7 July 1937 the escalating Japanese invasion met with resistance for the first time in the Lu-kou-ch'iao (Marco Polo Bridge) area near Peking. This marked the beginning of the nationwide War of Resistance, which lasted from 1937 to 1945.

was an extraordinary individual. According to Ch'en Tu-hsiu, he had absolutely no vices; unlike most military men he was gracious and urbane in manner, and very unassuming – he and his wife lived together in one room, without even a servant to look after them. When I first met him (through Ch'en Tu-hsiu), his wounds had already healed and he was about to rejoin his division. I formed a good impression of him, during our conversation. He was staunchly anti-Japanese, and felt very bitter towards the Kuomintang leadership. Six months of fighting in north China had taught him that unless the political consciousness of the troops was raised, there could be no effective resistance to the Japanese invasion, let alone final victory. Consequently, he had spent his convalescence reading whatever books he could get his hands on about the resistance and about social science in general. As a result of his reading and thinking, he had decided to invite a number of young revolutionaries to carry out political education among his troops. It was during his search for suitable candidates for such a mission that he came into contact with Ch'en Tu-hsiu. The two men got on well together, and General Ho looked up to Ch'en as a teacher. Needless to say he already knew what Ch'en's political position was, and it must have been obvious to him that we had differences with the Communist Eighth Route Army. For his own part, Ch'en made no attempt to pretend that he had any great forces at his disposal. As I recall the conversations that the three of us had at that time, Ch'en was always absolutely frank, explaining that he had long since broken off all relations with the CCP and did not even represent the Chinese Trotskyist movement; he said that he was acting solely in a personal capacity, as were those of us working with him. During the conversations at which I was present, the only question under discussion was the future direction of our political work in the division under Ho's command. We finally arrived at the following important conclusion: we would strengthen our military forces by mobilizing the masses through a limited agrarian reform programme, and thus prepare the way for victory in the resistance.

When P'u Teh-chih met General Ho for the first time, he too received a very favourable impression of him. However, both P'u and I doubted whether Ch'en Tu-hsiu's proposed measures would be of advantage to the Revolution. During the period 1925–7 there had been many instances of revolutionaries working as 'concubines' (as we called those who did political work in the armed forces during the period of the Northern Expedition) at various levels of the military structure, and their tragic fate was still fresh in our minds. Even fresher was the memory of the ill-fated marriage between the CCP and Feng Yü-hsiang. While I was still in Peking in 1926 I had personally witnessed the 'courtship' between Li Ta-chao and General Feng, and had afterwards read the famous 'Wuyüan Manifesto' which Feng wrote on his return from Moscow early in 1927. We had spent a lot of time doing 'political work' for him among the masses, trying to persuade them that he really was the 'peasant soldier' he claimed to be. But a few months later, in Wuhan, I had also personally witnessed this same Feng reuniting with Chiang Kai-shek to cause the collapse of the Wuhan Government, and saw his political workers arriving in the city by special train after he had sacked them from their jobs in his army. Afterwards many of these former political workers had joined the Opposition, and I was on good terms with a number of them, who had told me many stories of Feng's hypocrisy.

With these events in mind, but independently of each other, P'u Teh-chih and I began to voice the same doubts: what was there to prevent Ho Chi-feng from becoming another Feng Yü-hsiang, if on a smaller scale? Were we about to repeat the whole sad experience all over again? We expressed our reservations to Ch'en Tu-hsiu on returning home from our visit to the General. Ch'en said it would be absolutely wrong to characterize our activities as military opportunism. 'The present situation is entirely different,' he said. 'We are not the Third International, we have no resources of our own, nothing at all that Ho Chi-feng could trick us out of. What is more, we are not joining his army with the aim of replacing him as commander, or of winning him over as a revolutionary. We have already had experience of dealing with military men. From now on we must clearly understand that our most important task in the army is to educate the rank-and-file soldiers and bend all our efforts towards creating revolutionary conditions among the masses. This means that we must do all we can to launch agrarian reform in the area under our control, thus also speeding the revolutionization of the troops themselves. Finally, it seems to me that Ho Chi-feng is not as devious as Feng Yü-hsiang, and that there is even a chance of making a genuine revolutionary out of him. If he were to become one, then his not inconsiderable forces could easily come under our political leadership. If not, then the fact that we have never made any attempt to

hide our aims or beliefs means that we would be free to withdraw at
any time with no harmful consequences.'

I agreed with what the old man had said. However, our next step
immediately led to a new dispute with him. P'u and I thought that
for the project to develop favourably we should infoim the provisional leadership in Shanghai and seek their approval, so that they
could fit it in with our work nationally and send some reinforce-
ments to Wuhan. But Ch'en Tu-hsiu disliked the Shanghai comrades,
and therefore opposed our proposals. He thought it would be better
for us to wait until we had achieved some results and then if
necessary pass on a request for extra forces. But we never resolved our
differences, because even before we had begun to carry our plan into
practice the whole venture came to a sudden and unexpected end.
We had already completed all the necessary preparations: P'u Teh-chih,
myself, and another young comrade from Honan called Ma were
about to follow Ho Chi-feng to Neihuang, where his divisional headquarters were; I was to act as his chief political adviser and P'u
Teh-chih as his staff officer. We had already bought our tickets for the
Peking train when suddenly, on the eve of our departure, Ho Chi-
feng was informed that he had been relieved of his command and
instructed not to return to Neihuang. We guessed at the time that the
Blueshirt secret agents must have found out about his relations with
Ch'en Tu-hsiu, and had taken this step to forestall the radicalization
of his forces.

The bubble had burst: our hopes of infiltrating the army had not
materialized. After that we never had another chance to put our plan
into practice. During the whole period of the War of Resistance, the
Chinese Trotskyist movement taken as a whole never engaged in
military struggle. As far as I know the only two exceptions were
Wang Ch'ang-yao and his wife Chang San-chieh, who led a guerrilla
column some two thousand strong in Shantung which was eventually
destroyed by a CCP attack from the rear during an engagement with
the Japanese; and Ch'en Chung-hsi, who led a guerrilla detachment
in Chungshan county in Kwangtung and was killed in battle by the
Japanese. In retrospect, our failure to participate in the military
resistance was one of the main failures of the Chinese Trotskyist
movement. We should have admitted that it was a big mistake to
oppose all military activities and place ourselves outside the mainstream of the resistance simply for fear of committing a 'military
opportunist' deviation.

One of the most important lessons of the mass movement that has emerged in most backward countries since the Second World War is that, when the ruling class is becoming more and more reactionary and the system more and more militarized, no revolutionary party can hope to seize power unless it engages in armed struggle. This is not a new discovery: one of the basic differences between Leninism and reformism in all its guises lies precisely in this recognition of the importance of military force. Today, as bourgeois democracy continues in its decline, it is increasingly important to recognize this principle.

Ch'en Tu-hsiu's estimate of Ho Chi-feng did not prove wrong. After this episode none of us had any contact with him for many years and the next time I heard his name was in 1948, during the great Huai-hai battle in which the Kuomintang forces north of the Yangtse were destroyed. One of the main contributing factors to this brilliant and decisive victory of the People's Liberation Army was Ho Chi-feng's active collaboration with them from within the Kuomintang camp. It was a direct result of the rebellion of the forces under his and Chang K'o-hsia's command that Huang Pai-t'ao's army group was surrounded and destroyed. Ho is at present a member of the CCP's National Defence Council.

At the same time as we were preparing our military venture, Ch'en Tu-hsiu was making contacts with the Third Party (a small organization led by Chang Po-chün), with the National Salvation Association (an anti-Japanese movement of intellectuals founded in 1936), and with some 'democratic personages' whose names I no longer recall. His aim was to set up a united front with them, and fight in the resistance camp for democracy and freedom under a banner independent of both the Kuomintang and the CCP. There was a wide basis of support for such a programme in Wuhan at that time. The Kuomintang Government was so unpopular that not only the workers, the peasants, and the broad masses of the petty bourgeoisie, but also a section of the traditionally pro-Kuomintang bourgeoisie, were moving rapidly into opposition, pinning their hopes more and more on the CCP in Yenan. Naturally the CCP did not allow such a situation to pass by, and either openly or secretly it helped in the formation of a united front of the democratic parties. Ch'en Tu-hsiu, with his sharp political instinct, considered that we (he always used the term 'we Trotskyists', although he denied that he was any longer a member of the organization) should participate in this movement in order to extend our influence and break out of our isolation, which was in some ways self-imposed. Moreover, by participating in the movement we could prevent it from being utilized by the Stalinists.

P'u Teh-chih and I firmly rejected Ch'en's analysis and proposals. We considered that the so-called democratic parties were in reality nothing more than a handful of worthless politicians without any real mass following, and that we should therefore maintain our independence instead of entering into an alliance with them; our real task should be to win over any groups or individuals who might have illusions about them. I once again proposed that we should start up a paper of our own.

Ch'en Tu-hsiu was furious at our attitude. He told me that I was a dogmatist with no idea of political reality, and that I and the Shanghai comrades were 'jackals of the same lair'. He asked me to attend a conference with the three democratic groups as his representative, but I refused; he then asked P'u Teh-chih, and got the same reply. It was at that point that Lo Han turned up in the city, thus resolving the question.

After Lo Han's return from his fruitless mission to Sian, he had gone back to Ihsing county to resume his career as a pottery teacher. Ihsing was soon engulfed by the war, and Lo Han, not prepared to leave his students behind, made his way to Nanking with a group of twenty or thirty of them. (This was some time before I was released from prison.) When he got there he found that the trains, buses and steamships were full to overflowing with rich men or high officials and their families, so he got hold of a pair of rafts, built cabins on them, lashed them together, stocked up with provisions and sailed slowly up the Yangtse to Wuhan. For security purposes he also managed to get hold of two rifles. His little flotilla was a month or more on the water. After numerous dangers and adventures, he eventually reached Wuhan some time in January 1938. The first thing he did when he set foot on dry land was to try to sell his two rifles at an inflated price to his old friend Yeh T'ing, one of the newly-appointed commanders of the Communist forces. With the money from the sale he hoped to help his students settle down in their new environment. Despite the fact that Lo Han was officially an 'enemy', Yeh T'ing found it hard to turn down his request. Although it was impossible for him to buy the rifles (which in fact he handed over to the Kuomintang authorities) he managed to raise a small sum of money to enable his kind-hearted old friend to find accommodation for his pupils.

Most of the leaders of the democratic parties were old acquaintances of Lo Han, so he was in a better position to deal with them than I was. But by nature he was far from being a politician of that sort; he was too honest and straightforward, and completely unversed in the diplomatic arts. Therefore, after a few meetings with the members of the other groups involved, he tendered his resignation to Ch'en Tu-hsiu. Ch'en then turned to the veteran Trotskyist Kao Yü-han, who was at that time living in Ch'angsha, and asked him to take over as his representative; but before Kao could get to Wuhan the democratic parties suddenly broke with Ch'en. Thus the whole venture, like our military plans, came to nothing; but this time it was thwarted not by the Kuomintang, but by the CCP. In order to contain the political influence of the Chinese Trotskyist movement, the CCP intimated to their 'democratic' allies that they should immediately break all links with us, at the same time launching a shameful and hysterical smear campaign against Chinese Trotskyism in general and Ch'en Tu-hsiu in particular in the pages of the newly-founded *Hsin-hua Daily*. The man who directed and master-minded this campaign was none other than our old friend Wang Ming, who had recently returned to China from Moscow and was in charge of CCP contacts with the Kuomintang in Wuhan.

At this point a short account of developments in the factional struggle in the CCP in the period before 1938 is needed. At the Tsunyi meeting of the Central Committee in January 1935,[1] the Wang Ming group had lost its dominant position in the Party, and Mao Tse-tung, Liu Shao-ch'i, and their supporters took over the leadership – a position which they maintained right up to Liberation and beyond. But Mao's victory over Wang Ming at Tsunyi was neither complete nor decisive, and the latter's influence continued to linger on for a number of years; moreover, this struggle is still not over yet, even as I write these lines.[2] The reason why Wang Ming's group

---

[1] Tsunyi Conference. An enlarged Politbureau conference held during the Long March in January 1935 at Tsunyi, Kweichow province. At it Mao won back his control of the military from the Wang Ming group.

[2] In 1957 (ed.)

in China was defeated but not crushed is not hard to understand. Wang Ming was an authentic Stalinist, always looked upon by whoever happened to be in charge in the Kremlin (whether Stalin or Khrushchev) as the Soviet Union's most trustworthy agent. The CCP, despite the fact that it is led by a 'nationalist' like Mao and has grown strong roots of its own, is still forced to rely in many ways on Soviet aid, and is therefore obliged to tolerate Stalin's favourite Chinese son. This delicate relationship explains why Wang Ming was purged but not liquidated, and criticized but still awarded a seat (albeit the lowest ranking) on the Central Committee. After the Tsunyi meeting, he continued to hold the top position in the Chinese community in the Soviet Union. Occupying a high position in the Comintern, he spun Stalin's instructions into 'theories', and wrote long articles in Russian for the press of the international Communist movement. He passed himself off as the chief spokesman of the CCP, prided himself on being a confidant of the 'great leader' and used Soviet aid to bolster his own position in the Chinese Party, all with the aim of maintaining remote control over the direction of the Chinese Revolution. After the outbreak of the war against Japan in China he raised a number of proposals which diverged from Mao Tse-tung's line for the Party, and attempted to win back his old position in the leadership. Up to now I have not been able to get hold of any of Wang Ming's basic documents of that period, but according to Mao the 'second Wang Ming line' was actually 'a revival in a new situation of Ch'en Tu-hsiu's right opportunism during the period of the civil war'. According to Party histories the lines of Mao Tse-tung and Wang Ming were clearly opposed to each other, but in my opinion it would be more accurate to say that this confrontation was in fact a protest by the revolutionary wing of the CCP (possibly including Mao Tse-tung himself) against the directives which Stalin was issuing from Moscow. Of course, Wang Ming invariably and unconditionally supported each and every position that Stalin adopted, unlike most of the other leaders of the Party in China.

When Hitler's Germany threatened the Soviet Union as a formidable new military power in the West, and the Japanese militarists were behaving more and more aggressively in the East, Stalin finally gave up hope of saving the Soviet Union through revolutions abroad and sneeringly described the world revolution as a 'tragi-comic misunderstanding'. Communist Parties outside the Soviet Union were treated as small change in the dealing that was going on between Moscow and the foreign powers, and their fate depended on whether or not Stalin could reach an agreement with the bourgeoisies in their countries. If any power, fascist or democratic, wanted reconciliation with the Soviet Union (reconciliation which was both temporary and unreliable), Stalin did not hesitate to order the Communist Party in that country to submit to and support its ruling class. In the Far East this policy was carried out in the most barefaced way. On the one hand, he 'demanded that the CCP make concessions to the Kuomintang and its anti-popular policies, restrict its activities within the limits which the Kuomintang and Chiang Kai-shek were prepared to tolerate, completely integrate the Eighth Route Army and the New Fourth Army into the Kuomintang forces and carry out the line of unified command, unified organization, unified armaments, unified discipline and unified military activities'.[1] On the other hand, for fear of scaring Chiang Kai-shek and the Kuomintang away from the anti-Japanese camp, he opposed going all out to mobilize the masses for the struggle, expanding the liberated areas, and arming the popular masses in the Japanese-occupied areas. (See Hu Ch'iao-mu's comments on the 'Wang Ming line' – in reality Stalin's line for China – in the Chinese edition of *Thirty Years of the Chinese Communist Party*.) In short, Stalin wanted the CCP leaders to beg Chiang Kai-shek on their knees to tie down Japanese imperialism and prevent it from attacking the Soviet Union. At the same time, Stalin was flirting even more ardently with the Japanese themselves, in the hope of getting them to sign a mutual non-aggression pact. He finally achieved his aim in 1942, when he and Matsuoka Yosuke – a representative of Japanese militarism, but in Stalin's own assessment a 'moral Communist' – embraced in Moscow.

Stalin's shameful sell-out of his foreign comrades inevitably gave rise to protests among those people who were still to one degree or another true to the Revolution. During the War of Resistance the CCP by and large obeyed Stalin's directives, but made a number of revisions in their tactical implementation. I would argue that this is what is really meant by the 'two lines'.

The 'Wang Ming line' failed to succeed in the Party, and was denounced at the Sixth Plenum of the Central Committee in October 1938. Nevertheless, Wang Ming continued to play quite a

[1] Hu Ch'iao-mu, *Thirty Years of the Chinese Communist Party*, p. 41, reprinted by the People's Publishers, Canton, July 1951.

role in the CCP as a Kremlin-appointed Inspector-General.[1] One manifestation of this was the smear campaign launched in Wuhan against
the 'Trotsky–Ch'en Tu-hsiu liquidationists'.

When I first arrived in Wuhan, Wang Ming was still in Yenan. The
two men in charge of the Eighth Route Army office in the city and
secretly directing the work of the CCP in that area were Tung Pi-wu
and Ch'in Pang-hsien (Po Ku). Tung's relations with us Trotskyists
could be described as friendly. Lo Han was a frequent visitor to the
Eighth Route Army office and used to put all kinds of naïve proposals
to Tung, Ch'in, and the others, which either embarrassed them or
made them laugh. Tung Pi-wu even told my friend P'eng Ch'e-san
that he would like to meet Ch'en Tu-hsiu some time, and that when
Chou En-lai came to Wuhan he hoped that the two men could get
together for a discussion. This was not just a typically Chinese polite
remark; it also reflected in some ways the fact that at that time the
CCP had not yet decided to attack the Trotskyists as enemies. But

---

[1] I had indirect evidence of the authority which Wang Ming enjoyed
after he arrived in Wuhan in early 1938. I was very close to a group of
young refugees from Kiangsu and Chekiang. They came from many
different sorts of background: some were ex-members of the CCP, others
were only just becoming involved in politics for the first time, and others
still were members of the Kuomintang's Three People's Principles Youth
Corps, but the bulk of them were first-rate young men working in the
resistance through the National Salvation Association. In order to find
work and to stave off the threat of starvation, they spent most of their time
chasing around after influential people in the Kuomintang and the democratic groups. I found them an invaluable source of information. Once,
when a group of them came back from an interview with the democratic
leader Shen Chün-ju, they told me how excited he had been after a meeting
with Wang Ming. According to them, Shen Chün-ju was greatly moved by
that 'brilliant and capable man, with his deep theoretical understanding'.
The democratic groups really did think that Wang Ming was the CCP's
'most outstanding talent'. On another occasion, I was told that Dr. H. H.
K'ung, at that time head of the Kuomintang's Executive Yüan, had specially
arranged for an interview with Wang Ming, since according to my friends
'he considered that it was Wang Ming who was the real representative, he
was the direct representative of the Third International'. Hearing them, I
could not help recalling an occasion in Lung-hwa prison in Shanghai six
years before, when I had learned from my fellow-prisoners that Wang Ming
had at last achieved his goal of controlling the Party. Now it was clear to me
from what my young friends told me that Wang was 'down but not out'.

when Wang Ming arrived in the city, the situation changed abruptly. All social contacts with the Trotskyists ceased at once. A vicious smear campaign was started up, at first secretly but later openly, against Trotskyism in general and Ch'en Tu-hsiu in particular. Wang Ming was said to have launched this movement on the direct orders of Moscow, to co-ordinate with Stalin's world-wide offensive against all left-wing revolutionaries and in particular with his criminal policy of liquidating a whole generation of Old Bolsheviks within the Soviet Union. Under the influence of this campaign the so-called democratic groups (which had all along followed the lead of the Communist Party) hastened to cut their links with us and swell the anti-Trotskyist choir.

Thus Ch'en Tu-hsiu's plans for joint activities with the democratic groups were thwarted, and he was forced to carry out a struggle against the growing slander campaign against him. When I left Wuhan in February 1938, however, the campaign had still not formally begun. My main reason for leaving was that it seemed to me that there was nothing that could be done there, especially since all Ch'en's plans had fallen through. A second reason was that I had failed to arrive at any agreement with Ch'en on various questions relating to the war and the future course of the resistance. I found that even though I agreed with him on some practical questions, my positions were generally much closer to those of the Shanghai comrades. Finally, after nearly a year of terrible hardship I wanted to see my wife and children again. For all these reasons I decided to return to Shanghai and take part in the underground resistance there.

Ch'en Tu-hsiu was strongly opposed to my going, mainly because he thought that once I got to Shanghai I would inevitably fall back into the old way of working which he described as 'three months' work, three years' gaol'. But my mind was already made up, and there was no holding me back. Just before I left he handed me thirty dollars for the journey and said he hoped that I would return to the Kuomintang rear in six months' time and work together with him again. By now the Japanese armies were advancing along the Yangtse river towards Wuhan, and the Kuomintang Government had already pulled some of its offices back to Chungking in Szechwan province in the south-west of China. At the same time, people were busy making plans to leave Wuhan. Ch'en Tu-hsiu was preparing to leave for Szechwan, and P'u Teh-chih and Lo Han intended to go to Yünnan and Hunan respectively. I was the first of us to leave: my journey took me through Hunan and Kwangtung, and in Hong Kong I took a boat back to the International Settlement in Shanghai.

Soon after I got back there, Wang Ming's anti-Trotskyist and anti-Ch'en campaign hit the front page of the CCP's *Hsiu-hua Daily* in Wuhan, On 15 March 1938, that same Party organ republished an article by K'ang Sheng (who had returned to Yenan from Russia together with Wang Ming only a few months before) from the *Yenan Liberation Weekly* entitled 'Uproot the Trotskyist gangsters – the spies of the Japanese bandits and the common enemy of our nation'. In support of the allegation that the Chinese Trotskyists were spies in the service of Japanese imperialism, K'ang Sheng wrote:

After the 18 September Incident of 1931, the Japanese imperialists occupied the three north-eastern provinces of China. At the same time, Japanese agents in Shanghai were negotiating with the Trotskyite gangster centre made up of Ch'en Tu-hsiu, P'eng Shu-tse, Lo Han and others. . . . As a result, the Japanese agreed to give Ch'en Tu-hsiu three hundred dollars a month through T'ang Yu-jen (a high-ranking official in the Foreign Ministry of the Kuomintang Government at that time). It was Lo Han who actually took the money on Ch'en's behalf.

The charges were so utterly absurd and contrary to common sense that as soon as they were made public not only Ch'en Tu-hsiu's friends but also many people who had never before been involved in politics were outraged. A number of pro-Communist intellectuals also felt that these allegations went too far, and expressed their astonishment and disquiet. In reply to Wang Ming's deceitful campaign, Ch'en Tu-hsiu compiled a pamphlet refuting all the charges made against him. It was published by the Oriental Book Company in Shanghai.

In acting in this way, Wang Ming appears to have confirmed the charge of 'dogmatism' which Mao Tse-tung had laid against him, for he had clearly failed to recognize that Wuhan in 1938 was not Moscow, that the *Hsin-hua Daily* could not play the same role as *Pravda*, and that Chinese public opinion would never accept such charges against a universally recognized revolutionary. Like all his other miscalculations, this could ultimately be traced back to Stalin. The year 1938 was the high point of the Moscow trials, when Bukharin, Rykov, and other Old Bolsheviks in Moscow were on trial for their lives as 'Trotskyists'. It was typical of Stalinism that whatever developments took place in the Soviet Union or the Soviet

Communist Party were automatically transplanted to Communist
parties throughout the world. Wang Ming was simply making a
clumsy and foolish attempt to copy what was going on in Moscow.

But there was another, and hidden, motive behind Wang Ming's
smear campaign. At the time we were only vaguely aware of the
factional struggle that was going on in the CCP, and therefore interpreted Wang's campaign as an attempt to whip the leftist-inclined
lower cadres into line at a time when the Party as a whole was moving
rapidly to the right. There was some truth in this explanation; at the
time of the CCP–Kuomintang 'remarriage' there was indeed widespread dissatisfaction and confusion in the Party ranks, and to stifle
such dissent the leadership decided to drag out the old Trotskyist
bogey. But it is clear from material published since Liberation that
another of the targets of the campaign was Mao Tse-tung himself, and
that Wang Ming was using it as part of his attempt to regain power
in the Party. History has shown that he failed in his aim, but had he
and his friends succeeded in the intra-Party struggle, and ousted
Mao Tse-tung and Liu Shao-ch'i from the leadership, it is almost
certain that the latter, like Zinoviev and Bukharin in the Soviet
Union, would have gone down in Chinese history as members of the
'Trotsky–Ch'en gang'. From the time of the first Moscow trials in
1934 right up to Stalin's death in 1953, the victorious factions in the
Communist parties have always claimed the mantle of Marxism–
Leninism, while all the defeated factions have been denounced as
'Trotskyist gangsters', in confirmation of the adage known to
Chinese in the form 'all victors become kings, all losers are bandits'.
Wang Ming's aim was to kill two birds with one stone; but, unluckily
for him, he missed his target and the stone fell back down on to his
own head, in the shape of Mao's accusation that he was 'reviving
Ch'en Tu-hsiu's right-opportunist errors in a new setting'. The fact
that Wang Ming was branded only as a 'Ch'en Tu-hsiu' and not a
'Trotsky' confirms that he had been defeated but not yet routed.

. The CCP also attempted to spread its anti-Trotskyist campaign to
Shanghai, in an even more shameful way but with even less success.
The course of events was as follows: Li Kuo-chieh, grandson of the
famous Ch'ing dynasty viceroy Li Hung-chang, became a collaborator with the Japanese and took up a post as general manager of the
Japanese-controlled China Navigation Company in Shanghai; soon
afterwards he was assassinated by underground resistance fighters. A
few days later the Communist-controlled newspaper I-pao carried a

report that before his death Li Kuo-chieh had been seen in the company of the Trotskyist P'eng Shu-tse. This scurrilous news item was
meant both to suggest that the Trotskyists and the collaborators were
working together and also to prepare the ground for the assassination of P'eng Shu-tse, either directly by Communist agents or indirectly by the Kuomintang, and thus to 'prove' the original charge.

We took the following countermeasures: P'eng Shu-tse left home
for a while and went to live elsewhere; at the same time we asked a
foreign lawyer by the name of Jowishoff (a German Jew who had
fled the Nazis) to write to I-pao on P'eng's behalf and demand a re-
traction of the defamatory statement. (We asked Jowishoff to represent us firstly because as a friend of the foreign comrade Li Fu-jen he
offered us his services free of charge, and secondly because the
Chinese lawyers in Shanghai were afraid to touch the case.) As a
result, I-pao published Jowishoff's letter and thus brought the whole
sordid affair to an end.

On my way back to Shanghai I had stopped off in Hong Kong, where
for the first time I met Liu Chia-liang, a member of the provisional
leadership of the organization and chief organizer in the Hong Kong
area. The first thing he asked me was what I thought of Ch'en Tu-hsiu.
He also fired a number of other questions at me, demanding that I
answer yes or no. The atmosphere was so hostile that I felt as if I was
back again in the old factional situation of the early 1930s. It was
impossible under the circumstances to hold a real discussion, and in
addition I had already bought my ticket for the journey by boat to
Shanghai, so we discontinued our talks and hurriedly parted. Rather
depressed, I walked back to my hotel on the Hong Kong waterfront
with Ch'en Chung-hsi. On the way, Ch'en unburdened himself to me.
He told me that in his view Liu Chia-liang's main aim seemed to be
to create an artificial division between the young and old generations
in the membership, and to rally the newer recruits under his own
leadership. Ch'en went on to say that Liu took a very hostile attitude
towards himself, Lo Hsin, and other older comrades, and discriminated against them in the work of the organization. I now realized
that the reason Liu Chia-liang had treated me so brusquely was
because he regarded me too as 'old and worthless'. I advised Ch'en
not to worry too much about being discriminated against. I had
always considered that the best way of dealing with petty factionalism
was to refuse to reciprocate, to avoid sterile classification into

abstract categories such as young and old, and to concentrate instead on political questions and on the more long-term interests of the Revolution, so that the problem would eventually disappear of its own accord. Ch'en Chung-hsi had never received much of an education, but his nobility of character and his long experience of struggle enabled him to place himself above any narrow-minded considerations. He saw me to the ship and we said goodbye to each other. Unfortunately we never had a chance to meet again. Six years later Ch'en Chung-hsi, by then the leader of a Trotskyist guerrilla unit, was killed by the Japanese during a battle somewhere in Chungshan county.

On my return to Shanghai, I had a joyful reunion with my old friends Ch'en Ch'i-ch'ang, Lou Kuo-hua, and others. It was one of the happiest periods in my life. Only just under a year had elapsed between my arrest and enforced departure from Shanghai in May 1937 and my return to the city via a circuitous route in late February 1938, but it seemed to me that more things had changed in those few months than in the whole of the preceding half century. The International Settlement and French Concession of Shanghai had been turned into an island, cut off from the surrounding world by barbed wire beyond which demons and monsters danced fiendishly together, a world of ghosts and evil spirits. I myself had passed through numerous terrible hardships and had been within a hair's breadth of dying – it was a nightmare to think back on my experiences. But here I was back among old friends again – it was like being born a second time. Wang Meng-tsou, the publisher, was very pleased to see me back in Shanghai, and invited me and a few old friends round to his office for a meal. Among the other guests were P'eng Shu-tse and his wife Ch'en Pi-yün (Pi-lan). A few days after I returned to the city, however, my one-year-old daughter, who had been born one month before my arrest, died of measles. I desperately needed money for my family, and every day our plight was worsening. In spite of the fact that my health had been badly damaged and I needed time to recuperate, the situation was so pressing that I immediately set about translating Malraux's *Les Conquérants* for a Shanghai publishing house. On top of this, I also had my political work to do. The functions of the old provisional committee had by now been taken over by the editorial board of *Struggle*, and I was asked to resume my position on it. Thus a new period in my life began, in which my activities were mainly given over to translation and writing.

Ten years of working in the Opposition had left me with a hearty dislike for factional wrangling. During my long period of imprisonment I had had the opportunity to reflect on many things. I regretted none of my past political activities, which even to this day I maintain were absolutely worthwhile; but there are certain things which, when I think back on them, sadden me, in particular the energy we wasted on factional struggle. While I was in gaol I often used to sigh and say to myself or my friends: 'If only we could have spent all our energies on deepening our theoretical understanding, and translating Trotsky's writings into Chinese, instead of wasting time winning people over to factional positions.' My sheer good fortune in getting out of Nanking gaol alive made me swear all the more firmly to put my remaining years to the best possible use and translate as many of Trotsky's writings as possible into Chinese. I used to think it was a paradox that, although Trotskyism had existed in China for ten years now, Trotsky's writings on the Chinese Revolution, which had been one of the main bases for the formation of the international Trotskyist movement after 1927, had still not all been translated into Chinese; and some of the translations that did exist were very poor. I promised myself that I would do my best to remedy this deficiency.

The period was one of swift and dramatic changes. Any serious revolutionary could not help but realize that whether or not one's projects and proposals became an active element in the situation would be determined not so much by literary activity as by political and especially military work. I entirely agreed with Ch'en Tu-hsiu's emphasis on these points, and gave him my whole-hearted support. But as our efforts in this direction never got off the ground, and I was back in Shanghai, where more active work was impossible, my interest once again turned to translation and writing.

Immediately after arriving back in the city, I received visits from Ch'en Ch'i-ch'ang and Han Chün. From them I learned that in Shanghai too there was a division between 'old' and 'new' members, and that Han Chün, the leader of the 'young generation', had rallied support mainly on the basis of fighting against Ch'en Tu-hsiu's opportunism. At the same time this group discriminated against the whole of the 'older generation' in the organization – those comrades, P'eng Shu-tse among them, who had survived from the period of the unification of the four groups. Several days later I discovered that this move to drive a wedge between the generations had been jointly initiated by Liu Chia-liang and Han Chün, the former from his base in Hong Kong and the latter in Shanghai. There was one comrade in particular in Shanghai, Chiang Chen-tung (one of the leaders of the Shanghai insurrection in 1927), who thought like Ch'en Chung-hsi in Hong Kong that Liu and Han's factionalist activities could only harm the organization, and should therefore be exposed and halted. I advised Chiang Chen-tung not to take these goings-on too seriously, and argued that no faction could last long or play a really active role in the revolution unless it was based on a clear political or organizational conception. To call all 'old men' corrupt and reactionary was just as meaningless as to say that 'new' equals 'good'. To oppose Ch'en Tu-hsiu's political ideas was a very different thing from opposing all 'old men' who may for a longer or shorter period of time have had anything to do with him. Moreover, as I pointed out earlier, for the period from the autumn of 1937 to the spring of 1938, a clear distinction must be drawn between Ch'en Tu-hsiu's political ideas and his more practical projects, and much of what he had to say was worthy of our consideration. Han Chün and Liu Chia-liang were both promising revolutionaries. Han Chün in particular was an extremely hard-working comrade, in the excellent activist tradition of the CCP's middle and lower cadres. He was universally admired by all the younger comrades in the Opposition.

As for the 'old men', by the time the War of Resistance broke out there were not very many of them left in the ranks of the Trotskyist movement, and those that were still there were for the most part apathetic, and given more to empty talk than to action. They would rather sit around reminiscing than work out the future prospects of the organization. Others devoted themselves entirely to their wives and children, and their own individual interests and pursuits. Under the circumstances, it was understandable that those young people who had joined the organization on the eve of the War of Resistance should want to brush aside such obstacles and move quickly forward. But the problem was that the really apathetic 'old men' had in fact left the movement of their own accord, and there was therefore no need to take active steps to exclude them from the organization. As for that tiny handful of veteran Trotskyists who had remained members of the organization and were nominally represented on its leading bodies, they were only too ready to make way for more active comrades and it was therefore pointless to talk of 'edging them out'.

Apart from these two categories, those veteran Trotskyists who – far from being an obstacle to the further development of the organization – were actually one of its most valuable assets, numbered less than a dozen. Given this situation, it was not only unnecessary but positively harmful to want to set up an independent centre with the aim of squeezing out the 'old men'. Even though Han Chün and Liu Chia-liang may have been acting from the best possible motives, their behaviour was clearly detrimental to the interests of the movement. Fortunately the 'Liu-Han centre' was short-lived: by the summer of 1938 Liu Chia-liang was forced by the British authorities to leave Hong Kong, and Han Chün took over in the colony from where Liu had left off; shortly afterwards the two men fell out with one another, and the 'Liu-Han centre' ceased to function. As a result, this little episode of unprincipled factionalism did no lasting damage to the organization.

But this is not to say that there were no differences of political principle within the Chinese Trotskyist movement at the outbreak of the War of Resistance to Japan. Broadly speaking, there were three main political divisions at the time: Ch'en Tu-hsiu's position, which can be described as unconditional support for the War of Resistance; Cheng Ch'ao-lin's position, which opposed support for the war on the grounds that the Sino-Japanese conflict was from the very beginning an integral part of the imminent world war; and the position of the overwhelming majority of the Chinese Trotskyists, which can be summarized as support for the war, but criticism of the leadership. This third position drew support from 'young' and 'old' comrades alike, and was backed not only by P'eng Shu-tse, but also by Ch'en Ch'i-ch'ang and myself. These differences were serious, and could by rights have been expected to give rise to major confrontations within the movement, but in fact Ch'en Tu-hsiu had already openly declared that his views were his own and not those of the Chinese Trotskyist movement, and there was no one in the organization who completely supported his position; as for Cheng Ch'ao-lin, he lived in a remote part of the Anhui countryside, and had never seriously tried to put his views to the membership or to win influence. This meant that from the failure of the attempt to divide the movement by age-groups, until the outbreak of the Pacific war in the winter of 1941, no ideological or factional struggles split the Trotskyist movement.

The period from the winter of 1937 to the winter of 1941, when

Shanghai was cut off from the Chinese hinterland by the Japanese invasion, saw a boom in political publications by the various groups active in the city. During those years, the Japanese imperialists and their Chinese collaborators did not control the International Settlement and the French Concession, and the British and French authorities took advantage of their neutral status to give a certain protection to resistance activities. As long as a newspaper or journal was nominally published by a British or American citizen, it could be openly in favour of the resistance without fear of Japanese interference. At that time all newspapers and magazines in Shanghai, whether run by the Communists or by the Kuomintang, used to announce themselves as being either American or British concerns. Some of the Englishmen and Americans who acted as front men for these publishing businesses only did so for the money, but most of them genuinely sympathized with the aims of the resistance.

It so happened that a young American photographer in Shanghai by the name of Buckman was a sympathizer with the Trotskyist movement, and two or three relatively well-off Chinese sympathizers were willing to contribute a hundred dollars a month towards the cost of bringing out a Trotskyist journal; so the way was open for us to resume our public propaganda. With Buckman as our publisher, we launched a monthly journal in July 1939 under the name of Tung-hsiang (Tendency). Its main contributors were the poet Wang Tu-ch'ing, Ch'en Ch'i-ch'ang, P'eng Shu-tse, Liu Chia-liang, and myself. I edited the journal, and Lou Kuo-hua looked after the technical side, including fund raising and circulation. At two thousand copies a month the circulation of Tung-hsiang was not particularly big, but – considering that it was confined to Shanghai – its influence was not inconsiderable. Even though we only managed to bring it out for a few months, it quickly got results: our correspondence was so large that we could dispense with the usual practice of writing our own 'readers'' letters, and we made contact with many who shared our ideas.

Unfortunately, however, Japanese agents forced us to cease publication after only four issues. At that time it was illegal for any publication to be printed unless it carried the name and address of its publisher. We had an arrangement with the Shanghai Children's Newspaper whereby we used their address and they used Buckman's name as their legal cover. Of course, the Japanese gendarmes were only too aware of the true meaning of 'American Limited Company', and after a while they began to put pressure on the publishers of *Children's Newspaper* through their Chinese collaborators in the Settlement, threatening them with bombs unless they stopped publishing *Tung-hsiang* from that address. Unwilling to run the risk, our 'hosts' immediately complied with the Japanese demands. The Japanese also began to put diplomatic pressure on the Settlement police and the American Consulate in Shanghai, with the result that Buchman was no longer able to act as our legal front man. Though *Tung-hsiang* died an early death in October 1939, it had many mourners who wanted to see it resurrected somehow, including some who were willing to contribute money towards such a venture, so we decided to continue publication in pamphlet form and thus avoid the need for registration. We brought out two pamphlets: *P'o-hsiao (Daybreak)* that October, and *Hsi-liu (Against the Stream)* in January 1940.

During this same period we managed to bring out a number of Trotsky's writings in Chinese, including *The Revolution Betrayed*, a collection of articles on the Hitler–Stalin Pact, and Victor Serge's *From Lenin to Stalin*. At the same time we published fourteen pamphlets, some by Trotsky and others by Chinese comrades, through the Shanghai-based Oriental Book Company. These pamphlets achieved quite an impact, and circulated as legal publications throughout all those parts of China not under Japanese occupation. The most influential of these was Trotsky's *On the Eve of a New World War*, which sold over 10,000 copies and was the best selling publication we ever produced.

Shortly after the publication of *P'o-hsiao*, Cheng Ch'ao-lin arrived back in Shanghai from south Anhui. His arrival was a great help in our publication work. He was a brilliant linguist although a poor speaker, and proficient in nearly all the main European languages, in particular French and German. It was he who translated Bukharin and Preobrazhensky's *ABC of Communism*, the earliest and most influential Marxist textbook in the Chinese language, in the 1920s. He had great stamina as a translator, and was both accurate and prolific. He had come to Shanghai partly because he had now recovered from his long imprisonment and was eager to get down to work again, and partly because we had asked him to share in translating Trotsky's monumental *History of the Russian Revolution* into Chinese. This was our most ambitious literary project ever, and took me and Cheng Ch'ao-lin a full year to complete. Ever since 1929, when I produced a full-length translation of Plekhanov's *From Idealism to Materialism*, I had earned my living as a translator of numerous books and articles. But since my main aim had been to make money and most of the books I worked on were chosen for me by my publishers, I had come to look upon translating as forced labour and had taken neither pride nor interest in much of my work. But now things were different. Both Cheng Ch'ao-lin and I got down to work with all the creative zeal of writers. We worked with the utmost care and attention, referring not only to the Russian original but also to the French and English translations. Afterwards we checked over each other's drafts, in order to reduce errors in the text to the very minimum if not to remove them altogether. The same sort of care was put into the proof-reading, and we eventually discovered fewer than ten printing errors in a book of over a million characters.

While the work was still in progress we informed Trotsky, who was by then in Mexico, and asked him to write a special preface for the Chinese edition. With great pleasure, Trotsky agreed. In order to fit in with our own publication dead-line, he dropped everything he was doing and settled down to write a short introduction to our translation. But tragically, he was never able to complete the task, since soon afterwards his genius was struck down in its flower by a Stalinist assassin. When we came to print the *History* we left four pages blank at the beginning of the first volume, to mark our deep sense of loss. But just before we finished, something very unexpected happened: Trotsky's wife came across a part of the draft preface among her husband's posthumous papers, and immediately posted it on to us in Shanghai; with a mixture of grief and joy, we translated it into Chinese and included it as an appendix to the third volume.

We printed two thousand sets of the *History*, but had only sold two or three hundred of them when the Pacific War broke out and the Shanghai International Settlement was overrun by the Japanese, who immediately set about confiscating and destroying all anti-Japanese and other revolutionary literature. We did everything possible to prevent the remaining copies of the *History* from falling into their hands, but when the Japanese gendarmes finally threatened to search all the warehouses in Shanghai the owner of the building where we were keeping the books lost his nerve and we were forced to burn them – nearly a thousand copies in all – in the courtyard. Even today it hurts me to think of this enforced act of vandalism. After the war we did a photographic reprint of the original and ran off two hundred sets of the three volumes, but the technical quality was far below that of the original.

Even the books we published seemed to be under the same curse as the Chinese Trotskyist movement as a whole. Despite all our efforts Trotsky's *History* was never able to achieve the influence we had hoped for. But, looked at in a broad perspective, we still had grounds for being satisfied with what we had achieved. Truth will prevail, and none of the many books that have been written on the October Revolution can hope to match Trotsky's *History*. Sooner or later, historians and Communists are bound to want to know the truth, and Chinese Communists will be no exception to this rule. In the course of their search, Trotsky's *History* will become a beacon to light up the ocean of darkness. We can console ourselves with this thought.

Just as I was checking through the final draft of the *History* I fell ill with tuberculosis. I was coughing up a lot of blood, and it was vital that I should get some rest. While I was on my sick-bed the Pacific War broke out.

CHAPTER 11

The Pacific War and a New Split
in the Organization

◒ ◒ ◒

A new split came about in the Chinese Trotskyist organization in
1941, on the eve of the Pacific War. It resulted mainly from two
factors: a political dispute on how to characterize the War of
Resistance and what attitude we should adopt towards it should
China be drawn into the wider international conflict; and, later,
organizational problems in relation to the status and rights of the
minorities in the Party.

The War of Resistance was by now two and a half years old and
the Kuomintang Government had fled to the south-west corner of
China, where but for the outbreak of the war in Europe it would
almost certainly have joined the Japanese-sponsored 'Greater East
Asia Co-Prosperity Zone'. The European war gave Chiang Kai-shek a
new lease of life, and the more complicated international situation
increased his room for manoeuvre. In the early stages of the war he
had relied on Soviet aid (hence his co-operation with the CCP) to
improve his bargaining position with the Japanese, but the course of
the conflict, the balance of class forces at home, and the nature of
China's relations with other countries prevented him from doing a
deal with Japan and resulted in the prolongation of the resistance.
When it became obvious in mid-1939 that the outbreak of a new
World War was imminent, the Chinese bourgeoisie, headed by the
Kuomintang, made the fundamental change to an alliance with the
democratic powers, linking its fortunes to the United States. The
domestic policy of the Government underwent a sudden and obvious
change: it began to suppress all leftist groups, soon turning against
its CCP allies – whose support it no longer needed – and partially
destroying their New Fourth Army. This trend hardened after the
Russo–Japanese pact of April 1941, the increasing tension between
Japan and the United States, and the German invasion of the Soviet
Union in June of the same year.

Early in 1940 one question was uppermost in our minds: once

the War of Resistance to Japan became an integral part of the World War, would it undergo a change in character, and if so should our attitude towards it change accordingly? Some time in the autumn of 1940 I wrote an article on this subject for *Struggle* under the title 'The Pacific War and the Chinese War of Resistance'. My main conclusions were as follows: once the Pacific War broke out, the Chinese resistance (insofar as it was controlled by the Kuomintang) would have to be seen as an integral part of the wider imperialist war, since the Kuomintang, as junior partner of American imperialism, would have to accommodate its plans to the grand strategy of the US Supreme Command; as a result, the aim of national liberation would of necessity become subordinate to American ambitions to take over from Japan as the dominant power in East Asia. As long as China's struggle against Japan was waged more or less independently of all imperialist powers it would remain progressive, but once it became enmeshed in the World War its progressive aspect would dwindle away to insignificance or disappear entirely. After the Pacific War broke out, our attitude towards the Kuomintang-led war should correspond more to the revolutionary policy advocated by Lenin during the First World War. We would lay more stress on the victory of the revolution than of the war.

Apart from P'eng Shu-tse, who had just left Shanghai for Hong Kong, all the other members of the editorial board – Ch'en Ch'i-ch'ang, Cheng Ch'ao-lin (who had been co-opted into it after his return from south Anhui, as a member of the original Central Committee elected at the unification conference in 1931), Lou Kuo-hua, and Liu Chia-liang – expressed their agreement with the article when it came up for discussion. At about this time, P'eng Shu-tse adopted a completely different position in an article published in the Hong Kong Trotskyist organ *Huo-hsing* (*Sparkle*). He argued that the War of Resistance would remain progressive, regardless of whether it became caught up in the wider imperialist conflict, unless – and this was his sole reservation – British or American troops fought against Japanese troops on Chinese soil, in which case that part of the war would not be progressive.

A fierce and long-drawn-out internal dispute therefore broke out as soon as P'eng got back to Shanghai. At first it was confined to the editorial board, but later it spread to the whole organization. At first the line-up in the leadership was five to one, but later Liu Chia-liang went over to P'eng's position to form a minority of two. In the course of the discussion in the branches of the organization in Shanghai and Hong Kong most of the rank and file at first sided with the majority on the editorial board; but after the foreign comrade Li Fu-jen arrived in Shanghai with a resolution drafted by himself, adopted by the Pacific Bureau of the Fourth International and broadly in keeping with the positions of P'eng Shu-tse, the majority of the membership swung the other way, although the line-up on the editorial board remained unchanged. This controversy raged for several months, covering an ever wider area and delving more and more deeply into the various issues involved, so that it was not without a certain political and theoretical value. I presented my own positions on the ideological disputes of that period in my introduction (written in 1947) to our edition of Trotsky's *Problems of the Chinese Revolution*.

The subsequent split in the organization, however, came about for other reasons. In the summer of 1941 P'eng Shu-tse and his followers sponsored the so-called Second National Delegate Conference of the Chinese Trotskyist movement. I was too ill to attend, while Cheng Ch'ao-lin, Ch'en Ch'i-ch'ang and Lou Kuo-hua boycotted the meeting because of the way that it had been prepared; as a result, the only participants were a small number of activists from the Shanghai area and four or five comrades from Hong Kong and Kwangsi. The conference elected a new leadership body made up of P'eng's wife and other supporters of the pro-P'eng majority, although immediately afterwards two of its five leading members came over to the minority. Naturally we were not satisfied with the conference arrangements and the procedure adopted there, but we agreed to accept its outcome and to function as a minority within the organization. At the same time we demanded that a column should be set aside in our paper *Struggle* for a continuation of the discussion between the two tendencies, so that the issues at stake could be clarified. Our request was turned down, as was our later request for a continuation of the debate in the *Internal Bulletin*. We therefore decided to bring out our own bulletin, which we later called *Internationalist*, declaring that we would cease publication the moment that the new Central Committee allowed us a discussion column in *Struggle*. Once again P'eng and the other members of the standing committee rejected our overtures, claiming that our activities were in violation of organizational norms. They added that if we continued to publish our bulletin they would declare that we had left the Chinese Trotsky-ist movement of our own accord.

In this way the Chinese Trotskyist movement, which had united on 1 May 1931, split once again in May 1941, since when two separate organizations have continued in existence right down to the present day.

All this happened many years ago, and I have no intention of reckoning up old scores in the spirit of bitter or narrow-minded sectarianism. It seems to me, however, that the concept of the rights of factions and minorities within the Party to exist and advance their views retains its force and is of enormous significance not only for Trotskyists but for the revolutionary socialist movement as a whole.

Many of Stalin's worst crimes were committed under the spurious banner of 'Leninism'. Among the principles he most commonly abused was that of 'iron unity', which in his vocabulary meant the prohibition of all factions within the Party and other parties outside it. It would be absurd to imagine, however, that a large organization will be free from many differences of opinion.; and it would be equally absurd to think that disagreements of this sort will not eventually result in opposing factions. The organizational principles elaborated by Lenin (including a part of his theory of the state) are not a crude negation of the traditions of bourgeois democracy, but a critique and further development of them. Although Lenin poured scorn on bourgeois parliamentarism, the soviet system he advocated did not deny in principle the plurality of political parties. Immedi-ately after the October Revolution other socialist parties were active alongside the Bolsheviks in the soviets. One-party rule was not a necessary feature of the system but a product of the unprecedented intensification of the class struggle during the civil war. Leninist democratic centralism in the Party did not deprive minorities of their right to exist, or prevent their supporters from speaking up for themselves both within the Party and outside it. Lenin had often found himself in a minority in the Russian Social Democratic Party, and always insisted on minority rights so that he could continue to struggle for his own positions.

The resolution which banned factions, passed at the Tenth Congress of the CPSU in March 1921 as an emergency measure at the time of the Kronstadt Uprising, was transformed by Stalin and his friends into an immutable and iron law of organization. At first, it was a crime to start a faction in the Party, and later it became a capital offence to hold a different opinion from that of the General Secretary. Lenin's system of democratic centralism was transformed at the cost of innumerable lives into a despicable caricature of Hitler's 'one State, one Führer'. The perversion of Lenin's principles of organization and the wiping out of a whole generation of revolutionaries by the bureaucracy was rooted in deeper historical causes than Stalin's personal inclination to abuse power, but it is undeniable that the Stalinist interpretation of 'Leninism' smoothed the way to Thermidorian reaction.[1] Principles of this sort can lead to show-trials, bloodbaths and reaction in a country where the revolutionary party has already won state power, and to endless splits and organizational wrangles in a party which has not yet done so, as the tragic experiences of the Soviet Union and the Stalinist parties over the last thirty years show.

Although it is not my intention here to offer a full appraisal of P'eng Shu-tse as a revolutionary, I feel that a few words are in order. P'eng is undoubtedly a revolutionary, but his defects outweigh his virtues. His greatest defect was his acceptance of 'Leninism' in its Stalinist garb, in particular the Stalinist norms of organization.

Shortly after the split in the movement, the Pacific War broke out. The entry of the Japanese army and gendarmerie into the International Settlement area made our work even harder. From December 1941 to the Japanese surrender in August 1945 it was hardly possible for us to develop any field of work, and difficult to maintain even a bare existence. Our links with other countries and other parts of China were severed and our activities restricted in scope. Since our organization was small and weak, we made no attempt to engage as a group in any sort of direct armed confrontation against the Japanese oppressors. Faithful to our working-class orientation, we continued to devote ourselves to activities among the workers, with the aim of educating and organizing them. In that respect, the recruitment of the lawyer Chang Teh-tse and his sister Chang Teh-han into the group is worthy of mention, since with the help of their generous contributions we were able to finance the running of the two schools in the workers' district in west Shanghai, and thus deepen our contacts with the working class. The workers in the silk-weaving factories in this area had long been in contact with the Chinese Trotskyist movement. Chiang Chen-tung, one of the

[1] See footnote on p. 102 above.

leaders of the famous Shanghai insurrections of 1927, assisted by my nephew Wang Sung-chiu, was in charge of these schools, which were staffed exclusively by Trotskyist teachers. Through them we managed to extend our influence among these workers, whose children made up the majority of our pupils. Through the links which we established we succeeded in leading a number of struggles directly under the noses of the Japanese imperialists. We also built a base among the tram-workers in the French Concession during this period.

In spite of the priority we continued to give to the working-class struggle, various individual comrades joined anti-Japanese guerrilla detachments in north and south Kiangsu, and unknown to us played quite an important role in them. More significantly, two groups of Chinese Trotskyists, led by Ch'en Chung-hsi in Kwangtung, and by Wang Chang-yao and his wife Chang San-chieh in Shantung, succeeded (again without the knowledge of the Shanghai centre) in organizing guerrilla detachments several thousand strong and carrying on fighting against the Japanese for nearly two years. Unfortunately, as mentioned earlier, both were annihilated, either by the Japanese (in Kwangtung) or by the combined forces of the Japanese and the CCP (in Shantung).

Taken as a whole, however, our guerrilla activities during the period of the Japanese occupation were of little account. Our efforts in Shanghai as usual centred on education, propaganda, writing, and publishing. Considering the unbearable conditions, this was not easy. At great risk to our lives and despite enormous difficulties, we managed to bring out some fifteen issues of *Internationalist* during this period. *Struggle*, which had first been published in 1936 and had the longest run of any Trotskyist journal in China, was taken over by P'eng's new Central Committee after the split, but it folded up during the occupation of the International Settlement of Shanghai. Apart from a short interval at the beginning, P'eng's group published no organ whatsoever during the Japanese rule of the city. The pages of *Internationalist* carried commentaries on current political developments, anti-Japanese propaganda, and many theoretical analyses of the war and of the inevitability of revolution. Most of the important articles were written by Cheng Ch'ao-lin. Cheng had long been famous as a contributor to the CCP press but it was only now that his talents as a creative theoretician began to bloom. During those darkest years he wrote his most brilliant and substantial pieces, including *Dialogue Between Three Travellers* (a theoretical treatise of revolution written in novel form), a book of memoirs (an inner history of the CCP from the early 1920s through to 1930), and the *ABC of the Theory of Permanent Revolution*.

But the one work to which he devoted most care and attention was his *Critical Biography of Ch'en Tu-hsiu*, which – to judge from a reading of the manuscript – was the most brilliant history of modern Chinese thought to have been written to date. The pity of it was that apart from the *ABC*, none of his manuscripts from this period ever saw the light of day. When the Chinese Trotskyist movement was destroyed during the nation-wide round-up in December 1952, they were locked up by Mao's political police together with their author.

Ch'en Tu-hsiu died on 27 May 1942 in Chiangchin, Szechwan province. His death was not unexpected, since we had known for a long time that he was suffering from incurable sclerosis, but it still saddened us immensely. Before the outbreak of the Pacific War we had regularly received letters from him in which he kept us informed about his state of health, and on the basis of these reports a doctor we knew in Shanghai used to prescribe medicine which we then posted on to him via Hong Kong, since it was by that time unobtainable in the interior of the country. Those of us who had been on intimate terms with Ch'en Tu-hsiu experienced the loss more keenly than those who had never known him. Ch'en Tu-hsiu's thinking in the final years of his life was already far from Trotskyism, as shown by his *Last Articles and Letters*, but I was not alone in thinking that, had he lived longer, he would almost certainly have progressed beyond these views and, under the pressure of events, returned to the Trotskyist camp, since he not only had all the attributes of a genuine revolutionary but also was a shrewd and brilliant observer. Even though we on the *Internationalist* editorial board were further from Ch'en's views – especially on the question of the war and the resistance – than P'eng Shu-tse's group, we nevertheless looked upon him as a comrade and even a teacher, and published two articles (one by Cheng Ch'ao-lin, one by me) in mourning for the death of this giant of the modern Chinese Revolution. At the same time, P'eng Shu-tse denounced Ch'en in a mimeographed issue of *Struggle* for 'failing to maintain his integrity in later life'.

P'eng then attacked us for the 'non-political' attitude we had taken in going out of our way to sing the praises of a former comrade who ideologically had gone over to the enemy camp. We disagreed with him at the time, and today I am even more firmly convinced that we were right in what we had done, since the very act of making an appraisal of Ch'en Tu-hsiu as a person involved questions which were, primarily, not ideological but political. In assessing and mourning him we had to bear in mind that, in their own narrow Party interests, the CCP and the Kuomintang combined to destroy his reputation – the former either by passing over his death in silence or by besmirching his memory, and the latter by paying him false compliments and distorting his ideas. Their aims were essentially the same: to deprive him of his rightful place in history, and in so doing to strike a mortal blow at Chinese Trotskyism.

In mourning Ch'en Tu-hsiu, we had to do everything within our power to restore him to his rightful position as the most outstanding figure in the history of modern Chinese thought and the embodiment of the entire period of western political thought from Rousseau to Marx, and point out that the adoption by such a man of Trotskyism showed that the historical role of our movement in China was to act as a link between the revolutionary traditions of the past and the promise of the future. We therefore had to stress his positive and progressive sides and his great contribution to cultural and political life over the previous thirty years. His later ideological differences with us (differences which, it should be added, never had any effect whatsoever on the actual political life of China) were of minor importance. In the face of our bitterest enemies, it was only right that we should screen the weaknesses of our old comrade-in-arms.

The struggle to restore Ch'en Tu-hsiu to his rightful place in history, inseparable as it is from the struggle to rehabilitate the name of Chinese Trotskyism as a whole, will be even more important in future years. Mao Tse-tung understands this point well, which is why to this very day, despite his own great victory and despite the fact that Ch'en died many years ago, he has never once relaxed the struggle against him.[1] The first Chinese translation of the autobiography Mao related to the American journalist Edgar Snow, published in Hankow in 1937, contains a frank acknowledgement of the influence that Ch'en Tu-hsiu had on him; and it would be no exaggeration to say that Mao, both ideologically and personally, sat

[1] During the last years of his life Mao himself never said anything about Ch'en Tu-hsiu. Through the so-called Gang of Four, however, Ch'en was bitterly denounced during the Cultural Revolution as a 'traitor' and a 'Confucianist'.

at the feet of Ch'en. In the original interview Mao deliberately played down this influence, but after the launching of the Moscow-inspired campaign against Ch'en and Trotsky even this small acknowledgement was enough to get the book withdrawn from circulation. From then on intellectual circles in Yenan and fellow-travellers in other parts of China systematically began to falsify the history of modern Chinese thought, and in particular the history of the May Fourth Movement, with the main aim of playing down the role of Ch'en Tu-hsiu. For Mao to pass in silence over the role of Ch'en Tu-hsiu, when listing the names of progressive thinkers in China in his 1949 article 'On the People's Democratic Dictatorship', was equivalent to the Bolsheviks' naming of only the Decembrists and the Narodniks as their forerunners, and their denial of the role of Plekhanov as their immediate predecessor. Ch'en Tu-hsiu's position in the history of Chinese revolutionary thought can at least be put on a par with that of Plekhanov, and even if we concede that he 'failed to maintain his integrity in old age', then this was at worst a failing that he shared with his Russian counterpart. But after the October Revolution Lenin repeatedly expressed his admiration for that 'father of Russian Marxism' and urged young people to make a careful study of his philosophical writings, which he described as 'the best of their kind in international Marxism'. On one side of Red Square there is a memorial dedicated to progressive forerunners of the revolution, on which Plekhanov's name figures as the last in line and direct predecessor of the Bolsheviks. Why then, does not Mao Tse-tung treat China's Plekhanov – a comparison if anything flattering to the Russian – with similar justice? The answer is quite simply that Ch'en Tu-hsiu's thought ties in with that of Trotsky, the most implacable enemy of Stalinism, the transmitter of the true values of Marxism and the October Revolution, and for that very reason the gravedigger of the Stalinist system.

A year or so after Ch'en Tu-hsiu's death we suffered another tragic loss: Ch'en Ch'i-ch'ang died at the hands of the Japanese, after withstanding several months of the most terrible torture. Ch'en Ch'i-ch'ang was a martyr of Chinese Trotskyism, and had been one of China's foremost revolutionary veterans. Born in Loyang in Honan province, he joined the Chinese Communist Party while a student at Peking University in 1925, and carried out secret activities for the party among students and workers. During the months and years after the defeat of 1927 he worked as a middle- and then a high-ranking member of the Party. On becoming a Trotskyist in 1929 he was expelled. He devoted the rest of his life to the activities of the Chinese Trotskyist movement. Like many other of my comrades, he earned his living by writing articles and editorials for various newspapers and magazines in Shanghai. Among the books and pamphlets published by the Oriental Book Company in Shanghai, he was responsible for editing and translating Trotsky's I Stake My Life and for writing and compiling The Truth About the Moscow Trials and The Verdict of the John Dewey Commission. He also wrote a book called The Great Migration of the Chinese Nationalities, and was one of the main contributors to Struggle: most of the articles on economic questions came from his pen. He had all the qualities of a first-rate revolutionary. He knew how to endure poverty and hardship, and was never interested in the luxuries of life; he hated evil in all its forms, and had a great compassion for all oppressed and downtrodden people; he could not stand pretentiousness, and had none of the affectations of a 'leader'. He always placed himself in the front line whenever danger threatened and was a strange mixture of new-style comradeship and the old-style loyalty to his friends of a Chinese knight errant; he was so concerned about the safety and welfare of his comrades that he was known to everyone as 'elder brother'. Between 1931 and 1937, when the Kuomintang white terror was at its most intense and the organizations we had established in China were being destroyed one after the other, it was he who provided the continuity in our repeated attempts to re-establish the movement. He was extremely vigilant in underground work, never once relaxing his guard; more than once his courage and alertness saved the organization from destruction. I described in Chapter 9 how he managed to shake off the two secret agents who were trailing him and make his way back to Han Chün's house to raise the alarm. He was the complete opposite of those 'revolutionaries' who are so obsessed with their own importance that they put personal safety above all else, fleeing and leaving their comrades to their fate at the slightest hint of danger. Ch'en Ch'i-ch'ang was especially contemptuous of behaviour of this sort.

Ch'en was arrested not as a Trotskyist but as a participant in the anti-Japanese underground resistance. After his arrest, however, the Japanese gendarmes discovered a large quantity of Trotskyist literature in his home, and his 'crime' immediately became more serious.

He was subjected to terrible torture by his captors and asked the names and addresses of the other members of the organization, but refused to submit and was eventually secretly executed in the gendarmerie headquarters.

Early in 1945 Han Chün died in Hong Kong under the Japanese occupation. Although, as I explained above, we never got on very well, I must say that he was also a first-rate revolutionary, an able organizer, and a man of experience in leading the mass struggle. He had originally been a leading member of the trade-union-based Ho Meng-hsiung faction of the CCP, and had an expert knowledge of the Chinese labour movement. As a Trotskyist, he served three years in gaol under the Kuomintang. When the Japanese army occupied Hong Kong, Han was the leader of the branch of our organization there. Although all the other anti-Japanese activists (both Kuomintang and CCP) fled from the former British Colony, Han decided to stay with the Hong Kong workers to whom he was so closely linked, living as a labourer, suffering and struggling together with his friends and comrades, and finally dying of terrible poverty and starvation. He was the husband of the most outstanding woman revolutionary in the Chinese Trotskyist movement, Li Ts'ai-lien.

Li Ts'ai-lien, who had in fact died in 1936, was born into a poor working-class family in Hankow. Her father died while she was still a baby and her mother eked out a living by taking in laundry. When the Northern Expedition reached Wuhan in 1927 Li Ts'ai-lien, although only a girl of fifteen, plunged headlong into revolutionary work and was active as a trade union organizer in the workers' district of Ch'iao-k'ou. After the defeat of the Revolution, she was sent to study at Sun Yat-sen University in Moscow, where she had a wide circle of admirers and was known as the 'Beautiful Sparrow'. Though courted by the sons of high Kuomintang officials (who despite their fathers' break with the CCP were still living in Moscow), she contemptuously spurned her suitors and ended up marrying a student called Lu, who had absolutely no links with the Kuomintang bureaucracy. After the factional struggle in the CPSU spilled over into the Chinese community in Moscow, she became a member of the underground Left Opposition. She returned to China with my group in 1929, worked for a short period in the Party and was expelled at about the same time as I was. During the period in which four separate Trotskyist organizations were in existence she was a member of the October group.

After the destruction of the unified organization in 1931, her husband Lu went over to the Nanking Government. At the time of his defection Li Ts'ai-lien was giving birth to a son in a Red Cross hospital in Shanghai, but when her husband told her of his decision she secretly decided to break with him and fled the hospital soon after. To her great sorrow she was forced to leave her child behind. It was a cruel choice to make, but she had no money to settle accounts with the hospital authorities and was afraid that if she lingered a moment longer she would be sent to Nanking together with her husband. After this incident she became even more firmly committed to the Revolution, tirelessly throwing herself into the struggle at grass-roots level and diligently studying the writings of the great masters of Marxism. She had a frail constitution and lived in great poverty, but, as Confucius said of his disciple Yen Hui, 'others could not bear to see such suffering, but he himself was always happy.' At first Ts'ai-lien had been loved mainly for her looks, but after she became a fully-fledged revolutionary this rather superficial love gave way to feelings of deep respect and honour. We were amazed that such a strong will could inhabit such a frail body. However, extreme poverty gradually took its toll of her health, and she was found to be suffering from pulmonary tuberculosis. Like the rest of us, she was penniless and had no chance of receiving treatment, so her condition gradually worsened.

When I saw her again in early 1935 (after four years of separation) she had already lost her voice, and had to lie on her bed all the time. But I was astonished by her high spirits, her continuing sense of fun and her complete confidence in our cause. We all fervently hoped that her strong will would enable her to overcome her physical exhaustion, and that she would recover her health, or at least survive to see Han Chün come out of gaol. But will-power cannot hold back the laws of nature for ever, and one evening in the early summer of 1936 she died suddenly while staying at a comrade's house, at the age of twenty-four. The extent of our grief can be judged from a letter Ch'en Tu-hsiu wrote at the time to Chao Chi. It made a deep impression on me when I read it, and I believe I can quote correctly from memory: 'Ts'ai-lien's death grieved me deeply. Although many of my closest comrades have met an early death, I have never before experienced such sorrow. Perhaps it is because I am getting old. . . .' But the key to Ch'en's sorrow must have lain elsewhere than in his age, for we younger comrades were no less grief-stricken than he.

The untimely death of a loyal revolutionary is always hard to bear; all the more so, that of an outstanding woman comrade. Historical conditions have up to now meant that women militants are invariably outnumbered by men, so that they are all the more treasured, and their loss the more keenly felt.

I have described only a few of the Trotskyists who died and suffered during that period. Many, many more were oppressed, thrown into prison and even murdered for their beliefs, not only by the Japanese invaders but also by the Kuomintang Government and the CCP authorities. In the Kuomintang areas, particularly Chungking, Trotskyist workers in the arsenal and other factories were arrested and some, including Wang Shu-pen, one of the leaders of young Trotskyists, were imprisoned and murdered in the notorious Hsi-feng concentration camp in Kweichow province. In the areas controlled by the CCP, those Trotskyists who had gone there of their own accord (for example Wang Shih-wei) were brutally persecuted and eventually murdered. All of these comrades equally deserve to be remembered, but unfortunately space does not permit me to do so. All I have done is to give some examples of how Chinese Trotskyists lived and struggled during these years.

CHAPTER 12

From War To Revolution

● ● ●

When the Japanese surrendered in August 1945 there was a sudden surge of activity among the people of the occupied areas. I had never before seen such an abrupt and dramatic transformation in the mood of the masses after a long period of inactivity. Overnight their mood changed from deep despair to exhilarated optimism, and at the same speed from optimism to angry dissatisfaction when they saw their hopes dashed by the Kuomintang. Ever since the launching of the War of Resistance in 1937 we had been firmly convinced that a revolution was inevitable, that war was the mother of revolution. There was therefore an impoitant difference between us and Ch'en Tu-hsiu, and even between us and the 'majority' around P'eng Shu-tse, since we stressed the need not only to prepare, but – even more importantly – to *prepare ourselves for*, the revolution. But despite our firm conviction that the revolution was imminent, we found ourselves ideologically and organizationally unprepared for it when it actually broke out.

When the masses began to show their readiness to act, there was no strong revolutionary Marxist party to give them shape and direction. The CCP had long since withdrawn its cadres from the cities of southeast China, and the various 'democratic parties' could do little more than show the flag. There was therefore a vacuum of revolutionary leadership. If the Chinese Trotskyist movement had had several hundred or, better still, several thousand basic cadres, I believe we would have been in a position to fill that vacuum. Even if the forces of the CCP had then re-entered the cities to dispute the leadership of the mass movement with us, we would not necessarily have suffered a smashing defeat; and even though they might still have ended up by winning control of the whole of China, at least the political situation in the Kuomintang areas in the period from 1945 to 1949 would have gone down in history in a very different form.

But although we were few, and weakened by the split, we successfully intervened with our small forces in the post-war movement, rapidly growing in strength and influence. This was mainly because the political situation in China favoured our position. Having suffered terribly during the eight years of war everyone was eager for peace, but the 'victorious' Kuomintang was actively preparing a new all-out war against the Communists which rapidly led to economic crisis and ruin. People in the Kuomintang-controlled areas, especially the students and the working masses, angrily rose up against the government around the slogans 'no civil war', 'no dictatorship', and 'no starvation'. These slogans fitted in perfectly with the revolutionary democratic programme for which the Chinese Trotskyist movement had been struggling for over fifteen years.

Shortly after the war we in the Internationalist group began to edit a daily supplement to Ch'ien-hsien Jih-pao (Front-line Daily), a Shanghai newspaper whose chief editor was Huan Hsiang (at the time of writing, Chinese Chargé d'Affaires in London). Everyone with any literary ability in our group was mobilized to write for it on militant themes. We achieved quite an impact among students and workers in Shanghai, and for that reason the Kuomintang Department of Social Affairs in the city intervened after only a few weeks to silence us.

By this time we were no longer publishing our mimeographed Internationalist. Now that new newspapers and periodicals were springing up on all sides, we decided to bring out a properly printed and openly distributed fortnightly of our own called Hsin-ch'i (New Banner). The first issue came out in July 1946. The main responsibility for writing and editing fell on Cheng Ch'ao-lin and myself. This meant that the two of us were under a great deal of strain. Just before the sixteenth issue appeared, the paper was banned by government decree, so that the news-stands would not take it and our commercial printers refused to print it. Unwilling to bow to Kuomintang pressure, we rigged up a printing press which though small (and similarly operated) was bigger than the one on which we had printed Struggle, and got two of our comrades to do the typesetting. We brought out a further six rather unattractive, hand-printed issues of Hsin-ch'i. Because of printing difficulties the paper no longer appeared as regularly as before, so we switched our main efforts to books and pamphlets, publishing under the name Hsin-ch'i Library. As far as I remember we brought out Cheng Ch'ao-lin's ABC of the Theory of Permanent Revolution, his translation of Trotsky's The Permanent Revolution and his abridged translation of Trotsky's My Life. I put together an edition of Trotsky's articles and letters on China, calling it

Problems of the Chinese Revolution. We also brought out the photographic reprint, mentioned earlier, of the Chinese translation of Trotsky's *History of the Russian Revolution.*

During the same period, the members of the 'majority' also resumed their publishing activities. At first they brought out an academic periodical called *Ch'iu-chen (Seeking the Truth),* later joined by a smaller magazine initially called *Ch'ing-nien yü fu-nü (Youth and Women)* and afterwards renamed *Hsin-sheng (New Voice).* These two publications also had a certain influence, particularly among students. They differed in their editorial policy from our own *Hsin-ch'i.* In order not to fall foul of the authorities they blurred their true positions and concentrated their fire on the CCP rather than the Kuomintang.

The organizational work of our group also developed during this period, partly because many old comrades who had lost touch with us during the war found their way back into our ranks, but mainly because through our propaganda we recruited many new members in the mass upsurge then taking place. Many old friends returned to Shanghai, among them Ho Tzu-shen, whom I had last seen in Soochow Gaol fifteen years before. He brought with him Ch'en Tu-hsiu's posthumous manuscripts and papers on philological and political subjects which he intended to publish in Shanghai. Many of our old friends scattered throughout the remote south-eastern provinces of China (Szechwan, Yünnan, and Kwangsi) came to Shanghai for a short stay to re-establish links, and the rest resumed contact through correspondence.

They were inevitably rather discouraged to learn of the new split in the movement. Most of them looked forward to early re-unification, and they held discussions with both groups to probe the depth of the differences that separated us and the possibility of fusion. But when they discovered that re-unification was out of the question (for the time being at least) they had to opt for one of the existing organizations. All the 'veteran cadres', apart from Yin K'uan, who sat on the fence, joined the 'minority'.

Through our post-war publishing activities we made contact with a number of young revolutionaries. Although *Hsin-ch'i* had a print-run of only 2,000 we managed to distribute copies to readers in Shanghai and other parts of China, so that it had quite an influence among both people we knew and others we did not. During the Japanese occupation a youth group had been set up in Shanghai called I-she (Society of Tomorrow). Most of its members were university students, teachers in middle and primary schools, and shop and office workers; there were also several artisans and factory workers. Under the cover of being a centre for social and academic activities it was an anti-Japanese political organization, whose leaders at first inclined towards the CCP but were gradually won over to Trotskyism. By the end of the war, when we began to publish Hsin-ch'i, practically the whole group had come over to our side, living and working in close contact with the younger members of our own organization. They also set up a correspondence society and published their letters in a weekly symposium. The discussion evolved informally, so that everyone engaged in it could take part in a free exchange of opinions. This correspondence society was afterwards re-organized into a Marxist Youth League under our political guidance, and was one of the main forces behind the numerous mass protest movements launched by the Shanghai students in the years 1946 to 1948.

The 'majority' developed along more or less similar lines and engaged in similar work, but preferred Stalinist-style cultural and recreational activities, such as folk-dancing, singing and picnics.

As they were growing in influence, each of the Trotskyist organizations began to move at about the same time towards founding a party. Neither of the rival leaderships really wanted re-unification, so that despite a strong wish for reconciliation among the rank and file, the two Chinese Trotskyist groups moved rapidly towards becoming two parties. The 'majority' held a national delegate conference in August of 1948 which adopted the name of Revolutionary Communist Party of China. We made similar preparations and held a national delegate conference six months later, on 27 and 28 April 1949, when we passed a number of resolutions on organizational and political questions, set up a Standing Committee composed of Cheng Ch'ao-lin, Ho Tzu-shen, Lin Huan-hua, comrade Y. (the leader of the I-she group),[1] and myself, and adopted the name of Internationalist Workers Party of China. Our membership was tiny: we had sixty-four comrades in Shanghai and a little over a hundred in China as a whole, although we

---

[1] Y. stood for Yu Shih-i. I dared not mention his whole name when I first wrote these lines, for I had been misinformed that he was the only member of the leadership to escape arrest in the nation-wide purge of Chinese Trotskyists in December 1952. But in 1981 I was told that in fact he had been the first to be arrested and had later died in an asylum in Shanghai (Wang Fan-hsi, 1990).

had a rather larger number of sympathizers. The 'majority' party's membership was probably bigger than ours, but not by much. The two parties together had a membership roughly half the size of that registered at the Unification Conference in 1931, and less even than the number of Chinese Trotskyists active in the Soviet Union in 1929. But despite its small resources, Chinese Trotskyism, now exactly twenty years old, was clearly heading for a revival after suffering repeated blows from all sides. Had the rise of the revolutionary mass movement among the students and urban poor not been interrupted and brought under control by the unexpectedly rapid military victory of the Chinese Communist Party, the Chinese section of the Fourth International might have grown into a powerful political force.

But unfortunately events did not develop in the way we would have liked. The Kuomintang regime emerged from the war much more corrupt than it had gone into it. The whole ruling class around the Kuomintang had been transformed into a gigantic group of speculators, smugglers, parasites, and plunderers, alienating itself from nearly every other class of Chinese society. But just how rotten and isolated it had become was still not apparent. With the support of US imperialism it looked very powerful. Only when it was put to the test of civil war was the awe-inspiring regime of the Kuomintang revealed as a building riddled to the core with termites. The speed with which the whole Kuomintang system collapsed not only shocked the Chiang Kai-shek clique and its patrons in Washington, but also took Stalin and to some extent even Mao Tse-tung by surprise. We Chinese Trotskyists, needless to say, were also caught unawares.

Thus at the end of 1948, with the People's Liberation Army threatening Nanking after their brilliant victory in the Hsüchow area, P'eng Shu-tse continued to insist at the Emergency Conference of his Party that the Chinese Stalinists could not and would not achieve victory on a national scale, although he and his followers resolved at the same time to transfer their central committee and other leading members from Shanghai to Hong Kong.

By the time we held the founding conference of our Party in April 1949, the Communist armies had already crossed the Yangtse River and occupied Nanking and were marching on Shanghai along the Nanking–Shanghai railway line. The victory of the CCP was certain, and all our discussions of political and organizational questions took it as their starting point. As I lost all the relevant documents when I was arrested and expelled from my 'sanctuary' in 1949, I cannot say exactly what was in our political resolutions; but I do remember that we approved a series of guidelines, drawn up in a programmatic resolution by Cheng Ch'ao-lin, on our fundamental positions concerning the proletarian revolution, and also appointed a programme commission to work out their political content in more detail. I myself drew up the political resolution, but am unable to reproduce its contents from memory. The organizational resolution drawn up by Comrade Y. discussed the lessons of the split with P'eng's group at some length, and for the first time ever in the literature of the Chinese Communist movement officially stated that according to our interpretation of the Leninist principle of democratic centralism, minorities in the Party have the right to form factions or tendencies on the basis of their different political positions; that minorities should subordinate themselves to the majority in action; and that the majority should respect the rights of all minorities.

The main question before the conference was how to continue our work under CCP rule. We decided not to move the organization out of China. This was not because we had the slightest illusions about the 'magnanimity' of the CCP or were unaware how easily the CCP's system of mass-based political surveillance could crush our small organization. It was based on the simple conviction that it was better for a revolutionary organization of the working class to go down fighting than to quit the field without a contest. Although this conviction was widespread in the organization and could not be attributed to any one individual, Cheng Ch'ao-lin was its staunchest upholder. Even if we leave aside Cheng Ch'ao-lin's other strengths, his Peter-like spirit of martyrdom alone will ensure him a lasting place in the history of the Revolution. Our dilemma was similar in many ways to that of the early Christians under Nero – should we stay in the capital or flee to a safe place? Some approached the question mainly from the point of view of their own fate, others from the point of view of the future of the organization as a whole; but Cheng Ch'ao-lin did not wait for a voice from the heavens to ask '*Quo vadis?*': his mind was made up from the very outset.

In no sense was our attitude one of collective suicide. After we had decided to stay, we turned to the problem of how to work in the changing circumstances. In brief, we decided to dissolve our organization into a collection of discrete units, breaking off all horizontal links and establishing a co-ordinating centre in a safe place beyond the reach of the Chinese Communist Party. I was chosen to man the co-ordinating centre and therefore had to leave Shanghai. As I was no deserter, I must admit that I was moved by the spirit of St. Peter and retreated to my 'safe place' only with extreme reluctance.

Ironically, the place to which I had gone proved in the space of a mere four months to be anything but 'safe'. The authorities there, hypersensitive as a result of the dramatic changes that were taking place in China, did not allow me to stay, while the comrades who had stayed behind in 'Rome' continued in operation until the night of 22 December 1952.

During the three and a half years between the Communist takeover of Shanghai late in May 1949 and the nation-wide round-up of Trotskyists in December 1952, our comrades worked in many varied fields. The younger members of the Internationalist Workers' Party continued to bring out a journal with the title *Marxist Youth*, never flinching to raise criticisms of the new regime wherever necessary. Many of our comrades took an active part in the agrarian reform movement, and not a few joined the PLA, to fight in its campaigns to liberate the rest of the country. Those in industry led many strikes against capitalist employers, thus challenging the new Government's policy of collaboration between workers and capitalists. In many areas they became leaders of the masses, not only because they acted as staunch champions of the workers' interests but also because the workers who came under their influence were deeply impressed, in a period where Marxism was much in vogue, by their command of revolutionary Marxist politics. In Canton, Lin Huan-hua became one of the principal leaders of the Kwangtung Print-Workers Union; in what had earlier been the French Concession in Shanghai, a group of comrades led a series of strikes; and other comrades also engaged in various struggles in the Shanghai textile industry. Some of our members were inevitably dazzled by the Communist success and either openly or secretly renounced their beliefs and went over to the Government. A smaller number betrayed the organization to the authorities, so that from early 1950 a series of raids was carried out against our members, particularly in the Shanghai and Wenchow areas, in which we suffered serious losses. For example, Lien Cheng-hsiang, a worker in Wenchow, and two former members of the organization in Kwangsi province, died in front of firing squads. But, generally speaking, the CCP did not yet appear to have taken a firm decision to destroy our organization. In some cases they clearly knew the whereabouts of certain leading comrades, but refrained from any moves against them. In other cases they even made approaches to some of our older comrades through intermediaries. For example, the head of the CCP's United Front Department, Li Wei-han, sent the ex-Communist Shih Fu-liang to try to persuade Cheng Ch'ao-lin to do some translations for the Government. But we continued to grow both in numbers and in influence throughout those three and a half years, which is the main reason why the CCP's secret police finally carried out their nation-wide raid on the Trotskyists in December 1952.

Since my links with the movement were automatically severed by the raid, I do not know exactly how many were arrested. A conservative estimate would be two to three hundred, but, since many of our sympathizers and relatives of known Trotskyists were also taken into custody, the actual number was almost certainly much higher. To take my own case as an example, my two nephews and my brother-in-law, who – apart from occasionally reading our newspaper – had no connection with the Trotskyist movement, were taken off to gaol; worse still, a number of their friends, who were not even readers of *Hsin-ch'i*, were rounded up by the police. My wife, a totally non-political person, was also detained for a short period.

The raid was carried out in great secrecy, and the CCP has never once publicly acknowledged that it took place. In the four and a half years since then our comrades have not yet been publicly brought to trial. Nor have any been set free so far – they are in prison or labour camp, and some of them may have been executed. As 'counter-revolutionaries', they are forced to share their cells with genuine counter-revolutionaries and common criminals, so that on top of their physical oppression they have to endure an even more painful spiritual oppression. It cannot be often enough said that these men and women have done absolutely nothing to deserve such treatment, and that they are genuine Communists who have given their best years to the cause of the emancipation of the working class. The reason for the CCP's fear to give them a fair and open trial is clearly that Mao Tse-tung, Liu Shao-ch'i, Chou En-lai, Li Wei-han, and others know their 'old friends' very well and realize that if their revolutionary life-histories once became public, they would win the sympathy of Chinese workers and revolutionaries everywhere.

The immediate effect of the CCP victory was to send a shock-wave
through the ideological life of the Chinese Trotskyist movement.
The period from late 1949 to early 1950 saw an unprecedented upsurge in the level of theoretical activity – there was hardly a comrade
in China who was not pondering the problems raised by the new
developments. Cheng Ch'ao-lin in Shanghai and I in a sea-port off the
south China coast began at almost exactly the same time to carry out
a re-examination of the nature of Stalinism and the Soviet Union and
an assessment of the reasons for the CCP's victory and the nature of the
newly-established state. Both of us put down our conclusions in
writing, and secretly distributed them throughout China and beyond
as reference materials to further the discussion. P'eng's group (the
Revolutionary Communist Party of China) also underwent a period
of intense ideological ferment and produced a number of articles on
political themes, the first of which to appear in book-form was Liu
Chia-liang's *The Present and the Future of China.* Two years later P'eng
Shu-tse wrote his lengthy 'Report to the International Secretariat of
the Fourth International'.

Since then more than six years have gone by. In the meantime, a
whole series of colourful and complex events have taken place, both
in China and on a world scale. The time has now come to make a
comprehensive and thorough-going assessment of the various
opinions each of us advanced in the period immediately following
the CCP victory, to decide which of them have stood the test of time
and which have failed. I hope to make such a study, which would be
beyond the scope of this book, at some future date.

CHAPTER 13

Thinking in Solitude

At the time of writing these lines, in July 1957, I am fifty years old. For the past eight years I have been living on a tiny island off the south China coast, with more than a little time to think. To earn my living I have had to devote much of my energy to writing plays, but this has in no way changed my basic calling. I have remained a revolutionary, keeping a close watch on the changes that have taken place in the world at large and particularly in China. Since December 1952, when my comrades inside China were rounded up by the CCP's secret police, I have no longer been able to play an active part in political life, but this has not prevented me from thinking. In absolute isolation and solitude a person's thinking usually gains in intensity, and so it was with me. The pity is that so much of my time has been taken up with the problem of earning a bare living that up to now I have never had the chance to record all my thoughts over these last few years.

Although I have no intention in what is essentially a book of memoirs of making a detailed examination of the recent development of my thinking, still a short account of some of the problems I have engaged will not be altogether out of place here, particularly since thinking has been more or less my sole political activity in recent times. In an epoch such as ours, however few people may actually share my positions, there must be many addressing similar questions and searching just as anxiously for answers to them. To such people, I hope that my opinions will be of some value.

My thinking over the last few years has focused mainly on two questions. Why, if in terms of overall strategy the Chinese Stalinists were wrong and the Chinese Trotskyists were right, did they end up victorious and we in defeat? And what are the main lessons for the world socialist movement of their victory and our failure?

"Ah-Q-ism"[1] is a harmful affliction, particularly in a revolutionary, but revolutionaries are particularly prey to it, for the very qualities that mark them out – perseverance, tenacity, and an unbounded confidence in one's cause – often prevent them from recognizing their own defeats and admitting their enemies' successes. It is hard, of course, to draw a clear distinction between self-confidence of this sort and revolutionary firmness, for the one is an essential ingredient of the other. But carried to excess, what may originally have been a virtue ends up as "Ah-Q-ism" of the worst sort. To defend one's beliefs blindly and to dress up others' victories as defeats and our defeats as victories is positively harmful to the revolution. A fact remains a fact whether or not we recognize it as one. People who deliberately close their eyes to reality sooner or later end up bumping their heads against it, whereupon they usually surrender unconditionally to the very facts that only yesterday they so stubbornly denied.

True revolutionary confidence comes only on the basis of a cool assessment of how things really are. To recognize defeat is not at all the same as to surrender to the enemy: there is no reason why it should automatically lead to demoralization. In all social struggles – particularly the bitter and complex struggles of modern class society – victories and defeats invariably alternate, so the path to socialism is never straight but zigzag and uneven. Those who travel it must be able to draw the lessons of the defeats through which it inevitably passes.

"What is known as calamity is often good fortune in disguise. What is called good fortune is often a cause of calamity." This is Mao Tse-tung's favorite quotation from the ancient Chinese philosopher Lao Tzu; he often took heart from it in his darkest hours. Perhaps we too can profit from an examination of the "good fortune" of the Chinese Stalinists and the "calamity" of the Chinese Trotskyists in the light of Lao Tzu's teaching. But good fortune is only bestowed on those capable of grasping reality. Here Lao Tzu reminds us of Spinoza's "not to laugh, not to cry, but to understand" – advice we would do well to bear in mind in attempting any such assessment.

---

[1] Ah-Q is the antihero of Lu Hsün's "The True Story of Ah-Q." The usual meaning of Ah-Q-ism is to seek consolation by fantasizing defeat into victory.

As I said earlier, the Chinese Trotskyist movement entered a period of intellectual ferment in late 1949 and early 1950. Shaken to the core by the unexpectedness of what had happened (for none of us had ever reckoned with the possibility of a CCP victory), we began in the light of the new situation to reconsider our fundamental positions and beliefs. In this atmosphere of intense turmoil and in the heat of events, I made my own attempt to come to grips with the causes of the CCP victory, and noted some of my conclusions in a booklet published in early 1950.[2] In it I said that the Soviet Union had turned into a bureaucratic collectivist state, and the Stalinist party into a party of collectivist bureaucrats. From this I concluded that the victory of the CCP was merely the victory of a collectivist bureaucratic party and in no way the victory of a Chinese proletarian party, i.e. of proletarian revolution.

This analysis seemed to me to explain many features of the Stalinist parties and to solve the riddle of the CCP victory. Gradually, however, I discovered that for all its advantages and its theoretical consistency, once applied to revolutionary practice (e.g., which side to take in the civil war between the CCP and the Kuomintang) it proved to be wholly inappropriate and plainly wrong. Armed with this discovery, I returned again from the realm of politics to sociology and from practicalities to theoretical research, and eventually I arrived at the conclusion that among the numerous theoretical analyses of the Soviet Union and Stalinism advanced both inside and outside the Fourth International, Trotsky's was by far the strongest and in the best interests of socialist revolution. I had launched my soul onto unknown seas only to land again at the port where I had embarked. Some may mock me for this. Let them. All that matters to me is the search for truth, and for the key to the completion of the revolution.

To tell the whole story of how I traveled this ideological circuit, with its various periods and stages, would require more lines than I have room for here, and in any case I intend to devote a special study to this question.[3]

[2] I-te, Su-lien yen-chiu (A Study of the Soviet Union). Hong Kong, 1950.

[3] This study, titled Ssu-hsiang wen-t'i (Some Iedological Questions) was mimeographed in 1962 and printed in Hong Kong in 1982. It consists of three articles: "On Ch'en Tu-hsiu's Opinions Expressed in His Last Years" (1957); "On the

So I will confine myself here to a brief discusson of the class nature of the CCP and the historical role of Stalinist parties in general, for it was on these two questions that we Chinese Trotskyists developed a number of positions from which flowed our wrong analysis in and around 1949. Perhaps this discussion will serve as a warning example of how easy it is for revolutionaries to fall captive to their own prescriptions if they do not continually check them against events.

For many years up to and even after 1949 we Chinese Trotskyists had beleived that the CCP represented the interests of the petty bourgeoisie (mainly peasants and intellectuals) and was no longer a party of the working class. None of us had ever considered why – we simply took it as self-evident. That the CCP had withdrawn from the big cities, lived in and drawn its forces from the country-side, and abandoned class struggle in favor of class peace was more than enough to confirm us in our opinion.

It is impossible to say who first advanced this analysis. In his report to the International Secretariat of the Fourth International in November 1951, P'eng Shu-tse tried to attribute it to Trotsky, arguing that "beginning with 1930, Trotsky repeatedly pointed out that the CCP had gradually degenerated from a workers' party into a peasant party."[4] But this assertion is quite groundless. In the letter to the Chinese Left Opposition that P'eng quotes ("Peasant War in China and the Proletariat"), Trotsky never once argued that the CCP had "gradually degenerated from a workers' party into a peasant party." Instead he simply talked about the possible outcome of the struggle between the two factions of the CCP, i.e., if a civil war were to break out between a peasant army led by Stalinists and a proletarian vanguard led by Leninists "the Left Opposition and the Stalinists would have ceased to be communist factions and would have become hostile parties, each with a different class basis." But he went straight on from this theoretical hypothesis to ask if such a perspective was inevitable. His answer was unequivocal: "No, I

Twentieth Anniversary of the Transitional Programme" (1958); and "A Letter to Friends" (1958).

[4] P'eng Shu-tse, "The Causes of the Victory of the Chinese Communist Party over Chiang Kai-shek, and the CCP's Perspectives," in P'eng Shu-tse, *The Chinese Communist Party in Power*, edited by Les Evans. New York: Monad Press, 1980, pp. 71–137, at p. 108.

don't think so at all. Within the Stalinist faction (the official Chinese Communist Party) there are not only peasant, i.e. petty bourgeois tendencies, but also proletarian tendencies."[5]

Trotsky's letter was written on September 22, 1932, nearly a whole year before he decided to call for new communist parties and a new International. So at a time when we still considered ourselves a faction of the CCP, Trotsky was allegedly arguing that this same CCP had degenerated from a workers' into a peasants' party!

It was precisely our wrong understanding of the class nature of the CCP that to a large extent determined our positions on it – in particular the significance of its eventual victory over the Kuomintang – both before and after 1949. Having once established that it was a petty bourgeois party, we were logically driven to conclude that it could never lead a genuine revolution, still less lead to victory: for it is a fundamental theorem of Marxism (and of Trotsky's theory of permanent revolution in particular) that in the modern age and in a backward country even the bourgeois-democratic tasks of the revolution can only be solved by a thoroughgoing revolution led by the proletariat and its party. Even during the civil war between the CCP and the Kuomintang from 1946 to 1949 we invariably argued that a peasant army led by a petty bourgeois party was almost bound to lose, and that even if by some remote chance it won, it would inevitably end up in a blind alley. When facts proved otherwise and the revolution led by the CCP not only triumphed but deepened, we remained tightly bound by our old preconceptions. Instead of promptly recognizing the revolution for what it was, we continued to cling to our old assessment and to look for theoretical supports to bridge the growing gap between what had really happened and what we thought had happened. We now argued not only that the CCP was no longer a proletarian party but that it was not even a petty bourgeois party; instead, it represented the interests of an entirely new class – a class that Cheng Ch'ao-lin called state capitalist and I called bureaucratic collectivist. We believed that such classes were the product of a whole series of defeats of the revolution on a world scale and of the overgrowth of the capitalist system, so they were powerful but reactionary. Unlike the petty bourgeoisie, they were strong enough to overthrow

[5] *Leon Trotsky on China*, edited by Les Evans and Russell Block. New York: Monad Press, 1976, p. 530.

the old bourgeois regimes – in China, the Kuomintang – and to turn society on its head. But unlike the proletariat, they were incapable of moving onward in the direction of socialism, and would at best establish a regime of state capitalism or bureaucractic collectivism.

In this way, Cheng Ch'ao-lin and I built further on our old assessment of the CCP.

P'eng Shu-tse and a number of his followers responded to the situation in a different way, clinging to the same old formula and flatly denying that China had had a revolution. For two whole years, right up to November 1951, P'eng argued that the new regime was "actually a naked Bonapartist military dictatorship of the petty bourgeoisie and bourgeoisie, based on the armed peasantry," and that "such a military dictatorship will never change its bourgeois character."[6] In May 1952, however, he suddenly discovered that it had lost its bourgeois character and acquired a "dual character" because "the worker elements have increased in number in the last two years . . . (during the agrarian reform and the campaign against corruption, etc.)"[7] However, he continued to insist that the party up to then had been a party of peasants, and that its earlier seizure of power had been not a revolution but an accident resulting from a conjuncture of exceptional historical circumstances.

Like Cheng Ch'ao-lin and me, P'eng was unable to wrench himself free from the old formula, but unlike us he continues to insist to this day that we Chinese Trotskyists were absolutely right to apply it to the theory and practice of the Chinese revolution at each stage in its development. I am not concerned here with whether P'eng's claim to infallibility is valid, and will return to it in a future study.[8]

I said earlier that we had based our assessment of the CCP on the observation (a) that it had withdrawn from the cities into the

[6] Quoted from "The Political Resolution," written by P'eng on January 17, 1950, and adopted at a meeting of P'eng's group in Hong Kong. In his report to the Third Congress of the Fourth International, P'eng formulated the same idea in a slightly different form. See P'eng Shu-tse, *The Chinese Communist Party in Power*. New York: Monad Press, 1980, p. 110.

[7] P'eng Shu-tse, *The Communist Party in Power*, p. 136.

[8] See "On the Causes of the Triumph of the CCP and the Failure of the Chinese Trotskyists in the Third Chinese Revolution."

countryside and recruited its forces almost exclusively from the peasantry rather than the working class and (b) that it had capitulated in 1937 to the Kuomintang in the name of unity against Japan, by declaring its conversion to Sun Yat-senism, accepting the reorganization of its armed forces into the armed forces of the Kuomintang, and promising to give up class struggle. On the face of it, this was decisive enough proof of the charges we were making: a party that had torn itself away from the working class, left the main battleground, and given up its revolutionary platform could no longer be called working class.

So when we first declared in the mid-1930s that the CCP had degenerated into a party of the petty bourgeoisie, we were acting on entirely reasonable assumptions. Where we went wrong was in failing to check our assessment against reality, and in closing our eyes to developments that might falsify our analysis. Looking back, I can now see that we ignored four key facts. First, the CCP withdrawal from the cities was neither voluntary nor deliberate, but mainly the result of Kuomintang persecution and repression, so it could not be taken as proof that the CCP had committed itself to a new strategic orientation toward peasant war rather than proletarian revolution. Second, after withdrawing into the countryside the CCP did not forsake, in either words or deeds, the platform of "a revolutionary united front under the leadership of the proletariat." Third, while it is true that the CCP abandoned class struggle during the second united front, i.e., it called off land revolution and submitted to the leadership of Chiang Kai-shek in a decisive turn that we rightly denounced at the time as a final capitulation, by and large the turn was at the level of tactical maneuver rather than of strategy and was never carried to its logical conclusion, the main reason being that there were still revolutionary tendencies in the CCP that opposed Stalin's policy of capitulation. Fourth, during both the "soviet and Red Army" period and the "united front and Eighth Route Army" period, the CCP all along remained an organization of highly disciplined revolutionaries and carried out its recruitment (both political and military) on a class basis. If we Chinese Trotskyists had kept a closer eye on these developments and constantly checked our assessment of the CCP against them, we would have understood the true meaning of the victory of the CCP and would have made fewer mistakes in developing our own work and ideas.

Lenin once said something of relevance in this connection. Discussing the problem of British communists joining the Labour Party, he said: "Of course, most of the Labour Party's members are working men. However, whether or not a party is really a political Party of workers does not depend solely upon a membership of workers but also upon the men that lead it, and the content of its actions and its political tactics. Only this latter determines whether we really have before us a political party of the proletariat. Regarded from this, the only correct, point of view, the Labour Party is a thoroughly bourgeois party . . .".[9]

Following Lenin's method, we Chinese Trotskyists should have paid more attention to the "men that led" the CCP. We should have kept a close eye on the struggle between the various tendencies (particularly the Maoists and the Wang Mingites) in its leadership and tirelessly analyzed the "content of its actions and political tactics." But instead we put too much emphasis on its social composition, which was overwhelmingly peasant, and so concluded that it was a petty bourgeois party; which later led me to adopt the theory of bureaucratic collectivism. So we were unable to foresee a great many of the developments in the Third Chinese Revolution or to understand them even after they had happened. Had we followed Lenin's method, we would early on have developed a different view of the CCP. We would have admitted that in spite of its massive bureaucratic degeneration and its oppressive internal regime, its overwhelmingly peasant composition, its unprincipled maneuvers, and its distortions of Marxism, it was still a working class party of sorts, though it was more so in some periods than in others and it acquired a number of grotesque and repellent features.

It is precisely because we failed to follow this procedure that we fell so wide of the mark in our criticism of the CCP in the 1940s and immediately after the establishment of the new regime.

The extreme confusion sown in the ranks of the Trotskyist movement in both China and the world by the victory of the CCP in 1949 was due not only to our wrong analysis of the class nature of

[9] Speech on Affiliation to the British Labour Party, delivered on August 6, 1920, at the Second Congress of the Comintern. Published in V. I. Lenin, *Collected Works*. Moscow, 1966, vol. 31, p. 257.

that party but also to one crucial mistake in our view of the historical role of Stalinism in general.

Ever since the task of creating a new International was first broached in 1933, we had analyzed the Third International as historically spent and no longer capable of playing the role of headquarters of the world revolution. The parties affiliated to it, organizationally and ideologically rotted by the Stalin canker, could no longer be renovated or revitalized into revolutionary parties. They never led a revolution to victory, and they would go out of their way to sabotage, betray, and suppress any revolutionary upsurge not under their direct control. However incredible it might seem, they not only could not but would not take victory for themselves, for any victorious revolution outside the USSR would in the long run weaken and destroy Moscow's bureaucratic control over its "vassals and dependencies" in the Third International.

This analysis is fundamentally sound and was in the main borne out by a number of events of world importance between 1934 and 1945. However, in our exaggerated and mechanical interpretation of it, the view that Stalinist parties will refuse to make revolution even if it puts the helm of state into their hands developed into a sheer prejudice, and explains our utter confusion in the face of the CCP victory in 1949.

This is not the place for a detailed account of the overall evolution of Trotskyism on a world scale—how it grew from a faction of the Communist Party into an independent organization, and how it broke from the Third International and launched the Fourth. Suffice it to say that in the summer and autumn of 1933, after Stalin's "Third Period" policy had paved the way for Hitler's triumph in Germany and the whole of the Third International had supported his positions, Trotsky's decision to call for new communist parties and a new International was just as necessary and had the same historical significance as Lenin's call for a new (Third) International in 1914, when the parties of the Second International came out in support of their respective ruling classes in the imperialist war.

In making the analogy, however, we should note that the history of the past twenty years has shown that the actions of the Third International (which we declared dead in 1933) have differed in significant ways from those of the Second International after 1914. There are a number of fundamental differences between the parties of Stalinism and of social democracy. Even today the former are actually still not reconcilable with capitalism, for they fight to maintain and consolidate state property in the Soviet Union and at the same time work for the creation of a similar system in the capitalist countries. To judge by what they say and write, they are scarcely distinguishable from classical Menshevism, but whereas classical Menshevism is a position of principle and strategy, "Menshevism" of the Stalinist variety has (at least since 1930) been little more than a series of tactical measures, a smokescreen behind which to carry out political maneuvers. We Trotskyists have never taken this difference seriously, so we have tended to overlook or underestimate the anticapitalist aspect of Stalinist parties and have been taken unawares by at least three important developments over the past ten years: First, instead of reverting to capitalism (as we had predicted), the system of state property in the Soviet Union emerged from the Second World War stronger than ever; second, the economic and political system of the Soviet Union was exported (at bayonet point) to Eastern Europe; third, the Chinese Communist Party defeated the Kuomintang and began to reconstruct the Chinese economy on the model of the Soviet Union.

So we must admit that we have underestimated the anticapitalist potential of these parties, which even now is still not entirely exhausted. What then of Trotsky's decision to establish a new International?

Judged from the point of view of the long-term interests of world socialist revolution, we were right to argue that the Third International no longer had any positive role to play, that its thinking, politics, and organization had degenerated to the point where it would never again complete a revolution like the one in Russia or establish a workers' government like in the early days of the Soviet Union. The path of internal reform had been blocked: A new revolutionary International had become necessary.

This was the only conceivable solution to the problems posed by historical circumstance, and we must continue to defend it now and in the future as stubbornly as we ever did in the past.

But the way in which we understood and interpreted the 1933 decision must be judged separately. Our contention that the Stalinist parties would do no more than serve the Kremlin directly and the world bourgeoisie indirectly, squander the fruits of revolution (especially state-owned property) in the Soviet Union, and betray or crush revolutions that might break out elsewhere in the world even where this would place state power in their hands was demonstrably wrong.

Perhaps one of the two of these views can be ascribed to Trotsky, but most of them are mechanistic derivatives from or even caricatures of Trotsky's original positions. Here I am not interested in who authored these mistakes. What does concern me is that over the last twenty years or more precisely these views have decided our attitude as Trotskyists toward Stalinism throughout the world; and we Chinese Trotskyists were at the very least among their most stubborn proponents.

This is why, even after the CCP's stunning victories around Hsüchow and Pengpu in late 1948, Trotskyists like Liu Chia-liang argued that the Chinese Stalinists would never inflict a nationwide defeat on the Kuomintang; why, even after the fall of Canton in the autumn of 1949, they declared that the CCP would decline to reap the fruit of victory; and why, even after the new regime had been established in Peking and land revolution had been extended throughout China, they asserted that the CCP was not only unable but unwilling to retain state power, and that agrarian reform would (for some unspecified reason) stop at the northern bank of the Yangtze River.[10]

But if we renounce such seemingly essential parts of our analysis of Stalinism, how can we continue to argue that the 1933 decision to create a new International was and remains correct and necessary? Should we not admit that since the analysis upon which this decision was based has been undermined, the International should disband and surrender to the Stalinists?

No few Chinese Trotskyists have done so, including veterans like Li Chi and Liu Jen-ching. A few surrendered under pressure, but most did so from conviction. Before they finally went over to the CCP in the early 1950s I had a chance to discuss this with a number of them, either face to face or through letters. My arguments can be more or less reduced to the following two points.

First, while it is true that Stalinist parties are far less easily rec-

---

[10] Liu Chia-liang, *Chung-kuo-ti hsien-chuang yü ch'ien-t'u* (*China's Present and Future*). Hong Kong, 1949.

onciled to capitalism than are the social democratic parties, there is still no reason to believe that they can adopt a strategy and tactics of the sort that is necessary for socialist revolution.

Second, even if Stalinist parties can under certain circumstances fight capitalism and carry out a revolution, we should not neglect the equally fundamental question of how they do so, and what sort of regimes they form. As the newly established Stalinist states multiply, this aspect of the problem will increasingly eclipse the other in importance.

Yes, revolutions cannot be made to order and along a predetermined path, but we should still recognize that goal and means are interdependent and that means to no small extent determine goals. The difference between one means and another can amount to hundreds of thousands of human lives, so the choice between them is crucially important and deserves our closest consideration. Moreover, bureaucratic rule will never create a truly socialist society. In the absence (however unlikely) of a successful antibureaucratic upsurge by the workers, bureaucratic rule, with its inevitable interstate wars and conflicts, will spell the collapse into barbarism of human society as a whole.

Needless to say, I did not succeed in convincing my old friends or in preventing them from going over (some from Hong Kong) to the new regime in China. To their great misfortune and disappointment, the authorities doubted the sincerity of their conversion, so few of them got jobs and some were even arrested and cast into jail. In the light of their own experience and of recent developments in the Soviet Union, Poland, and Hungary, most of them must now realize that their deicision to surrender to the Stalinists was wrong.

The Yugoslavian experience, Khrushchev's exposure of Stalin's crimes at the Twentieth Congress of the CPSU, and the tragic events in Poland and Hungary have posed in all its immediacy the problem of how to establish and maintain genuine workers' power.

In his famous speech of December 7, 1956, E. Kardelj, Vice-President of the Federal People's Assembly of Yugoslavia, said: "It should be noted that since the progressive socialist forces have thus far lacked experience in combatting bureaucratism, to induce a form of true democracy from experience is out of the question. Before the Twentieth Congress of the CPSU only the Yugoslavian party had ever seriously searched for and eventually found a series of political measures to resolve the contradictions of the period of transition and established institutions of mass self-management in various areas of social activity, thereby enabling our society to get rid of those political forms and measures used by bureaucratic elements in their attempt to reduce the whole of society to stagnation."[11]

Kardelj rightly emphasized the importance of combatting bureaucratism (though it is another question whether Yugoslavia itself has succeeded in doing so). But he forgot to say that Trotskyism was born from precisely such a struggle and has accumulated valuable experience from the fight for a "form of true democracy." For though the Fourth International has so far achieved little of real significance in practical politics, it has contributed richly to theoretical research into the problems of the transition to socialism, in which sense it represents the pinnacle of contemporary Marxism.

Recent experience in the Soviet Union and Eastern Europe shows that there has been no serious or successful attempt to resolve the problems of bureaucratic rule, though the struggles that have broken out there have in general been against bureaucracy. This suggests that without the program advocated over the years by the Fourth International, the efforts of those currently raising a hue and cry against bureaucratism will surely fail. But though such people have still not broken in practice with Stalinism, what they say is still encouraging. It proves that we Trotskyists have not been fighting in vain over the last thirty years, that our ranks will swell and that Stalinist domination of the world communist movement is coming to an end. In coming years whether we actually achieve anything will depend in part on how far we succeed in intergrating our program and membership with antibureaucratic mass movement in countries under communist rule. But we must never forget to check our positions in the light of events, to hold firm to those that are right, and to right or discard those that are wrong. A Fourth International full of life and energy is more necessary now than it ever was, and must be strengthened and expanded. We

---

[11] This quotation is retranslated from the Chinese.

have no reason to be pessimistic, still less to desert our organization.

We first launched the campaign for a new International in 1933, mainly because of our political appraisal of Stalinism but also because of the internal structure of Stalinist parties, which brook no opposition. Now, however, we have begun to notice for the first time (beyond the isolated example of Yugoslavia) that a general process of differentiation is taking place within the Stalinist parties and the countries under their rule, so there is a slight prospect of some degree of internal reform. Should we change our attitude toward them accordingly? Should the world Trotskyist movement return to its old pre-1933 position, which looked to reform existing communist parties rather than set up new ones? I think not. The events in Hungary in 1956 showed how stubbornly those in power in the party and the state will fight to defend themselves and that they will not make the slightest concessions except under the direct revolutionary pressure of the mass movement. So we should continue to propagate unwaveringly the necessity of anti-bureaucratic political revolution in these countries. But at the same time we should avoid interpreting and applying this position mechanistically. The various communist parties and the states that they control are no longer Stalinist to an identical degree, and conflicts and struggles are breaking out among them. We should not stand aside from these fights, like passive onlookers. Rather than indiscriminately attack each side with equal force, we should distinguish between them and tirelessly pay attention to the conflicts and struggles, no matter how small, that divide them; and we should give critical support to those that prove the more progressive. In so doing, our revolutionary attitude toward the faction or party concerned should be fairly flexible in its tactical application.

In sum, with our fundamental tenets unrevised, i.e., sticking firmly to the position of preparing political revolution in all degenerated or deformed workers' states (whether Stalinist, semi-Stalinist, or "de-Stalinized") by siding with the toiling people in their fight for democracy and against privilege, we should at the same time pay more attention to the specific application to different circumstances of our basically identical position. A right policy is not enough – it must be supplemented by elastic and flexible tactics.

Is the CCP a Stalinist party, to what extent has it been Stalinized, and what position does it occupy within Stalinism as a world system? Is Mao a Chinese Tito, or will he become one? What is the nature of the People's Republic of China and what stance should we adopt toward it?

These questions have haunted me in recent years, so I will briefly deal with them. I pointed out in an earlier chapter that it is clear from the history of the factional struggle in the CCP ever since the mid-1930s that Mao has never been a Stalinist in terms of faction. The Stalinists would never have recruited anyone as opinionated as Mao into their inner circle, and he is in any case by nature incapable of acting like a Wang Ming. I have never had the chance to work closely with Mao, but we have no few mutual friends, among them Hsü Chih-hsing (Mao's childhood friend) and Ho Tzu-shen (who worked closely with Mao for many years and has been in prison under him since 1952). From them I learned many things about Mao's character, his learning, and his way of thinking and working. Combining these indirect impressions with my own knowledge of Mao's life and writings, I conclude that as a man he has many traits in common with Ch'en Tu-hsiu, the founding father of Chinese communism. Both had their first love of learning in Confucianism; both built their ideological foundations in the Chinese classics; both acquired their knowledge of modern European thought, in particular Marxism-Leninism, in the same way, by building a rough superstructure of foreign style on a solid Chinese foundation at a time when they were physically as well as intellectually fully matured. So both Ch'en and Mao take "Chinese learning as substance, western learning for practical application" (to quote the words of the Ch'ing dynasty reformer Chang Chih-tung). They can never become "thoroughly Europeanized," nor will they ever cast aside that self-conceited pride peculiar to old-style Chinese scholars. I pointed out in an earlier chapter that Ch'en Tu-hsiu had a poor opinion of foreign communists, all the more so after Moscow had shamelessly heaped the whole of the blame for the defeat of 1927 on his shoulders. He always spoke with hatred and contempt of those Chinese communists who kowtowed to foreign comrades, and he dismissed them as "red compradors." Mao, being more diplomatic, substituted the word "dogmatist" for "comprador," but he looked down just as deeply on men like Wang Ming who could only quote from the works of Marx, Lenin, and Stalin

and from resolutions of the Comintern. Ho Tzu-shen once told me
an interesting anecdote in this connection. While he and Mao were
carrying out underground work for the Hunan Provincial Committee of the CCP in Ch'angsha in the autumn of 1927, at a time when
the revolution was in chaotic retreat and hundreds of communists
were being sent to Moscow to study, Mao once said to him: "I
won't go to Moscow until the revolution triumphs."

Even at that early date Stalin must have been aware of the recalcitrance of this leader of equal ambition, desperately struggling for
survival in the faraway mountains of Kiangsi. That is why he unfal-
teringly placed his confidence in Wang Ming and finally planted
him as leader of the CCP and the Red Army in 1931. But this "red
comprador" proved unequal to the job, so Mao and other "indigenous" leaders squeezed his followers out of the leadership at the
Tsunyi (Kweichow) conference in 1935. After that Mao (in the words
of Cheng Ch'ao-lin) was a "Titoist before Tito."

Mao has all along remained outside the clique transplanted into
the CCP from Moscow, but that has not prevented him from being
a staunch Stalinist, just as it has not prevented the CCP from becoming Stalinized and the People's Republic of China from being
organized and constituted after an essentially Stalinist model. Historical and social factors are incomparably stronger than individual
likes and dislikes in determining the character of states and institutions. The extreme backwardness of Chinese economy and society, the peasant environment in which the CCP was forced to live
and grow, its protracted involvement in a predominantly military
struggle, the ebb of the world revolution, the ever-deepening bureaucratic involution of the Soviet state between 1930 and 1945,
and (last but not least) Mao's undemocratic disposition and training – all these factors combined to force the Chinese Communist
Party and its leading figure onto the Stalinist road. In *fundamental
ideological terms* Stalinism means the substitution of nationalism for
internationalism, of tactical interclass maneuvers for class struggle,
and of bureaucratic dictatorship for the democracy of the toiling
people. In practical terms, it means that all initiatives from lower
levels of party and government organizations are stifled, that everything is done according to instruction, that political and social life
is dominated by a frantic personality cult and a hierarchy of privilege, that all forms of thinking are controlled by the secret police,
that all oppositions are purged, that all factions and parties are for-

bidden, and so on *ad nauseam* – all these measures have already been copied from Stalin and the CPSU by Mao and the CCP.

I am told that some Marxists in the Fourth International believe that since the victory of the CCP was due mainly to its having broken successfully from Stalinism, or to its freedom from Stalinist influence and domination, the CCP can no longer be regarded as a Stalinist party. Such a view is onesided and unsound. True, under the direct impact of class struggle the CCP, with Mao Tse-tung at its head, tactically violated Stalin's directives and at crucial junctures took an opposite path to that of Stalin by going all out to mobilise the masses, giving a bold leadership to their struggles, and finally achieving revolution. In that sense, though the CCP remained a fundamentally Stalinist party, one of the main reasons it triumphed was because it failed to follow the line of Stalinism.

So Maoism and Stalinism are not direct equivalents. The different conditions of time and space in which the Russian and Chinese revolutions occurred, the different cultural backgrounds and traditions of those who made them, and the different personal qualities of a Stalin and a Mao have led to important differences in both the outlook and the practice of the two men. The elements of identity and difference between them make an interesting and important subject for investigation, from both an historical and a political point of view, to which I shall return in a separate study.[12] But for my present purposes I must insist: Checked off against my earlier list of basic characteristics of Stalinism as a political force and a political system, the CCP is still fundamentally a Stalinist party and Maoism is still fundamentally a variant of Stalinism.

One question that is worth discussing is what will become of the CCP now that Stalin and Stalinism are coming under fire in the Soviet Union and Eastern Europe and the Stalinist camp is beginning to differentiate.

Immediately after the victory of the revolution in China many people were inclined to think that Stalinism in the CCP would be shaken off much earlier and much more easily than in other Stalinized parties, and that in some branches of the new-born state

---

[12] See San Yuan (i.e., Wang Fan-hsi) *Mao Tse-tung ssu-hsiang yü Chung-Su kuan-hsi* (*Maoism and Sino-Soviet Relations*). Hong Kong: Hsin-ta ch'u-pan-she, 1972, and *Mao Tse-tung ssu-hsiang lün-kao* (*Studies in Mao Tse-tung Thought*). Hong Kong: Hsin-ta ch'u-pan-she, 1973, in which this question is expounded in greater detail.

machine Stalinist methods of rule and institutions would never be systematically established. Later developments showed this view to be naive. Judging from its reaction to "de-Stalinization" in the CPSU and its hostile attitude to the Hungarian Revolution, the leadership of the CCP sticks faster to Stalinism than many of us thought. It has not actively facilitated the breakdown of Stalinism, and in some ways it has even turned out to be a bulwark of this obnoxious doctrine and its reactionary practice.

But this is hardly surprising, for the CCP set out to construct socialism from a socio-economic level lower even than that of the Soviet Union in the early 1920s and based its policies on the Stalinist principle of nationalist autarchy. So Stalinism will persist and even grow in China, at least in the short term. However, there is an important difference between now and when Stalinism first emerged and consolidated itself as a system: Then the curve of world revolutions was downward, now it is upward. What's more, even though the Chinese Revolution is artificially confined by its leaders to strict national boundaries, it is impossible to prevent it from coming under the influence of revolutionary movements elsewhere in the world. The most obvious example was the tragicomic "Hundred Flowers" campaign, unthinkable but for the Hungarian Revolution of 1956. It would be naive to imagine that that campaign was in any way a real attempt to grapple with the actual problems of Stalinism, but even so there was a strong link between it and the events in Hungary.

The "Hundred Flowers" campaign showed that most top-level intellectuals in China plus many students and workers and practically the whole of the peasantry are deeply dissatisfied with the CCP's Stalinist regime. But their demands were ruthlessly suppressed during the subsequent "anti-rightist" campaign, and those called upon by the party to speak out were mercilessly persecuted. The result of this act of treachery will be (as Mao Tse-tung himself said in another context), to "make such a mess of things that it can never be cleaned up." If through the current anti-rightist campaign the CCP further strengthens the Stalinist system in all its aspects, the anti-Stalinist indignation of China's intellectual youth and of its workers and peasants will explode all the sooner and with all the more serious and wide-ranging consequences. Impelled by events both in China and in the world, a genuine and powerful left wing may come into being within the CCP, perhaps linking up with the forces of Chinese Trotskyism to channel all anti-Stalinist (i.e., anti-Maoist) movements in the direction of a new anti-bureaucratic revolution. Such a revolution would aim to establish a real government of workers and peasants and to ally with the world proletariat to speed the advance to socialism.

I believe that history will show that such a prospect, far from being a mere pipedream, is entirely realistic.

Epilogue

● ● ●

I have now more or less exhausted what I have to say. However, it seems to me that there is one question I have so far left unanswered: since I am a mere foot-soldier in the Revolution, how did it enter my mind to write a book of recollections of this sort, and what is there of value in it?

I should start by pointing out that many years ago, in Japanese-occupied Shanghai, Cheng Ch'ao-lin also set out to write his memoirs. Beginning with his early childhood, he traced his life down to 1927 and the defeat of the Revolution, when he attended the August 7th Emergency Conference of the Central Committee of the Party and began working in the underground with Ch'ü Ch'iu-pai. At that point he seemed to lose interest, devoting only a few pages to his conversion to the Left Opposition and the early days of the Chinese Trotskyist movement and eventually stopping altogether. We urged him to continue with the project, and it was then that he countered by saying that I should write about my own experiences in 1928–9, when nearly half the Chinese students in Moscow came over to the side of the Left Opposition. He argued that the events of that period were important in the history not only of the Chinese Trotskyist movement but of the Chinese Communist Party as a whole, and that, of those involved in them, I was the sole survivor and the best qualified to tell the tale. I was much moved by what he had said and agreed to his proposal, but more urgent work prevented me from carrying out my promise.

Since 1952, when Cheng Ch'ao-lin was thrown into Mao's prison, I have heard nothing more from him, and do not even know whether he is alive or dead. His memoirs, if not destroyed, are probably under lock and key in the archives of the CCP's secret police department. In recent years I have often thought back on the proposal that he made and felt guilty for not having fulfilled the wishes of a good friend: having lost my family, comrades-in-arms, relatives, and friends, I have been forced to live in a state of endless political idleness. My life seems to have ground to a halt, or to have lapsed into stagnation. In such a situation one is inevitably inclined to look back over the past. Events and people from bygone days have haunted me like ghosts, gripping my mind. Their memory has stuck – like a fish-bone in my throat; I could never feel at ease until I succeeded in dislodging it. It was for this reason that at one point I wrote several sketches of unforgettable old friends of mine. I also made a number of attempts to write a 'Chapter of My Life', dealing with the various factions among the Chinese Communists in Moscow, but never succeeded, either through pressure of other work or simply because of the inherent difficulty of the project.

It was the 20th Congress of the CPSU of 1956, with its decision to launch a 'destalinization' campaign and rewrite the history of the Soviet Party, that finally made up my mind to write the 'chapter'. My determination was further strengthened by the reaction of the CCP to the dramatic political turn in Moscow. After a close study of the literature published or released by the Chinese party, I began to realize that the struggle among the Chinese Communists in Moscow had not only left a deep imprint on the history of the CCP over the past twenty-six years, but would continue to reverberate throughout its activities for many years to come. Because of various internal and external considerations, the present leadership of the Party is in no position to write a frank and fair account of this period of history, and future historians who wish to do so may find it hard to come by the necessary first-hand materials. As a participant in the events of those days, I therefore decided to do my best to fill the gap.

With Cheng Ch'ao-lin's words resounding in my mind, and with the active help of Lou Kuo-hua, I set about my work in earnest. At first my plan was simply to write one chapter about my Moscow days, but this soon began to grow. Everything has its own logical development, even the writing of a short article. It is impossible to cut a cross-section from one's life as though from the trunk of a tree. To make any one episode comprehensible, one must say something about both its causes and its consequences. But simply to add a heavy crown and long roots to the original trunk would at best be to create a rather ugly tree. Thus willy-nilly my one chapter grew into a fairly lengthy autobiography.

This also explains why what purports to be an autobiography is not in fact mainly devoted to my own personal life. I only allowed myself a place in the whole story because I wanted some sort of thread to string together the various events of the last fifty years. To use a cliché, my aim was to see some aspects of a great epoch reflected in the mirror of an ordinary person's life. Nor is it a history of Chinese Trotskyism. Although what I have to say is closely connected with the course of that movement, it is recounted and presented merely from my own point of view, and limited to my own experience. What is more, since – to my great misfortune – I have not been in a position to refer to the documents and literature of the movement, my descriptions of events are largely taken from memory.

There can be no real place for private affairs, of course, in an autobiography which is not centred directly on the writer himself. Friends of mine, on reading the manuscript, have raised two criticisms of my writing. First, they have suggested that I should have offered a self-appraisal, since although I have given my opinion or impressions of many of the characters who have peopled my life, I have made no particular assessment of my own role in the movement. Secondly, they have pointed out that I should have said more about certain aspects of my private life, for example my love affairs. As I see it, however, neither of these subjects is worth treating here. I hate self-aggrandizement as much as I hate insincere self-depreciation, both of which are difficult to avoid in any self-appraisal. In my opinion, I have already displayed far too much of myself in the course of writing this book. In Buffon's words, 'the style is the man'. Since readers are already acquainted with my style, what need is there for a further description of the man? Moreover, to criticize is also in a certain sense to be criticized – when a mirror reflects an image, it at the same time reveals its own quality. As for my private affairs, I have if anything dwelled at far too great a length on them. True, emotional life has always made up the main and best part of most biographical literature, but this work must be an exception. I have no intention of placing my own strictly personal joys and tragedies on a par with the great issues of the epoch.

In short, I have written this work not for my own emotional satisfaction and still less for reasons of personal vanity, but for the very cause to which I have devoted the best years of my life. I have remembered not merely for the sake of remembering, but also, and more importantly, to help others understand the past and thus prepare better for the future. In this way, and this way alone, do I justify the writing of this book.

28 July 1957

Postscript

● ● ●

This work was completed in 1957, and the events it recounts came to an end in 1949. Almost a quarter of a century has elapsed between its completion and its publication in English. Since it is not an autobiography in the strict sense of the word, it does not cover the entire life-span of the author. But since it is also not an objective history, the reader naturally has the right to ask what has now become of its author. It seems that a few words are therefore in order.

After I was forced to leave Hong Kong in late November 1949, I lived in a peninsula of seven square miles extent on the south China coast until March 1975, when through the help of friends I managed to find my way to Europe. I spent the first three years after 1949 pondering and reassessing the ideological positions of our movement. During that time I kept close contact with my friends in China. After December 1952, when they were all arrested and imprisoned by the secret police of the CCP, my political activities came to an end in practical terms. I managed to eke out a living by teaching and writing plays, but this in no way stopped me thinking or changed my basic calling. I kept a close watch on the changes that were taking place in the world and more particularly in China. I kept a critical eye on each of the major events in China, including the Hundred Flowers campaign, the Great Leap Forward, the People's Communes movement, the Sino-Soviet debate and the Cultural Revolution, my aim being both to formulate and clarify my own ideas and to exchange opinions with like-minded observers. My writings during this period, which were published and distributed with the help of some of my old friends, took the form of articles, pamphlets and even a book-length study of Mao Tse-tung's thought (under the pseudonym 'Shuang Shan').[1]

But it was not until 1968 that our ideas and publications drew any real response. The glittering victories of the CCP and the unprecedented prosperity of the post-war western world combined to consign to the margins of major world developments what remained of

[1] See Translator's Introduction, p. xviii, n. 1.

revolutionary Marxism outside China, and – ideologically – to send it off course. The Red Guard movement launched in 1966 did provide a certain stimulus for overseas Chinese youth and partly shook off their political apathy. But it was only in 1968 that a fundamental change in the mood of a large number of young people became apparent. It was in that year that Hong Kong youth in particular, influenced by the powerful wave of radical thinking that shook the world as a result of the Vietnam war, began seriously to raise their efforts for personal success to the level of a struggle for the betterment of society as a whole, of China, and of mankind. They began both to feel a deep hatred for the capitalist world and to deplore the bureaucratic regime of the CCP. Not surprisingly, many of them tended towards anarchism. Before long, however, as a result both of their own experience and of the influence of other ideological tendencies, they began to differentiate among themselves, so that a majority of them eventually turned towards revolutionary Marxism.

During the next four or five years they grew greatly in influence, gaining new support not only in Hong Kong but also in Europe and north America. Now we are able to see quite a powerful movement springing up among Chinese youth, workers as well as students, all over the world, with the aim of redirecting the new China into channels which will genuinely benefit the interests of the toiling masses; and in June 1979 Cheng Ch'ao-lin and eleven other old friends of mine were released from gaol (though not rehabilitated) after twenty-seven years, as a result of the new turn in the policy of the CCP.

My role in preparing for this process of change was not particularly worthy of note, but neither was it entirely lacking. Now that I am approaching the end of my life's journey, I cannot but feel happy to find that what appears before me is not the darkness after sunset, but the bright glimmering of daybreak.

25 January 1980

Select Biographical Reference List

An Fu
A leader of the Chinese Trotskyists in Moscow. Arrested and exiled to Siberia in 1930.

Chang Ching-ch'en (1906–31)
Chairman of Peking University Students' Union in 1926. Studied in Moscow, returned to China in 1929, and was arrested and executed by the Yünnan authorities as a member of the Provincial Committee of the CCP in Yünnan.

Chang Kuo-t'ao (1897–1979)
A founder of the CCP and labour leader during the 1920s. Leader of the CCP's Fourth Front Army during the Long March, when he clashed with Mao. Left the CCP in 1938 and ceased political activity thereafter.

Chang Po-chün (1896–)
Returned student from Germany. Participated in the Northern Expedition and was a founder of the Third Party (Workers' and Peasants' Party of China). A leader of the Democratic Alliance after 1944. At one time Minister of Communications in the Peking Government. Purged during the Cultural Revolution.

Chang Shih-chao (1882–1974)
Lawyer and journalist. Opposed to the New Culture Movement and a bitter enemy of Lu Hsün, but died a supporter of Maoism.

Chang T'e
Joined the Trotskyist movement in Moscow in 1927. Left it in 1931 and was thereafter a supporter of the Kwangsi warlords.

Chang Teh-han (1918–1987)
Joined the underground Trotskyist organization in 1939 and carried out educational work among the workers in Shanghai. Arrested by the Maoist secret police in 1952, since when nothing has been heard of her.

Chang Teh-tse (1915–44)

A lawyer, who rendered valuable help to resistance fighters under the Japanese occupation in Shanghai. Joined the underground Trotskyist movement in 1939, and died of tuberculosis.

Chang Wen-t'ien (1902–76)

Alias Lo Fu, one of the 'Twenty-Eight Bolsheviks'. General Secretary of the CCP from 1935 to 1945. Purged together with P'eng Teh-huai as a 'rightist' in 1959.

Chao Chi (1905–)

Veteran Communist. Participated in the Northern Expedition as a political commissar. Became a Trotskyist in Moscow in 1928. Active during the early stages of the Trotskyist movement in China.

Chao P'ing-fu (1902–31)

Alias Jou Shih. Novelist and Communist after 1926. Intimate friend of Lu Hsün, who afterwards wrote an essay in his memory. Arrested and executed together with the 'Conciliationists'.

Ch'en Ch'ang-hao

One of the 'Twenty-Eight Bolsheviks'. Active in the Oyüiwan soviet area as a supporter and collaborator of Chang Kuo-t'ao. Nothing heard of him since the 1930s.

Ch'en Ch'i-ch'ang (1905–43)

A Peking student leader, and a member of the middle-ranking cadre of the CCP after 1925. Turned to Trotskyism in 1929, and became a leader of the Chinese Trotskyist movement.

Ch'en Chung-hsi (1908–43)

A Hong Kong worker, who joined the Trotskyists in 1930. As a Communist, he led an armed peasant struggle in Chungshan county, Kwangtung, towards the end of 1927. He was organizer of the Hong Kong Trotskyists in the mid-1930s and led an anti-Japanese guerrilla unit in Chungshan during the war of Resistance. Died in battle around 1943.

Ch'en Han-sheng (1897–)

Professor of History and Sociology, and CCP sympathizer.

Ch'en Hsi-ying (1895–)

A professor, and one of the main literary adversaries of Lu Hsün. Studied in England.

Ch'en I-mou (1907–31)
See under 'Ou Fang'.

Ch'en Ming-shu (1891–1965)
A military man of the Kwangtung group who was usually opposed to Chiang Kai-shek. Participated in the Fukien rebellion against Chiang in 1933. A member of the People's Republic of China State Council after 1949. Purged as a 'rightist' in 1963.

Ch'en T'an-ch'iu (1889–1943)
One of the twelve participants in the founding conference of the CCP in 1921 and a member of the Central Committee. Arrested and executed by Sheng Shih-ts'ai, warlord of Sinkiang.

Ch'en Tu-hsiu (1879–1942)
Editor of New Youth, leader of the New Culture Movement, founder of the CCP and its General Secretary until 1927.

Ch'en Wei-jen
A 'Frugal Study' student. His fate after 1931 is unknown.

Ch'en Wei-ming (1907–61)
Alias Sakov, one of the 'Twenty-Eight Bolsheviks'. At one time principal of the Academy of Arts in Memory of Lu Hsün in Yenan. A top literary official after 1949.

Ch'en Yen-nien (1900–1927)
The eldest son of Ch'en Tu-hsiu and a founder of the European branch of the CCP. A leading member of the Kwangtung Provincial Committee of the CCP until 1926. Executed by Chiang Kai-shek in Shanghai in May 1927.

Cheng Ch'ao-lin (1901–)
Writer and translator. Joined the CCP in Paris in 1922. Returned to China in 1924 to edit the party organ Hsiang-tao (Guide Weekly). A member of the Hupeh Provincial Committee of the CCP during the revolution of 1925–7, and a participant in the Emergency Conference of 7 August 1927. Became a Trotskyist in 1929. A founder and leader of the Chinese Trotskyist organization. Served seven years in prison under Chiang Kai-shek. Arrested by the Maoist secret police in 1952. Kept in prison without trial until 1979.

Chiang Chen-tung (1906–1982)
A textile worker and veteran Communist. One of the leaders of the Shanghai insurrections of 1927. Became a Trotskyist in 1929. Arrested by the Maoist police in 1952 for his dissident activities.

Chiang Kuang-jen (1906–   )

Alias Hu Feng, a disciple of Lu Hsün and a well-known independent left-wing Leader of the so-called Hu Feng clique. Purged in 1955 by Mao.

Ch'in Pang-hsien (1907–46)

Alias Po Ku, one of Pavel Mif's 'Twenty-Eight Bolsheviks'. Acting General Secretary of the CCP from 1932 to 1935. Died in an air crash in 1946.

Ching Heng-yi (1872–   )

Educationalist and nationalist. A minister in the revolutionary Wuhan Government, 1926–7.

Chou En-lai (1898–1976)

Joined the CCP in France in 1922. Most prominent organizer, negotiator and administrator of the CCP. A survivor of all the internal factional struggles. Premier of the People's Republic of China from 1949 until his death.

Chou Tso-jen (1885–1968)

Essayist. One of the main contributors to *New Youth*. Introduced Japanese and East European literature into China. Brother of Lu Hsün.

Chou Yang (1908–   )

Returned student from Japan. Left-wing literary leader in Shanghai in the years 1933–6. Principal of the Art Academy in Yenan during the War of Resistance. Vice-Minister of Culture after the victory of the CCP. Purged in 1966, and arrested in January 1967 as a 'capitalist roader'.

Ch'ü Ch'iu-pai (1899–1935)

Writer and translator. Veteran Communist and General Secretary of the CCP from August 1927 to July 1928. Executed by Chiang Kai-shek.

Chu Hsi (1130–1203)

Most famous Confucian scholar of the Sung dynasty. His textual commentary on the Confucian classics became standard.

Chu Tan-chi

See under Li Hsia-kung.

Fan Chin-piao (1904–?)

A leader of the Chekiang student movement, he participated in the Northern Expedition as a political commissar and afterwards as a leader of the peasant movement in Chekiang. He became a leader of the Chinese Trotskyists in Moscow, and was arrested there and sent to Siberia, where he died.

Feng Hsüeh-feng (1902–1974)
Poet and critic. Joined the CCP in 1927. A leader of the National Association of Writers and Artists after 1949. Purged during the Cultural Revolution.

Han Chün (?–1945)
A leader of the younger generation of Chinese Trotskyists. Active among Hong Kong workers throughout the period of the Japanese occupation of the colony, until his death in 1945.

Ho Chi-feng (1897–1980)
Rebelled against Chiang Kai-shek in 1948 while vice-commander of the Kuomintang's Third Pacification Area. After 1949 Ho became among other things vice-minister of irrigation and vice-minister of agriculture.

Ho Lung (1896–1969)
A legendary CCP military leader. At the time of the split between the Wuhan Government and the CCP, Ho was commander of the pro-Communist 20th National Revolutionary Army.

Ho Meng-hsiung (1898–1931)
A labour leader in north China during the 1925–7 revolution. Leader of the Kiangsu Provincial Committee of the CCP after 1928. Arrested and executed by the Kuomintang.

Ho Tzu-shen (1899–   )
A Peking student leader during the early 1920s. Participated in the Northern Expedition and was active in the Hunan Provincial Committee alongside Mao. Became a Trotskyist in 1929, and spent several years in gaol under the Kuomintang. Arrested by the Maoist secret police in 1952; reportedly died in prison in 1962.

Ho Tzu-shu
Returned to China from Moscow as one of the Stalinist 'Twenty-eight Bolsheviks' group. Died in a Kuomintang prison some time in the early 1930s.

Hsia Tou-yin (1884–1951)
Commander of a division of Kuomintang troops stationed at Ichang, Hupeh province, who on 6 May 1927 rebelled against the Wuhan Government in collusion with Chiang Kai-shek. His army was annihilated on the outskirts of Wuhan on 18 May.

Hsiang Chung-fa (1880–1931)

A worker-Communist and labour leader during the period of the Wuhan Government. He became General Secretary of the CCP at the Sixth Congress in 1928, and was arrested and executed by the Kuomintang in 1931.

Hsiang Ying (1894–1941)

An early labour leader. Member of the Politbureau after 1935 and leader of the remnant military forces in Kiangsi after the Long March. Became vice-commander of the New Fourth Army in 1938. Killed by a traitor shortly after the South Anhwei Incident of January 1941.

Hsiao Ch'ang-pin

Became a Trotskyist in Moscow in 1927. A founder of the Chinese Trotskyist organization. Active in north China, he left the movement in 1931.

Hsieh Chüeh-tsai (1893–1953)

Joined the CCP in 1925 and participated in the Long March. After 1949, became Minister of the Interior and then head of the Supreme Court.

Hsü Chih-hsin (1904–1983)

Novelist and Communist. An orphan adopted by Mao Tse-tung and brought up and educated under his care.

Hsü K'o-hsiang (1889–1964)

Garrison commander at Ch'angsha, where he carried out a coup against the workers' and peasants' organizations on the night of 21 May 1927.

Hsü Mao-yung (1910–77)

A close collaborator of Chou Yang, who became famous for his correspondence with Lu Hsün in 1936 concerning the slogan of 'literature of national defence'.

Hsü T'e-li (1877–1968)

Mao's teacher and a participant in the Long March. A member of the Central Committee of the CCP after 1945.

Hu Shih (1892–1962)

Philosopher and writer. Advocate of the vernacular literature. A supporter of the Kuomintang, and pro-American.

Hu Yeh-p'in (1903–31)

Novelist and husband of the well-known authoress Ting Ling. Arrested and executed by the Kuomintang together with other 'Conciliationists'.

Huan Hsiang (1910–)

Studied in Japan. A journalist during and after the War of Resistance. Delegate to the People's Consultative Conference in 1949. Chargé d'affaires in London from 1954 to 1962. Nothing heard of him since the Cultural Revolution.

Huang Kung-tu

Returned student from Moscow. Served as a political adviser to the Kwangsi military group when they adopted an anti-Chiang Kai-shek position, but was executed after they had compromised with Nanking.

Isaacs, Harold (1909–1986)

An American journalist who published *China Forum* in Shanghai in the early 1930s. Became sympathetic to Trotskyism and wrote *The Tragedy of the Chinese Revolution*, but left the movement before the Second World War.

Kao Jen-shan (1894–1928).

Professor of Peking University. Educationalist. Executed by Chang Tso-lin as a Communist.

Kao Yü-han

Veteran revolutionary and a political instructor at the Whampoa Military Academy. The first Communist who openly attacked Chiang Kai-shek. Became a Trotskyist in 1929.

Kautsky, Karl (1854–1938)

Leader of the German Social Democratic Party. Best known before 1914 as a Marxist theoretician. He opposed the Bolshevik revolution in 1917 on the grounds that a genuine socialist proletarian revolution could only be achieved by democratic means, i.e. by universal suffrage and not by the insurrection of a minority of the nation. He opposed Lenin's theory and practice of the dictatorship of the proletariat.

Kirov, Sergei Mironovich (1886–1934)

Old Bolshevik, elected to the USSR Central Committee in 1923 and the Politburo in 1930. A staunch supporter of Stalin. His assassination in 1934 was followed by the Moscow trials.

Ko Ch'ung-o (?–1931)

Became a Trotskyist in 1927 in Moscow and was expelled and sent back to China at the end of the same year. A founder of the Chinese Trotskyist movement. Arrested by the Kuomintang in 1931, and died in a Shanghai prison.

Ku Shun-chang (1895–1935)

A worker and leader of the Shanghai insurrections in 1927. Chief of the CCP 'special service' and member of the Central Committee. Arrested by the Kuomintang, and finally executed by Chiang Kai-shek despite becoming an informer.

Kuan Hsiang-ying (1905–46)

A printer, who joined the CCP in 1925. A member of the Central Committee until 1928. Ho Lung's political commissar during the anti-Japanese war.

Li Chen-ying

An activist in the labour movement and member of the CCP. He joined the 'Conciliationists' in 1931, and was arrested in the same year. He left politics after his release from prison.

Li Chi

Known as the first Marxist scholar in China. Author of *A Biography of Karl Marx*. Became a Trotskyist in 1929. Recanted after 1949.

Li Chi-shen (1886–1959)

Governor of Kwangtung during Northern Expedition. Suppressor of Ho Lung-Yeh T'ing army in September 1927. Head of the short-lived Fukien rebellion against Chiang Kai-shek in November 1933–January 1934. Expelled from the Kuomintang in 1947 when he organized the Kuomintang Revolutionary Committee, which supported the CCP.

Li Ch'iu-shih (1903–31)

Writer and member of the Communist Youth League of China. Arrested and executed with the 'Conciliationists'.

Li Chung-san

A veteran Kuomintang revolutionary, active in north-west China. Became a Communist in France and went over to Trotskyism in 1929 together with Ch'en Tu-hsiu.

Li Fu-jen (1901–1987)

Pen name of a foreign journalist in Shanghai. A leader of the Chinese Trotskyist movement from 1934 to 1938.

Li Hsia-kung

Li Hsia-kung, Wu Chi-hsien, and Chu Tan-chi were communists who worked in the Kuomintang before being sent to Moscow. On their return to China, Li left the Party and joined the Kuomintang Revolutionary Committee in the mid-1940s, later becoming an official under the Peking Government; Wu, nephew of Ch'en Tu-hsiu, became a Trotskyist; and Chu was last heard of as a participant in the Fukien rebellion against Chiang Kai-shek in 1933.

Li Li-san (1899–1967)

Veteran Communist and labour organizer. Elected to Politburo in 1927. Chief executor of Stalin's ultra-left line in China during the period 1929–30; removed from the leadership in 1931 as a scapegoat for its failure. Detained in Russia until 1945. Attacked during the Cultural Revolution, when he reportedly committed suicide.

Li P'in-hsien (1887–?)

A military commander under T'ang Sheng-chih. Became one of the leaders of the Kwangsi military group.

Li Ta-chao (1889–1927)

One of the founders of the CCP, who died for the cause.

Li Wei-han (1897–1984)

Alias Lo Mai. Joined the CCP in France in 1922 together with Chou En-lai and others. Head of the Orgburo in 1936. After 1949 he was mainly in charge of the Party's United Front work. He was accused of 'anti-Party' activity in December 1966 and purged in June 1967.

Liang Ch'i-ch'ao (1873–1929)

Journalist and historian. A constitutional monarchist who became leader of the so-called 'Study Clique' after the downfall of the Ch'ing dynasty.

Liang Kan-ch'iao

Studied in Moscow after graduating from the Whampoa Military Academy. Active in the Chinese Trotskyist movement for a few years, but became a leader of Chiang Kai-shek's 'Blueshirt Clique'.

Liang Po-tai

Veteran Communist. Returned to China in the early thirties and worked for a while in the Kiangsi soviet area, but little has been heard of him since then.

Lien Cheng-hsiang (1928–51)

A young Trotskyist student in Wenchow, Chekiang, shot by the Maoists in 1951.

Lin Huan-hua

A leader of the student Trotskyists in Kwangsi province in the early 1930s. In charge of printing for the Trotskyist centre in the mid-1930s and a member of the Executive of the Printworkers' Trade Union in Canton until his arrest in December 1952.

Lin Po-ch'ü (1885–1960)

Veteran Communist and member of the CCP Politbureau. After 1949, vice-chairman of the National People's Congress.

Lin Yü-nan (?–1931)

A CCP labour leader and secretary of the National Federation of Labour. Arrested and executed by the Kuomintang, together with Ho Meng-hsiung and other 'Conciliationists'.

Liu Chia-liang

Liu Chia-liang, Ssu Ch'ao-sheng, and Wang Shu-pen were three of the leaders of the second generation of Chinese Trotskyists. Liu died in a Vietnamese prison sometime in 1950, Ssu left the movement long before that, while Wang was executed by the Kuomintang in a concentration camp on the eve of their military débâcle.

Liu Jen-ching (1899–)

A founding member of the CCP and General Secretary of the Socialist League of Youth. He joined the Left Opposition in Moscow and visited Trotsky in Prinkipo, Turkey, in 1929. After returning to China he played a part in organizing the first groups of Chinese Trotskyists, and helped Harold Isaacs write his book The Tragedy of the Chinese Revolution. He was arrested in 1934, and recanted in prison.

Liu Pan-nung (1891–1934)

Poet and linguist. One of the main contributors to New Youth.

Liu Po-chuang

'Frugal Study' student. He turned to Trotskyism in 1929, but became a professor soon afterwards and left the movement.

Liu Shao-ch'i (1889–1969)

Veteran Communist and prominent Chinese labour leader of the CCP from the mid-1940s on. Head of State of the People's Republic of China after 1959, but purged during the Cultural Revolution.

Liu Yin, alias Li Mai-mai

A leader of the Wuhan student movement during the 1925–7 revolution. Studied in Moscow. Active for a while in the Chinese Trotskyist movement, then became a publicist for the Kuomintang.

Lo Han (1898–1941?)

Joined the CCP in 1922 in Paris. Active in the Kuomintang army until March 20th Incident (1926). Became a Trotskyist in 1928 and a leader of the Left Opposition of the CCP. Died in Chungking during a Japanese air-raid.

Lo Hsin

A Hong Kong worker who became a Trotskyist together with Ch'en Tu-hsiu.

Lo I-yüan (1893–1931)

Leader of the peasant movement in Kwangtung and member of the Central Committee of the CCP. Arrested in Shanghai, and executed despite his recantation.

Lo Teng-hsien (1901–33)

Leader of the famous Hong Kong–Canton general strike of 1925–6, member of the Politbureau after 1928 (?), Party leader in Manchuria after 1931, and organizer of anti-Japanese guerrilla detachments in that area. Returned to Shanghai in 1933, when he was arrested and executed by the Kuomintang.

Lominadze, Vissarion (1898–1934)

Known as 'Stalin's prodigy'. Comintern representative in China from July to December 1927. He masterminded the August 7th (1927) Emergency Conference and together with Heinz Neumann directed the December 1927 Canton insurrection. Fell into disfavour after 1930 and committed suicide in 1934.

Lou Kuo-hua (1906–)

A Communist since 1925, he became a Trotskyist in 1928. He is one of the few survivors of the first generation of Chinese Trotskyists, and has been the chief publisher of Trotskyist literature in Chinese.

Lu Hsün (1881–1936)

Modern China's best-known novelist, essayist, and critic, known as 'China's Gorky'. Original name Chou Shu-jen.

Lu I-yüan

Studied in Moscow. A translator who later left the movement.

Ma Yü-fu

A CCP labour activist who became a Trotskyist in 1929 and defected to the Kuomintang a year later.

Mao Hung-chien

A leader of the Kwangsi Trotskyists in the early 1930s. A member of the Central Committee of the International Workers' Party after 1949. Left the movement in 1951.

Mif, Pavel (1899–?)

Patron of the so-called 'Twenty-eight Bolsheviks' at the Sun Yat-sen University in Moscow. Arrested in 1937 and disappeared during the purges.

Ou Fang

With Ch'en I-mou, Sung Feng-ch'un, and Shih T'ang, one of the four main founders of the first Trotskyist group in China. Imprisoned by the Kuomintang on returning from Moscow. Ou and Ch'en died in prison, while Sung and Shih left the movement after their release.

P'an Hsün (?–1928)

Poet and novelist. CCP member. Arrested as a Communist, and died in Tientsin gaol.

P'an Wen-yu

A returned student from Moscow and collaborator with Li Li-san. Later purged by the Wang Ming group.

P'eng P'ai (1896–1929)

Leader of the peasant associations in Hailufeng, Kwangtung, after 1922. In October 1927 he organized a peasant insurrection and led the armed peasant struggle in that area. After the defeat he fled to Shanghai, where he was arrested and executed by the Kuomintang.

P'eng Shu-tse (1896–1983)

Otherwise known as Peng Shu-chih. A returned student from Moscow and a member of the Central Committee of the CCP after 1925. Chief editor of the Party organ during the 1925–7 revolution. Expelled together with Ch'en Tu-hsiu in November 1929 for supporting Trotskyism.

P'u Teh-chih (1908–   )

Alias Hsi Liu. Joined the CCP in 1926, and was active in literature and the theatre. Became a Trotskyist in Moscow in 1928. Arrested together with Ch'en Tu-hsiu in 1932 and released from prison in 1937.

Radek, Karl (1885–1939)
Went over to Stalin in 1929 and was defendant at the second Moscow trial. Died in prison.

Remmele, Herman (1880–1937)
A leader of the Communist Party of Germany who fled to the USSR in 1933. Arrested and executed by Stalin in 1937.

Roy, M. N. (1887–1954)
Indian nationalist and Communist. Went to China in May 1927 as the representative of the Comintern.

Shen Tse-min (1890–1934)
Studied in the Soviet Union, active in the Oyüiwan soviet area in the 1930s. Member of the Central Committee of the CCP.

Shih T'ang
See under 'Ou Fang'.

Shih Ts'un-t'ung (1889–1970)
Afterwards changed his name to Shih Fu-liang. Participated as a member of the CCP in the 1925–7 Revolution, but left the Party after its defeat. Remained an opponent of Chiang Kai-shek and a CCP sympathizer.

Shumiatsky, B. Z.
Old Bolshevik of worker origin. An expert on Far Eastern affairs.

Ssu Ch'ao-sheng
See under 'Liu Chia-ling'.

Su Chao-cheng (1885–1929)
A seaman, and leader of the famous 1925–6 Hong Kong–Canton general strike. Chairman of the short-lived Canton Soviet Government in December 1927.

Sun Fo (1891–1973)
Minister of the Wuhan Government and member of the State Council.

Sun Yat-sen, Madame (1892–1981)
Maiden name: Soong Ch'ing-ling. A member of the State Council of the Wuhan Government. Continued to favour collaboration with the CCP even after the Left Wing of the Kuomintang split with the Communists.

Sung Che-yüan (1885–1940)

Originally a high-ranking general under Feng Yü-hsiang. Commander of the 29th Army on the outbreak of the anti-Japanese war in 1937. With Chiang Kai-shek's approval he became head of a pro-Japanese administration in north China.

Sung Feng-ch'un
See under 'Ou Fang'.

Tai Chi-t'ao (1891–1949)

Leader and theoretician of the Kuomintang Right Wing (organized in the Society for the Study of Sun Yat-sen-ism). Committed suicide when the Communists came to power.

T'an Tsu-yao (?–1927)

A Peking student leader, and member of the Peking Committee of the CCP in 1927.

T'an P'ing-shan (1887–1956)

An early leader of the CCP, expelled in 1927. He joined the Kuomintang in 1937 and later became a supporter of the Revolutionary Committee of the Kuomintang, which backed the Peking Government after 1949.

T'an Sheng-chih (1889–1970)

Commander of the 8th Nationalist Army during the Northern Expedition. He became the military bulwark of the Wuhan Government when the latter split with Chiang, and then turned with Wang Ching-wei against the CCP.

T'ao Hsing-chih (1891–1946)

An educationalist and disciple of John Dewey. A leader of the Democratic League of China, persecuted by the Kuomintang.

Thaelmann, Ernst (1886–1944)

Joined the German Social Democratic Party in 1903. Became a Communist in 1920. Leader of the Communist Party of Germany after 1925. Carried out Stalin's ultra-left line, leading to the victory of Hitler in 1933. Arrested in March 1933 and murdered in Buchenwald eleven years later.

Trang Malaca

After the Second World War, when the Dutch East Indies achieved independence as the state of Indonesia, Trang became leader of the Indonesian Trotskyist movement. He disappeared during the 1950s, probably executed by the Sukarno regime.

Ts'ai Ho-sen (1890–1931)
A leader and martyr of the CCP. Author of *The History of Opportunism in the CCP*.

Ts'ai Yüan-p'ei (1868–1940)
Veteran Kuomintang leader and important liberal educationalist. Sponsored the New Culture Movement around 1919 in his capacity as President of Peking University.

Tung I-hsiang
Writer and veteran Communist. Reportedly murdered in Sinkiang together with Yü Hsiu-sung and others by Wang Ming because of his Trotskyist sympathies.

Tung Pi-wu (1886–1975)
Veteran Communist and Central Committee member after 1945. Vice-head of state. Member of the Politbureau after 1966.

Wang Ch'ang-yao
A returned student from Moscow who became a Trotskyist in the early thirties. Active in the Peking student movement before he returned to his native province of Shantung, together with his wife, Chang San-chieh, to organize an anti-Japanese guerrilla detachment.

Wang Chia-hsiang (1904–1974)
Close friend of Wang Ming; became a Mao supporter in 1932. Member of the Politbureau during the Long March. First Ambassador of the People's Republic of China to the Soviet Union. Purged in 1966.

Wang Ching-wei (1883–1944)
Veteran member of the Kuomintang and at first leader of its Left Wing. He later compromised with Chiang Kai-shek and ended up a Japanese puppet.

Wang Jo-fei (1896–1946)
Joined the CCP in 1922, and was a member of the Central Committee until 1945. A member of the Communist Party delegation to the Comintern in 1928. Died in an air crash in 1946.

Wang K'o-ch'üan
A Shanghai labour leader and member of the Central Committee of the CCP. Purged by the Wang Ming group in 1931 for belonging to the 'Conciliationist' grouping.

Wang Meng-tsou (1897–1953)
Publisher friend of Ch'en Tu-hsiu and supporter of all progressive movements in China since the beginning of the century.

Wang Ming (1906–74)
Pseudonym of Ch'en Shao-yü. Stalin's main supporter in the CCP. His group dominated the Party after 1931, but was defeated during the Long March. His influence was finally eliminated at the 7th Congress of the CCP in 1945.

Wang Shih-wei (1907–47?)
Writer and translator. Author of the well-known article 'The Wild Lily'. First victim (in Yenan) of the CCP's literary policy. It was later revealed by Mao that Wang was killed, probably in 1947.

Wang Shu-pen (?–1949)
See under 'Liu Chia-liang'.

Wang Sung-chiu (1922–1952)
Young Trotskyist educator and organizer in Japanese-occupied Shanghai. Arrested by the Maoist secret police in 1952 and committed suicide in prison.

Wang Te-lin
A leader of the anti-Japanese guerrilla forces in Manchuria after 1931. Wang's units were chiefly active in the southern part of Kirin province.

Wang Tu-ch'ing (1898–1940)
A poet and one of the four founders of the Creation Society. A professor at Chungshan University in Canton. Went over to Trotskyism in 1929 together with Ch'en Tu-hsiu. Died of typhoid.

Wu Chi-hsien (1898–1940)
See under 'Li Hsia-kung'.

Wu Chih-hui (1865–1953).
Ex-anarchist, veteran member of the Kuomintang, and one of the sponsors of the Society for Frugal Study by Means of Labour.

Wu Fu-ching
A leader of the Moscow branch of the CCP in 1927–8. Worked under Chou En-lai after being sent back to China.

Wu Li-p'ing (1906–   )
Returned student from the Soviet Union, and translator of several Marxist classics. At one time Mao's secretary and interpreter.

Wu Yü-chang (1878–1966)
Veteran Communist and educationalist. A member of the Central Committee after 1938, and later a member of the Standing Committee of the National People's Congress.

Yang P'ao-an (?–1931)
A Communist working in the Kuomintang as a member of its Central Committee and Central Control Commission. Stayed loyal to the CCP after the split between the two parties and was arrested and executed by the Kuomintang.

Yaroslavsky, Y. M. (1879–1943)
One of Stalin's literary henchmen. Author of the charges on which the Left Oppositionists were expelled from the Party in 1927.

Yeh Chien-ying (1898–1986)
Professional military man who participated in the Northern Expedition and the Canton Insurrection of December 1927. Chief of Staff of the CCP's Eighth Route Army after 1937. Now Defence Minister in the Peking Government and member of Politbureau Standing Committee.

Yen Chung
A Kuomintang general of leftist persuasion. He was sacked by Chiang when his division reached Hangchow, capital of Chekiang, and reportedly left politics after that.

Yin K'uan (1900–1967)
Veteran Communist who joined the CCP in France together with Chou En-lai and Ch'en I. Active in the Central Committee and the Anhui Provincial Committee of the CCP in 1925–7, and became a Trotskyist in 1929. Twice arrested by the Kuomintang for his revolutionary activities. Arrested by the Maoists in 1952.

Yü Hsiu-sung (?–1937)
Veteran Communist and early leader of the Chinese students in Moscow before Wang Ming. Said to have been murdered by Wang Ming in Sinkiang in 1937 as a 'Trotskyist'.

Yün Tai-ying (1895–1931)
A political instructor at the Whampoa Military Academy, and a member of the Central Committee of the CCP. One of the most respected leaders of the

Party among revolutionary youth during the revolution of 1925–7. Executed by the Kuomintang in 1931.

Yün Yü-t'ang (?–1931)

A returned student from Moscow and trade union activist. Arrested and executed together with the 'Conciliationists'.

Index

◉◉◉